PRAISE FOR
SLAYING DIGITAL DRAGONS

"This interactive, comprehensive guide helps teens thrive online and off. *Slaying Digital Dragons* trusts teens to make the right decisions for themselves and gives them the information and tools to do so, while also calling on them to use their abundant empathy to make the world a better place."

—Dr. Michele Borba, parenting and bullying-prevention expert, author of *End Peer Cruelty, Build Empathy*; *Thrivers*; and *Unselfie*

"*Slaying Digital Dragons* illuminates one of the dimmest, least understood, most impactful domains of life today, especially in the lives of children and teens: screens. Alex J. Packer breaks new ground in this authoritative, impeccably researched but also highly engaging, funny, and practical manual on how to take advantage of the huge upsides of the digital world while avoiding the diabolically dangerous traps it sets for the unsuspecting. This is an important and much-needed guide on how to navigate and thrive in the world young people inhabit and absorb every day."

—Edward M. Hallowell, M.D., founder of The Hallowell Centers; author of *ADHD 2.0*

"This book is truly the *War and Peace* for teens and anyone who spends a vast amount of time on their screens. Alex J. Packer's manifesto for slaying the *digisphere* is a lifesaver. Join the resistance and share this powerful book. It will help you and your friends retool, regroup, and set healthier standards for abating the dark forces beyond your control."

—Nancy Chuda, co-founder and president emeritus of Healthy Child Healthy World

"Teens are on their phones and screens for seven and a half hours every day. Most of them know that they are either addicted to their devices or in danger of getting addicted, but when their parents bring the subject up, kids react defensively and angrily. In his funny, straight-talking new book, *Slaying Digital Dragons,* Alex J. Packer offers teens a way to think about their relationships to their devices. Relying on cutting-edge research and his deep insights into children, Packer is by turns supportive and challenging, humorous and dead serious. If you want your teen to examine their smartphone use, if you want to have a productive conversation with your child about social media, you should buy this book for yourself and your child."

—Michael Thompson, Ph.D., *New York Times* bestselling coauthor of *Raising Cain: Protecting the Emotional Life of Boys*

SLAYING DIGITAL DRAGONS

Tips and tools for protecting your body, brain, psyche, and thumbs from the digital dark side

ALEX J. PACKER, PH.D.

free spirit
PUBLISHING®

Library of Congress Cataloging-in-Publication Data
Names: Packer, Alex J., author.
Title: Slaying digital dragons : tips and tools for protecting your body, brain, psyche, and thumbs from the digital dark side / Alex J. Packer.
Description: Minneapolis, MN : Free Spirit Publishing Inc., [2021] | Includes bibliographical references and index. | Audience: Ages 11 & up
Identifiers: LCCN 2020055317 (print) | LCCN 2020055318 (ebook) | ISBN 9781631985966 (paperback) | ISBN 9781631985973 (pdf) | ISBN 9781631985980 (epub)
Subjects: LCSH: Internet and teenagers—Juvenile literature. | Social media—Psychological aspects—Juvenile literature. | Teenagers—Mental health—Juvenile literature. | Data protection—Juvenile literature. | Time management—Juvenile literature. | Health behavior in adolescence—Juvenile literature. | BISAC: YOUNG ADULT NONFICTION / Computers / Internet & Social Media | YOUNG ADULT NONFICTION / Social Topics / Values & Virtues
Classification: LCC HQ799.2.I5 P33 2021 (print) | LCC HQ799.2.I5 (ebook) | DDC 004.67/80835—dc23
LC record available at https://lccn.loc.gov/2020055317
LC ebook record available at https://lccn.loc.gov/2020055318

Reading Level Grade 8; Interest Level Ages 13 & Up
Fountas & Pinnell Guided Reading Level Z+

The "Do I Have an Achilles Heel?" challenge on page 48 is adapted from The Gaming Disorder Test (Pontes, Halley M., Bruno Schivinski, Cornelia Sindermann, et al. 2019. "Measurement and Conceptualization of Gaming Disorder According to the World Health Organization Framework: The Development of the Gaming Disorder Test." *International Journal of Mental Health and Addiction*. doi.org/10.1007/s11469-019-00088-z). The term "gaming" was changed to a blank space that teens can use to assess any problematic screen activity. The parenthetical examples of significant problem areas in Question 4 were altered slightly to better represent the experiences of young people. The backward-looking timeframe cited in the instructions was modified from twelve to six months to acknowledge a younger audience with frequently shifting screen habits. The scoring information guidance was also changed to eliminate clinical terms, create three general self-assessment categories along a continuum from healthy to problematic screen activity, and to reflect the self-assessment/empowerment focus of this book.

Edited by Eric Braun and Alison Behnke
Cover and interior design by Shannon Pourciau
Illustrated by Jon Davis

10 9 8 7 6 5 4 3 2 1
Printed in the United States of America

Free Spirit Publishing Inc.
6325 Sandburg Road, Suite 100
Minneapolis, MN 55427-3674
(612) 338-2068
help4kids@freespirit.com
freespirit.com

FSC
www.fsc.org
MIX
Paper from responsible sources
FSC® C005010

Dedication

For Mateo, Leonie, and Emily
and the
Resistance Generation

Acknowledgments

"Acknowledgments" is where you thank the "team"—the people whose advice, expertise, and encouragement contributed to making this book possible. (See page 310 on thanking the team.)

I would like to express my appreciation to Max Banta for providing a helpful "young person's" perspective on the gaming parody in Chapters 2 and 3; neurologist Shelley Cross, M.D., for reviewing and sharpening Chapter 4; James Hallowell for his astute reading of the manuscript and willingness to tell me which jokes bombed and had to go; Alex Lobo for creative inspiration and sharing the fruits of his decades of work with teenagers; and David Waterman for sparks of insight that ignited my motivation whenever it flagged.

I would also like to thank MaryLouise Bailey, Philip Banta, Susan Banta, James Chuda, Nancy Chuda, Michael Clarke, Angel Colón, Patricia Colón, Brad Furman, Betsy Gabler, Stephanie Haines, Edward M. Hallowell, M.D., John Houchin, Norm Jenkins, Sharon Johnson, Jon Kerlin, Constance Kim, Suzanne Laberge, Sandi Pei, Jean Peters, Sherman Todd, and Suzanne Winter. They have no idea how much their friendship, emails, calls, meals, and/ or timely *"How's-the-book-going?"* inquiries kept *me* going and stopped me from giving up and throwing my laptop out the window.

I am deeply indebted to the many journalists, reporters, and tech experts whose fascinating and provocative articles and podcasts on technology, privacy, and social media provided me with invaluable context, data, and tips: Tim Biggs, Brian X. Chen, Geoffrey A. Fowler, Tristan Harris, Tim Herrera, Kashmir Hill, Cade Metz, David Pogue, Kevin Roose, Kara Swisher, Charlie Warzel, and Amy Yee.

I wish to thank the entire staff at Free Spirit Publishing—many of whom I have never met but whose behind-the-scenes contributions were essential. I especially wish to acknowledge Eric Braun for his initial yeoman's work in shaping and editing the manuscript and for listening empathically to my laments, complaints, and frustrations; Alison Behnke for "getting" the book and reflecting its tone and message in her incisive editing, for being open to my perspectives and pushback, and for reining in or excising my most outrageous and/or cherished paragraphs (like Le Pétomane—look him up!), with such tact, empathy, and positive bookending;

Alyssa Lochner for casting her eagle eyes on every word, line, comma, quotation mark, and dot; Amanda Shofner for her marketing and publicity smarts and efforts; Shannon Pourciau for creating such a beautiful book and being open to my two cents' (or two fonts') worth of design requests; and Judy Galbraith, president of Free Spirit Publishing, for her courage, dedication, and values as a publisher, her encouragement and candor as a friend, and especially for protecting Pokey the Turtle's dignity.

I am grateful to Jon Davis, whose exuberantly zany and witty illustrations bring so much life to the book.

And finally, I wish to thank Big Tech itself. I wish to thank them for the miracles of technology: word processing, email, video calling, file sharing, search algorithms that generate 34,010,000 results or help me find a pig emoji, and endless playlists like Spotify's *Quiet Background Jazz for Authors Named Alex Working on Books for Teens*. But even more, I wish to thank Big Tech for the constant reminders it provided as I worked on this book—reminders of the countless companies, platforms, apps, and advertisers whose arrogant, invasive, bullying, assaultive, deceptive, manipulative, greedy, and addictive tactics kept me inspired and motivated throughout the course of this project. (And, no, Google! I will not comply with the order to "Add birthday to your Google account now." Not until you say "Please.")

CONTENTS

PART III: RESET

LIST OF FORMS

See page 407 for instructions for downloading digital versions of these forms.

PART I

REFLECT

START SCREEN

Joining the Resistance

I don't need to tell you how wonderful smartphones are.

> **Something tells me you're about to.**

Snuggled in a pocket or purse, your phone is a ticket to the world. You can use it to do homework, learn how to fix a bike, and connect with friends. You'll find clever vids and *whatever* kids. Cute cats and snooty rats. You can query Siri and perplexa Alexa. You can be a gamer or lion tamer, learn the guitar or make an avatar. Take pics or watch flix. Send Snaps or check maps—

> **Is this a book or a poem?**

—plan trips or post clips, play tunes or draw baboons, buy clothes or—who knows?!

Who knows? You do. That's because most teens spend hours a day on their phones, tablets, gaming consoles, or laptops. And if you do, you know how wild, wacky, and wonderful the digital world can be. The world at your thumb tips. Music. Movies. Friends. Games. Videos. Questions. Answers. Yup, you can find anything and everything online anytime.

Well, not quite. You can't inhale the smell of brownies baking in the oven. You can't watch the sunset until the last sliver of purple disappears. You can't ruff-ruffhouse with your dog or give your best friend a hug. You can't get in the zone on a long run or stare up at the stars and wonder if there's life in outer space.

Think of some of the things you enjoy doing the most. Things that fill you with joy, put a smile on your face, make you feel good about yourself, make your parents * proud of you, cause your younger siblings to look up to you. I bet a lot of those things—maybe even all of them—happen offline.

＊FAMILY PHANTASMAGORIA

In a perfect world, the term I use to refer to the adult(s) with whom you live would exactly describe *your* particular domestic circumstance. But that would mean that every time I mention these creatures, I would have to say "your parents, or parent, or grandmother or grandparents, or aunt and uncle, or mom and stepdad, or dad and dad, or foster parent, or two moms, or dad and stepmom, or adoptive father and his girlfriend, who's from Saturn (but that's a secret)." And *that* would mean by the time you finished reading this book you could have teenage children of your own.

So please know that whatever term I use, it's meant to refer to *your* family life and the people who take care of you. This book will work for you whether you live with one, two, three, or four-and-a-half adults (Uncle Albert being *very* immature); whether your folks are divorced, separated, unmarried, twice married to each other, gay, straight, transgender, or gender fluid; whether you share a roof with one mom, two great-grandparents, three siblings, four stepbrothers, five cats, thirteen hamsters, or . . . I think you get it. Got it?

Got it!

Along with the magic and information, the connections and games, the friendships and support, the texts and tweets and tags and shares and likes and posts—along with all the wonderful, positive things smartphones, social media, and the internet have made possible, there's another side to them.

The Dark Side.

You may have encountered it. Smartphones and social media can be used to hack and attack, tattle and rattle, brag and nag, hurt and blurt, roast and ghost, feud and brood. People can be mean and obscene, gross and morose; they can lie and defy, cheat and mistreat, steal and conceal, hate and berate.

They can also make waaayyy too many rhymes.

The internet is full of misinformation, scams, viruses, phishing, blackmail, fake stories, fake videos, and fake people. That "nice kid" who says he's in tenth grade at a school in your town and wants you to send him photos of yourself may be a 70-year-old who lives 5,000 miles away. Not everything you find is true. Not everyone you meet is who they say they are.

You may be rolling your eyes and thinking . . . *if one more person tells me not to send naked selfies; that anything I post lasts forever; that there's no privacy online; or that I shouldn't put my home address, social security number, and combination to my locker in my profile . . .*
I'M GOING TO SCREAM!!!

. . . *and* post a video of it.

I hear you.

(It was a loud scream.)

I know *you* probably know about all these risks and the precautions that go along with them. But not everyone does. Some people spend so much time online, they can't imagine life without smartphones. And they shouldn't have to. These devices are great and here to stay. But the digisphere✶ offers so much pleasure, opportunity, information, social connection, and fun that it's easy to forget or deny its dark side—the side of surveillance, scams, hacking, subterfuge, manipulation, and invasion of privacy.

✶*Digisphere* is the term I use to mean all things digital: phones, tablets, laptops, gaming consoles, apps, social media, the internet, etc.

You—Bot and Sold

In the grand scheme of things, we're still just beginning to understand the consequences of social media and a world in which anyone, anywhere, can use the internet to do just about anything they want. Even though the digisphere can be a place of hope, positive action, and connection, it can *also* be used to spread hate, lies, and bigotry; to bully and shame; to undermine elections and democracies; to distort truth, facts, and reality.

Here's something else to consider. Just by using the internet, *you* have become a product. You're not a customer. You're a commodity. Governments and Big Tech—that's the major companies like Apple, Google, Amazon, Facebook, Microsoft—watch you online. They can scan your messages and calls. They know where you go and what you do. They know what you like, what you buy, what you search for, what you worry about. They have a file on you—millions of data points—that they share with and sell to other companies. They invade your devices, placing tracking cookies inside your phone and tablet and laptop to monitor you. They design their platforms and games to manipulate you—and, yes, addict you—for your clicks, likes, attention, and money.

Teens for Sale

Nutrition Facts	
Serving Size 1 Teenager IP 17.22.481.01	
Servings Per Device 1 (age 15 5'7" 60kg)	
	% Daily Value
Total Time 7.5 hours	**330%**
Saturated Social Media 4.5 hours	**220%**
Trans Insta Fat 0 hours	
Polyunsaturated Texting 0.5 hours	**26%**
Sodium Snapchat 2 hours	**98%**
Gender Female	
Sexuality Questioning	
Likes Granola Koalas Leggings Yellow Soccer	
Dislikes Rain Nose Rings Pimples Torn Jeans	
Total Mood Fiber	
Depressed 0.5 hours	**2.5%**
Lonely 1.5 hours	**15%**
Happy 4.5 hours	**50%**
Scared 0.5 hours	**2.5%**
Confident 3 hours	**30%**

Life online can threaten you from the outside—cyberbullying, bogus information, mean comments, ransomware attacks. Scammers, politicians, governments, and corporations can intentionally try to hurt or use you for their own benefit. Too much time spent online can also harm you from the inside, just between you and you—affecting the way you feel, learn, grow, and relate to people—and yourself. It can affect your moods, grades, self-image, self-confidence, and self-control. It can change your brain and the way you think. It can affect your health—even your posture!

Social scientists (those are scientists who *really* like to party) have studied whether screen time affects kids and teenagers in negative ways. There's data that suggests yes and data that suggests no. It may take decades more to know for sure, since certain effects can only be identified through long-term studies. It's similar to what happened with tobacco. There were indications as far back as 1920 that cigarette smoking was harmful and might cause cancer. But it wasn't until 1964 that the US Surgeon General's report linking it to cancer finally came out. And it took decades longer after that for laws and societal attitudes and behaviors to push back against the dangers of smoking.

I don't smoke.

Glad to hear it.

I believe that in 5, 10, or 30 years, we will have evidence that digital devices and platforms are also causing developmental and societal harm (even while offering many benefits), and then we will wonder why people didn't rise up earlier.

In one sense, though, it doesn't matter what the research finds. It doesn't matter if 20 percent, 50 percent, or 80 percent of teens experience certain negative (or positive) consequences. All that *really* matters is what YOU experience. Think of allergies. Some people have none. Some people have a few allergies that are easy to avoid or ignore. And some people have allergies so severe they can be life-threatening. If YOU have an allergy, whether common or rare, then it's irrelevant to you how other people react to pollen, dog hair, mold, or bee stings.

The same holds true for people who may experience "allergic" reactions from their exposure to the digital world. It doesn't matter what the research says or how it affects other people. The reaction that counts is your own. The good news is that this book will provide you with knowledge and self-awareness you can use to assess whether you might be having an unhealthy "allergic reaction" to any aspects of your device use. And if you are, you'll discover how to strengthen your online immunity and protect yourself from the worst aspects of Big Tech.

By now, my point of view may be sneaking up on you.

How about crashing into me like an 18-wheeler.

I do believe that digital devices, social media, and the internet—as useful, essential, miraculous, and even life-saving as they are—also have the potential to harm teens (and adults) and society. I believe they *have* done harm, and will continue to do so.

Whether this is the case for you, I don't have a clue. This is because (sadly) I don't know you. I don't know how much time you spend on a screen, how you use it, what else is going on in your life, what kind of personality you have, whether you're a cat person or a frog person, what your family is like, whether you put ketchup or mustard on a hot dog.

Perhaps you aren't consciously aware of whether your digital life is causing you harm, either. I say "consciously" because I believe teens are deeply intuitive. They often know something in their gut long before they know it in their head. Meanwhile, their gut may be causing them feelings of stress, guilt, worry, or fear, leading to conflicts and problems. Moving "knowledge" from your gut to your head is one of the best ways to deal with negative or troublesome feelings. That's why keeping a journal, talking to a friend or trusted adult, or seeing a therapist can be so helpful. They are all processes that bring thoughts and feelings into the light of day.

> ***My* gut is telling me I shouldn't have eaten that third burrito.**

When I hear that a Common Sense Media survey found that roughly 40 percent of all teens say they "feel addicted" to their phones, I suspect that many of those teens have unexamined, troubling feelings in their gut. They may feel confused, ashamed, helpless, scared, or out of control. They may wonder why they can't cut back despite wanting to; why their willpower lets them down. Disturbing as these feelings can be, they are a perfectly natural response to the power and manipulations of Big Tech and social media. The important thing to remember is that you *can* take charge. Using the smarts in your head (and this book), you'll be able to reap the best—and repel the worst—of the digital world.

Tech Alert!
LEFT TO YOUR OWN DEVICES
You'll see the words *phones* and *smartphones* throughout this book. In some cases I mean specifically that little device you take everywhere and use to say, "Hello, hello, can you hear me?" In other cases, which you'll know because you're clever, I mean any digital device with a screen, whether a smartphone, tablet, watch, laptop, gaming console, or television, that you use to make calls, send messages, visit social media, play music, browse the internet, play games, watch videos, etc.

Join the Resistance

Don't get me wrong. The internet's riches are beyond imagination. Social media is an incredible way to connect with people. Smartphones are technological miracles. Together, they have saved many people's lives and improved life for even more people. The COVID-19 pandemic revealed how interwoven these technologies are into the fabric of our existence. Without them, there would have been no remote learning. No working from home. No online shopping and contactless deliveries. No rapid-fire data crunching, no complex modeling of disease trajectories, no medical breakthroughs in record time, no videos of country singers serenading their cockatoos.

And because of the digisphere, we were able to stay in touch with friends, teachers, and grandparents; to be inspired by stories of courage, sacrifice, and triumph; to be saddened by stories of tragedy, despair, and heartache; to separate fact from fiction, truth from spin, genuine hope from magical thinking; to hear balcony arias; to be mesmerized by a cascade of 100,000 falling dominoes. The internet kept millions of people from going bonkers while being confined to their homes for weeks and months. Think of all the wonderful memes and videos that linked the world as millions of people shared them. Kind of gives new meaning to something going *viral*.

But the underside of these worlds—the things we don't know, and how these devices and the time we spend on them are affecting us as individuals, communities, and societies—is . . .

Chilling.

It's *so* chilling I have to wear my parka even when it's 80 degrees out.

People are just beginning to realize the extent to which digital devices, social media, and spending hours a day online have the potential to change human behavior, emotion, communication, interaction, and attitudes in both positive and negative ways. That a few giant corporations now control how we think and feel, what we do, and what we buy would have been unimaginable 20 years ago. That social media can be used by anyone, anywhere, to dispense lies, promote division, and influence elections is a destructive force that early innovators never contemplated. (At least I hope they didn't. Although I wish they had.)

I'm not saying this to scare you (well, maybe a little) or to tell you that these devices are inherently "bad" (they're not). But their misuse can hurt you and people you care about. It can stain your life and future in ways that you may not be able to undo.

The internet is a vast, unknown world. To make sure you're the master of your devices and online life—to make sure your smartphone is *your* tool, and you're not *its* tool—you need to be aware of the risks and dangers, so you can stay healthy, safe, and wise.

And that's what this book is about.

Putting you in charge. So that your phone works for you. And not the other way around.

Menu

To accomplish this, the book is divided into three parts.

Part 1: REFLECT

These first three chapters will get you thinking about the issues. You'll encounter a series of nine **challenges** and **missions** that will reveal to you the nature of your screen scene. The intel you gather will encourage you to reflect (get it?)—

> Yeah, I get it.

—on how you use your devices and how that may be affecting you for better or worse. If the challenges reveal or reinforce concerns you have about your screen time, you'll be able to use that intel to tune up your digital life, using strategies discussed later in the book.

Part 2: RESIST

These six chapters look at ways screen time can affect your body, brain, relationships, psyche, privacy, safety, reputation, and life balance. Some of these ways you may already know or sense. Others will be new—and maybe even disturbing—to you. You'll find tons of tips that will help you to resist (get it?)—

> Jeesh! Yeah, I get it.

—and protect yourself from Big Tech's meddling with your mind, emotions, and future.

Part 3: RESET

This is where you pull it all together. In these final three chapters you can combine the intel you gathered about your screen scene with the boundless knowledge you've gained to—

> Lemme guess. Reset.

> You got it!

—your digital life. No matter where you find yourself along the continuum of screen time, whether 36 minutes a day or 36 hours a day, you'll find steps you can take to give yourself an App-endectomy—

> Give myself a WHAT-endectomy?!?

> App-endectomy. That's an operation where you cut out any unhealthy aspects of your screen scene. Get it? APP? APP-endectomy?

> Are you gonna do this throughout the whole book?

> Count on it!

—to ensure that your screen scene enhances, rather than harms, your life.

Book Alert!

If you are especially observant, you may have noticed that this is a, er, how to put it, a *longish* book. But I don't think you'll find it long and *boring*. On the contrary, I think you'll find it's full of useful, interesting, and important information. So I hope you'll read it from front to back (I don't recommend reading it back to front). But if you're not sure, if you're still thinking *them there's a lotta pages,* it's fine to dip into the book. (Pretend it's guacamole and you're the chip.)

You could start with chapters 2 and 3, which have lots of challenges to get you thinking about your device usage and habits.

> **Those are good. I peeked.**

You could then dive into the RESIST chapters that interest you most. You'll find loads of information on how screen time can affect you, and tips for living a healthier online life and not being Big Tech's sucker (or lollipop). And if you think you might like to make some changes in your digital life, check out the RESET chapters. They'll show you how.

So, feel free to hop, skip, and jump in and out of the book. There's no rule that you have to start at the beginning and finish at the end. (I checked.)

The resistance has begun. It's in its infancy. But people are waking up. They're realizing how digital devices affect emotions, health, and human interactions. They're exposing the motives and misdeeds of tech companies that influence and control our lives. These internet revolutionaries are reducing or eliminating their own presence on social media. They're turning off their phones at night. They're taking steps to fight back against Big Tech and Peeping Tom corporations.

Use your phone. Love your phone. (I know I do.)

> **You love MY phone?!?**

> No. MY phone!

Play your favorite games, post on your favorite apps, text your favorite people. Find ways to use that time to do good in the world and bring joy and encouragement to yourself and others. But join the resistance. Be empowered. Learn how to slay the digital dragons—to thwart the people and companies trying to control and profit off of you. Learn how to stay safe. And, especially, learn how to protect your goodness, identity, self-confidence, and future from . . .

The Dark Side.

And now, if you'll excuse me, I need to go online to buy some navy-blue shoe polish and a blow torch for making crème brulée, text a friend a photo of the albino skunk I just saw in my yard, see if it's going to rain tomorrow, and find out if bears can carry coronaviruses.

Check Out My Profile

You may be wondering why you should pay any attention to what I have to say.

> I am DEFINITELY wondering that.

Well, many people, having read my books and attended my talks, extol (and truly, it makes me blush to even mention this) my brilliance and expertise #humblebrag. But beyond that, I have a Ph.D. (pronounced "Phidd") in educational and developmental psychology. I was the head of a school for 11- to 16-year-olds and president of an organization that provides substance abuse prevention programs for middle and high schools across the United States and in over 65 countries around the world.

I've written 11 books for teens, parents, teachers, counselors, and youth care professionals, including *How Rude! The Teen Guide to Good Manners, Proper Behavior, and Not Grossing People Out.* (So you can be sure that I will be very polite in offering advice.) Speaking of advice, mine is often sought, and I have spoken at schools and conferences around the world to the point that I often don't know whether I am coming or going. Or going or coming.

So, as a psychologist, educator, and expert in dependency and addiction who has been #soblessed to know and work with teens over the years, I come at the issue of screen time from many different and useful angles.

My greatest qualification, though, may be that I spend a huge amount of my own time on devices. I never thought of myself as someone who might be overdosing on screens. Never, that is, until I began to write this book and learn more about how the internet and digital technologies affect users. I figured, because I don't spend 10 hours a day glued to social media or playing video games; because I don't send and receive 300 texts a day or watch tons of video clips, my digital device use was moderate and "safe."

But then I realized that, on an average day, I spend at least 10 to 11 hours looking at a screen—writing, reading the news, doing research (e.g., do stinkbugs hibernate? What's the origin of the word *posh*? What rhymes with King Kong?), organizing photos, shopping (bear spray, ginger preserve, hand sanitizer, red high-top sneakers, used books, a BugZooka™), streaming TV, doing email, watching cable news (which depresses me), and clocking out with late night comedians (who cheer me up) right before bedtime. (Always try to go to bed laughing!)

> **What DOES rhyme with King Kong?**

I don't think of myself as "addicted" to screens. The way I use my online time seems healthy, reasonable, and necessary to function in the world. Offline, I see friends, make phone calls, wash my truck, go to the hardware store, talk to the deer, cut the grass, put off things I don't like to do, exercise, swear when I drop something on my toe, listen to music, read, and eat. It *feels* balanced to me.

But still . . . 10 to 11 hours!?! I was shocked! Flabbergasted! Gobsmacked! The more I looked into the effects of screen time for this book, the more I realized that I do experience many of the negative consequences I was learning about. My eyes get dry. My vision gets blurry. My fingers hurt. My neck aches. My friends ask if I'm okay because they haven't heard from me. I sit for hours at a time without getting up or moving. I go online to buy a book and two hours later realize that I have 14 books in my cart and it's 1 a.m. Need I go on?

> **Please do!**

I see all these great things I'd love to buy, but they cost too much. I see all these people having such great lives and it gets me wondering about my own. If I'm bored, my first instinct is to beeline for my computer to entertain myself. It's easier than tackling any of the more challenging projects I know I'd enjoy if I only started them.

My point is that I am not approaching this topic all holier-than-thou trying to convince you of anything. If I hear a notification, I, too, instantly reach for my phone. (But I am training myself to turn them off if I need to concentrate.) I'm not saying that smartphones and screen time are terrible. I *love* what I do online. I'm not preaching or judging anything. I'm not saying you should do one thing or not do another thing. That's for you to decide. What I am saying, as I have learned from looking at my own use, is that your screen time and its effects are uniquely yours. Some of them may be great, some may be *meh*, and some may be harmful. I just hope that you will reflect, resist, and, if you feel it makes sense for you, reset.

Ding-dong.

Huh?!?

Rhymes with King Kong.

Ping-pong.

Singsong.

Tech Alert!
THE CONSTANCY OF CHANGE

There's a lag-time between when I'm writing this and when you're reading it, and during that period governments may have passed new tech regulations; Apple may have further strengthened its anti-tracking privacy features; Google may have eliminated third-party cookies; Big Tech companies may have been broken up; new, better apps may have appeared; some apps I mention may have fallen out of favor; other apps may not support certain operating systems; rampaging hordes of elves from Outer Roboland may have infected the internet with earwax-craving viruses, a particular app may react glitch-ily with your phone, and what this all means is that you should do your own research, look at reputable reviews, be cautious about what you install on your devices, and, most important of all, not send me angry emails saying the tech landscape has changed, or you followed my suggestions and your tablet turned into a shape-shifting, mutant, mobile monster.

Dude, that was one LONG sentence.

Did you get through it all right?

No problem!

CHAPTER 2

YOUR SCREEN SCENE

Decoding Your Digital Life

Do your parents ever say, "We're worried about how little time you spend on your phone"?

Didn't think so.

It's more likely they say, "Can't you put that thing down for one second!?!"

Many families argue about how much time kids spend on their phones. Some parents think it's too much. Other parents think it's WAAAAAAY too much.

What do you think? Do you feel in control of your phone? Or do you sometimes wonder if *it* controls *you*?

In this chapter and the next, you'll find nine challenges for exploring your relationship to the digital world. Each focuses on a different aspect of screen time. With the successful completion of each challenge, you'll gain valuable insights that will allow you to complete more difficult missions, teleport across biomes, and earn R-Bucks (R for Reflect, Resist, and Reset!) that you can use to purchase sorcerer secrets, lava swords, and the newest skin for a Battle Royale against Big Tech.

> Really?

> No, of course not. This is a book, not a video game.

I'm presenting the nine challenges as a video game parody for a reason. Many video games (and social media apps and other platforms) are *consciously* designed to addict you. (You'll hear much more about this in chapter 9.) Your attention, your digital trail, and, ultimately, your money, is the treasure Big Tech is after. They use every trick in the book to hook you: psychology, emotional manipulation, brain chemistry, colors, sounds, rewards—you name it. Think of Snapstreaks. What a (deviously) brilliant way to get you coming back to Snapchat day after day

> Okay! I get the point.

Well, if you get the point, let's get to the challenges. Let's play **ScreencraftNITE.**

CHALLENGE 1: WHAT'S *YOUR* SCREEN SCENE?
Level 1: Dawn of Enlightenment
Mission 1: Searching for the Beacon of Knowledge

The following questions are about your screen time over the *past six months*.

"Screen time" means any activity (texting, messaging, emailing, streaming, surfing, shopping, Snapping, viewing, gaming, reading, writing, chatting, posting) . . .

. . . that involves a device with an electronic screen (smartphone, tablet, laptop, e-reader, watch, gaming console, television) . . .

. . . that you do online and/or offline, by yourself and/or with others, whether for school, work, or pleasure.

There are no right or wrong answers here. No good or bad. It's a judgment-free zone. The purpose of the challenge is simply to see how *you* feel about your screen use. I promise I haven't placed cookies in this book to track your responses. (Although I did eat a few while writing the book.) Nobody but you will know your answers. So, reflect on your screen time and be as honest and self-aware as you can.

The challenge that follows is also available for download at freespirit .com/dragons.

CHALLENGE 1: WHAT'S *YOUR* SCREEN SCENE?

Your mission is to place a checkmark in the column that represents your response to each statement. The lines are electrified, but there's a secret challenge for avoiding them that will award you triple XP if you succeed . . . trust me.

	Never	Rarely	Sometimes	Often	Very Often
I spend more time online than I plan to.					
People close to me complain or express concern about how much time I spend online.					
When I'm not online, I think about what I'm missing and can't wait to get back online.					
I lie, feel ashamed about, or hide what I do online or how much time I spend online.					
When I see or hear a notification, I check my phone right away, even if it interrupts what I'm doing.					
I use my phone when I know doing so is impolite, against the rules, and/or a safety hazard.					
I worry that I may be spending too much time on my phone.					
I sleep with my phone on and within reach.					
I wish I could reduce the amount of time I spend online and/or have tried to do so without success.					
I use screen time to escape my feelings or problems in real life.					
Things I do online make me feel sad, anxious, lonely, uncool, empty, and/or depressed.					

CONTINUED ›

	Never	Rarely	Sometimes	Often	Very Often
I lose sleep due to nighttime phone use.					
I neglect chores, relationships, and/or responsibilities due to the time I spend online.					
My schoolwork (grades, homework, relationships with teachers) has been harmed by my screen time.					
I have stopped seeing friends or doing activities I used to like as a result of my screen time.					
I feel it's easier to relate to people online than in person.					
I turn to my phone by default when I am bored or have nothing better to do.					
I feel nervous, uncomfortable, or like I'm missing out on something when I don't have my phone.					
I prefer to be online rather than do things with friends or family members.					
I have trouble focusing, remembering, being organized, and/or finishing tasks when I'm offline.					
Total number of checkmarks for:	Never	Rarely	Sometimes	Often	Very Often
	X 1 point =	X 2 points =	X 3 points =	X 4 points =	X 5 points =
		=	Total Points		

Compute Your Score: Assuming you weren't electrocuted by touching a line, here's how to figure out your score: Add up the checkmarks in each column and multiply that number by the point value for that response. For example, if you answered "Never" to all 20 questions, your score would be 20 (20 answers x 1 point). If you answered "Sometimes" to 5 questions, "Often" to 5 questions, and "Very Often" to 10 questions, your score would be 85 (5 "Sometimes" answers x 3 points = 15; 5 "Often" answers x 4 points = 20; 10 "Very Often" answers at 5 points = 50 (15 + 20 + 50 = 85).

Interpret Your Score: If your score is less than 40, it's a good bet you're in the "safe" zone when it comes to screen time. You're in charge of how much time you spend on your devices, and it's in healthy balance with other activities. If your score is in the 40–60 range, you may sometimes have difficulty controlling your screen time. If your score is greater than 60, your screen time is likely interfering with your life, relationships, and/or responsibilities in ways that are bothering you on some level.

▥➡ **Last But Not Least:** Wait, you thought you were through? NOOOOOOOOOO! Before a new game begins and resets your answers above, go back and circle any statements where your response is of concern to you. These may be statements where you answered "Often" or "Very Often." We'll refer back to these later.

Having completed the What's *Your Screen Scene?* challenge, you are now a *Brave-Hearted Apprentice Oracle of Awareness*. With this badge, you may pass through the portal to the next level. The Razor Laser Saber you have earned will give you a better, but still slim, chance of surviving your next mission: Slices of Truth. But first, you must cross the perilous Sea of Words between here and chapter 3 without disappearing into the Alluring Abyss of Alliteration, from which few readers ever return.

This is dumb.

You don't feel the slightest pride in having completed the first challenge?

No.

Not even a mini-morsel of curiosity about the next challenge? The dangers lurking?

No.

Come on . . . Not even the teensiest, itsy-bitsy-est sense of accomplishment? Not even a microscopic molecule of curiosity?

Well, maybe an atom's worth.

AHA!!! Big Tech has you in its claws.

The Aforementioned Perilous Sea of Words

You now have an initial sense of your Screen Scene. Your score fell someplace between "no sweat" and "pools of perspiration." The reason the Screen Scene challenge is useful is because it is based on *warning signs.* In the World of Psychology, of which I am a member, a warning sign is a clue that provides information about a person's health. The clue can be physical (like frequent headaches or low energy), social (like getting into fights or losing friends), emotional (like feeling depressed or having low self-esteem), or cognitive (like getting poor grades or not being able to focus on a task). You get the idea.

The more warning signs a person shows, the more likely it is that they are experiencing a particular problem. But since these clues only reveal *symptoms,* further detective work is often necessary to figure out the *cause.* For example, if somebody's nose is running, it could be the result of allergies, flu, a cold, or forgetting to turn off the faucet. If somebody is isolating themselves and doesn't want to see other people or go to school, the cause could be anything from a video gaming addiction to bullying to depression to an abusive parent to a passionate, all-consuming interest.

The Screen Scene challenge asked you to indicate how often you experienced thoughts, feelings, and/or behaviors that are warning signs for possible negative consequences of excessive screen time. If you responded "Never" or "Rarely" to a question, you're not exhibiting that warning sign (or you're in denial about it). By the same token, answering "Often" and "Very Often" means you are experiencing it. (I hope the World of Psychology doesn't kick me out for revealing these secrets.) The more warning signs you experience, the more likely it is that the nature and duration of your screen time may be causing problems.

If your answers place you in a "worry" zone, don't panic. You've already taken a great first step—increased self-awareness. You can use that to re-balance your online and offline lives. You'll see how to do this in chapters 10 and 11. But because warning signs only indicate symptoms, we (or, more to the point, *you*) need to reflect more on the nature of your screen time, and how it affects you, to get a better understanding of the causes.

May the Force of Wisdom be with you as you pass from the Overworld through the Page-Turn Portal to the challenges of chapter 3.

Searching for the Beacon of Knowledge

Dear Alex,

"My mom is always bugging me about how much time I spend on my phone. I think she should be happy I'm not using drugs or stealing from stores. Why does screen time even matter?"

It doesn't. UNLESS it interferes in negative ways with your daily life and healthy development. Then it becomes a problem. Balance is the key. Happy, healthy, responsible teens tend to balance the different areas of their life such as school, friends, family, sports, work, play, chores, sleep, creative projects, social media, vegging out, and "real" versus virtual. If any of these get in the way of other needs and responsibilities, your balance may be threatened.

But I do agree with you. No matter how much time you spend on your phone, your mom should be grateful that you are not a drug dealer, kleptomaniac, serial killer, sword swallower, or mutant zombie.

Dear Alex,

"Is all screen time the same? I admit I spend lots of time online and at my computer. (Like maybe nine or ten hours a day.) But I'm mostly doing stuff like making movies and videos. Can you tell my dad that's okay?"

I'm not the Internet Police. So I'm afraid you'll have to make the case to your dad yourself. But maybe this will help.

Screen time is tricky. Like you, lots of teens spend many hours a day in front of a screen. How you spend that time does make a difference. For example . . .

- Are you creating or vegetating?
- Are you a passive spectator, or are you digging deep into your mind, feelings, and imagination to learn, connect, grow, and express yourself?
- Is your screen time a *healthy* balance of homework, staying in touch with friends, playing games, learning, posting on social media, and watching videos—or are you spending eight hours a day killing space invaders, evading Creepers, mining Obsidian blocks, outbuilding noobs in Salty Springs, spamming boogie bombs on enemies for a game clip, trying to become Twitch famous, and catapulting angry zombie chunks at a bunch of pig-shaped falling tiles while battling Blazes and Wither Skeletons to prevent famine and build a portal to the Nether?

- Does your time online make you feel happy, valued, productive, and close to people you know in real life? Or does it make you feel depressed, lonely, guilty, uncool, or insecure?

- Is your screen time focused and meditative (as in editing a film), or does it bombard you every few seconds with a cacophony of sounds, lights, banners, pop-ups, notifications, and attention-grabbing "got-chas" across multiple open windows?

- When you're *not* staring at a screen, are you physically active, seeing friends, spending time with your family, and keeping up with your other responsibilities?

- Is moss growing on you?

Thinking about these questions, you can see that not all screen time is the same in how it affects your feelings, productivity, relationships, and future. You could probably make a good case that your screen time is creative and productive, and could help you become a rich, famous movie director who will buy your dad a beautiful car and a beach house and take care of him in his old age. (I'm trying to help, here.)

But even if your screen time is "healthy," **you're still experiencing life electronically through a device for many hours each day.** While the tech industry may like that, it is not a recipe for optimal human functioning and fulfillment, and it can have negative physical, social, mental, and emotional consequences no matter how you're spending that time. It's not just a question of *what you're doing online*. It's also a question of what you're *not doing offline*.

So, it's a complex equation, and you have to look at the entire picture in order to assess whether your screen time is healthy or not. (Don't forget to invite me to your movie premiere.)

CHAPTER 3

GATHERING INTEL

Exploring the Valley of Appland

If you are reading this, it means you bravely crossed the Sea of Words. You outwitted octopi, evaded eels, silenced Sirens, pilloried piranhas, and beheaded hydra without being sucked into the Alluring Abyss of Alliteration. The Dawn of Enlightenment arose in you, and you are now, armed with your Razor Laser Saber, ready to confront the next challenges.

> Not this again.

Onward! By way of ancient Greece.

Socrates was a Greek philosopher (philosophers are people who think a lot) who said, *"The unexamined life is not worth living."* I couldn't agree more. In fact, I'd love to invite him to dinner and tell him so personally, except he died over 2,000 years ago after being sentenced to death for expressing ideas that didn't sit too well with the ruling powers of Athens.

What Socrates (@hemlock399BCE) meant was that wisdom comes from knowing oneself. The more knowledge and self-awareness a person has, the more that person will be able to make ethical, wise choices that bring true happiness and contribute to the well-being of society. This is expressed in another Socratic meme: *"To find yourself, think for yourself."*

While Socrates's thoughts on screen time and social media were never recorded, I'm pretty sure he would have said, "The unexamined digital life is not worth living." He would have agreed with me—great minds think alike!—that you are not some passive jug of olive oil to whom life does its thing. You're in the driver's seat of your own chariot. Of course life will throw tridents and detours your way (I'm sure it already has). Some of them may be easy to sidestep. Others—such as those resulting from racism, discrimination, ignorance, economic hardship, family troubles, or systemic social inequalities—are much harder to overcome. But you have the power and the right to find friends, mentors, and paths (and yes, they are out there!) to help you steer your life in the direction of your dreams, passions, and goals. You have the wisdom and the responsibility to take good care of yourself and others, and to avoid potholes. (Don't worry, there'll still be lots of potholes to hit—and learn from—and maybe even be thankful for someday.) For now, think of excessive screen time as one of the potholes you'll run into. And think of Socrates looking down from the Cloud, encouraging you to examine your life and relationship to the digital agora.

Next up: Eight more challenges for examining your screen time. There's no right or wrong here. There's only what is best for you. If you recognize yourself, for better or worse, in the pages of this book and the questions in this chapter, use that knowledge to make informed choices—to lead an *examined life*.

Mind the Gap

Maybe you've heard that phrase before.

> Nope. Can't say I have.

> It's used all over the world to warn train and subway passengers to be careful and pay attention when stepping across the gap between the car and the station platform.

You're about to mind a different sort of gap, where you will:

1. **G**ather intel
2. **A**nalyze data
3. **P**lan your operation

For one week, you're going undercover. And I don't mean crawling into bed under three blankets. I mean you're going to spy on yourself. You're going to do a stakeout of your screen time and digital device use each day for seven days. Everything from the nuts and bytes of where you go and what you do to why you do it and how you feel about it. You'll use state-of-the-art tools and tradecraft and end up with a screen scene profile of "me, myself, and my devices." Doing your stake-out for seven days is important to ensure that you include weekdays and weekends and that any atypical days that skew your screen time way up (or way down) have a good chance of being evened out.

This profile will allow you to identify aspects of your digital life that you find most helpful, necessary, and pleasurable, as well as areas that cause you concern or harm. By gathering intel, analyzing the data, and planning an eventual opera-tion—which I call an App-endectomy—you will be able to press the reset button to achieve a healthier relationship with your devices.

So, grab your back bling, don your Battle Robe, mount your glow jet, and may the time travel begin.

CHALLENGE 2: HOW DO I SPEND MY SCREEN TIME?
Level 2: Slices of Truth
Mission 2: Terminating Time Trolls

Here's a pie. Lemon meringue, to be exact (minus the meringue). The pie challenge is also available for download at freespirit.com/dragons.

CHALLENGE 2: HOW DO I SPEND MY SCREEN TIME?

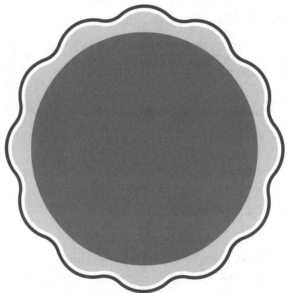

Instructions

Your mission is to "cut" the pie into pieces that represent the proportion of time you spend each day, on average, on each activity. Here are some of the ways you may use your devices:

- playing games
- texting, messaging, video chatting
- using social media
- streaming movies or tv shows
- watching videos
- doing homework
- creating (e.g., writing, drawing, composing, coding, designing, filmmaking, photo editing)
- web surfing
- shopping
- other _____
- other _____
- other _____
- other _____

If you don't do any of the above activities, don't put them on your pie. If you spend time doing things online that are not on this list, *do* be sure to include them. Label each piece by category and average time spent per day. If an activity strikes you as *combining* categories (for example, talking with teammates while gaming online), decide which category seems dominant to you, and give it that label.

This mission is primarily focused on the time you *choose* to be on a screen. In other words, *do not include screen time during the school day if it's required for a class you're in*. But *do* include all other in-school screen time you *choose* to spend (for example, social media during a free period, watching videos at lunch).

Also be sure to count how much time you spend on homework *outside of school*.

> **WAIT!!!** You said this was about time you *choose* to be on a screen. I don't choose to do homework. I mean, I do. But I don't. You know what I mean. Right?

I know exactly what you mean. Homework *is* required. But often, homework time is also Snap time, YouTube time, Insta time, texting time, and checking-out-a-vid-of-a-trained-octopus-that-can-open-eight-jars-at-once time. This can turn three hours of homework into six hours of "homework."

So, even if homework feels less like a choice and more like a teen's job description, it's still part of your overall outside-of-school, personal screen scene. So it's important to quantify it.

As you think about this, don't distinguish between your devices. For example, if you play games and use social media on your phone during the day, but do it on your laptop at night, add up your gaming and social media time across all devices.

Feel free to adapt the pie chart to make it most useful and informative to you in providing a profile of your screen time. You might want to add notes, invent new categories, draw emojis, or sprinkle coconut flakes if it will give you a clearer understanding of your typical daily device use. *To earn extra R-Bucks, use your Razor Laser Saber to slice the pie.*

Here's the pie chart of one kid who spends about seven hours a day on her devices.

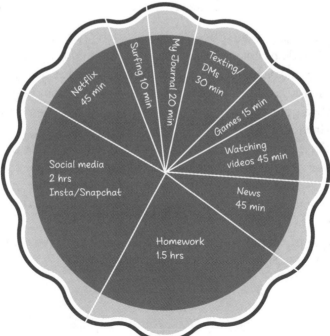

Having traversed the treacherous tempests of time, you are now a *PIE-oneering Protector of the Past, Present, and Future.* You drove the time trolls out of their dark lair and into the light, using your Razor Laser Saber to slice and dice their Minute-Menacing Madness into a mushy mess to feed the Kind Villagers of Evermere.

And now, armed with the Starship Spatula, which you have earned, you may travel to The Temple of Time.

> Um . . . Starship Spatula?

CHALLENGE 3: HOW MUCH TIME DO I *THINK* I SPEND?
Level 3: Temple of Time
Mission 3: Shape Shifting into a Grand Guru of Guessing

Instructions

After you've cut up your pie, use your Starship Spatula to transfer each slice to the following table. (Try not to make any crumbs.)

For each of the categories, fill in the "Estimated Time per Day" column with how much time you *think* you spend on average per day. Add up your figures and enter the total estimated screen time at the bottom of the table. Be sure to include any additional "other" categories you created.

Don't worry about the "Actual Time per Day" or "Is This a Concern for You" columns yet. We'll get to those later. And don't forget to answer the Bonus Question.

This challenge is also available for download at freespirit.com/dragons.

CHALLENGE 3: HOW MUCH TIME DO I *THINK* I SPEND?

Activity	Estimated Time per Day	Actual Time per Day	Is This a Concern for You?
Social media—all apps total			No ☐ Yes ☐
Playing games—all games total			No ☐ Yes ☐
Texting, messaging, or video chatting			No ☐ Yes ☐
Streaming movies and TV shows			No ☐ Yes ☐
Watching videos			No ☐ Yes ☐
Creating (e.g., writing, drawing, composing, coding, photo editing)			No ☐ Yes ☐
Doing homework			No ☐ Yes ☐
Web surfing			No ☐ Yes ☐
Shopping			No ☐ Yes ☐
Other:			No ☐ Yes ☐
Other:			No ☐ Yes ☐
Other:			No ☐ Yes ☐
Other:			No ☐ Yes ☐
Time Totals			No ☐ Yes ☐

Bonus Question	Estimated # of Times	Actual # of Times	Is this a concern for you?
How many times a day, on average, do you pick up/ unlock your phone?			No ☐ Yes ☐

You courageously infiltrated the Temple, stealthily using your Starship Spatula to levitate Slices of Truth onto the Tablet of Time. As a *Grand Guru of Guessing*, you have earned the Emerald Shield of Enchantment, and may cross the Moat of Doom to track the Soul Stealers. Wear diamond armor and maintain sapphire vigilance. The Dragons of Algorithm will be stalking you.

> **Moat of Doom? Dragons of Algorithm? I'm outta here.**

> Not so fast. Big Tech is stalking your every move. To keep you from quitting, they're going to give you some easy wins and rewards.

> Here are 2,000 bonus R-Bucks, a redstone hut, and a Battle Pass.

> That's all?

> You drive a hard bargain. Here's a pair of astral supersonic tracker wings.

> I'm hungry.

> Jeesh. Fine, have some golden carrots. Now go replenish your hunger bar and PLAY!!!

CHALLENGE 4: HOW MUCH TIME DO I *ACTUALLY* SPEND?
Level 4: Tracking the Soul Stealers
Mission 4: Time Travel to the 4th Dimension

Most people significantly *under*estimate their screen time and how often they pick up their phone. To really understand your screen scene, it's important to know *exactly* how much time you're spending and how you're spending it. You can't change habits without understanding what they are. The last challenge asked you to make a guess. This challenge will provide you with solid data—the best intel—should you decide to hit the reset button on your digital life.

Your mission is to use a screen time tracker to get an accurate picture of how you use your devices. If you have an iPhone or iPad, or use an Apple computer with macOS Catalina or later, the tracker is called Screen Time. On Android phones, it's called Digital Wellbeing. Both are free. For Windows users there's Microsoft Family Safety, also a free app. This works across Xbox, Android, and all Windows 10 devices. While Microsoft describes it as a tool to allow parents to monitor, limit, and/or manage their children's screen and gaming activity, there's no reason *you* can't use it to produce weekly activity reports of your screen time, and, based on what you discover, set up notifications, create schedules, and/or establish time limits for specific apps to help you achieve any screen scene resets you'd like to make.

Another app is RescueTime, which includes FocusTime (I think whoever came up with these names was missing their space bar). It's a powerful, time-tracking/distraction-blocking app that helps you to manage your device use and is available for most operating systems. There's a free version called RescueTime Lite, as well as a paid version with additional features.

These should allow you to track and coordinate your use across multiple devices with the same operating system. Similar free trackers exist for Chrome and other devices. If a tracker isn't preloaded on your phone, tablet, or computer, you can go to the appropriate app store for your device to look for and install one.

These apps have features to help you understand and manage your screen time. On a daily and weekly basis, you can track such activities as screen time across various platforms and categories, the number and types of notifications you receive, and how often you unlock your phone. Based on what you learn, you can use these tools to block certain apps or websites, limit use to certain hours or up to certain amounts of time, turn off some or all notifications, and even "wind down" to ensure a good night's sleep as you get closer to bedtime.

It's possible that your mom or dad set up these apps as "parental controls" on devices you use in an attempt to limit where you go, what you do, and how long you spend on your phone. I say "attempt" since it's well known that many kids (certainly not you) figure out in a matter of minutes how to outfox these controls. Now, of course, I can't condone that and must say, "Tsk, tsk, you shouldn't try to get around the limits your parents place on your phone use." Really. I should say that. But I cannot tell a lie: It makes me smile to think that teens (and maybe even some nine-year-olds) might be outsmarting Silicon Valley engineers.

> **You shouldn't say that.**

> Say what? I didn't say that. In fact, I have no idea how it ended up in this book. I think I've been hacked.

If there's already a parental control on your phone, tell your mom or dad about your mission to track your online time and activities, and they can help set that up.

Nothing is more precious than your time. Don't let Big Tech steal it with their sneaky algorithms and psychological manipulations. Save yourself from the Soul Stealers! Put on your Emerald Shield of Enchantment, cross the Moat of Doom, sling your Raptor Satchel across your shoulder, and watch out for the Dragons of Algorithm who will be stalking you.

And now, while I figure out how I got hacked, you can launch your next mission.

Instructions for Challenge 4: How Much Time Do I *Actually* Spend?

1. Track your screen time per day/week—how much time you spend on various platforms and activities. Set up your screen-time tracker to provide data that matches, as closely as possible, your uses and the table for Challenge 3: How Much Time Do I *Think* I Spend? (page 30).

   Depending on the tracker you use, the data generated may not correspond exactly to the categories listed on the table. So you'll need to do your best to create "like-to-like" comparisons. Ideally, your tracker will monitor your use of specific apps (e.g., Snapchat, Instagram, FaceTime), as well as general categories (e.g., "social media," "entertainment"). If you need to, you can add up the weekly times you spend on individual apps to come up with totals for a particular category.

2. Track the number of times you pick up/unlock your phone per day/week.

3. Track the number and sources of your notifications per day/week.

4. At the end of the week, record your total actual screen time, phone pick-ups, and notifications over the previous seven days in the appropriate "actual" categories on the table for Challenge 3: How Much Time Do I *Think* I Spend? (page 30).

Note #1: Monitor your use for one week. If possible, this should be a *typical* week, not one where you're cramming for finals, sick in bed, or climbing Mount Everest. Your tracker should provide data on both a daily and weekly basis. Daily stats are useful for seeing if your use changes from day to day. Weekly totals will even out your average in case you have one day when you're spelunking in a cave for six hours with no phone reception, and another day when you gorge on social media.

Note #2: If you use multiple devices—say, a phone and a laptop—it's important to track the above information across all of them. Otherwise you won't have a full picture of your screen time. You want to use a tracker that will collect and aggregate data across all devices with related operating systems, for example, an iPhone and a MacBook. Screen Time and Digital Wellbeing, for example, should be able to do that. If, however, you use an iPhone, a Chromebook, a Windows PC, *and* an Android phone, I'm stumped. I guess you'll have to ask a nine-year-old what to do.

That's a pain!

Look, do you want the Soul Stealers to win? Do you want greedy corporate mobs devouring your time and attention?

No.

> That's the spirit. Here's a turbo coil tracker tusk so you won't leave the game. Now hop on the Battle Bus. We're about to drop!

I know that's a major computational undertaking, but it's important to do. Now you can compare your original guesses with the actual figures from the screen-time tracker. How'd you do? Were your guesses close to your actual use? If not, were you over or under? Wherever you came out, no worries. If you decide you want to make some changes in your screen time, chapters 10 and 11 will show you how.

⫸ Don't forget the most important step: Now is the time to complete the Column of Concern. For each category, circle "Yes" or "No" to indicate whether your answer is of "concern" to you. Is it something you worry about? Something that triggers a bad feeling? Something that makes you feel overwhelmed, powerless, guilty, or unhappy? Something that reminds you of problems in your life? If so, that's a "yes" answer.

Right now, you're simply flagging items of concern. Later, if you decide to do a reset of your digital life, you'll examine more closely the specific nature and source of the concern. That will give you valuable intel for creating your reset plan.

In tribute to your death-defying diligence and mind-blazing mathematical manipulations, you are now an elite *Freedom Fighter of the 4th Dimension* and may enter the Cave of Calculations to receive your reward of FIVE GOLD STARS and the *Crown of the Addition Avenger*. You earned it! With those stars, you have ascended to the level of *Crafty Creative Computationalist* and may seize the Valley of Appland to secure enough blocks to build a village and enough pufferfish, slurp juice, and cake to replenish your health bar for eternity.

CHALLENGE 5: HOW 'APPY AM I?
Level 5: Time Suckers
Mission 5: Exploring the Valley of Appland

Your next mission is to explore the Valley of Appland. You will *appr*aise your *'app*iness by *appr*ehending the *appr*oximate *appo*rtionment of your *app*etite for apps. You will discover which apps and activities are constructive, positive, and life-enhancing and which might be harmful, negative, time-sucking, and life-curdling. As you explore Appland, beware the Demons of Denial seeking to obliterate your self-awareness.

The challenge asks how you feel before and after using various apps. You may not have thought about that. But those feelings can be important clues for understanding your screen scene and making choices about any device-use resets you might want to make. For example, when you think of using certain apps you might feel stoked, curious, anxious, creative, excited, fearful, or ashamed. *After* using them you might feel supported, joyful, proud, enlightened, exhilarated, guilty, worried, embarrassed, angry, or creeped out.

Another question asks if you lose track of time when using an app. That means, do you open the app thinking you'll just be on for a few minutes or half an hour, and then discover that much more time went by than you planned to spend?

Instructions: Fill out (please) the following table using your lifetime of accumulated expertise for how to answer surveys, take tests, fill in blanks, complete sentences, select multiple choice answers, and circle, check, and/or color to indicate your response. As with the "pie" challenge, feel free to add comments, notes, and explanations to make the table as personalized and helpful as possible.

This challenge is also available for download at freespirit.com/dragons.

CHALLENGE 5: HOW 'APPY AM I?

My top 10 apps, in descending order starting with the one I use the most each day, are:	Actual Average Daily Time	How I Feel Before Using App	How I Feel After Using App	I Often Lose Track of Time Using This App	Overall Impact on My Life of Using This App
1.				No ☐ Yes ☐	☺ ☐ 😐 ☐ ☹ ☐
2.				No ☐ Yes ☐	☺ ☐ 😐 ☐ ☹ ☐
3.				No ☐ Yes ☐	☺ ☐ 😐 ☐ ☹ ☐
4.				No ☐ Yes ☐	☺ ☐ 😐 ☐ ☹ ☐
5.				No ☐ Yes ☐	☺ ☐ 😐 ☐ ☹ ☐
6.				No ☐ Yes ☐	☺ ☐ 😐 ☐ ☹ ☐
7.				No ☐ Yes ☐	☺ ☐ 😐 ☐ ☹ ☐
8.				No ☐ Yes ☐	☺ ☐ 😐 ☐ ☹ ☐
9.				No ☐ Yes ☐	☺ ☐ 😐 ☐ ☹ ☐
10.				No ☐ Yes ☐	☺ ☐ 😐 ☐ ☹ ☐

Your *app*-titude for self-discovery is *app*reciated and *app*lauded! You are now an *Ace of Apps* and have earned Golden Wings of Willpower. With them, you can soar over the Swamp of Temptation. If you found Time Suckers and Denial Demons, they must be crushed. This will be a Battle Royale, but the Angel of Honesty will watch over you, whispering in your ear, *"Don't worry, be 'appy."* You will derive strength from her belief in you. But will it be enough to survive the Invasion of the Brain Snatchers? Only time, and the next challenge, will tell.

The average teen spends approximately nine hours a day on a screen. And that doesn't include schoolwork. That comes to 63 hours a week, or 3,276 hours a year, which equals 136.5 days a year!!! If you are that teen, it means approximately 37.5 percent of your life is experienced through a screen.

But wait. Those figures are based on all 24 hours in a day, when you're both awake and asleep. To make a more meaningful analysis, we should analyze those numbers based on the time a teen is awake. If the average teen gets seven hours of sleep a night, let's compute the percentage of conscious *waking* hours these numbers represent. Hmmm, 24 hours, 9 hours on screen, 7 hours sleep, subtract, borrow a 10, carry the 1, add 0 to the denominator, 17 divided by 9 x 1 + 24 minus the square root of 11—GOT IT!

Nine out of 17 waking hours—or 53 percent of the conscious existence of the average teen—is experienced through a screen. To put it another way, on average, half of the time a teen is awake is spent on a screen.

> And now, please excuse me while I pick my jaw up from the floor.

> You're excused.

Okay. I'm back. I know all that time is not monolithic. It's not as though you're spending 136 days a year watching cat videos or even watching cats making videos. You're engaged in thousands of different ways online, doing thousands of different things.

And of course, unforeseen events sometimes change the equation. The COVID-19 pandemic that began in 2019 forced most of us to spend many more hours on screens than usual. And much of what we were doing was vital to our lives *and* to our mental health, whether we were working or learning from home; connecting with friends and family through gaming, social media, or video calls; or getting our entertainment through screens rather than in person.

But still, there's the overarching reality that, even in "normal times," you are living a huge proportion of your life through a screen.

Think of it this way. If you heard of a teen who spends over half of her waking time with her head buried in a book, reading thousands of wonderful books a year, would that give you pause? Her passion for reading is admirable, but such a disproportionate amount of time means she's not doing other things that might be beneficial to her optimal physical, social, or emotional development.

Or think of a teen who spends over half of his waking time—every minute when not in school—cooking tens of thousands of meals for people who are homeless. Would *that* give you pause? Of course what he's doing is noble. But wouldn't you wonder about what he *wasn't* doing? About how *not* hanging out with friends, *not* expanding his mind in other ways, or *not* having a more balanced life might limit his growth?

Now, don't get me wrong. If I met these teens, I would take my hat (or, more accurately, my cap) off to them. I would tell them how much I admire their commitment, their passion, their *compassion*. But then I'd say, "I hope you'll also be sure to spend some time trying on new and different aspects of life." And that's what I'd say to a teen experiencing much of their life through a screen. "Try on as much of life as you can. Analog life. Life that triggers your senses directly, not digitally."

CHALLENGE 6: AM I UNDER ATTACK?
Level 6: Invasion of the Brain Snatchers
Mission 6: Nuking Notifications

"Don't interrupt!" That's one thing almost all parents try to teach their kids. But sadly, Little Naughty Notifications never got the message while growing up. That's why you're bombarded with pushy notifications dozens or hundreds of times a day. *How rude!* These notifications can be everything from texts and messages to emails to phone calls to social media posts to app updates to photo uploads to ads from companies or websites. All clamoring for your attention.

Your mission is to decipher the attack strategies of these Brain Snatchers. Lurk in spectator mode and spy on their war games. Knowing their habits and intentions will allow you to resist the Attack of the Alerts, and nuke notifications into the next universe.

Instructions

1. Fill out the table with your best guesses for how many notifications you receive on average per day from the 10 apps that send you alerts most frequently. Then, estimate the total number of alerts you receive from all other miscellaneous apps combined. Enter those figures in the "*Estimated* Number of Notifications per Day" column. Add them up to get your total *estimated* notifications per day. (Remember to count across all devices you use.)

2. Now check your screen-time tracker for its tabulation of how many notifications you *actually* receive per day and week. Enter those figures in the "*Actual* Number of Notifications per Day" column. (Here, too, make sure the count includes all your devices.)

3. Finally, choose "No" or "Yes" to indicate whether your answer is of concern to you.

   This challenge is also available for download at freespirit.com/dragons.

CHALLENGE 6: AM I UNDER ATTACK?

App Name	Estimated Number of Notifications per Day	Actual Number of Notifications per Day	Is This a Concern for You?
Top App #1:			No ☐ Yes ☐
Top App #2:			No ☐ Yes ☐
Top App #3:			No ☐ Yes ☐
Top App #4:			No ☐ Yes ☐
Top App #5:			No ☐ Yes ☐
Top App #6:			No ☐ Yes ☐
Top App #7:			No ☐ Yes ☐
Top App #8:			No ☐ Yes ☐
Top App #9:			No ☐ Yes ☐
Top App #10:			No ☐ Yes ☐
All Other Miscellaneous Apps:			No ☐ Yes ☐
Total Number of Notifications per Day			No ☐ Yes ☐
Total Number of Notifications per Week			No ☐ Yes ☐

How'd you do? Were your guesses close to your actual counts? Did you overestimate or underestimate your daily notifications? Were you surprised by the total number? It would be interesting to figure out how many notifications you receive on average every hour. (And how many greet you first thing every morning.) I'm math-ed out at the moment. But if you're not, play with the numbers. Do a little analysis. See what they tell you about your screen scene.

You are now a *Notifications Knock-Knock Knockout Ninja*. You possess the secret codes to nuke notifications and avenge yourself against Attention Abductors and Brain Snatchers ransacking your time and focus. You may wear the *Crested Cape of Awareness* you earned with pride. May it protect you as you brave the Jungle of Alerts in search of the Hellscape of Hidden Habbit-Creatures. If you find the Motivation Microscope, grab it! You will need it for the next challenge.

> This is hard! I think I need another reward or I'm going to switch to a different book.

> Big Tech's secret algorithms have detected your flagging interest. To keep you from leaving, how does a Death Star Destroyer sound?

> Cool.

> Look out, Big Tech. This kid is going to be a heroic resistance fighter against your manipulations, addiction bait, and snooping.

CHALLENGE 7: WHAT ARE MY PHONE HABITS AND TRIGGERS?
Level 7: Hellscape of Hidden Habbit-Creatures
Mission 7: Taming the Triggers

People reach for their phones throughout the day. Some people do it relatively few times (yes, such people really do exist!), while others do it dozens or hundreds of times a day. For some people it's an occasional behavior; for others it's a habit; and for still others it may be an addiction—a compulsive behavior they can't seem to stop.

Checking or picking up your phone doesn't happen by accident. The phone doesn't magically levitate to your hand. (At least, not *yet.*) When you pick up your phone, you do it for a reason. Something *triggers* that action. It may be:

- **A reflex or reaction:** answering an incoming call, turning off an alarm, responding to a notification
- **A habit:** you *always* check your phone as soon as you wake up; you *always* check your phone between classes
- **A practical need or desire:** taking a photo, texting your mom that you'll be late, confirming a plan, following directions, checking the weather
- **An emotion or mind-state:** curiosity, joy, loneliness, boredom, anxiety

You may not have given much thought to *why* you pick up your phone. You just do. This mission, if you succeed, will reveal your most frequent triggers and habits—both practical and emotional. You will need X-ray vision to uncover the hidden Habbits burrowed deep inside you. These strong, resourceful creatures are mostly content to remain invisible and lead simple, predictable lives. But if anything threatens their comfort or security (or meals), they will cleverly and courageously fight to protect their way of life. That's why you need to befriend the Habbits within you. Get to know them. They can be kind and loyal. Just make sure they support, rather than thwart, your best self.

This challenge represents the most difficult level yet—hard-core SELF SEARCH mode! Your X-ray vision, plus the Motivation Microscope (which I hope you found crossing the Jungle of Alerts), will help you discover your Habbits and examine your triggers. To acquire clues, you will need to Practice the Pause. This means:

Anytime you pick up your phone, **PAUSE**—and try to remember what happened immediately before you picked it up.

Did a thought fly through your head? Did a feeling fly through your heart? Did you think of a particular person? Did someone say something that made you want to check an app? Did you witness something hilarious or weird or beautiful and crave a photo? Did you see someone else pick up their phone and then, by reflex, reach for yours? (Yawns are like that; just try watching someone yawn without ending up yawning yourself.)

Practicing the Pause will enhance your powers to complete this challenge. Knowing when you're most likely to use your phone and what triggers it—a habit, feeling, or need—will be essential information should you wish to craft a plan for resetting your relationship to your digital devices.

Instructions: To enter the Hellscape of Hidden Habbit-Creatures, first respond to the "My Phone Habits" statements. Then see if you can come up with at least four triggers in each of the practical and emotional categories. Feel free to come up with more. List them in order of frequency. So, the number-one trigger will be the one that causes you to pick up your phone most often. If a trigger seems both emotional and practical, make your best guess as to which element is dominant, and place the trigger in that category. If you think of a trigger that doesn't fit in either category, feel free to list it or create a new category at the bottom of the answer box.

You can also download this challenge at freespirit.com/dragons.

CHALLENGE 7: WHAT ARE MY PHONE HABITS AND TRIGGERS?

My Phone Habits

I check my phone last thing before going to sleep.　　　　No ☐ Yes ☐

I sleep with my phone on and within reach.　　　　No ☐ Yes ☐

I charge my phone overnight near my bed.　　　　No ☐ Yes ☐

I check my phone during the night.　　　　No ☐ Yes ☐

I sleep with a dog.　　　　No ☐ Yes ☐

> **What does that have to do with smartphones?**

> Nothing. I was just curious.

I check my phone first thing in the morning.　　　　No ☐ Yes ☐

I almost always have my phone with me.　　　　No ☐ Yes ☐

I keep my phone on the table when eating with my friends.　　　　No ☐ Yes ☐

I keep my phone on the table when eating with my family.　　　　No ☐ Yes ☐

I check my phone while doing homework.　　　　No ☐ Yes ☐

I check my phone during class.　　　　No ☐ Yes ☐

CONTINUED ›

My Triggers **Practical Triggers** I am most likely to reach for my phone when . . .	1. 2. 3. 4.
Emotional Triggers I am most likely to reach for my phone when I feel . . .	1. 2. 3. 4.
Other Triggers	1. 2. 3. 4.

You have journeyed deep into the Hellscape of Hidden Habbit-Creatures and returned to tell the tale. You have been knighted a *Titan of Trigger Taming*. Your courage to endure the Precipice of Pause has brought you great wisdom. Good thing—you will need it to survive the Dungeon of Digital Abuse. Shed your armor of defensiveness, drink a strong potion of humility, and venture, if you dare, into the next challenge to seek your Achilles Heel.

At various points in your life, you're likely to look back on a period and do a "self-debriefing." This might happen after a two-week backpacking trip. Or sophomore year. Or a relationship. Milestones, partings, and endings often trigger this sort of *examined life.* (Socrates would be proud of you!)

It's natural after, say, experiencing your first summer with a driver's license, graduating from high school or college, or leaving your first job, to reflect on what you experienced. What was wonderful? What was valuable? What made you feel most alive and happy? What was horrible? What did you regret? What would you change if you could?

One of the best self-care steps you can take at any stage of your life is, instead of asking questions about your life *looking backward*, ask them now, *looking forward*. For example, while you're beginning middle school, or approaching the end of high school, or entering college, or starting your first job, ask yourself:

Thinking about these next years between now and [pick your milestone] . . .

. . . What would I like to be able to say about myself?

. . . What would I like to do or accomplish?

. . . How would I like to see myself?

. . . How would I like other people to see me?

. . . How would I like to spend my time?

. . . How would I like to treat others?

. . . What would I like to do for the world?

. . . What would help me feel I am living each day to the fullest?

These are tough questions, and it's fine if you're not sure how to answer or if your answers change over time. I'm also not saying that you (or a parent) should program every second of your day with things that will make you stronger, smarter, happier, more productive, more skilled, or more likely to get accepted by a school or hired for a job. Not at all. Indeed, I'm a definite believer in the importance of play, daydreaming, goofing off, and watching sunsets. (All in balance, of course.)

But one of the saddest things I can think of—and sorry if this brings you down—is people at the end of high school, or college, or even their lives, looking back, who have long lists of wishes and regrets: *I wish I hadn't spent so much time watching blooper videos. I wish I hadn't been so mean to Lucy Lollapalooza in tenth grade. I wish I had spent more time with my children. I wish I had become a teacher instead of a hedge fund arbitrageur. I wish I had followed my dream of becoming an actor. I wish I had learned to play jazz ukulele instead of spending so much time weeding the garden.*

And now, as all things must, this comes around to healthy screen time. You're spending some proportion of your waking hours using digital devices. I don't know how much time you spend, what you do with it, or how it affects your life.

But what I do know is that this would be a great time to leap ahead in your mind to, say, the end of your next milestone. Pretend you're looking back from that future vantage point, and ask yourself:

When I look back on those years . . .

. . . What would I like to be able to say about my screen time?

. . . Is there anything I might end up regretting about my current phone use?

. . . Would I wish I had spent less (or more) time online?

. . . If I could rewind the clock and get back the accumulated nine months I spent on social media during high school, would I use that time differently?

. . . Would I wish that, instead of playing video games, I had used that time to study harder, practice my guitar, join a team, get to know more people, do volunteer work, learn a language, or build bird feeders out of popsicle sticks?

As Socrates would say, "The unexamined WiFi is not forgiving."

CHALLENGE 8: DO I HAVE AN ACHILLES HEEL?
Level 8: The Dungeon of Digital Abuse
Mission 8: Avoiding Kryptonite

Even the strongest, most courageous heroes can be laid low by one vulnerability. For Superman it was kryptonite. For Achilles, it was his heel. (The moral of that story is: *Parents, if you're going to dip your kids in the River Styx to protect them from harm, don't forget to dip the heel you're holding them by.*)

Ever wonder if a particular element of your screen time is kryptonite for you? That's always a good thing to be wondering. It might not be a big worry. It might just be a quiet, sneaking suspicion. You may feel on top of your life and responsibilities—yet, when it comes to _____ (fill in the blank with a digital activity, habit, or temptation), you seem to lose your self-control, good judgment, and ability to make your behavior follow your mind's instructions. Or maybe there's an activity your parents bug you about. Or that interferes with doing your homework. If you'd like to reassure yourself that an activity or app is healthy and constructive—*or* if you'd like to discover once and for all that it's putting your life balance out of whack—this challenge will help you figure it out. You will need to summon searing honesty, along with deep faith in your fortitude. With those twin powers, you may be able to step into the Dungeon of Digital Abuse long enough to take your measure.

Instructions: Fill in the blanks in the next paragraph and the challenge template with *one* app or online behavior you're concerned about or that takes up a large portion of your screen time. For example, you could enter "social media," "Insta," "texting," "gambling," "binge-watching," "pornography," "YouTube," "gaming," etc. *If you're concerned about more than one online activity, complete separate challenges for as many as you like.*

The questions in this challenge are about your _____ activity over the past six months. "_____ activity" means any _____-related activity you engaged in on a computer or laptop, a console, or any other kind of device (e.g., mobile phone, tablet), online and/or offline, either solo or with others.

Indicate how often the following issues occurred on average over the past six months. Place a checkmark in the column that represents your answer.

This challenge is also available for download at freespirit.com/dragons.

CHALLENGE 8: DO I HAVE AN ACHILLES HEEL?

	Never	Rarely	Sometimes	Often	Very Often
I have had difficulties controlling my _____ activity.					
I have given increasing priority to _____ over other life interests and daily activities.					
I have continued _____ despite the occurrence of negative consequences.					
I have experienced significant problems in my life (e.g., school, family, friends, work, health, moods) due to my _____ behavior.					
	Never	Rarely	Sometimes	Often	Very Often
	1 point	2 points	3 points	4 points	5 points
	____ +	____ +	____ +	____ +	____ +

Adapted from The Gaming Disorder Test. Pontes, Halley M., Bruno Schivinski, Cornelia Sindermann, et al. 2019. "Measurement and Conceptualization of Gaming Disorder According to the World Health Organization Framework: The Development of the Gaming Disorder Test." International Journal of Mental Health and Addiction. doi.org/10.1007/s11469-019-00088-z).

= **Total Points** _____

Compute Your Score: Add up the checkmarks in each column. Multiply that number by the point value for that response. For example, if you answered "Never" to all four statements, your score would be 4 (4 answers x 1 point = 4). If you answered "Sometimes" to two statements and "Very Often" to two statements, your score would be 16 (2 answers x 3 points = 6, plus 2 answers x 5 points = 10; 6 + 10 = 16).

Interpret Your Score: If your score is between 4 and 8, you are in control of that activity (with, perhaps, a rare exception). That doesn't necessarily mean the activity itself is "good" or beneficial for your development (compared to other on- or offline activities), but it suggests that it is not harming you, and it might even play a positive role in your life.

If your score is between 9 and 14, it means the activity *sometimes* causes problems, negative consequences, loss of control, and/or imbalance in your life that pushes out other interests and responsibilities. That doesn't sound too healthy.

If your score is between 15 and 20, it suggests that you may have an unhealthy dependence upon the behavior. It's likely that the activity is interfering with your life, because you continue to engage in it despite experiencing significant negative consequences often or very often.

You entered the Dungeon of Digital Abuse, completed your mission, and emerged as a Destroyer of Deadly Denial Demons. Whether you discovered an Achilles Heel, tumbled into a sinkhole of Kryptonite, or avoided landmines of dependency entirely, your reward is the *Warlock of Warning's Secret Quiver of Poison-Tipped Number 2 Pencils.* You will need these if you are to escape with your life from the next and most dangerous challenge of them all. May you summon all your powers of endurance, focus, and daring, pray to the gods of luck and benevolence, and hope to survive. You are about to meet the Dark Energy.

CHALLENGE 9: AM I AT RISK?
Level 9: Warnings of Doom and Despair
Mission 9: Facing the Dark Energy

Sharpen your poison-tipped pencils! You are at the final precipice of your screen scene quest. You have chased the Beacon of Knowledge, discovered the lair of Time Trolls, entered the Temple of Time, tracked the Soul Stealers, explored the Valley of Appland, repelled the Brain Snatchers, and conquered the Hellscape of Hidden Habbit-Creatures. All that remains is for you to Face the Dark Energy. To stare into the eyes of . . .

The Warning Signs of Treacherous Screen Time

You already know many warning signs, like:

Having thumbs the size of cantaloupes from too much texting

Walking into telephone poles because you're buried in your phone and not watching where you're going

Asking a doctor to turn your palm into a touch screen

Speaking in emojis

However, other signs of excessive screen time may not be as obvious as these. This final challenge presents a wide spectrum of warning signs that may be new to you. For your Mission, I've broken these down into six categories that correspond to the six upcoming RESIST! chapters. (You're welcome.)

- Chapter 4: Protect Your Body: Physical warning signs
- Chapter 5: Protect Your Brain: Cognitive warning signs
- Chapter 6: Protect Your Relationships: Social warning signs
- Chapter 7: Protect Your Privacy, Safety, and Reputation: Responsibility warning signs
- Chapter 8: Protect Your Psyche: Emotional warning signs
- Chapter 9: Protect Your Life Balance: Dependency warning signs

For each category, you'll see a number of behaviors and/or attitudes. You may look at these and feel they don't apply to you. But it's still helpful to be aware of them so you'll be alert to any future changes in your digital health, and also so you can recognize if a friend or family member may be in screen-time trouble.

If you do engage in or experience any of these, that's a sign that you may be spending too much or the wrong kind of time on a screen. In the corresponding RESIST! chapters and in chapters 10 and 11, you'll find strategies for addressing any areas that concern you and decreasing your screen time if you decide that's something you'd like to try.

Some tips will be specific to a particular warning sign. For example, if your eyes get tired, there are exercises for perking them up. If you're not sleeping well, you'll find tips for getting a better night's sleep. But there is one solution that can be applied to virtually every warning sign—and that is to reduce your screen time. This can be stated as a math equation: If excessive screen time is causing negative consequences, less screen time will result in fewer negative consequences. Mathematically, that's expressed as . . .

$$f(x) = a_0 + \sum_{n=1}^{\infty} \left(a_n\, ZZZZZzzzzz\, \frac{n\pi x}{L} + ws_n \sin \frac{n\pi x}{L} \right)$$

. . . where (x) = Screen Time, ZZZZZzzzzz = falling asleep in class, and (ws_n) = Warning Sign, and all the rest of the stuff I don't have a clue about but I know it's important. Especially the part about "sin."

And now, if you dare, it's time to *Face the Dark Energy* and stare down the *Warning Signs of Treacherous Screen Time.*

Instructions: Read each Warning Sign. (Please.) If you've experienced or engaged in it to the extent that it is a concern for you, place a checkmark in the "Yes" category. If it's not a concern, check "No." To keep the list as short as possible, I've grouped some items on the same line. For example, under "Physical Warning Signs," I list "Dry eyes, blurred vision, or eye strain." If none apply, check "No." If any of them apply, even if it's just one, check "Yes." You'll know which warning sign you had in mind.

Are you ready? Then venture forth, O *Destroyer of Deadly Denial Daggers.* You can also download this challenge at freespirit.com/dragons.

CHALLENGE 9: AM I AT RISK?

My Warning Signs	Is This a Concern for You?
PHYSICAL – Chapter 4: Protect Your Body	
Disrupted sleep. Tired. Low energy. Fall asleep during the day.	No ☐ Yes ☐
Painful, stiff, or achy neck, shoulders, or back. Sore fingers, thumbs, or wrists.	No ☐ Yes ☐
Dry eyes, blurred vision, or eye strain.	No ☐ Yes ☐
Hunched shoulders. Poor posture.	No ☐ Yes ☐
Poor nutrition and eating habits. Skipped meals. Excessive weight gain or loss.	No ☐ Yes ☐
Headaches.	No ☐ Yes ☐
COGNITIVE – Chapter 5: Protect Your Brain	
Forgetful. Memory problems.	No ☐ Yes ☐
Disorganized.	No ☐ Yes ☐
Trouble paying attention or concentrating.	No ☐ Yes ☐
Unmotivated.	No ☐ Yes ☐
Easily distracted.	No ☐ Yes ☐
Difficulty finishing tasks.	No ☐ Yes ☐
SOCIAL – Chapter 6: Protect Your Relationships	
Uncomfortable in real-life social situations.	No ☐ Yes ☐
Withdrawal from offline social activities and relationships.	No ☐ Yes ☐

CONTINUED ›

My Warning Signs	Is This a Concern for You?
Conflicts with others over screen time and phone use.	No ❒ Yes ❒
Prefer being online to doing things with friends or family members.	No ❒ Yes ❒
Hide or lie about screen time and/or internet use.	No ❒ Yes ❒
Prefer to text, message, or video chat instead of communicating face-to-face.	No ❒ Yes ❒
RESPONSIBILITY – Chapter 7: Protect Your Privacy, Safety, and Reputation	
Post things you later come to regret.	No ❒ Yes ❒
Don't use privacy settings as much as you should.	No ❒ Yes ❒
Reveal too much personal information.	No ❒ Yes ❒
Rarely think about the trail you leave online.	No ❒ Yes ❒
Get sucked into negative emotions.	No ❒ Yes ❒
Respond to emails or messages from strangers without exercising caution.	No ❒ Yes ❒
EMOTIONAL – Chapter 8: Protect Your Psyche	
Feel depressed, lonely, sad, or self-hating after being online.	No ❒ Yes ❒
Quick to get angry. Upset by small things.	No ❒ Yes ❒
Use internet to escape real-life problems and feelings.	No ❒ Yes ❒
Mood swings without knowing why.	No ❒ Yes ❒
Often feel stressed out. Can't cope.	No ❒ Yes ❒
Feel anxious, irritable, angry, moody, or empty when not able to use phone.	No ❒ Yes ❒
DEPENDENCY – Chapter 9: Protect Your Life Balance	
Screen time keeps increasing. Lose track of time when online.	No ❒ Yes ❒
Efforts to cut back on screen time have failed.	No ❒ Yes ❒
Constantly think about online activity. Can't wait to get back online.	No ❒ Yes ❒
Keep using phone despite negative consequences.	No ❒ Yes ❒
Always checking phone, even when it's unsafe or against the rules.	No ❒ Yes ❒
Phone is default activity when bored.	No ❒ Yes ❒
Total Number of "No's" and "Yeses"	No: Yes:

⫸ You may have chosen all "No's," all "Yeses," or a three-way combo of "No's," "Yeses," and a side of fries. Now, in each *category* where you said "Yes" once or more, ***choose the one warning sign that concerns you the most***. If you only chose "Yes" for one sign in a category, choose that one and circle it, mark it with a check, or make a note next to it. After you're done, you should have chosen anywhere from zero (if you didn't say "Yes" to any) to six signs in each category. As a final act of bravery, add up the total number of "No's" and "Yeses," and enter it at the bottom of the table. The two together should add up to 36.

With courage and derring-do, you confronted and vanquished the *Dark Energy of Treacherous Warning Signs*, earning your *Warnings Warrior Sun Wings*. This completes your initial dangerous quest into the depths of your screen-scene soul to gather intel on your digital life. You have amassed a fortune in R-Bucks, which you can use in the next six chapters to purchase Resistance Immunity Bars that will protect you from internet infestation, digital diseases, and psychic seizures at the hands of Big Tech. And, finally, in chapters 10 and 11, you can use your bounty of self-awareness and knowledge to create a personal plan for maintaining or restoring your digital health.

So, let's move forward to discover more about your relationships with Big Tech and your digital devices, how healthy (or harmful) those relationships are, and how, if you decide you need to, you can RESIST!

> **Wait! That's it? Where's my reward?**

>> Reward? You have the greatest reward of all—INSIGHT. REFLECTION. SELF-AWARENESS. KNOWLEDGE.

> **That's cheap.**

Behold your treasure. March onward. Drink from the Fountain of Protection. Strengthen your immunity to internet-spread infections.

Dazzle your friends. Amaze your parents. Surprise yourself with your protective powers.

That's still pretty cheap.

Dear Alex,

"I don't have a problem with screen time. Why should I bother to read this book?"

Good question. Let's see if I can give you some good answers.

1. If your screen time is fine and dandy, learning more about what makes it so will reinforce that healthy relationship by showing you *why* you're in good digital shape.

2. Forewarned is forearmed. If your screen time should ever become less healthy in the future (I know it's unimaginable, but humor me), knowing the warning signs will help you hear the alarm sooner and do something about it.

3. You may have friends or family members whose screen use worries you (and maybe them). You'll be in a better position to help if you know the warning signs of too much screen time, along with steps people can take to change their behavior and attitudes to achieve a healthier digital life.

4. You may be in denial about your own screen time and its consequences. It happens, and it's nothing to be ashamed of. Still, digging deeper could help you reach a more accurate understanding of your use and its consequences. Think of it this way: If you told somebody who sits on her couch 12 hours a day watching Sesame Street reruns and eating popcorn that you were worried about the harmful effect that was having on her life, would she say, "Me, too"? I doubt it. She'd probably say, "There's nothing wrong. Mind your own business," and throw the tub of popcorn at you. That's called denial. And a waste of popcorn.

PART II
RESIST

PROTECT YOUR BODY

How Screen Time Affects Your Body and Your Health

Suppose that day after day, week after week, month after month, year after year, you sat at a sewing machine for six, eight, even ten hours a day. You made tapestries and flags and blankets, amazing clothes for yourself that people raved about, presents for friends, a cape for your mom, even a tuxedo for Hot Dog, your dachshund. You loved sewing. You saw it as an important part of your life and identity, and clearly much good came from your efforts. And yet in spite of all these great benefits of sewing so much, there was a downside: the fine motor control and postures sewing requires took a toll on your body.

This would be true of *any* activity with repetitive motions, physical exertion, and/or positions maintained for hours at a time, whether you're building models, weeding a garden, playing tennis, or using a smartphone. Doing anything like that too much would wreak havoc on your body.

Yup, using smartphones and spending time on screens for hours at a time, day after day, can cause physical consequences. It can affect your muscles and bones. It can affect your eyes. It can disrupt your sleep. It can lead to safety risks such as Death by Earbud. It may even cause you to call in the fatty fish (more on that later) or produce sperm with a banana-shaped head (if you're a sperm-producing person). If this doesn't get you curious, I don't know what will. So read on to learn about these possible effects on your body and their warning signs.

Signs That Screen Time Is Affecting Your Body

If you are experiencing any of these, your body might be in distress due to overusing smartphones and other devices.

 You Have Upper Body Stiffness, Aches, and/or Pains.
Some days, you feel like the Tin Man from *The Wizard of Oz*. Your neck, back, and/or shoulders are so stiff they need oil. You have trouble turning your head. You experience serious pain when moving your head or twisting your upper body. Your shoulders ache so much you want to spray silicone lubricant under your arms. You get headaches or pains behind your eyes or temples. Some days, your fingers even tingle or feel numb.

 You Have Poor Posture.
Your head hunches forward and it feels like you have an anvil sitting on your neck. You think you'd make a great anteater since you often look down when you walk. Your shoulders droop. People are always telling you to "stand up straight." (They say this because they care about you, but that doesn't make them any less annoying.) You tell them it's because your backpack is so heavy, but no one's buying it. They say it's because you're always looking down at your phone.

 You Feel Out of Shape.
You don't like seeing yourself in the mirror. You're embarrassed if you have to get undressed in a locker room. You weigh more or less than you'd like. Physical exertion rarely makes an appearance in your daily routine. You don't get enough exercise (although your thumbs are really jacked from all the reps they do on your phone). Junk food is your best friend. You often skip meals, and your attitude toward good eating habits is—"whatever." Your screen time goes hand in hand, or should I say "hand in mouth," with high-calorie snacking time.

 You Stink.
Well, *YOU* don't, and even if you did, I would never phrase it so indelicately. But I thought it was an attention-grabbing warning sign for poor personal hygiene. What does that look (and smell) like? You wear crumpled clothes past their expiration date. Your hair is a mess. Your fingernails are dirty. Dried boogers hang out of your nose. (Not really, I just like using "boogers" in a sentence.) Your odor sets off smoke detectors. You rarely have interest in—or time for—looking your cleanest, freshest, snazziest best.

If you want to learn more about how an overdose of screen time can cause physical symptoms (or if you want to see if I use "boogers" again in a sentence), read on.

> **I definitely want to see if you use boogers again.**

Here is more information about how these warning signs might affect you, along with tips for reducing or preventing any lasting damage they might cause.

Got Tech Neck?

Take the Tech Neck Body Check:

- Do you ever feel pain in your neck? (As opposed to being *called* a pain in the neck.)
- Do you ever have achiness, stiffness, or reduced mobility in your neck, shoulders, or upper back?
- Do you ever experience headaches or pain behind your eyes or temples?
- Do your fingers ever tingle or feel numb?
- Do any of these symptoms get worse if you move your head forward and down?
- Do people tell you your posture is bad and to put your shoulders back?
- Does your phone ever say, "How dare you look down on me"?

If you answered yes to any of these, you may have tech neck, a condition that results from spending too much time looking down at your tablet or smartphone. (This is not to be confused with Shrek Neck, which comes from binging Shrek movies.)

What causes tech neck? It's all in your head. Literally! The median weight for 13- to 18-year-old heads ranges from approximately 8 to 12 pounds, with the weight increasing as you get older, and presumably have heavier thoughts. (Airheads weigh less; swelled heads weigh more.) When your head tilts forward to look down at a tablet or smartphone, it places additional force—as much as 60 pounds!—on your neck, since your head is no longer aligned with your spine. Necks aren't designed for that much continuous weight. Think of your arm. When it's hanging down, you don't feel its weight. But if you raise your arm straight out from your side, you quickly feel how much it weighs, and your muscles begin to tire.

| 0° = | 15° = | 30° = | 45° = | 60° = |
| 10–12 pounds | 27 pounds | 40 pounds | 49 pounds | 60 pounds |

Given how many hours a day many kids spend with their heads tilted down, it's no wonder that more and more of them have poor posture and hunched shoulders, and report neck, shoulder, and/or upper back pain, achiness, or stiffness. Using two hands on your phone is the biggest culprit since this rounds your shoulders and brings your head even more forward. That position makes it harder to breathe deeply, reducing oxygen flow and energy levels.

Keep tech neck in check.

If you think you might have tech neck, or you want to lower the chances you'll get it, here are some strategies for minimizing strain on your neck and spine.

- Reduce the amount of time you spend each day looking at your screen.
- Space out your device use over the day so you're not in the same position for too long at once.
- Avoid holding your phone at chest or waist level. Hold it at eye level. (But not while you're walking.)
- Take a break every 15 to 20 minutes for 2 or 3 minutes. Do a lightning round of exercising, stretching, dancing, hydrating, or bathroom-ing.
- Take a longer break every hour. Go for a walk or run. Make a snack. Do the chore you've been putting off. Do anything except commune with a screen.
- Pay attention to your posture.
  - Sit or stand up straight. Shoulders back. Ears in line with shoulders.
  - Don't tilt your head forward or look down.
  - Keep your feet flat on the floor. (Especially when standing—no floating off the ground!)

- When seated, place a folded towel or blanket (about 3 inches thick) between your lower back and your chair. This helps support your spine.
- Get a chair with a high back or headrest and keep the back of your head in contact with it. This forces you (politely) to look up and ahead, rather than down. And you'll feel cheerful since things will be looking up.

Try exercises that can help.

To take things a step further, which you may want to do if you're experiencing any of the negative consequences of tech neck, you can do some exercises that target your neck, shoulders, chest, and upper back. Here are a few good ones you can do quickly and easily just about anywhere, any time.

Chin Tuck

- Sit or stand up straight. (Your ears should be centered directly over your shoulders and remain attached to your head at all times.)
- Place your forefinger on the front of your chinny-chin-chin. (Think of it as the "hmmm" gesture.)
- Looking straight ahead, pull your head and chin straight back. Don't tilt your head up or down. (Your finger will now float in space a couple inches in front of your chin.) You'll feel the stretch at the top of your neck.
- Hold this position for 5 seconds.
- Release the stretch and bring your head forward so your chin again touches your finger.
- Repeat 10 times. The whole exercise will only take 1 minute.
- Do this exercise at least 5 times throughout the day.

Neck Extension

- Sit up straight with your shoulders back.
- Tilt your head all the way back until you are looking up at the ceiling or sky.
- With your hand, push your forehead down to increase the stretch. (Gently—you don't want to snap your head off.)
- Hold the stretch for 15 to 20 seconds.
- Repeat 5 times.
- Do this exercise twice a day.

Side Neck Stretch

- Stand or sit up straight.
- Tilt your head to the right, trying to touch your right shoulder with your right ear. (Don't lift your shoulder.)
- Hold for 10 seconds.
- Return your head to an upright position.
- Repeat 5 times.
- Do the same exercise in reverse: Tilt your head to the left, hold for 10 seconds, and repeat 5 times.
- Do this exercise twice a day.

TIP: Technically speaking, you can do any of the above exercises while sitting in class. It's true that some teachers might frown upon it, but I think it's at least worth trying once, if only to see how they react to you swiveling your head around like you're going through a slow-motion exorcism. If all goes well, who knows, maybe the teacher will invite you to share the exercise with the other students and institute Chin-Tuck time at the beginning of the class.

And if things didn't go so well, here's a great exercise to do if you're told to go stand in the corner.

Corner Stretch

- Pretend you're a hypotenuse and face the corner of a room.
- Keep your feet together.
- Stand 2 feet away from the corner.
- Put your forearms flat against each wall. Your elbows should be a couple inches below your shoulders.
- Lean forward. You'll feel your chest and shoulders stretch.
- Hold the stretch for 40 to 60 seconds.
- Repeat 4 or 5 times throughout the day.

This next exercise should only be done on days when your underarms are sweet-smelling.

I'm always sweet-smelling.

Don't mean to be nosy, but what deodorant do you use?

Chest Stretch

- Place the palms of your hands behind your head with your fingers locked.
- Pull your elbows backward as far as you can.
- Hold for 40 to 60 seconds.
- Repeat 4 or 5 times a day.

If you get in the habit of doing these exercises, you should feel an improvement. If, however, your symptoms remain, or you experience pain while doing the exercises, talk to a doctor or your school nurse.

THINK ABOUT IT

Picture the body language of athletes prepping for a game or competition. They reach for the sky with outstretched arms. Stretch. Jump and dance. Expand their chests. It's as if they can't contain their energy, self-confidence, and feelings of POWER. These expansive postures are sometimes called "high-power poses."

Now picture somebody who's feeling sad, lonely, or disappointed. They fold in upon themselves, curl up, hunch their shoulders, hang their head, cross their legs, make themselves physically small. These are "low-power poses."

What this means is that feelings—whether happy or sad—influence posture. Scientists wondered if the reverse could happen: Could the posture you assume affect your feelings? Some research suggests that the answer is yes.

And what does all this have to do with smartphones? Using a phone often places you in a "low-power pose." Your head droops, your hands come together, your shoulders round, you bend forward. Could this have anything to do with the feelings of sadness, depression, loneliness, stress, and poor self-esteem many kids who spend lots of time on their phones report?

Think about it. And while you're thinking, put your shoulders back. Uncross your legs. Sit up straight. Raise your head. Hold your phone at eye level. Assume a power posture.

Feeling Floppy?

Fitness flagging? Fortitude failing? Focus flailing? Do you feel physically fit and active? Do you spend a lot of time being sedentary? Are you a healthy weight? In many countries, the percentage of children (and adults) who are overweight or obese has increased dramatically over the past several decades. Being overweight or obese in childhood and adolescence can harm a child or teen's physical, social, emotional, and academic well-being, and may predispose a person to health problems later in life.

While there are many factors that can contribute to poor physical health and an unhealthy weight—genetics, stress, family practices, sleep patterns, poor nutrition, lack of exercise—research suggests that increased levels of screen time are associated with being less physically fit and active, being at an unhealthy weight, and reporting poorer quality of life and family relationships. On the flip side, research also shows that reducing screen time for schoolchildren results in their losing weight.

Why is more screen time associated with poorer physical health? One obvious reason is lack of physical exercise. Unless your screen time is spent doing online aerobics or playing Pokémon Go at breakneck speed, you're sedentary. In addition, kids and teens tend to see a lot of ads online for high-calorie, sugary foods and beverages, and eat them (the food, not the ads) while at their screens. In fact, a study in the *Journal of Pediatrics* examined YouTube "kid influencers"—children (even toddlers) who have millions of social media followers. The study found that videos from these kids, showing them reviewing toys, conducting experiments, doing taste tests, playing games, or going to fun places, were crammed with product placements and endorsements. Some of the kids' accounts (typically run by parents) rake in *millions* of dollars a year by promoting fast food and sugar-stuffed snacks and beverages. Ninety percent of the products displayed were considered unhealthy by nutritionists.

And, if that's not bad enough, lots of screen time, especially before bed, disrupts sleep and body chemistry, triggering cravings for salt, sugar, and junk food. Combine this with low energy levels that make you want to veg out during the day, mix well, and you've got a (high-sugar) recipe for disaster that serves six.

While too much screen time is associated with being overweight or obese, it's also possible that excessive screen time can lead to being unhealthily *under*weight for some teens. This can happen if you skip meals or forget to eat.

So, for all these reasons and more, physical health is an important reason to monitor and control screen time. Teens who are physically active are more likely than teens who spend a lot of time on screens to feel good about themselves, perform well cognitively, experience elevated moods, and enjoy cardiorespiratory fitness.

Of course, optimal physical health is a function of many elements. If I gave you detailed information on every factor, this book would be 18,907 pages long and you wouldn't be reading it (because I would still be working on it). But you can learn the basics of what you need to know by searching for "teen fitness guidelines" at an authoritative source such as MyPlate or the Centers for Disease Control and Prevention. If you need more help, talk to your school nurse or a doctor.

Physical health is a foundation of well-being. So monitoring the basics is essential:

- Get lots of exercise.
- Eat a nutritious diet.
- Engage portion control to seek and maintain your optimal weight (one size *doesn't* fit all when it comes to body size).
- Minimize your intake of high-calorie, high-sugar snacks, beverages, and meals.
- Don't eat in front of a screen.

Do You P.U.?

I admit it. I'm writing this section with a clothespin over my nose so I don't have to smell the stinky rooms of odoriferous teens who may be neglecting personal and environmental hygiene in favor of screen time. This is a common-sense warning sign of TMST.✱ If your personal environment (AKA "your room") is decorated with vintage food and dirty clothes; if fresh air is extinct and tidiness is in hibernation; if your parents wear gas masks when entering; if the police have placed "Crime Scene" tape on the door—these are signs that you've created a toxic dump.

✱ TMST: Abbreviation for "Too Much Screen Time"—pronounced "Timst," or "TimsTee" depending on whether you live in the southern or northern hemisphere.

While this toxicity may have other causes than TMST, like, say, being a slob, you should examine cause and effect to see if it might have something to do with, or be exacerbated by, spending too much time online. Unclean, unsanitary, and chaotic spaces contribute to:

- being disorganized (because you can't find anything)
- being late (because you can't find anything)

- being in trouble with your parents (because they can't find you)

- being in trouble at school (because you're disorganized, late, and arguing at home)

See how everything in life connects?

The other aspect of this is personal hygiene. If you neglect washing, scrubbing, scenting, deodorizing, trimming, combing, brushing, and other good habits of personal hygiene, you are engaging in air pollution and creating an eyesore. If you rush to school looking like a disheveled hurricane with earbuds, you're doing yourself (and those who sit next to you on the bus) a disservice. So, be alert to fainting passersby as a warning sign that your personal hygiene may not be up to snuff. Or up to sniff.

Signs That Screen Time Is Affecting Your Sleep

If you asked people who know about these things,

"What is the one thing teens can do to most benefit their health, mood, energy, emotional balance, and academic performance?"

. . . I am sure they would say, "Get enough sleep."

Some might say, "Exercise," to which I would reply, "Well, you can't exercise if you fall asleep in the middle of soccer practice." And some might say, "Eat right," to which I would say, "Well, you can't eat right if you nod off on your plate of quinoa porridge and free-range eggs."

So, I would definitely go with the importance of "sleep" for keeping teens in tip-top tempo. Here are some warning signs that screen time is interfering with this essential good-health habit.

HYGIENE HIJINKS

There once was a teen name of Newt
Who frequently failed to ablute
He didn't give a hoot
So germs did pollute
His moldy and furry young snoot.

Another lad called himself Fritz
Neglected his pores and his pits
His 'rents called it quits
At the end of their wits—
"That boy's never staying at the Ritz!"

Now here's a young lass christened Joan
Whose nasty hair-don't was well known
Addiction full blown
("JUST LEAVE ME ALONE!")
She couldn't get off of her phone.

So what does this story portend
For teens who do naught but click send
Whose odors offend
Whose psyches distend
Whose virtues suspend
I would recommend
Step in as a friend
Say, "Please comprehend
The screen time you spend
Must come to an end
To stop this sad trend
And get you, my friend, on the mend."

You Don't Get Enough Sleep.

Every day it's late to bed and early to rise. And then you crash on weekends, sleeping to noon if your dad doesn't pour a jug of cold water on your head to get you out of bed earlier. If sleep were money, you'd be broke. You have trouble falling asleep. Your mind is wired; you don't feel tired. You have trouble staying asleep and often wake during the night. Come morning, tearing yourself out of bed feels like swimming to the surface of a pool of molasses with a 250-pound weight on your consciousness.

 You Always Feel Tired.

The first time you heard the expression *chronic fatigue*, you thought, "That's me! Low energy is my middle name." You always feel tired and slog your way through the day. You seem to get sick a lot, and frequently fall asleep in class, in carpool, on the bus, or when doing homework. And, scariest of all (which you've kept a secret), you almost fell asleep driving and would have run off the road if the rumble strip hadn't jolted you awake.

> ZZZZZzzzzzzz.

You're Stressed Out and Have Trouble Concentrating.

The fog of fatigue makes it hard to focus and think clearly. Your grades are falling; you forget things. Half the time your mind just doesn't seem to want to work. You live on coffee and would take an intravenous caffeine drip if they'd let you. Add it all up and you're frequently anxious, irritable, depressed, and frustrated.

If you recognize any of these symptoms, it could mean you're sleep-deprived. Certainly, poor school performance, feelings of depression and anxiety, and even low energy could come from other causes, but for teens who experience these warning signs, sleep habits would be a good place to look.

Sleep experts (these are doctors who spend all their time sleeping) recommend that teens get eight to ten hours of sleep a night, with nine hours being the "sweet spot." If you're thinking . . . *I wish!* . . . I bet you're one of the seven out of ten teens who are seriously sleep deprived, getting seven or fewer hours of sleep a night.

Why aren't teens getting enough sleep? Lots of reasons. You're busy with tons of things you have to do and want to do. You may need to wake up at 6 a.m. or earlier to get to school on time. And then, between school, sports, clubs, jobs, homework, chores, friends, and family time, the day rushes by and before you know it, you're crashing into bed, only to wake up five, six, or seven hours later. But these activities and demands have been a part of teenagers' lives for decades without causing anywhere near the levels of sleep deprivation experienced by today's teens.

So, what changed?

> **Lemme guess. Smartphones?**

Right-a-roni. I knew you'd get it. Smartphones. Screen time. Studies of teen sleep patterns since portable, wireless, digital devices saturated their lives show a steep increase in the number of teens getting seven or fewer hours of sleep a night. In other words, as more kids got phones, average shut-eye decreased. More screen time = less sleep time.

Research backs this up. One study examined the total amount of time per week young adults spent on social media, as well as the number of times they logged on during the week. The study participants who spent the most *time* on social media were twice as likely as those who spent less time to experience disrupted sleep. Even more interesting, the subjects who checked their social media most frequently during the course of the study were *three* times more likely to experience sleep disturbances compared to those who checked less often (even if they spent more time on social media). This suggests that the *frequency of checking* social media during the day is a greater disrupter of sleep than the *amount of time* spent.

In another study, the more devices teens used, the more likely they were to feel tired during the day and have trouble sleeping at night.

> **Well, duh, I could have told them that.**

I'm sure you could. You know firsthand how much time you spend online during the day. And suddenly it's 9 p.m. and you haven't started your homework, and you stay up until midnight to finish it. Or, you had your homework all done by 10 p.m., and now it's time to text your friends, post some pics, play some games, watch some videos, catch some episodes and, oh no, it's 1:30 in the morning!

Feeling Blue

Now, for all you medical science fans, here's why too much screen time disrupts sleep far beyond the actual number of hours it steals from slumberland. Both natural and artificial light send information to your brain that affects your body's sleep-wake cycle. Every night, a few hours before bedtime, the pineal gland in your brain begins to release melatonin, which makes you feel sleepy. This hormone is nature's way of telling your body that it's nighttime and beddy-bye is on the horizon. Think of it as a wake-up call to go to sleep.

This message to your brain is caused by the disappearance of "blue light." Daylight is blue light. So, as darkness falls, blue light fades, triggering the melatonin melody that serenades your body. For centuries, blue light only existed in nature during the day. For nighttime illumination there were candles, fires, and, eventually, incandescent light bulbs. These produced reddish-yellow light which, along with darkness, caused the brain to send its sleepy-time signals. All was well.

So, what changed?

> Lemme guess. Smartphones?

> Smart kid!

Electronic screens radiate blue light. So, if you're on a screen for hours before bedtime, your brain senses it as "daylight," it doesn't produce melatonin, and you don't feel sleepy. Your circadian rhythms get confused. It's like jetlag minus the jet.

What makes it even worse, beyond just the blue light, is that the things you're doing on your phone or tablet are stimulating, not calming. You're not spending two hours watching swans glide across a still pond while snow falls gently in the background and mellow music soothes your soul. You're texting, talking, playing games, checking feeds, and switching back and forth between screens vying for your attention with obnoxious "hey, look at me!" pop-ups, strobes, and flashings. There's a good chance you'll get caught up in a social drama; see an upsetting post, message, or news story; and/or learn something that gets your mind whirring a million miles an hour late at night.

So, not only is the screen's blue light keeping you awake, but the visual, auditory, physical, and emotional stimulation from what you're doing on that screen can also trigger thoughts or feelings that prevent you from falling asleep.

These blue-light nocturnal emissions (not to be confused with other emissions) also reduce the *quality* of the sleep you do get. The suppression of melatonin keeps your body from entering REM (rapid eye movement) sleep and deep-sleep phases for as long or as often as needed. This makes it difficult for sleep to do its important job of "processing" the day, dreaming, and carrying out the "housekeeping" in the brain that solidifies learning and memory, discards experiential "clutter," reduces levels of anxiety and fear, and makes you feel refreshed and rarin' to go in the morning. If you can't imagine "you" and "rarin' to go" ever being in the same sentence, you are likely sleep-deprived.

> Only thing I'm ever rarin' to go to is sleep.

Bad Things Happen

When you don't get enough sleep, bad things happen. This is because sleep affects almost every system, tissue, and organ in the body. Sleepyhead teens are more likely to be irritable, anxious, depressed, moody, forgetful, and overweight. They're more likely to exercise poor judgment, lose self-control, and suffer from chronic fatigue. They are less able to learn and retain information, concentrate, think clearly, and tolerate frustration. And they are more likely to have at least one risk factor for suicide. In fact, nearly three out of four teens who report feeling sad, unhappy, or depressed also say that they feel tired during the day and don't get enough sleep. When you don't get enough sleep, your body chemistry changes. You tend to crave sugar, salt, and junk food; your production of infection-fighting T cells is lowered, making you more likely to get sick; and altered hormone levels can even make your skin more susceptible to zits.

> Zits? I'm getting into bed right now!

The cumulative effects of sleep loss and its negative consequences have been associated with weakened immune functioning and an increased risk of diabetes, high blood pressure, heart attack, stroke, and obesity later in life.

Add it all up and teens who are sleep deprived are more likely to do poorly in school, get into conflicts with friends and parents, become sick, have car accidents, and feel tired throughout the day. Chronic fatigue can lead to unhealthy use of caffeine, nicotine, alcohol, or other drugs to stay awake, which further interferes with sleep.

And if all this hasn't convinced you, think about this: How do you think your bed must feel when it isn't getting enough quality time with you? Do you really want to cause such hurt and rejection when your bed's always been there for you?

Sleep isn't just "down time." It's restore, refresh, and reinvigorate time. Your body, your brain, and your spirit need the nourishment sleep provides. Here's how to get it.

Tips for Getting a Good Night's Sleep

I know you'll look at some of these and say "fat chance." You'll think some ideas are ridiculous in terms of your life. I understand and respect that. But see how many of these tips you *can* apply. It may involve changing some behaviors and priorities, but the goal is to make you feel more healthy, energetic, centered, and able to enjoy each day and meet any challenges that come your way.

If you conscientiously practice these tips and still have problems sleeping, it's best to talk to a doctor if you can. There may be other causes that you need to explore.

Establish a regular schedule for when you go to bed and get up. A routine reinforces your body's natural sleep-wake rhythm. Try to stick to the same schedule on weekends. I know it's tempting to sleep in on Saturday and Sunday—and maybe stay up even later than you do during the week. But your body couldn't care less what day it is. It likes a regular pattern. Plus, catching extra sleep on the weekend isn't like a credit you can carry forward into the week to dole out if you're sleep deprived on Wednesday. So, if you must cheat on weekends, try to keep it in check so I don't find out.

Don't eat large meals before bedtime. If you're hungry, have a light, sugar-free snack.

Avoid caffeine late in the day. Many products other than the usual suspects (coffee, tea, soda, energy drinks, chocolate) contain caffeine in varying amounts, such as gum, breakfast cereals, and even pain relievers and "decaffeinated" coffee. Always check ingredients, especially if you are highly sensitive to caffeine. You don't want to be jittery or wired before bedtime. Nicotine, vaping, and alcohol should also be avoided late in the day. And early in the day. And midway through the day. This is because such substances and activities are either addictive, illegal, risky, or all three. Their use, especially during the teen years, can interfere with healthy physical, emotional, social, and cognitive development.

Refrain from high-intensity exercise within an hour or two of bedtime. Strenuous physical activity gets the adrenaline pumping, which increases your heart rate and blood flow. Adrenaline (also known as epinephrine) is a stimulant like caffeine, so this can make it harder to fall asleep and sleep soundly.

Turn your bedroom into an oasis of serenity as night falls—a space that says, "Sleep, come and get me." Extinguish bright lights. Lower shades. Turn on a lamp with red-yellow light-tones. If you share a room with someone who likes stadium lighting and music blasting, you'll need to negotiate and be creative. Experiment with headphones and focused task lights. Use blankets, sheets, cardboard, or curtains to create personal spaces to dampen sound and individualize lighting.

Engage in calm, relaxing activities as you get closer to going to sleep. Read a book in hard copy (not on a screen). Meditate. Do yoga or gentle stretches. Sit comfortably, close your eyes if you'd like, and picture yourself in a place of serenity, safety, and beauty. Avoid things that are likely to agitate, upset, or stimulate you.

Keep a journal or diary (pen and paper, please). Writing down what's on your mind can get troubling emotions, worries, and/or relationships "out of your system." Journaling not only helps you sleep, but can reduce depression, stress, and anxiety, and promote healing after a traumatic or sad event.

Create a bedtime ritual. Having a before-bed routine tells your body and brain that you're coming in for a landing at Sleepy-Time Airport. The routine can be anything calming: a phone call review of the day with a best friend (landline if your family has one, please—otherwise, voice only, and definitely no FaceTime). A shower or bubble bath. Lighting a candle or incense. (Just make sure it's in a safe container and that you don't fall asleep with anything burning.) Playing a favorite mellow song on your guitar, or listening to one. (Quietly, in case other people in your home are already asleep.)

> Just reading these tips is making me sleepy.

Remove or cover up all those tiny lights that everything seems to have these days. I can't tell you how annoying I find them. Have you ever stayed in a hotel room? When I do, I take a roll of black electrical tape with me so I can block them out. That may seem weird, but I just don't like 20 mini-spotlights keeping me up at night. There's the battery light on the smoke detector; the standby light on the television; the obnoxious clock; the red "power on" indicator on the extension cord plug strip; the LED display on the thermostat; the glow from the modem; the microscopic night-lights built into every outlet. What—do they think I'm going to get up in the dark at 3 a.m. to plug something in?!? Why do I need these narcissistic lights telling me they're on standby and wasting electricity? I do not. I like to sleep in total darkness, and so should you for the best zzzzzzzzzzzzs. (By the way, I remove the tape before checking out, since I *am* the Manners Guru to the Youth of America.) So, either remove light-emitting objects from where you sleep, wear an eye mask, or use tape, stuffed animals, toy cars, ancient Dr. Seuss books, or dirty socks to cover those polluting pinpricks of light so you can get a good night's sleep.

That said, if you have monsters under your bed and need a nightlight on to keep them from crawling out (or to see them if they do attack)—or if you just generally feel safer sleeping with a nightlight—I'll allow it, as long as you sign an affidavit that it helps you fall asleep.

If you listen to music as bedtime approaches, make it mellow, melodic, and meditative— not something that's bashing your brain with noise.

Turn down the temperature if you can. Cooler rooms, where you're under the covers, snug as a bug in a hug, are more conducive to sleep.

Get out of bed if you can't fall asleep. You want your body and brain to associate being in bed with sleeping. Tossing and turning with anxiety, caffeine, adrenaline, or a melatonin deficit doesn't help to make the bed = sleep connection. If you can't get to sleep, try writing a letter or read a book. The kind of book—

> I know. The "real" kind, with pages you turn.

But whatever you do, don't turn on your phone or any screen.

Use an old-fashioned electric or battery-powered alarm clock.

> Why would I need an alarm clock? I use my phone to . . .

> OH NO! NO WAY!

Yes, sorry, but at least I saved it to the end: Turn off your phone and all blue-light-emitting devices at least two hours before bedtime. More hours would be better, but I'm trying to be realistic (and to not have you throw this book out the window). Remember, blue light from screens prevents your body from getting the message that sleepy-time draws nigh.

If you must use a digital device late into the evening, reduce the amount of blue light hitting your eyes. Look under settings for "Display" to find options for turning on night modes that do this. There are also apps that reduce blue light on your screen as you get closer to bedtime, and physical filters you can place over a screen.

Another good idea—and this may feel like twisting the knife—is not sleeping with your phone in the room where you sleep. This will reduce the chance of your turning it on for one last look before bed or during the night.

"Don't you dare turn me off!"

"You'll be sorry!"

Now, of course, your phone or tablet, upon hearing you intend to turn it off well before bedtime, is sure to have a wild temper tantrum, call you bad names, and taunt you with late-night posts, pings, texts, and notifications, daring you to resist. Which you can, if you're the one in charge.

So what you'll need to do is recognize that your phone feels threatened and hurt. Those feelings are natural. It's hearing that *your* health is more important than its being able to bother you at all times of the day or night. While that's true, it's still hurtful for your phone. So let your phone know you understand how it feels. But you mustn't give in. Instead, create a bedtime ritual for your phone.

Speak quietly and soothingly. "Okay, little fellow, time for beddy-bye."

Slip him into his iJammies. Put his sleeping cap on. (You can ask the kid from page 58 who sews 10 hours a day to make one.) Carry him to the comfy, soft bed you made in the living room out of a shoebox and old socks with holes in them. Tuck him into bed and tell him a story. My favorite is a fairy tale about a little girl named Goldilocks.

Once upon a time, Goldilocks walked up a hill with Jack and Jill just in time to see Hansel throw a bowl of too-cold porridge at Gretel who ducked so it hit Humpty Dumpty in the face who then fell off the wall while Gretel stole Hansel's cell phone for revenge (before midnight so she wouldn't turn into a pumpkin) and hid it behind a clock on the mantle of the three little pigs' brick house where Little Red Riding Hood found it and was just about to check her social media feed when the wolf came down the chimney but the pigs were too busy texting to notice so the wolf swallowed the phone (and Little Red Riding Hood and the three little pigs). The End.

At this point, your phone should be in sleep mode and you can turn it off for the night.

Signs That Screen Time Is Affecting Your Eyes

Eye don't know about you, but Eye think my i's are important to protect. Here are some warnings signs to alert you if you begin to experience iSores in your head.

⚠ **You Have Dry Eyes.**
Your eyes often feel scratchy and dry. You blink but it doesn't seem to help much. It's as if your tear ducts are having a drought. While you don't want to go through the day crying, you wish you had more moisture in your eyes.

⚠ **You Experience iStrain.**
Your eyes always feel tired. And that makes the rest of you feel tired. When your eyes are strained, you find it hard to focus on a book or a screen. You sometimes close your eyes to give them a rest, and end up falling asleep.

⚠ **You Have Blurred Vision.**
You stare at the page, and it's as if somebody spread a layer of petroleum jelly over your eyeballs. Everything's blurry. You try to open your eyes wider, adjust your angle—still blurry. This could be why you often get headaches.

iStrain is a common warning sign for TMST (Too Much Screen Time). If your head aches or your i's become dry, blurry, tired, twitchy, or red after using your devices, you may have Computer Vision Syndrome. This is the name people who like to name things created for ailments linked to staring at screens for extended periods. If you're a screen starer, chances are good you have some of the symptoms. (I know eye do!)

Tips for Better Eye Health

Fortunately, there are a number of easy steps you can take to minimize screen-related eye problems. (The steps are easy. The discipline to do them is harder.) Start with the ones that are simplest and don't cost anything to try. If your eyes perk up and thank you, great! If not, you'll need to step up your efforts and consider some of the ideas that require shelling out some cash, and/or coming up with some creative workarounds.

Blink often.

People blink about one-third as often when staring at a screen as they normally do. This leads to dry eyes since blinking lubricates your eyes and prevents irritation. To keep your eyes moist, blink frequently when using a screen. Your eyes will feel better, and your computer may think you're flirting.

Adjust your device settings.

The goal is to make objects on your screen as easy to see as possible.

- **Brightness.** Set the brightness of your display to match the brightness of your work station. You want even illumination, so your screen isn't like a stadium light shining in your face. Turning brightness down as it gets later at night may help to counter the effects of blue light and make it easier for you to fall asleep.

- **Contrast.** Increase the contrast on your display. Contrast is the ratio between the brightest white and the darkest black that can be produced on your screen. *Higher* contrast, where the, er, contrast between light and dark is greatest, makes it easier to focus.

- **Zoom, zoom.** Enlarge the size of text and images on your screen. Larger print and pictures are easier on the eyes since you don't have to squint as much to see them.

- **Zoom, zoom, zoom.** If you can, use a bigger monitor. The larger the screen, the less your eyes have to strain to see the images. While I realize it's not practical to carry a 34" monitor around with you, having access to a large screen at home to which you can connect your device will make extended screen time easier on the eyes.

Experiment with night modes.

On page 70 you saw how blue light in the hours before bedtime affects your sleep in negative ways. Many digital devices come with features, usually accessible through display settings, that allow you to reduce blue light, increase warmer tones of the light spectrum, and lower screen brightness. Use these night modes and other tips from pages 72–75 as you get closer to bedtime for a smooth slide into slumberland.

Use a humidifier.

If the air in your room has low humidity, the dryness speeds up the evaporation of tears in your eyes. A humidifier increases the moisture content of the air, which can be helpful in combatting dry eyes. (This is almost definitely the origin of the

Low-Cost
Humidification System

expression, "There's not a dry eye in the house.") Mini-humidifiers for a small space start at around 10 dollars. You can also often find them for less at a thrift store.

Use artificial tears.

These are drops designed to lubricate eyes. Since there are many different eyedrops for different purposes, and since your eyes are so precious, don't put anything in them without first consulting your school nurse or another healthcare professional, such as an optometrist or ophthalmologist.

Try computer eyeglasses.

These are eyeglasses designed to reduce glare, increase contrast, and block as much as 50 percent of the blue light emitted from digital screens, all factors in causing eye strain. Because they reduce blue light, they'll also help you fall asleep at bedtime. You can get them with or without prescriptions, and as clip-ons if you already wear glasses. If you use contact lenses, computer glasses can help reduce the dryness and discomfort you may experience from extended screen time. There are many different types of lenses, filters, and anti-reflective coatings, so talk to your school nurse, a doctor, or an optometrist to decide which might be right for you.

Minimize glare.

Glare is to Eyes as:

    a. Gluten is to Kale

    b. Cheddar is to Toe Cheese

    c. Static is to Ears

    d. Kerfuffle is to Brouhaha

Sorry, I had an unexpected flashback to my SAT days. The correct answer is "C." Glare is like visual static. It creates optical "noise" that makes it harder to see what's on the screen. This causes iStrain. Harsh interior lighting (such as fluorescent bulbs) and light on the screen from above or behind you (such as sunshine) are the worst offenders. So, think like a cinematographer. Use the tools of your trade. Create optimal lighting for the film of your life.

Get anti-glare filters to place over the screens of your digital devices. If you're outdoors, move into the shade. Change the angle of your screen.

If you're indoors . . .

- Close or adjust curtains, blinds, or shades.
- Turn off bright ceiling lights.
- Use lower intensity tubes and bulbs.
- Adjust the angle of floor and desk lamps.
- Place yourself where light bouncing off of walls or finished surfaces isn't going to cast reflections on your display.
- Strive for soft, even, indirect lighting.

Perfect your desk or workstation.

Lighting is just one element of a healthy, productive workstation. To minimize the chance of developing iStrain or tech neck, your computer screen should be 20 to 24 inches from your eyes. The top of the screen should be at or just a bit below eye level. The idea is to keep your head level and aligned with your spine, so you're not looking down. If you work on a tablet or laptop, you have two options:

1. Connect a monitor that you can locate at a proper distance and height.
2. Connect a keyboard which then allows you to place your tablet or laptop screen at the proper height and distance.

If you need to refer to printed material while working at your computer, try using a document holder or book stand. This minimizes looking down at pages on a desk or table, which can strain your neck. Make sure the printed material is well lit, without causing glare on your screen.

Exercise your eyes.

Nothing like a few retina thrusts, lens lunges, pupil planks, and jumping cornea jacks to energize your eyes. Staring at *anything* a set distance from your eyes for long periods of time is bound to cause eye fatigue. But it's even worse when that "anything" emits blue light, forces you to zoom in on tiny print and images, and throws shiny moving objects at your retina to get and keep your attention. Eyes weren't designed to do that. Here are some exercises you can mix and match to reduce digital eye strain when using your devices:

Follow the 20-20-20 rule. Every 20 minutes, shift your gaze to something 20 feet away for 20 seconds. This relaxes the focusing muscles inside your eyes. (Now, can you put on your Sherlock Holmes cap and deduce why it's called the 20-20-20 Rule?) When you perform this exercise, no cheating with 22-20-18. Although you will get extra credit for 15-20-22!

Focus pocus. Try this so your eyes don't "lock up." Look at a faraway scene or object for 10 seconds. Then focus on something, like your index finger, just a few inches from your face for 10 seconds. Repeat 10 times. I call this the 10-10-10-10-10-10-10-10-10-10-10-10-10-10-10-10-10-10-10-10 Rule.

Lazy eights. Focus on a point on the floor 10 feet away (like a knot or stain or dead bug). With that point as the center, trace a figure eight with your eyes. Do that for 30 seconds. Then, reverse the direction and trace for 30 seconds. All done.

Put on the breaks.
Make sure you take a total break from device use at least once every hour. Do some of the stretches, exercises, or activities described in the Tech Neck section on page 62. Stepping away from the screen for a period of time will ease iStrain by allowing you to change focus, clear your head, go outdoors, splash water on your face, and recharge your (non-lithium) batteries.

Get an iExam.
Even if you're not experiencing any vision problems, it's a good idea for teens to get their eyes checked every one to two years. If you already wear glasses or have contact lenses, an annual exam will catch any change in your vision. If you've diligently tried the above tips and still experience eye strain, blurriness, dry eyes, and/or headaches, tell your parents that you'd like to see an iCare specialist if possible. Be sure to tell them about your screen activities.

Take fatty fishy supplements.
According to the famous Mayo Clinic (and, no, that's not short for mayonnaise), taking fish oil, which contains omega-3 fatty acids, can reduce dry eye symptoms. These fatty acids are not produced by your body. You find them in fatty fish such as mackerel (holy or not), trout, salmon, sardines, tuna, and your favorite, anchovies. They're also found in such shellfish as mussels, oysters, and crabs. (And in capsule form in drug stores, supermarkets, and natural food stores.)

If you consume several portions of fish a week, you should be getting enough omega-3 fatty acids. But if not, you can consider taking these natural supplements, which are likely to not only reduce dry eye symptoms, but help lessen the risk of heart attacks, strokes, blood clots, and cholesterol problems, and it never hurts to get an early start on that sort of prevention. I know this sounds fishy, but if you're not getting enough omega-3 fatty acids from your diet (and I apologize for the yicchy-sounding name), think about giving them a try. Be sure to talk with a parent or healthcare provider first.

Screen Behaviors That Can Lead to Taking Physical Risks

Personally, I consider injury and death to be negative effects of screen time. While such occurrences are rare, I'd hate for you to become a statistic. Here's how to make sure you don't.

Death by Selfie

Fatal accidents have befallen people who took risks to get the perfect selfie. They climbed too high, backed up too far, balanced too precariously, even got electrocuted using a selfie stick during a lightning storm.

Don't let the lure of an amazing selfie pressure you into taking dangerous risks. No photo is worth it.

Death by Distraction

Distraction can also lead to injury or death. This happens when you combine phone use with tasks that require your full attention: driving, biking, skateboarding, operating dangerous machinery. You might not notice a car, a pedestrian, or a deer leaping into the road. Unlike fatal selfies where you're most likely to be the victim, distraction often causes the injury or death of innocent *other* people (or deer).

To keep yourself from being or creating a death-by-distraction statistic, don't let your attention get divided. If you absolutely have to check your phone, pull over. Stop driving, pedaling, or mowing. Find a safe place, and *then* check your phone. A delay of even a second in seeing and reacting to a hazard could be the difference between safety and a serious accident.

Less dramatically, inattention while walking may lead you to bump into people, run into lampposts, trip on steps, or walk into potholes. In fact, researchers in Japan conducted a fascinating experiment to study the impact of distracted walking on crowds of pedestrians. First they filmed groups of students passing along a walkway in both directions. The students moved at a normal pace, intuitively and effortlessly forming lanes and making subtle course corrections to navigate through oncoming pedestrians. Then these sneaky scientists introduced three new students into the group, instructing them to do math problems on their phones while walking. Just these few distracted walkers completely messed up the movement of the entire crowd of more than 50 people. The group's pace slowed dramatically, with students forced to dodge and sidestep one other. The researchers theorize that our gaze broadcasts our predicted path to oncoming passers-by. People looking down at their phones instead of "watching where they're going" deprive oncoming "traffic" of those visual clues, causing ripples of pedestrian pandemonium.

To avoid becoming a clod with a throb, be alert to your surroundings. Don't use your phone at times and in places where there are people and conditions that require your attention. Be present. Take a walk on the wild side: Go electronically naked.

TALES FROM THE DIGITAL FRONTIER

I cannot tell a lie. When I'm walking along the sidewalk and I see somebody coming toward me on a collision course because they're buried in their phone, I refuse to alter my direction. I think of it as a form of protest.

I think of it as being a jerk.

I prefer my interpretation.

I don't feel it is my responsibility to move out of the way when they're the ones not paying attention. If they're in a public place, it's their civic duty to watch where they're going. So I just keep walking toward them.

The suspense of whether we're going to have an actual pedestrian pile-up is excruciating, but what always happens is, at the last minute, like when they're 18 inches away, they sense an obstacle in their path and look up. Then, *they* make a course correction. Often, they'll say, "Excuse me," or "Sorry," which redeems them quite a bit in my eyes. Sometimes in life, you have to take a principled stand. And this is one of mine.

Death by Earbud

Sounds—whistling trains, wailing sirens, clanging railroad crossing bells—alert us to potential threats. It's what tells us to look up, step off the tracks, get out of the way.

Don't get me wrong. I love being my own DJ and selecting the perfect music to accompany me whenever I'm taking a walk, mopping a floor, or working out at the gym (a rare occurrence). But I always make sure I can hear any approaching dangers such as 300-pound bodybuilders who say, "Spot me?" To which I politely reply, "Where do you want the spots?"

To avoid Close Encounters of the Unheard Kind, keep the volume of your music and other earbud emissions low enough that you will be sure to hear audible alerts. And don't forget, listening to loud music can cause hearing loss in teens. In fact, it's believed that one in five adolescents suffer some degree of impaired hearing from overdosing on decibels. That's because the sound on personal listening devices can be as loud as motorcycles, power saws, leaf blowers, and crying babies. So how loud is too loud? It's too loud if:

- You can't hear background noises and conversations.
- Somebody near you can hear the sound.
- You're at greater than 60 percent of maximum volume for more than 60 minutes.

When it comes to earbud volume, less is more. Your ears will thank you.

Death from Exploding Phones

A student in South Korea suffered burns to his fingers and butt when a lithium battery caught fire in his back pocket. Another unfortunate fellow in Florida had a spare battery explode in his pants. I don't know if he was a liar, but his pants were definitely on fire.

Phone charging generates heat. If that heat has nowhere to go, as when charging under a pillow or blanket, it can ignite a fire. While this is a rare occurrence, if I can save just one teen from a bonfire in the behind, it will have been worth it. If you don't want firefighters climbing in your window at 3:00 AM, the following tips will help ensure that your body and your dreams remain flame-free:

- Don't use knock-off phones, batteries, or chargers. Use parts listed by a qualified testing laboratory and authorized by the manufacturer of your device.

- Don't charge or use any device where it doesn't have proper ventilation for heat dissipation.

- Never combine water and electronic devices that are charging or plugged in. You could be shocked or electrocuted. While you can replace a fried phone, you can't replace a fried you.

Toasty Testicles and Overcooked Ovaries

Do I have your attention? In addition to all of the more immediate physical risks described in this chapter, there is a more subtle, potentially more dangerous risk to your physical health. But we all need to be mature here because it's time to talk about scrambled eggs and baked balls.

> I can be mature. Can you?

> I doubt it. But we'll see.

This isn't about breakfast recipes, but rather, whether exposure to radio frequency electromagnetic radiation (RF-EMR) from carrying cell phones and hands-free Bluetooth devices in pants pockets can negatively affect fertility.

Effects on Fertility

To look into this question, scientists have conducted experiments with humans, rabbits, mice, albino rats, and chickens. Let's stop right there. Making assumptions about effects on humans from studies involving non-humans should be viewed with caution since non-humans are not humans. (You may quote me on that.)

But these scientists really got into it. In one study (and I have to tell you this since I may never get another chance to write about cell phone calls to chicken eggs), researchers investigated the effect of RF-EMR on fertile chicken eggs by

placing a cell phone in the "call" position in their incubator and "repeatedly calling a ten-digit number at three-minute intervals during the entire period of incubation." Yes, you read that right.

The eggs exposed to the calls had a significantly higher embryo mortality rate than another batch of eggs next to a phone in the "off" position. This suggests a negative effect from RF-EMR, assuming you consider dead embryos a negative effect (which I do). We could get into a discussion of cruelty to animals and research ethics, and differences between the morality of conducting *scientific experiments* on chicken eggs versus *eating* eggs for breakfast—

> **But let's not.**

I'm not sure how these scientists determined that the cause of the embryo mortality was electromagnetic radiation as opposed to the eggs experiencing toxic rage from being called every three minutes. Nonetheless, I tell you about this research so you can see how deeply this issue has been investigated.

As for female fertility, some studies suggest an adverse effect, others do not. So, a conclusive eggsplanation of the relationship between electromagnetic radiation and human female fertility will have to wait.

To investigate the research involving cell phones and male fertility, I learned that:

Flow cytometry studies were used to examine caspase 3 activity, externalization of phosphatidylserine, induction of DNA strand breaks, and generation of ROS in ejaculated, density-purified, highly motile human spermatozoa exposed to mobile phone radiation.

I kid you not.

What that means is that a bunch of scientists ran a bunch of studies to examine a bunch of characteristics of ejaculated (you may know what *that* means) sperm exposed to cell phone radiation.

I further learned that male mice exposed to RF-EMR had "significantly more sperm head abnormalities (knobbed hook, pin-head and banana-shaped sperm head)." I don't know about you, but I, for one, would not want to be producing pin-headed sperm!

> **I think you're getting immature.**

To summarize the findings of these many human studies on the radio-phrequency -phone-phallus-phertility-phenomenon, there is reason to believe that keeping your cell phone in talk mode in your pants pocket may decrease semen volume, sperm count, sperm concentration, motility, and viability, impairing male fertility. In other words, the ability to reproduce.

One thing the scientists all agree on is that further research is needed. For example, what are the differences between having your phone in talk, silent, or standby mode? Is the potential decrease in sperm quality a concern for all males or just those who are already at the borderline of infertility? Do effects vary based on how long you talk each day? Or whether your phone is in your front or back pocket? Or how tight your jeans are?

In the meantime, a German company is manufacturing underwear that it says will absorb 98 percent of cell phone radiation and 70 percent of WiFi radiation. That's good news for gonads, but now people will ask if you wear "Boxers, briefs, or anti-EMRs?"

Other Electromagnetic Effects on Your Body

If we can now turn our attention from private parts to public parts, you may have heard about other possible effects of electromagnetic fields (EMFs) on the body, such as whether cell phone use can cause cancer or brain seizures. There are no definitive answers yet since the relationship between manmade EMFs and human biology is complicated, and it often takes many decades to see long-term effects.

Keep in mind that cell phones are not the only generators of EMFs. Other sources include power lines, TVs, WiFi routers, dimmer switches, "smart assistant" devices, cordless phones, fluorescent lights, electric blankets, air conditioners, hair dryers, electric shavers, and even your neighbor if their apartment is a strong source of EMFs. Microwave ovens are big offenders since they use EMFs to cook your food. (So never stand near a microwave while it's running, and make sure the seal around the door is tight.) **YIKES!** I'm moving to a cave.

The radiation from most of these sources is low and considered safe, as long as you don't walk around all day with your electric blanket on and wrapped around your head. But we do know that children absorb radiation more readily than adults and are more sensitive to environmental toxins and radiation precisely because their bodies are growing, contain more water, and have thinner skulls, which makes their brains and tissues more vulnerable than those of adults.

Your body's brain, nerves, heart, skin, and muscles produce their own electromagnetic fields. Studies have shown that the EMFs from wireless devices affect the EMFs produced by the heart and brain. So, it's not a stretch to imagine that man-made EMFs may be messing with the nuanced functioning of your body's EMFs by creating stress and disrupting information transmission. Think of it as "jamming" your body's electromagnetic systems. Possible effects from this may include the aforementioned impaired fertility, disrupted sleep, changes in heart rate, high blood sugar, retinal damage, tissue inflammation, and impaired cognitive functioning.

> Now you're being *too* mature. Could you lighten it up?

> I don't think so. I'm on a roll.

Solid research on the relationship between mobile device EMFs and the human body is difficult to do since there are so many variables to consider: amount, frequency, and duration of exposure; strength, wavelength, and proximity of signals; whether subjects are or were previously exposed to human-made EMFs from other sources (work, microwave ovens, transformers, LCD screens, radiation treatment); and human variables such as age, overall health, and genetics.

The more complex the variables, the harder it is to compare and replicate research. That's why some research shows EMFs negatively affecting the body, and other research doesn't. And that makes it difficult to come to definitive conclusions.

But there is one sensible conclusion: Where there's smoke, there's probably fire. As long as there is a reasonable possibility that prolonged exposure to EMFs (like nine hours a day for the average teen) *might* cause cancer, reduce fertility, and/or create other health problems, doesn't it make sense to take some simple precautions to reduce your exposure?

Tips for Reducing Electromagnetic Bad Stuff

If you, like me, find yourself in the "better safe than sorry" camp, here are some protective measures that minimize the likelihood of having tech testes, irradiated ovaries, fried brains, and jammed genetics.

Be a careful carrier. Do not put RF-EMR-emitting devices like cell phones in your pants pockets or close to your reproductive organs (like in a front-facing, low-slung belt bag). Keep it in a backpack or purse or, better yet, attach it to a kite and fly it behind you.

Use an anti-radiation protective case on your phone. This won't eliminate all radiation, since you need some for the phone to work. But it will reduce your exposure via a flap that shields you from the front side of the phone while you're making calls. Be sure to avoid shoddy products from unreliable companies that have difficulty writing coherent product descriptions and instructions. Look for good quality items from reputable sources that list test results and lab certifications.

Seek out strong signals. Poor reception forces your phone to use more power and emit more EMF radiation. If you have a weak signal (anemic bars) and the call isn't essential, wait to make it until you have more bars.

If you have a choice, use a landline to make calls. You could even go retro with an old rotary or *Princess* phone. Très chic! And worthy of a pic to post on social media.

Use speakerphone to keep your device farther from your brain and body. A distance of even a few inches reduces radiation significantly. Putting your phone even farther away on a table or desk is even better. Don't, however, put your device on speakerphone when you're in public. Do that and people will treat you like *you're* radioactive.

Turn off WiFi and/or put your phone in Airplane Mode whenever you can. This will cut the radiation way down.

Use a desktop computer when possible. Desktop computers do produce EMFs, but not at the same level as smartphones, tablets, and laptops, which are usually closer to your body.

Avoid the burst. When you make a call or answer your phone, wait a second or two to place it next to your head. There is a burst of radiation as the call seeks a tower and connects. By waiting, you will be able to avoid the surge. Don't worry if the person on the other end says, "Hello? Hello? Are you there?" Anticipation makes the heart grow fonder.

Did I just say to place the phone next to your head? I take it back. Don't do that. Use a *wired headset* with a microphone. This allows you to keep the phone farther from your body. Radiation will still travel from the phone through the wires in the cord to your head, but it's much less than placing the phone at your ear, giving the radiation a direct route into your brain.

Wait, did I just say to use a wired headset? Don't do that either. Get an *air tube headset*. These plug into your phone just like a regular headset, but the cords, instead of having radiation-conducting wires in them, are hollow. They conduct the sound through air, like a doctor's stethoscope, significantly reducing radiation.

Get a ferrite bead. It's impossible to eliminate *all* radiation. A ferrite bead is an inexpensive, er, bead, that you attach to the wire of your headset. It works like a little dam to absorb the radiation traveling through the wires from your phone to your body. Placing your phone at a distance AND using a headset AND using a ferrite bead—you can see how it all begins to add up.

Ration your use of Bluetooth wireless earpieces. While they're better than holding a phone to your ear, they still emit some radiation. They're not meant to be glued to your ears. So wean yourself off of them a bit to reduce the zap attack on your brain.

Don't put laptops on your lap. I know the name suggests that putting them on your lap is exactly what you should do. But don't. The heat generated by the laptop may nuke your nuts or overheat your ovaries to a degree that could affect fertility. Use your laptop on a desk, or place a large book on your lap to block the heat. Or, if you want to sit in a comfortable chair, use one of those breakfast-in-bed stands for the laptop.

Text, don't talk. I *really* didn't want to include this, since I'm such a fan of "real" talking instead of texting. But in the context of reducing potential negative physical consequences of cell phone radiation, I am compelled to say that texting allows you to keep the phone away from your brain, which reduces EMF transmission to your precious little gray cells.

The final way to reduce radiation infiltration from your phone is to use it less. Heh, heh.

Play It Safe(r)

By now you can see the theme in these various physical dangers and why I included them in this chapter. What they all have in common is the potentially risky combination of digital devices and, well, you.

Nature gives you this wonderful prefrontal cortex, which is the part of the brain that's responsible for good judgment, reasoned thinking, and self-control. But it isn't fully developed until you're well into your twenties. That's why teens sometimes do impulsive things despite "knowing better"—things like drinking and driving, sexting, blurting out an unkind tirade, taking a dangerous selfie. You know, the types of things that lead parents to say, "Don't you ever think before you act?"

It's really evolution's dirty trick. It gives you increased skills, mobility, and independence in your teens, but holds back on the self-control app until you're much older. Fortunately, what I call Angels for Adolescents are out there doing their very best to protect teens from the risky activities they sometimes get up to. Or maybe it's just luck. Either way, these "angels" can't be everywhere, so that leaves *you* to try to think as carefully as you can before doing anything that might pose risks to your body and health—or that of others.

PROTECT YOUR BRAIN

How Too Much Screen Time Can Rewire and Mess Up Your Brain

Do you ever feel mush-minded? Muddle-headed? Brain befuddled? You sit down to read an assignment and can't stay focused. You try to remember what your teacher said in class and it's a hazy blur. You jump from one task to another so it takes forever to finish anything.

From time to time, everybody can be forgetful or distracted or find it hard to concentrate or get psyched. That's normal. But if you feel that way often, it could be that the amount and character of your screen time is affecting your brain in unhelpful ways. Here's how that can happen.

Smartphones are changing the nature and structure of your brain. That's not surprising. The brain goes through an amazing period of growth in the womb and during the first months of life. By age six, the brain's structure is 95 percent of its adult size. But size isn't everything, and the "thinking" part of the brain (known as "little gray cells") continues to develop and grow a lot of new connections throughout childhood and adolescence, and into your mid-twenties.

Other areas of the brain, such as the *corpus callosum* and the *cerebellum* also experience dynamic growth during the teen years. The prefrontal cortex, which is involved with decision-making, organization, planning, judgment, reasoning, goal-setting, and impulse control, goes through a second growth spurt right around puberty. This results in a new round of overproduction of neurons (brain cells) and synapses (connections between brain cells). Since the brain has more of these than it needs or can sustain, an important "pruning" or consolidation of connections takes place during the teen years that is just as essential to the brain's functioning as periods of growth.

I think my brain is pruning just from reading this.

Think of this exuberant period as giving your teenage brain a burst of potential. You get better at learning new skills, processing information, regulating emotions, understanding non-verbal communication, thinking "outside the box," creating, innovating, expressing yourself, and achieving goals—all of which sets you up in fine style for a fulfilling life.

But, since nutrients and available space in the brain are limited, only a small fraction of the new cells and connections will make it. They fight it out—in a "survival-of-the-fittest" battle—with the "last cells standing" influencing your brain's nature and capacities.

So, what determines which connections survive and which disappear? What determines which functions of the brain are strengthened and which are weakened? Four factors are key:

1. How you use your brain during these years

2. The proportion of your time and "brain power" you spend on each activity

3. Outside forces and stimuli that act upon your brain

4. Whether you floss like the dentist says.

(Well, maybe that last factor isn't *quite* so key . . .)

Every stimulation to your brain triggers neurochemical, electrical reactions. Those neural circuits engaged the most will thrive; those used least will weaken. This has to do with your brain's *neuroplasticity*—its ability to form new connections and discard old ones, essentially re-organizing itself. Brain scientists with major degree power in these areas describe this phenomenon in highly technical terms: "*Use it or lose it.*"

And that, my dear readers, brings us back, as you knew it must, to smartphones and screen time. Teens spend an average of nine hours a day on screens (not counting homework time). Doing *anything* for nine hours a day is going to influence the brain's development, just as spending nine hours a day hanging upside down would affect physical development even if, during that time, you also read a book, had a snack, watched a movie, talked to a friend, put together a jigsaw puzzle, and trimmed your nails.

The malleability of the brain during adolescence means this is a period of great opportunity—and risk—for your brain. What your brain experiences during this stage can shape its actual physical connections and hard wiring for years to come. Now, of course the connections in your brain continue to prune, rewire, and reorganize throughout your life. This "plasticity" is why you can learn a new language at the ancient age of 40 or recover cognitive functioning after a stroke or brain injury. But childhood and adolescence are the times when your brain is most actively developing, and the connections being made or *not* being made can have a powerful influence on later life. Think of acquiring a complex physical skill: Of course you can take up ballet or snowboarding or gymnastics when you're 30, 50, or 70. But it's much easier to learn and to become good at such skills if you start when you're young and your body is most pliable. You just don't hear about gold-medal athletes who took up their sport when they were 45 years old.

As humans grow from infancy to adulthood, they go through "critical periods" of development—"ripe" times when it is easiest to learn certain skills, concepts, and behaviors. These optimal periods for growth correspond to times when a child or adolescent's brain, body, and psyche are most pliable; when physical, cognitive, and social skills are developing most rapidly. Much of this learning takes place "automatically." A child's natural curiosity and desire for love and human contact, knowledge, and mastery motivates them to crawl, stand, and walk; speak and read; explore build, and play; acquire skills and form close relationships.

In a nurturing and healthy environment, this learning, while at times challenging, occurs naturally. But if the learning is thwarted during a critical period—as can be the case for children who grow up with social, sensory, or emotional deprivations *or* detrimental screen time habits—it can be harder to acquire the behaviors and knowledge later in life.

What does this have to do with phones? The pre-teen and teen years are critical periods for establishing neural connections; learning about yourself and other people; developing social skills; forming friendships; becoming more responsible and independent; embracing values to live by; expressing and controlling emotions; understanding one's sexuality; making good decisions, and much more.

How do you think your or your friends' screen time, social media use, and online relationships help or hinder these developmental tasks?

Signs That Screen Time Is Negatively Affecting Your Brain

You can control the changes in your brain to a large extent, which is exciting and empowering. The first step in doing so is to understand the potential negative effects of too much screen time on teenage brainology. We can think of these effects in terms of their warning signs.

 You Have Trouble Paying Attention.

You're in class and the teacher is explaining important material that's going to be on a test. Or you're doing homework. Or listening to a coach talk about the upcoming season. You know it's important to listen. But your mind seems to have a mind of its own. It won't focus. You want to pay attention, but you can't. You force yourself to concentrate, but seconds or minutes later, your mind is off and running again. It might be a daydream, a worry, or a desire to get back online. But it's definitely not what you know you should be focusing on.

 You Have Memory Problems.

You often—um—oh, sorry, I forgot what I was going to say. Oh yeah, I remember. Being forgetful is another warning sign of cognitive cloudiness. You find it hard to remember appointments, conversations, or obligations. You listen to a teacher explain a problem, but later, at home, you can't remember anything she said. You have it in your head that your dad is picking you up at school, but then you forget and take the bus home. It's as if your mind gets overloaded, and things you need to know and remember get pushed aside.

 You're Easily Distracted.

Your mind won't stay focused on what's important. Any stimulus—a noisy truck going by, a bird outside the window, a classmate dropping a pencil, a conversation between your mom and your sister—interrupts your concentration. And then it's almost impossible to bring your focus back to the task at hand. It's as if every little thing yanks your mind in one direction and then another. Okay, finally, you're able to concentrate. Wait—is that a helicopter going by? And you jump out of your seat to run and take a look.

 You Have Difficulty Finishing Tasks.

You always seem to have seven, or is it 17, different projects in various stages of completion. Or *non*-completion, to be more accurate. There's that paper you have to write that's been half-done for weeks; that book you haven't finished reading; that box of old toys your mom asked you to go through before she gives them away; that problem with your bike gears you started to work on. You have no problem *starting* a project. But when it comes to finishing it, it's like you start a sentence and then somewhere about halfway through you just

 You're Disorganized.

Sometimes it feels like you spend half your life looking for things. Clothes, papers, keys, assignments. You've got study notes on your phone, on scraps of paper, on your

laptop, inside a notebook, inside another notebook. Stuff in your locker. Stuff in your backpack. Stuff at home. It's as if your life is fragmented across a thousand time zones and universes. It feels like you're drowning in disorder. If you could just make a list, order your life, get on top of things. But you can't seem to make it happen.

You're Unmotivated.

 In many ways, being unmotivated—feeling lazy, lethargic, bored, disinterested, and un-psyched for anything—is a logical result of losing focus, forgetting things, being disorganized and easily distracted, and having difficulty finishing anything. Put all of these together and they add up to a big *why bother?* If you know on some level that you won't be able to concentrate or follow through, and that anything you tackle is going to be frustrating and make you feel lousy about yourself, might as well not even try.

The thing you've probably noticed about all these warning signs is how interrelated they are. If you have trouble paying attention, you're likely to forget things you might have heard or been told. If you're disorganized, you'll have more difficulty finishing tasks. If you're easily distracted, you'll jump out of your seat when helicopters fly by and have trouble concentrating again. If your mind doesn't want to follow your commands, you're not going to be motivated to do anything that requires extended focus, logical thinking, memorization, or sustained mental effort.

How Screen Time Leads to Brain Drain

This cluster of warning signs relates to the prefrontal cortex, which you'll recall is the part of the brain essential to "higher" functions. If anything were to weaken its development, you would expect to experience disturbances in your ability to focus, ignore distractions, remember information, make good decisions, and get motivated to start (and finish) projects.

Guess what can weaken the functioning of the prefrontal cortex?

> Um, excessive, assaultive stimuli coming from my phone to my brain that bulk up not the higher cognition circuitry, but rather the amygdala, which is the region of the brain responsible for more primitive, instinctive, "fight or flight" responses?

> Couldn't have said it better myself.

To see how this works, let's watch a movie.

Have You Been Brainmoshed?

A 20-minute car chase. The hero races through narrow city streets. Cars and motorcycles roar after him. Bad guys chase, shoot, swerve, screech. BAM! WHAM! Side-swiped SLAM! Pedestrians scramble, 18-wheelers jackknife, cycles fly, riders smash into concrete, cars crumple, roll, explode. Flames, carnage, chaos. The hero yanks the wheel, downshifts, revs, plows through a row of food stalls, flies through a barrier, plunges down a steep stairway. Bad guys follow. Glass breaks, sparks fly, engines shriek, tires scream. Metal against metal. The hero slams on his brakes, scorches a 180, takes aim at his pursuers. It's a game of chicken as he pounds on the pedal—80–90–100 miles per hour—dead-heading for the cars pursuing him. At the last second before a head-on crash, the bad guys swerve, fly off cliffs, plow into gas pumps, car after car decimated. The hero rolls back his moon roof, puts on some mellow jazz, and drives off into the sunset. A stroll in the park.

And *you're* a nervous wreck. Your heart rate is through the roof. Blood pressure's off the charts. Your body's tense, you're literally on the edge of your seat. You know it's just a movie. It's not "real." But your brain and body couldn't care less. All they know is that you were under attack by a relentless flood of visual and auditory stimuli. Your nervous system went on high alert. The excitement, suspense, and *perceived* threat activated your primitive evolutionary response of fight or flight. The images, the overstimulation of your senses, were way more powerful than your submerged intellectual awareness that you were just watching actors and special effects on a screen.

It can take hours for your body to return to a restful state, secure that the threat is over. This state of hyperarousal is useful in the event of a real threat. When hunter-gatherers were roaming the plains 200,000 years ago, searching for wild goats, elephants, rhinos, bison, buffalo, and boeuf bourguignon, "fight-or-flight" was essential to survival. They needed to be alert to any and all predators and dangers, be it a hyped-up hippo, a lion, a tiger, or a kid on a skateboard barreling down the sidewalk. So, the brains of our prehistoric ancestors were always on the lookout for flashes of sound, color, and movement.

But fortunately, when not needing to be alert to danger, Paleolithic hunters were able to relax around a campfire after a hard day, making s'mores, sipping a glass of sparkling water with lime, doing yoga, and streaming Netflix. (You can tell I was a prehistory major in college.)

This down time is essential if bodies and brains are to return to a calm state that supports optimal functioning. Remaining in a condition of heightened stimulation, arousal, and threat (whether real or perceived), so that the nervous system is unable to re-regulate or (to use the scientific term) *chill*, can lead to chronic stress.

Think of times when you've had a terrible stomachache or other serious pain. Your psychic and physical energy gets diverted, and you aren't able to function normally. Or think of times you've had *something on your mind*. Your mind is so preoccupied with a problem or worry, you can't think of anything else. You can't concentrate or do homework. It's as if the worry takes over your brain and crowds out everything else.

Now, think of the hours you spend every day on screens. Don't think about *what* you do. Think about what it does to you. Think of it purely in terms of your brain and nervous system being under assault by a continuous barrage of stimuli, most of which attack through your eyes. Sort of like watching that intense movie scene, but for nine hours a day.

Trick or Tweet

The apps and sites you visit are designed to get your attention. The flashes, movements, colors, sounds, brightness, contrast, and visual "SHOUTING" are artificial. They are pixel creations that flood your brain through its primary portals—your eyes and ears. But your brain doesn't initially know whether these stimuli are ads, feeds, tweets, posts, pop-ups, video clips, notifications, ravenous crocodiles, charging elephants, or what. So it needs to assess the threat of each one and determine whether a fight-or-flight response is called for. When you think of the number of apps and pages you have open at a time; the speed with which you jump from one app to another; the quick shifts from one task to another; the unexpected sensory intrusions of flashing ads and strobing pop-ups, you can see how your brain has to stay on heightened alert. This triggers chemical and electrical changes that keep *you* in a state of heightened alert—otherwise known as stress.

The stimuli your brain receives from assaultive on-screen activities bulk up more primitive areas of the brain, the fight-or-flight areas. Those areas responsible for the highest levels of cognitive functioning do not get strengthened to the same extent. But it's not just the rapid, percussive, non-stop flood of stimuli that can compromise higher functions of the brain, creating difficulties in being able to focus, reason, and think clearly. It's also the speed and frequency with which many teens switch back and forth between apps.

One study of college students showed that they switched tasks on their computers an average of every 19 seconds. The majority spent less than a minute at a time on any given screen. That's a lot of rapid-fire task switching. And it's not good for your brain.

It's a bit like trying to watch four movies by flipping between them for a few seconds or minutes at a time. The lack of sustained concentration creates a superficial experience, nothing like what you'd feel by immersing yourself in each movie one at a time. And it would condition you to want to experience sensations in rapid-fire bursts. This type of "multitasking" is another source of the potential harm excessive screen time can cause to higher level brain functions.

THINK ABOUT IT

The number of teens diagnosed with attention deficit hyperactivity disorder (ADHD) has soared since the year 2000. Perhaps this is the result of greater awareness of the condition on the part of parents, teachers, and healthcare professionals, leading to more teens being diagnosed and seeking treatment. But there's another possibility. Certain characteristics of ADHD—impulsiveness, restlessness, problems sustaining attention, disorganization, poor planning skills, mood swings, difficulty completing tasks, forgetfulness, trouble dealing with stress—are exactly the same symptoms studies are now associating with excessive screen time.

What else has occurred over these decades? Soaring smartphone use with the vast majority of teens spending many hours a day on a screen.

Could it be (as shrinks like to say) that the type of stimulation coming from excessive screen time is rewiring the brain in a manner that creates symptoms similar to those of ADHD? Brain imaging studies that show which areas of the brain "light up" in response to various stimuli support that hypothesis (as shrinks like to say). This means that the neural pathways that facilitate concentration, communication, coping skills, social dexterity, emotional literacy, and self-regulation are the very ones being pruned during adolescence by excessive screen time.

Here's another clue. Traditionally, ADHD has been much more frequently diagnosed in boys than girls. Yet, over this same time period, there's been a dramatic increase in *girls* being diagnosed with ADHD. This doesn't make sense. Why would many more girls suddenly have ADHD? One explanation could be that girls are "catching up" by acquiring these ADHD-like symptoms and ADHD diagnoses as a result of screen-induced brain rewiring.

These clues, along with a growing body of research, are leading more and more doctors and psychologists (of which your humble author is one) to ask: How many teens might be seeking help or taking medication for ADHD when a more effective "treatment" might be less screen time?

The Myth of Multitasking

There's a common belief out there—I know because I run into it all the time at the supermarket and post office—that "multitasking" is this cool skill that lets you do multiple things at the same time, be more efficient, and get more done. To that, I say "Poo."

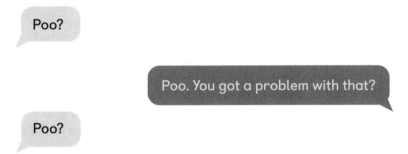

There's really no such thing as "multitasking" in the sense that you can do several things simultaneously. Oh, sure, you can sing while taking a shower, or eat popcorn while watching a movie, or listen to music while sweeping a floor. That's because the "tasks" in each pair of activities are different from each other and use different areas of the brain and/or body. But you can't sing while eating popcorn. Or read while talking to a friend. Or text while studying for an exam.

What we're really talking about when we say "multitasking" is "task *switching*." You change your attention from one task to a different task. If you do this frequently in a given period of time, if you jump from, say, reading an assignment to sending a text to taking notes to checking a feed to reading more of that assignment to watching a video to Snapping a friend to writing a report to checking email to posting on social media, you aren't being efficient by doing all those things at the same time. What you *are* doing is switching your attention quickly and repeatedly from one task to another. And this comes at a cost.

In one study of middle school, high school, and university students, researchers found that students studied for fewer than six minutes before switching to other tasks on their phones, such as social media or messaging. In another study, 50 percent of teens said that they used social media, 51 percent watched TV, and 60 percent texted while doing homework, but claimed that it didn't interfere with the quality of their work.

But it does.

Neuroscientists have conducted fascinating research into the effects of task switching on the brain and cognitive functioning. If you look at the studies, here's the sort of brain-freezing language you might find:

Operational media multitasking (OMM), as measured by a multimedia, multitasking, multi-index measure (MMMTMIM), when combined with a full-sample regression analysis (FSRA), revealed that heavy media-multitaskers (Hmm) manifested a significant negative relationship between media multitasking measures (M&M's) and semantic comprehension performance (SCLP), indicating Really Messed Up (RMU) neurocognition.

For those of you who don't speak psychobabble as a second language, what this means is:

The more you "multitask," the more likely you are to have trouble remembering things, thinking clearly, and focusing.

When researchers asked two groups of students to perform various exercises which required them to focus while viewing changing images, the "high multitaskers"—those with a history of frequent task-switching between different media (print, IM, texts, email, videos, photos, social media, games, apps)—did much worse than the "low multitaskers" at discerning the relevant information.

This might seem counterintuitive. Wouldn't you expect that people who "multitask" a lot would be better at zeroing in on what they need to pay attention to? If they focus on sending a text, and then focus on reading, and then focus on their social media, and then focus on a 10-second video, wouldn't that train their ability to focus? Nope. It trains their brain to hopscotch around, to attend to information in six-second increments, to skim the surface of paying attention, thinking, and engaging. The frontal part of the brain responsible for organization, memory, concentration, and logical thinking doesn't get the workout it needs.

Poo?

Remember how the neural connections in teenagers' brains are strengthened or weakened based on what their brains are experiencing? Well, if your brain experiences a cacophonous chaos of stimuli from frequent task-switching, it gets used to quick doses of information and doesn't develop the capacity for sustained focus and deep analytical thinking.

The practical effects of this can be profoundly negative for teens. High multitaskers have to use much more brain power to do tasks that low multitaskers do with ease. What this means is that students who *rarely* multitask are better at multitasking than are students who do it all the time. As the brains of high multitaskers are altered over time by the barrage of stimuli from frequent task-switching behaviors, these teens can suffer academic problems since their memory and ability to focus are compromised. You'll be more likely to make mistakes when taking a test. Writing a paper will take longer. Remembering what the teacher said in class will be more difficult.

Another even scarier example of how "multitasking" compromises attention has to do with driving. Obviously, safe driving requires full concentration. Yet magnetic resonance imaging of the brain while driving shows that if you add in one more activity, such as listening to music, your attention drops by 37 percent. You can think of your brain's capacity at any given moment as comparable to bandwidth. You know that on your computer, if you're trying to do too many things at once, it can slow down processing. Or if everyone in your house is gaming and streaming movies at the same time using the same WiFi router, things slow down since the bandwidth can't handle so much traffic.

Same thing with your brain. Listening to music takes bandwidth away from driving. Now imagine if the volume is high. And throw in a few friends who are rowdy, with everyone engaged in hilarious, fast-moving conversation. Handing snacks back and forth. "Can you turn up the AC?" "Hey, change the playlist." The more tasks you layer on top of each other, the less you can concentrate on any one of them. Combine that with being a new, less-experienced driver in heavy traffic. Talking on a cell phone—even hands-free—increases the risk of an accident. And I won't even mention texting while driving since I refuse to believe you would ever do something that dangerous. It's no wonder that the crash rate for 16- to 17-year-olds is almost double that of 18- to 19-year-olds, roughly 4.5 times higher than drivers ages 30 to 59, and 6 times higher than 60- to 69-year-olds. Injuries and fatalities are also much greater the younger the driver.

That's depressing.

Yup. But the good news is that teens can protect themselves and others by always paying attention, wearing seat belts, and never drinking, drugging, texting, or playing spin the bottle while driving.

If you think about aspects of your own life—particularly in school, such as paying attention in class, writing a paper, studying for a test, remembering important information, solving problems, making a plan—they all require the ability to concentrate, filter out distracting and irrelevant stimuli, and maintain goal-directed attention. Becoming skilled at anything—sports, playing an instrument, repairing cars, dancing, painting, designing, cooking, woodworking—requires hours of sustained, focused practice and repetition. And these critical brain functions and abilities seem to be those most neglected and harmed by heavy online multitasking during adolescence. *Use 'em or lose 'em.*

From Brain Drain to Brain Gain

Fortunately, there are things you can do to protect your brain from bandwidth bankruptcy, and retrain it to perform better on tasks requiring memory and concentration. Think of these ideas as a smorgasbord of options. Some may strike you as non-starters. Others may seem more practical and applicable to your life. Keep in mind that the more of these you engage, the greater the chances of protecting and enhancing your brain power and cognitive functioning.

Focus on One Thing at a Time

How much would you get done in a day if you spent 3 minutes in your garden, then 2 minutes on a painting, then 30 seconds practicing lay-ups, then 1 minute reading, then 5 minutes building a model, then 45 seconds making a casserole (creamy garlic chicken and broccoli), then 10 minutes watching a movie, then another 3 minutes in your garden, and 2 more minutes on your painting, followed by 30 more seconds of lay-ups, and 1 more minute of reading—with the cycle repeating itself throughout the day?

All that switching! You'd be wasting so much time going from one thing to another, figuring out where you left off, getting your materials out again, re-focusing, alternating between fine-motor-control tasks (like chopping broccoli) and gross-motor-control ones (like shooting hoops). Your day would be a model of start-and-stop inefficiency. Your lay-ups would never improve, your painting would never get finished, that book would never get read, and, worst of all, that casserole would never get made.

Now imagine if you spent 45 minutes in your garden, then 2 hours on the painting, then half an hour practicing lay-ups, an hour reading, an hour working on your model, 30 minutes making a casserole (still creamy garlic chicken and broccoli), followed by 90 minutes watching a movie.

> Can I make pizza instead?

I know this analogy may seem kind of absurd. But sometimes absurd analogies make important points. Many teens use their devices like this, bouncing around like kangaroos on caffeine, subjecting their brain to nonstop digital fireworks.

You can lessen the negative effects of this stimuli staccato by reducing your frequency of task-switching. Try to bundle your tasks into sustained time periods. Instead of switching between screens every 19 seconds, focus on doing one task—social media, playing games, watching videos, sending DMs—for increasingly longer periods without switching to another. Within these dedicated chunks of time there may still be a lot of fast moving, attention-clamoring lights, camera, and action. But their negative impact will be mitigated by lowering your rate of task-switching.

Some tasks, like texting, may defy this scheme and be harder to resist. That's because texting/messaging is the number-one smartphone activity for teens, many of whom send and receive hundreds of texts a day. Plus there's an expectation that texts will be read and responded to within minutes, if not seconds. Just the same, do as much as you can to consolidate how you spend your screen time. Turn off text notifications and, instead, check for texts every 30 or 60 minutes. See if it makes you feel even a little calmer and less fragmented. Your brain will thank you. And that casserole, er, pizza, will taste delicious.

Take Notes by Hand

Studies suggest that students who take class notes on laptops, compared to students who take notes by hand, do more poorly on tests and on answering questions that show their understanding and application of the material. This could be because laptop note-takers are switching between taking notes and other computer tasks. It could also be because laptops, much like smartphones, symbolize the world beyond the classroom, reminding students, consciously or subconsciously, of friends, plans, obligations, and things they're missing. This symbolic "presence" could be a distraction that gets in the way of learning and memory.

If you see room for improvement in your grades and schoolwork, and you currently take notes on a laptop, you might want to try taking notes by hand. Your teacher may wonder what's going on and ask when you became a Luddite. To which you can reply, *"Actually, Professor Pixel, I am conducting an experiment based on subliminal device symbology and distraction theory and its relation to frontal cortex synapsing to see if I can improve my performance on conceptual-application questions as well as strengthen my neurochemical encoding functions by using paper and pencil."*

Turn off Notifications

Almost three out of four teens say they feel a need to respond immediately to texts and notifications. That's not surprising. I mean, when's the last time somebody said:

"Knock, knock,"

and you didn't answer,

"Who's there?"

Notifications are your smartphone's way of saying:

"Knock, knock."

Forcing you to say:

"Who's there?"

"Tex."

"Tex who?"

"Text me."

"Knock, knock."

"Who's there?"

"Annie."

"Annie who?"

"Annie-body got a charger?

(I'll give you a moment to compose yourself.)

Notifications are almost impossible to ignore. It's as if someone taps you on the shoulder. How can you NOT turn your head to see who it is? Imagine trying to do homework with a younger sibling constantly interrupting you with questions and "Watch me!"

In that case, you might say, "STOP BOTHERING ME! I can't concentrate."

Just like a pesky sibling, your phone interrupts and nags you. It preys upon a human craving for novelty and stimulation, at the expense of "flow" and focus. Notifications are one of the most powerful tools of control and addiction apps use to demand your attention and make money. People who allow "push notifications" end up launching those apps more frequently. Well, duh! That's because the pushy apps are always interrupting what you're doing.

One of the best things you can do to protect your brain and your focus is to say NO to notifications. Turn them off if you need to concentrate or you're in a social setting where an endless stream of pings and pongs (if your phone is audible), or bright lights in a dark setting (if your phone is on silent), or bobble-heading (if you keep looking down at your phone) would be rude or distracting to others. Resist the tyranny of obnoxious alerts. Show your phone who's boss. Tell it *you're* busy.

TALES FROM THE DIGITAL FRONTIER

I admit it. If I hear a notification, I can't *not* grab my phone. Just like, if my nose itches, I can't *not* scratch it. (Even if it's a pandemic and I'm not supposed to touch my face.)

Every notification gets me curious and suspenseful. Is it a best friend texting hello? An alert about a package I'm waiting for? An email telling me I won a sweepstakes? So I reach for my phone. And you know what? It's almost always totally useless, like a text saying a bill was paid (which I already know), or I qualify for a new phone (which I don't need), or I haven't answered some stupid survey (which I don't care about). Or that they *really* need my feedback on how I'm liking the daily multivitamins I bought. REALLY? They're %&@#! vitamin pills. You think I have nothing better to do than spend my valuable time composing a review of multivitamins?!

Best vitamins I ever bought. Perfect shade of red. Bright, but not too shiny. Nicely packaged in a high-quality round plastic jar. Love the safety cap. They go down like silk when I swallow. I really get a jolt of energy within seconds. What an exhilarating combination of iron and riboflavin. I can feel my bones getting stronger with every passing minute. All essential vitamins and minerals in one tiny capsule. Amazing. Will definitely recommend to my friends.

Ninety-nine out of a hundred things I get notified about are either: a) bummers; b) not important; c) useless; d) annoying; or e) nothing I need to do anything about right away. So, since I have learned I can't resist notifications, I have also learned to turn them off when I need to concentrate.

Your notifications may be much more important and time-sensitive than mine. But no matter their content, they still interrupt concentration just as much as boring ones. And let's face it, even important notifications can likely wait 30 minutes or so for your attention without any ill effects.

Hide Your Phone

At any given moment, you have a finite amount of cognitive capacity. If something "takes up" some of that capacity, there will be less available for other tasks. Brainy scientists (these are scientists who study the brain), have found that the mere *presence* of your smartphone reduces your working memory capacity and functional fluid intelligence. Functional fluid intelligence isn't how much you know about liquids. It's the strength of your fundamental cognitive processes such as learning, problem-solving, logical reasoning, abstract thinking, and creativity (all good things to have).

It doesn't matter whether your phone is face-up or face-down, whether it's on, off, or silent. The effect is the same. And that effect—reduced memory and thinking capabilities—is stronger the more dependent you are on your phone. In other words, the more you feel *I couldn't live without my phone*, the more loss you'll sustain by its presence.

How can this be? How can your smartphone, even if it's turned off and buried in your backpack, reduce your cognitive firepower?

It has to do with the power and meaning of a smartphone in your life. It's your significant other. Chances are good that you never have it out of your sight or hearing. You check it dozens or hundreds of times a day. First thing in the morning. Last thing at night. You may sleep with it. It is you. You are it. No other device takes up so much emotional, social, psychological, or intellectual space in your life—even when you're not using it. Not even your electric toothbrush.

If this relationship with your phone is harming your memory and cognitive processes, that could make learning and test-taking in school more difficult. And it could be detrimental to your future, since your brain circuitry and cognitive abilities are being shaped to such a large extent during adolescence. It's not as though if, when you're 25, you realize that you really have trouble concentrating, completing tasks, and writing a report, you can rewind back to age 14 and rewire your brain.

What if you do it when you're 18?

That would be better. But how about not having to do it at all?

Can anything help? Or are you and your brain doomed to an eternity of mush-mindedness and dim prospects?

Fortunately, there is a solution. Those same brainy scientists found that separating yourself from your phone increased cognitive capacity and working memory. And, encouragingly, those who were most dependent on their phones benefited the most from separation and reduced digital distraction.

So, when you need to have your cognitive power functioning on all cylinders, turn off your phone. But don't stop there. Create an extreme separation. If you're taking a test in school, leave it in your locker. If you're doing schoolwork at home, put it in another room, as far from you as possible.

Give yourself a digital Heimlich. Say you're doing homework. It shouldn't take more than two hours. But with every ping you grab your phone. And before you know it, you've spent 30, 60, or 100 minutes doing "not homework." Finally, you switch back. But your mind is still thinking about the other tasks you just did. You've lost not only the actual time you spent doing those other things, but your concentration.

Many teens who complain about how long homework takes may not realize that it's because they are task-switching dozens or even hundreds of times while trying to work. In fact, 57 percent of all teens agree that social media distracts them when they should be doing homework.

To reduce the amount of time homework takes . . .

- Eliminate the distractions. Turn off notifications.

- Follow the *out of sight, out of mind* principle. Eject your phone. Propel it to another room where you won't see or hear it.

- If you're frustrated, if you need a break, don't liberate your phone. Instead, do some quick exercises, make a snack, tidy something up, tell your mom you love her.

These tips will help you to focus and soon you'll be as concentrated as a frozen can of lemonade mix. And that homework that used to take four hours? You'll do it in two.

Big Tech wants to spy on your brain. Companies such as Facebook and Elon Musk's Neuralink are working to develop hands-free, brain-computer interfaces (BCIs). This means you could scroll or type just by thinking. What that means, of course, is that in order to work, your device would be able to recognize what you are thinking. (Um, no thank you.)

Initial research on BCIs focused on medical uses for people with paralysis, damaged nerves, tremors, or Parkinson's disease. This would benefit millions of people whose mobility is limited because of nerve damage. But Big Tech has greedier aspirations than helping those in need.

Ray Kurzweil, a "futurist" and director of engineering at Google, believes it will be possible to upload our brains to computers and the cloud by 2045. He also thinks that our body parts could become mechanical by the end of the century. (Assuming that climate change hasn't put us all 20 feet under water.)

Elon Musk—who created Tesla and SpaceX along with Neuralink, and is a billionaire—is hot to see "some sort of merger of biological intelligence and machine intelligence." He envisions BCI chips being implanted in your brain—simply, quickly, as routine as laser eye surgery.

Hmmm. Mechanical human beings with computers for brains. Can you say R.O.B.O.T.? Well, call me fuddy-duddy . . .

> Fuddy-duddy.

. . . but that sounds pretty terrifying to me. The last refuge of privacy we have is our thoughts.

It didn't take long for advertisers to start salivating at the prospect of knowing your thoughts and moods. Imagine if they could understand your personal neurochemistry at any given moment. They could create new feedback loops by showing you text or images, and then track your neural activity and emotions. Social media companies could monitor your emotional journeys, just as they do your digital journeys, and sell that information.

Right now, a brain-computer interface requires you to wear a sort of "swimming cap" or have a surgical implant. So, you'd be pretty sure to know if a company were monitoring your thoughts. But, as artificial intelligence advances, it may become possible to create less invasive, less visible ways to control your devices with your thoughts. And vice versa.

So, for now, my advice would be:

- Don't put any weird-looking swimming caps on your head.
- Don't let anyone do elective brain-implant surgery.

Boredom Is Beautiful

"Mom, I'm bored."

"Then go find something to do."

"*Thanks*, Mom. Really helpful."

Sarcasm noted. But at least she didn't say, "Only boring people get bored."

There's another reason to reduce your time on screens besides saving the health of your brain (as if that weren't enough). It's to preserve the beauty of boredom in your life. What, boredom doesn't sound beautiful to you?

Boredom has a bad reputation—somewhere between poison ivy and b.o. People see being bored as shameful, and painful. Something to avoid at all costs, to be cured, kept at bay. That's one reason why many parents program their kids 25 hours a day with school and sports and lessons and tutors and afterschool activities. So there won't be a moment when the deadly claws of boredom can sink into their child's mental and emotional flesh.

But boredom can be a quiet moment of beauty, if you let it. It can be a gift to yourself, a time to reflect, pause, and be quiet so you can hear your inner thoughts and intuitions.

I wonder sometimes if boredom is dying. Oh, sure, you can still feel bored during class or a church sermon. But if teens have their phones handy, isn't it easier than ever to vanquish boredom, to send it packing with a click, a tap, a swipe, or a scroll? Take that, boredom! I banish you. I'll never be bored as long as I can dive into my digital dopamine distraction device.

Many teens feel that way. In a Pew Research Center survey, nine out of ten 13- to 17-year-olds said they use their phone sometimes or often as a way of "just passing time." In another Pew survey, 93 percent of 18- to 29-year-olds said they use their phones to keep from being bored.

If it's true, if boredom is an endangered species now that teens can easily drown it out with digi-noise, that's a shame. Because boredom—that panic-producing mix of overflowing emptiness, hopeful hopelessness, screaming silence, and ticking timelessness—is a blessing, a spark that ignites self-knowledge. It's the space where you get to know yourself. Here's why.

Boredom Is a Garden for Creativity

When people are bored, their minds wander. This can lead to creative thinking. Boredom researchers (not to be confused with boring researchers) have conducted studies in which participants were asked to complete a boring task, like copying from a phone book, or an even more boring task, like *reading* the phone book, or no task at all. All were then given exercises that measure creative thinking (like coming up with good excuses for being late or ways to use plastic cups). The more boring the task they were given, the higher participants scored on the subsequent creativity tests. The findings suggest that experiencing boredom increases the mind's desire to sink its teeth into a challenge and come up with novel ideas. This is why mindless moments like washing dishes, cutting grass, taking a shower, or lying outside and watching clouds go by can lead to creative inspiration.

Boredom Is a Gateway to Daydreaming

Teens get the message that if they're not busy and productive every minute of every day, if they're not learning and doing and making and building and striving, they'll end up a failure. Well, sure, you need to acquire skills and knowledge and participate in life to grow into a mature human being. But really, I think the opposite is even more true. To succeed in life, you need to find moments of idleness. Nothingness. *Boredom*. Moments when you can let your mind wander and see where it takes you. As a teen once told me, "If you don't daydream, you'll never get anywhere in life." Yes, daydreaming is important because it can lead to creativity and "aha" moments. But it also provides a time for repose, reflection, and recharging. (Recharging *yourself*, not your phone!) A time for hearing your thoughts, touching your emotions. And that's often where you find your values, deepen your self-knowledge, and discover your path.

Boredom Introduces You to Yourself

Imagine trying to get to know another person without communicating or spending time with them. Impossible. Same thing with getting to know yourself. Marie Josephine de Suin Beausacq, also known as Comtesse Diane (a 19th-century French countess and author I hadn't heard of either), said, "Boredom is the fear of self." That rings true. Some people can't stand the stillness of being alone with their interior life. They may be afraid of their thoughts. They may not want to be alone with themselves and their emotions, hopes, fears, or dreams. But any journey requires you to observe your surroundings to know if you're headed in the direction you want to go. Same thing with life destinations. You have to observe your inner surroundings. How you feel. What you think. What you're doing. What you're not doing. There's a temptation to avoid these thoughts by picking up your phone. Try to resist. Otherwise you may never get to know yourself. Or know what kind of self you want to be.

Boredom Tips You Off

To what? To knowing that you're not doing what you want to be doing. Sometimes it's obvious: you want to be shooting baskets but instead you're raking leaves. So you're bored. You want to be Snapping with a friend, but you're stuck listening to a lecture. Bor-ring! But other times when you're bored, there's discomfort. A feeling of blankness. A longing. For something. But you don't know what.

The Russian novelist Tolstoy (okay, he sounds kind of familiar) called boredom "the desire for desires." The void of boredom cries out for a passion to fill it. It's emptiness in search of a purpose. You just don't know what that purpose is. And that's the anguish and blankness of boredom. It's a paradox: * Your soul cries out for something, but there's nothing you want. That's because the boredom is paralyzing you. If you knew what you wanted, you'd act. You'd go after it.

*A paradox is not two doctors. It's a statement that seems contradictory or nonsensical on the surface but which, when you think about it, you realize may be true.

So the challenge of boredom is to discover what you want; to allow yourself to float in the emptiness. Don't change your inner channel to an external device. Alleviating the discomfort with digital noise won't lead to insight, revelation, or growth. Instead, walk barefoot in the depths of your soul and see what you feel. What you find.

What to Do When You're Bored

Next time you're feeling bored and left to your own devices (and I don't mean *that* one), try these tips.

Don't reach for your phone. (You knew I'd say that.) Resist the impulse. If you don't think you can, try to hold off for just one minute. Once that minute is over, go for another. Your phone will always be there. But this moment, this precious slice of time, will not. Don't let it go to waste. If you're willing to trust your internal life, it can take you to brave, interesting, exciting new places.

Adopt a new attitude. Don't panic. It's just boredom. It can be a friend. It can lead you to new interests and insights. Picture it as a treasure hunt. Or a door to the great unknown through which you will pass to a land of surprise and promise and . . . ?

Go for a walk or bike ride with no destination in mind. Just start moving. Let your body daydream. You'll notice new things. You'll discover new places. And in the course of your journey, you may find yourself on a mission or a mini-adventure.

Embrace the boredom. Lie on your bed. Climb a tree. Sit on a porch, a stoop, a bench, or a swing set. Experience and relish your boredom. Look inside your mind. Let it wander. Commune with your thoughts and feelings. This is how people set goals, make plans, and get in touch with their dreams.

Engage in a tedious task. Let the basic action of doing something mundane or repetitive, like raking leaves, shining shoes, or copying a phone book (remember?) free your mind. You'll be amazed where it takes you.

TALES FROM THE NON-DIGITAL FRONTIER

There was a time in my life when I was working on a screenplay. The writing was the easy part for me. The hard part was thinking about the story, getting inside my characters, figuring out the plot. During this period, I belonged to a gym. I went there three times a week. Prior to using the weights and exercise machines, I spent 30 minutes on an exercise bike to get the heart pumping. (Years later I realized I could just go for a bike ride.)

Few things are more boring to me than spending half an hour on an exercise bike. So I used the time to think about the plot and inhabit my characters' lives. I'd get inside their feelings and enter their world. Sometimes it felt so real, and their pain and losses were so profound, that it brought real tears to my eyes and down my cheeks.

"It's just sweat," I'd say to the person next to me.

"My eyes sweat a lot."

Eventually, over the course of many months and much pedaling, this journey into my imagination, combined with my writing sessions at home, led me to complete a screenplay that I was really proud of. I knew that, when I accepted my Academy Award, I would thank boredom.

When you're bored or doing something mindless, you can use that space to work on song lyrics in your head. Create a story. Disappear inside a book. You know, with real paper. Your mind can transport you anywhere.

> What happened with the screenplay?

Well, since you asked, it won first prize in a screenwriting competition. I got a free trip to Los Angeles to meet with agents. The prize included several free nights in a fancy hotel, the kind where a glass of orange juice costs more than an iPhone. So I didn't eat any breakfasts there.

The screenplay got optioned by a director. And nothing further happened.

But that's showbiz.

> Bummer.

> Bummer supreme. But I never regretted doing it. I got to spend time with my wonderful characters, explore another form of writing, and meet some great people.

Step out of character. Do something you've never thought of or done before. Do it precisely because you've never done it before. It could be anything: making a sketch; standing on your head for five minutes; creating a superhero; sending a handwritten, fully illustrated letter to a grandparent; picking up trash along your street; playing a new game with a sibling; going to a pet store; taking the subway to a station you've never been to and exploring (safely, of course); asking a parent about their childhood. Anything. That's the whole point. It's your chance to learn more, grow as a person, and expand your relationship with the world you live in.

Have a conversation with yourself. You're an interesting person. Get to know yourself better by asking yourself questions. Your answers will give you ideas for things you can do in that moment or the next time you're bored.

- If I were stranded on a desert island for six months, what one person would I want to be there with me? Why?
- What would I like to know more about?
- What skill would I like to learn?
- If I could do something kind today, what would it be?
- What one thing about my room would I most like to change?
- Did I do anything in the past day, week, month, or year that I regret? Can I do anything about it?
- Is there anyone I've lost touch with that I'd like to contact?
- Could I help out my mother/father/sibling/friend in some way? How?
- What would I like to work on about myself?
- What dreams, hopes, or goals am I aiming for and working toward?

Give your brain a break. Scan your senses. What do you hear, see, smell, taste, and feel? Whether it's birds or buses; ceiling stains or passing trains; burning leaves or saltwater air; baking cookies or bubbling sauces; sexual stirrings or stomach gurglings, there are marvels to behold, miracles to ponder, portals to pass through. Whether you're slogging along a sidewalk, twiddling your thumbs on a train, or dawdling in a doctor's office, there are sights, sounds, smells, details, layers, and sensations that you've never noticed.

Any one of these ideas could take your mind on an interesting journey or launch you into a plan or activity. I dare you. Be bored.

> Okay. I'll try it. But first I have one question.

> What's that?

> Poo?

PROTECT YOUR RELATIONSHIPS

How Screen Time Affects Your Social Skills, Relationships, and "Street Smarts"

People. Can't live with 'em. Can't live without 'em.

For most teens, other human beings provide more joy—and pain—than anything else. What could be better than a sleepover with a best friend, celebrating a win with teammates, being in love, hearing praise from a teacher, or getting a hug from your mom? And what could be worse than feeling betrayed by a friend, striking out with three runners on base, getting dumped by somebody you care about, having a teacher ridicule you in front of the class, or your mom chewing you out for breaking a bowl?

Yup, relationships and social interactions trigger the full spectrum of human emotions—joy, anger, resentment, heartache, longing, fear, desire—like nothing else. Think about it: Countless people have murdered someone in a fit of rage, jealousy, or lust, but I've never heard of anybody committing a crime of passion against shampoo. It's always a person.

It's natural that human nature—what it means to be "human"—finds expression in our online lives. We bring our innate qualities of thinking, feeling, and behaving into that world. So, as in "real life," we see the best and the worst of people online. But increasingly, as more people spend more time online, what we do there, what we experience there, how things work there, is creating a new arena of human nature: *online* human nature. And we are discovering that these new online ways of thinking, feeling, and acting have become so powerful and universal that they are now changing our *offline* human qualities and behaviors—often in troubling ways.

That's what this chapter is about.

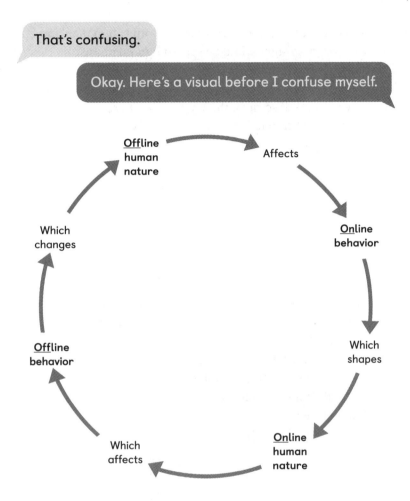

Signs That Screen Time Is Negatively Affecting Your Relationships

Social or interpersonal warning signs are good indicators of some of the profound changes in behavior that can result from living so much of our lives through screens. If you experience any of the following, it could mean that online socializing is interfering with your offline social life and skills. And if your offline social skills are impaired or never fully develop, that can make it harder to work out conflicts, negotiate with teachers, succeed at a job, express yourself, be assertive when appropriate, build positive relationships—romantic and otherwise—and create a fulfilling life for yourself.

Keep in mind that warning signs are simply a notification that "something is up." Many of these warning signs could be caused by something other than screen time, such as bullying, shyness, anxiety, depression, or problems at home. But given what we know about the possible consequences of too much screen time (or the wrong *kind* of screen time), if some of these warning signs ring true for you, your digital life is a logical first place to look for causes and clues.

 You Feel Uncomfortable in Real-Life Situations.
You often feel eye-shy and tongue-tied. You avoid looking people in the face, you don't know what to say. The thought of a "heavy" in-person conversation creates a feeling of dread or panic. You'd much rather do it by text or not at all. Talking about a problem with a parent, approaching a teacher after class with a question, telling someone how you feel, comforting a friend who's upset, ending a relationship—AGGGHHH!!!—you'd rather walk barefoot on hot coals through a tunnel of snakes while juggling wasps' nests.

 You've Withdrawn from Offline Social Activities and Relationships.
You used to participate in sports, clubs, afterschool events, and volunteer activities. You used to meet up with friends all the time. You used to enjoy doing things with your siblings, parents, or grandparents. But now, you've cut way back or stopped altogether. It just kind of happened. More and more, you realized that your offline life was interfering with your online life. One of them had to go. And away it went.

 You Have Conflicts with Others Over Screen Time and Phone Use.
Your teacher confiscates your phone during class. "I wasn't using it. I was just *checking it*." Your mom tells you 400 times a day to put down your phone. Your brother bugs you about what you're doing spending all that time online. Even some of your friends have complained that you pay more attention to your phone than you do to them.

These warning signs go hand-in-hand with research suggesting that more and more teens:

- Prefer to text instead of talk face-to-face
- Feel awkward in, and ill-equipped to deal with, real-life social situations
- Feel uncomfortable with eye-to-eye contact and in-person emotional exchanges
- Are withdrawing from social activities and real-life relationships
- Prefer being online to doing things with friends or family members
- Don't have good conversation skills

- Argue with friends and/or caregivers over their own screen time
- Hide or lie about their screen time and what they do online

Now, when I say "more and more teens," I don't necessarily mean all teens or the vast majority of teens. I mean "lots" of teens; seriously increasing numbers of teens. I mean that over recent years, as phone ownership and use by teens has skyrocketed to the point that 95 percent of all teens own or have access to a smartphone, profound changes in the social behaviors and "street smarts" of teens have occurred.

Declining Social Skills, Independence, and Confidence

Clearly, online socializing is affecting offline socializing. According to multiple surveys and studies, today's teens, on average, are less independent and more sheltered than teens of a generation ago. They are less likely to date; more likely to stay at home on Friday and Saturday nights. They do less volunteer work. They get driver's licenses at a later age. Fewer teens have paid jobs, participate in extra-curricular activities, attend parties, or go out to malls or movie theaters.

Sheltering in Place

In 15 years, over the period of time that smartphone use by teens soared to become almost universal, the number of teens who see friends in person every day or nearly every day dropped in half! Coincidence? I don't think so.

Teens stay at home more, and when they do go out, it is more likely to be with a parent. Now, don't get me wrong, I think parents are great, and my eyes become misty thinking of loving parent-child field trips to buy shoes at the mall. But an important task of adolescence is developing independence. Taking risks. Exploring. Building skills of self-sufficiency. Falling and getting up and dusting yourself off. (Assuming you fell in a dusty area.) In order to become—and feel—independent, confident, and capable, it's important for you to meet challenges and solve problems. You need to learn to listen to and communicate with other people, develop close relationships, and find your way through uncomfortable feelings.

You develop these skills and traits by being out there in the world. Planning a trip. Taking public transportation. Getting lost. Getting un-lost. If kids video chat instead of going to a friend's house, hitch rides with a parent instead of journeying on their own, stay home with devices instead of exploring their world, this delays "growing up." And, indeed, today's teens seem to be experiencing longer childhoods. They are more dependent on adults, and less assertive and comfortable solving their own problems, than were teens a generation ago. And let's not forget, many teens, armed with their phones, may not see any reason to go out when they can text, see movies, play games, shop, and connect with friends without ever leaving home. In fact, according to a Common Sense Media study of teens, social media, and social life, more teens now prefer to communicate with their friends by text rather than face-to-face. (This survey was conducted *before* the pandemic, when there was a choice.)

I'm not blaming teens for any of this.

> **You better not be.**

It's just another unplanned consequence of smartphones. These devices have made it much easier for parents to intrude on—I mean, be involved in—their kids' lives. Parents nowadays, just because they *can*, want to know at all times where you are (assuming they don't have a tracking app that *tells* them where you are), want you to check in with them, and want to be able to reach you any minute of the day or night.

Parental Preoccupation

Alongside the explosion of smartphones and all that they mean for keeping tabs on kids, plenty of parents are also tapped in to the 24-hour news cycle, which instantly alerts them about the one child that got kidnapped that day, rather than the 5,489,765,211 who did *not*, or pings them when a tornado touches down halfway across the country, rather than rhapsodizing about the beautiful weather right outside the window. This constant barrage of bad news has made parents ever more fearful that their kids will be the victim of some event or emergency that, in reality, has an infinitesimal, tinier-than-tiny chance of happening. This constant monitoring can have an unintended side-effect of making teens fearful and feel less confident of their ability to navigate life and work things out on their own. Now, to be fair, "helicopter parenting" began its take-off before smartphones arrived on the scene. But the emergence of smartphones reinforced the trend as parents gained the ability to monitor and reach their kids 24/7.

Of course, parents should be involved in their kids' lives. Kids of all ages benefit from parental love, support, and encouragement. And while some teens could use *more* of their parents' attention and guidance, others are "failure-deprived." If their parents are always hovering to protect them from disappointment or discomfort, if they are coached, tutored, monitored, and programmed to follow a narrow path toward "success," that can keep teens from developing the insight, inner strength, and social skills to analyze and power through the inevitable challenges they will encounter.

Thinking about these issues makes me recall my own childhood. Beginning when I was 11 or 12, my friends and I would set off on our bikes for adventure. We'd ride miles to a park, or go downtown, or even go to a museum if we felt we needed to see a diorama (not to be confused with diarrhea) of early colonial life. I can assure you my mother wasn't chewing her fingernails in a fit of worry until I returned, which I always did. She was thinking, *Oh good, a little peace and quiet for the afternoon.*

This tightening of the leash by some parents—not that I'm suggesting you are a bone-carrying member of the canine species—

> **You better not be.**

—in *combination* with teens experiencing more "virtual" than "real" life, has made many teens and young adults less independent, less willing to solve their own problems, and less able to confidently relate to and communicate with their peers than ever before.

To a large extent, teens experience their friends through texts, photos, and videos. And even video calls and group teleconferencing are different from being together in person due to transmission delays, freeze frames, freaked-out pixels, and getting distracted by the weird things on people's bookshelves. I'm sure you experienced that during the pandemic lockdowns. Online socializing was a lifesaver, but it also revealed how much you missed being with people in person. This trifecta of 1) "staying at home" (with or without a coronavirus); 2) parents minding *your* own business; and 3) primarily relating to other human beings through a device is narrowing teens' social skills.

Over the coming years, the impact of digital socializing may get even worse. I mean, what's going to happen as artificial intelligence, virtual reality technologies, brain implants, and mind-reading laptops take over? (Yes, it's all in the works.) Are we going to turn into programmed robots as face-to-face human contact becomes extinct? Sound far-fetched? Well, check back with me in 25 years.

TALES FROM THE NON-DIGITAL FRONTIER

I went away to a boarding school during high school. It wasn't that my parents wanted to get rid of me (I was a delightful child), but rather, they thought it would be a valuable experience for me to be more on my own, and that it would help me to become independent and responsible and also, I guess, well-educated.

This took place a number of years BCE (Before Cellphones Emerged). There was a pay phone in the basement of my dormitory. (You can learn what a "pay phone" was by googling "Stone Age Communication.") If I wanted to speak to my parents, I had to call collect (you might need to google that too) and hope they would accept the charges and pay for the call. (Fortunately for my self-confidence, they always did.)

If they wanted to call me, they had to hope that some kid hanging out in the basement butt room (no, this wasn't where students dropped their pants and displayed their butts; it was where kids with parental permission could smoke [yes, back then 16-year-olds could smoke, it was *that* long ago]); anyway, if my parents called the pay phone in the basement and some kid answered the phone, if he was lazy he'd just say I wasn't in the dorm, but otherwise, he'd yell up to the fourth floor, "PACKER!" and hope that I'd hear and come down.

My point in sharing this drive down memory lane is this: Going away to school as a teenager was tough. I was scared I'd fail my classes, and that people wouldn't like me, and that I'd hate it, and that I'd drop my tray in the cafeteria and everyone would point and laugh.

To this day I can remember and even *feel* that first night in the dormitory, lying in a strange new bed, in a strange new place, not knowing a soul, and how alone I felt. If I could have picked up a cell phone and easily called or texted my parents, maybe it would have helped. But maybe I would have begun to rely on them more than my own resources. Instead, with no cell phones, those feelings of aloneness motivated me to hang out with people, make friends, and realize, a few weeks later, that I no longer felt lonely. I had worked things out on my own, which, between you and me, gave me a little boost of confidence and pride.

Getting support from people who care about you is essential, especially when the stakes are high and mistakes could have serious consequences. But, as with many things, it's important to find a balance point where the support is enough to help you succeed on your own, but not so much that it *prevents* you from succeeding on your own. Have you found a balance point for yourself? If not, how could you start looking for it?

The Decline and Fall of Empathy

One of the most serious casualties of the rise in virtual relationships is the decline of empathy. Empathy is the ability to see things from somebody else's perspective; to imagine what they are thinking and feeling. It is the soil in which kindness, decency, good manners, and healthy relationships bloom. According to a study by a group of University of Michigan researchers, college students whose adolescence coincided with the explosion of smartphone use were 40 percent *less* empathetic than their peers of a generation earlier. At the same time, narcissism—an exaggerated sense of self-importance that makes people selfish, entitled, and infatuated with themselves—has increased by nearly 60 percent.

Empathy—the "we" trait—has declined, while narcissism—the "me" trait—has increased.

So? Why does that matter?

Empathy bonds people and societies together. Being able to imagine what others are thinking and feeling lies at the heart of healthy relationships and cultures. Empathy gives life to caring and compassion, to not hurting people's feelings, to hugs and encouragement and offers to help. Teachers need empathy to see things from their students' perspective. Students need empathy to see how their behavior, individually and as a class, affects teachers. Wealthy, powerful leaders need empathy to understand and support the lives of average citizens and people living in poverty. Teens need empathy to stand up to bullying or to give a booster shot of affection to a parent having a bad day. Empathy lies at the core of every healthy friendship and romantic relationship.

The decline in empathy and rise in narcissism are flip sides of the same coin. If you become more self-focused, that gets in the way of putting yourself in someone else's sneakers. Conversely (that's a subtle sneaker joke if you're paying attention), if you extend yourself toward others with kindness, commiseration, and support, you are less likely to see yourself as the exalted center of the universe.

What's Happening to Empathy?

Such profound, fundamental shifts in identity, emotion, behavior, and personality affect how we relate to ourselves, to others, and to the world. There are many possible reasons for this decrease in empathy and rise in narcissism.

- **Teens are more stressed.** When you're stressed, it's natural to focus on yourself more than on others. And research shows a dramatic increase in depression and stress levels for today's teens over the past several decades. This stress can come from school, parents, expectations (both your own and those imposed upon you), being overscheduled, having no time to daydream, and feeling you need to meet an idealized image based on what your friends post or what celebrity culture dictates. Throw in troubled times, pandemics, climate change, complicated problems like racial and social injustice, and fears about the future or getting a job, and, well, I'm getting stressed just thinking about all the stress teens are feeling.

- **Social media encourages narcissism.** While many teens use social media to extend empathy to others, the medium encourages an exhibit of "self." What will you say? How will you look? What experiences will you relate? What photos will you post? For many teens, this has little to do with who they really are and what they really feel. Instead it's an image; it's how they want people to see them. Or how they *think* people want to see them. It's a superficial relationship with themselves displayed for the world to see.

- **Teens don't read as much fiction as they used to.** (Bet you weren't expecting this one.) Fiction—getting lost in a book where you experience emotions, adventures, and new worlds through characters who may be similar to or different from you—allows you to imagine and inhabit other people's lives and feelings. The deep emotional experience of reading fiction contributes to the growth of empathy.

But the biggest culprit in the decline of empathy is the shift from in-person to online communicating. Empathy is nurtured by face-to-face interactions.

What Your Body Reveals

It makes sense that, with more and more interpersonal relating happening online, levels of empathy have fallen. Why? Because, according to research conducted over many decades, as much as 70–93 percent of communication is *nonverbal.* But rather than argue over the numbers and whether such studies are accurate, let's just go with the scientific term: "lots." Facial expressions, hand gestures, your appearance, how close to or far apart from someone you stand, whether your arms are folded or your feet are tapping—these are critical elements of communication that add immeasurably to the ideas or feelings being expressed. Yet they don't get conveyed in a text or DM.

Is someone fidgeting? Smiling? Looking nervous? Perspiring? Mumbling? These types of nonverbal clues, which can indicate anxiety, affection, discomfort, or even truthfulness or deception, often say much more than just the words coming out of someone's mouth.

What is the volume, emphasis, or pitch of the person's speech? Does their voice sound cold, distant, happy, downcast? Is the speaker putting on a funny voice?

Let's say you send a text to ask somebody how she is, and she texts back "fine." Is she sighing, or rolling her eyes, or being sarcastic when she says it? Is it an abrupt expectoration of the word which might signal anger? You just don't know.

Whenever you've had a video call with a grandparent or for an online class, birthday party, or gabfest with friends, prezoomably you've experienced frozen images, strange facial expressions, delayed audio, and jerky motions. This is frustrating and interferes with the quality of conversation, closeness, and comprehension. Unless you've got really weird friends, that never happens in face-to-face conversations.

Infants and early preschoolers who are not yet able to communicate verbally rely heavily on the facial expressions of caregivers for emotional cues. Children need to understand these cues to avoid potentially dangerous situations, interpret social interactions, and learn positive behaviors.

Touch is another element that is missing-in-action online. Think of how much is conveyed by a gentle arm around the shoulder or a clasping of someone's hand. Watch a parent with a young child in an affectionate moment. The parent will be cradling and embracing their child. Mussing his hair and rubbing his back. These physical actions are powerful communicators to the child, which are felt in the moment as love, security, attention, and approval, and, as the child develops, lay the groundwork for the later language of intimate relationships. But you can't hug somebody on a video call.

THINK ABOUT IT COVID-19 lockdowns and social distancing made us look at face-to-face relationships in a whole new way. On the one hand, social media and video conferencing was a lifesaver (maybe even *literally*) for many people during the pandemic. The ability to connect digitally kept us sane. It allowed people to work from home, participate in online classes, send and receive important information, and place orders for toilet paper.

At the same time, this 100 percent reliance on technology revealed how different digital interactions are from face-to-face ones. There must have been so many times during the lockdowns when you longed to go to a friend's house, meet people in a café, hang out at the mall, see a movie with a group of friends, or be with someone you care about. But you couldn't. Did you see the videos of principals and teachers who drove past the homes of their students to drop off cookies or diplomas? Or caravans of cars driving past somebody's house to wave or sing "Happy Birthday"? Being "in person," even from 20 feet away, was thrilling and emotional and gave all who participated a warm feeling and wonderful memories.

Still, our online lives came through in grand style to help us cope with the pandemic and the way it shattered our offline lives. Social media nourished us during a period of social starvation, even as not being able to be with people physically made us appreciate our in-person relationships all the more. It will be interesting to see if the pandemic changes how teens value in-person versus online relationships. Maybe face-to-face contact will reclaim its spot from texting as the number-one favorite way to relate to friends.

Empathy Eyes

You may have heard the expression "the eyes are the window to the soul."

> Uh, no.

Well, now you have. Eyes are our greatest physical reveal. (Much more so than the bellybutton.) Look at someone's eyes when they speak. Do they look dry, red, tired, and bleary (maybe from too much screen time, ha, ha)? Is the person looking you in the eye? Looking down? Do you see warmth or judgment in their eyes? Are they misting with tears?

If you want to feel the power of the eyes, sit facing a friend. Interlock fingers and hold each other's hands, resting them on your knees. Then, gaze into each other's eyes for at least 30 seconds. It may feel awkward or embarrassing at first, but push through. I guarantee you will feel something profound, whether it is closeness, sadness, love, concern, discomfort, attraction, or maybe even hilarity. Now, look down and stare at each other's left knee. I guarantee you won't feel anything except really strange.

Since I have a boundless supply of empathy, I am imagining you're thinking two things:

1. "But, Alex," you say, "I use video chat apps to talk to my friends. So we *do* see each other."

   To which I would reply, "That's better than not seeing each other, but it's still a poor substitute for the real thing."

   Think of it this way. You could spend days devouring online travel videos for a trip to Pago Pago. You could chat with 100 people who have visited there. You could learn everything about its history, geography, weather, tourist sites, and major exports. You're "seeing" and hearing about Pago Pago. But that would never replace the experience of going there in person. And video chatting will never equal or replace real-time, face-to-face conversations.

2. "But Alex," you say, "I don't see what's so bad about texting. Just because we don't see each other doesn't mean we're not sharing our feelings."

   To which I would reply, "I'm not saying that texting a friend to confirm what time you'll meet up after school is going to lead to the evaporation of empathy and evisceration of all your interpersonal skills."

What I *am* saying is that texting and messaging, which are designed for brief exchanges, will never allow for the full range and depth of human communication. This has led increasing numbers of young people, especially those who are neurodivergent and may face challenges interpreting linguistic cues, to use and request "tone indicators" when messaging. It's a type of shorthand placed at the end of a sentence that clarifies the sender's meaning, emotion, tone, and intent. For example:

/s = sarcastic
/j = joking
/t = teasing
/srs = serious

And if you want further proof of the limitations and ambiguities of texting, I present you with emojis. Emojis were created precisely to compensate for the inadequacies of online written messaging. Yes, they can be cute, funny, helpful, and clever, and yes, a microscopic winking face or a need-to-get-out-my-magnifying-glass-to-see-it eggplant or angel with a halo may add a bit of meaning to an otherwise confusing or ambiguous text, but they are still "manufactured," and a poor substitute for genuine expressions of human emotion. For me, life is too short to want to spend time figuring out what strings of emojis mean and whether the mouth in that ninth emoji is a spoon or a rattle.

Just in case you were wondering, this emoji string means: *A sad cat and an octopus who lost three arms in a scooter accident went to a Blue Man Group performance which they loved except when the bodybuilder in a thong stole a purse from a woman with a spoon for a mouth who erupted in anger because she no longer had money to take the bus to the merry-go-round that was closed due to a fire which got her so hot under the collar she went to the bathroom to take her temperature where she met Casper the grey snowman who was in a relationship with Pedro the diabetic penguin who gave himself a shot of insulin which he keeps under lock and key.*

At least, that's what I think it means.

How to Strengthen and Protect Your Relationships and Social Street Smarts

So, what do you do if you think some of these social warning signs apply to you?

First, congratulate yourself on being self-aware and honest. Not everyone is.

Second, recognize that many teens feel uncomfortable in face-to-face situations. That's natural. Teens have always felt this way, long before the internet ever existed. Talking to a teacher about not understanding something, bringing up a problem with a friend, or asking somebody to go out can feel awkward. No wonder many teens prefer to do these things online. If they want to end a relationship, they'll do it by text. (This is known as a data dump.)

Communicating with and relating to others with honesty, respect, warmth, dignity, assertiveness, flexibility, tact, and *empathy* . . .

. . . all while maintaining your values and beliefs . . .

. . . *and* being alert to nonverbal cues . . .

. . . *and* doing so with individuals who are bringing their own baggage, ego, prejudices, emotions, and perspective into the equation . . .

. . . is easily as complicated and challenging as the sentence you just read.

But the solution isn't avoiding these situations by hiding out online. It's confronting them. The fact is, human relating is messy. And I don't mean peeing on the toilet seat or not cleaning up after yourself in the kitchen. (As for peeing in the kitchen, that simply isn't allowed!) So don't be afraid to face your discomfort. And don't forget the importance of practice. Whether shooting baskets, playing piano, or communicating in person, you get better with practice. That's true of all skills. So take them on. Face-to-face. In real life.

> **Being online is part of real life.**

> You know what I mean. So don't be difficult. ;) *

*I had to use an emoji here. Because even with all the words I have at my disposal, and even with the context I created, and even with my masterly command of the English language, I realized that I couldn't be sure you'd know that I meant "So don't be difficult" as a friendly joke, and not as a judgmental scold. So, if I wasn't certain you'd take that phrase as I meant it—and I am, as I'm sure you know by now, an amazingly clever and creative and modest wordsmith and author, and I have more words at my disposal since this is a book and not a brief, thumb-twiddled text exchange, and this entire chapter serves as context—you can imagine how ambiguous, confusing, and incomplete online communications can be, especially since they are usually briefer, more quickly dashed off, and lacking in context.

"If One Train Spends an Hour on Insta, While Another Train . . ."

Online socializing doesn't only affect your offline social skills, it also affects your offline relationships. That's because if you spend a lot of time online, it means you're spending less time offline. This foundational principle of digispherical physics, known as the Pythagorean theorem of TikTok, is right up there with Newton's law of gravitation in how it has changed the world. As a scholar of mathematics myself, who won a set of colored pencils in third grade for being the first person in my class to learn his multiplication tables, let me explain what this formula means:

If you spend an hour online, you're not spending that hour offline.

This is expressed as . . .

$$(BT) = f \bigcup_{n=1}^{m} (L_n \cap W_n) \; \nabla \; + \; \Psi \, (1 + xst)^{nw} - \frac{fc}{1} + \frac{nr^2}{2} \div \frac{-k \pm \sqrt{D \, x \, hwh}}{2A}$$

. . . where *BT* (Big Trouble) is a function of *U* (Uh-oh) to the *m* (Mom) power where *L* represents *Leave Me Alone* and *W* represents *Whatever* and *n* represents *Nuh-Uh*, times ∇ (coffee filter in case you're thirsty) plus Ψ (pitchfork, in case you have to make hay while the sun shines) times 1 plus *st* (screen time) where *x* = total hours to the *nw* (No Way!) degree minus *fc* (forgotten chore) plus *nr* (neglected responsibility) squared, divided by negative *k* (karma) plus or minus the square root of *D* (your last grade in Chemistry) times *hwh* (Homework? What Homework?) over 2*A* where *A* = Android.

It's a simple equation illustrating how excessive screen time can lead to doing poorly in school, blowing off commitments, neglecting responsibilities, and disappointing friends. This often results in conflicts with important adults in your life. Here are three simple ways to get back on their good side. Okay, two simple ways and one complicated way.

Make lists. Every day, before you turn in at night, prepare a list of what you need to do or bring with you the next day. (Doing it the night before allows you to put together any supplies you might need and avoid a scramble in the morning.) Handwrite your list. By not looping it through all the distractions your phone represents, where it's just one more thing among thousands of stimuli, it becomes more personal.

First thing each day, check your list. This will anchor you in what you need to do that day, *before* your mind and emotions get distracted by your phone (or anything else). In other words, get in touch with yourself first.

Keep a calendar. This is a valuable tool for space cadets living in Flake City. It's also essential for responsible teens who need to remember they have band on Mondays, debate on Wednesdays, and babysitting Timmy Terror and his stepsister Nancy Nightmare every other Tuesday. Your phone, of course, has a calendar. But frankly, if you have a problem with excessive screen time, it's flirting with danger to keep your calendar on your phone. I recommend paper calendars. There's something primal about them.

Build pillars of trust. "Can't you be more responsible?" "Don't you *ever* think first?" These statements are in the Hall of Fame of Annoying Things Parents Say to Their Kids. They're annoying because they often ring true, and nobody likes hearing that their mom or dad is disappointed or upset with them.

If people are on your case for being irresponsible, it may be because the pillars of trust between you and others are crumbling.

For people to trust you, to see you as a responsible person, it helps to:

- Be honest
- Show up on time
- Honor commitments
- Keep promises
- Use good judgment
- Avoid risky behavior
- Respect confidentiality

I know, that's quite a hefty list. But at least I didn't include a lot of other things such as:

- Make wise decisions
- Do chores
- Clean up after yourself
- Treat people with kindness and respect
- Be sensitive to other people's needs and feelings
- Use good manners
- Take care of possessions

Yeah, I know. Sneaky way to get in some more trust pillars. But nothing is more important than building and keeping the trust of people who matter to you (and to whom *you* matter). If you strive to embrace these pillars of character and behavior in your relationships and life, you'll be seen as a responsible and trustworthy person (who doesn't get hassled by adults for not meeting your obligations).

Encouraging Truths

If you feel uncomfortable in real-life social situations, if you've withdrawn from offline social activities and relationships with friends, parents, siblings, or others, if you're having conflicts with others over your screen time, you may feel better if you keep a few basic truths in mind.

It's to be expected. These are the years when you're *supposed* to feel awkward, uncomfortable, and like a total doofus from time to time. You say something, and then wish you could take it back. You don't say something, and later wish you'd said it. You're with somebody and feel self-conscious, and worry you're coming across like an idiot. Totally standard operating procedure. All teens feel this way from time to time. Some just hide it better than others. (And, to let you in on a secret, most adults feel this way, too.)

You'll need to readjust the ratio between your online and offline socializing. That's a nice way of saying you're going to need to cut back on your screen time to make room for more offline activities. This means more time for being with people in person. There's nothing brilliant about this concept; it's simply a mathematical truth based on the fact that there are only 24 hours in a day.

Like everyone, you can get better with practice. While the ability to relate to others is influenced by personality, confidence, past experiences, temperament, hormones, and parenting, it is still a skill. And much of it needs to be learned, sometimes by seeing what others do, sometimes by simply taking the plunge. You become more comfortable by being willing to go beyond your comfort zone. It's only by extending yourself, by feeling the burn, that you expand your possibilities and your social confidence.

Teens don't automatically know how to have a deep conversation or how to read emotions. And why should they? These skills don't just appear out of nowhere. They take time and practice to develop. And practice, as we all know, makes perfect. Except it doesn't, really, because perfection doesn't exist. Practice makes "better."

If you feel minorly (or majorly) socially challenged, or if you just want to brush up on your skills, the next section will give you some ways to practice becoming a smooth and sage social samurai who puts people at ease, displays empathy and social grace, builds supportive, rewarding friendships, and gets invited to the best parties. Well, I don't know about that last one, but I do know people will want to be around you since you'll make them feel good.

Tips for Talking in Person

When teens are hesitant to talk in person, it's often because they feel they don't know what to say. So, here are some sure-fire (former) secrets for becoming more comfortable with offline conversation and socializing. Use these, and soon everyone will be saying, "Oh, Bartholomew [or Hortense or whatever your name may be] is the most erudite, intelligent, witty, delightful conversationalist I know!"

Secret #1: Disown the phone.

I bet you've been in situations with friends where you wish they'd pay more attention to you than to their phones. Your instinct is right on. Even if someone isn't constantly checking their phone, the mere *presence* of a cell phone lessens the quality of a conversation. But don't take it from me. Take it from a fascinating study that enlisted people for an experiment. The participants were divided into couples who were asked to have a conversation in a café on either a trivial or a meaningful topic. The couples were observed by the researchers, with particular attention paid to whether any of them held in their hand or placed on the table a mobile phone. The researchers then asked the couples to report on their conversation and experience.

The study found that couples with mobile devices within reach rated the conversation as less fulfilling and less empathetic than did couples having phone-free conversations. It didn't make any difference whether the couples talked about something meaningful or trivial. But the decline in empathy was more pronounced between participants *who were already friends with each other*, than between people who just met.

Why would just the visual presence of a phone reduce the quality of a conversation, even if the phone is never checked or used?

Phones are not only functional, they're symbolic. They represent connection, communication, information, drama, news, games, obligations, relationships, things you need to do, the world "out there." The presence of a phone creates an "absence" that makes you aware on some level of everything you're missing. Is the phone going to ring? What does the notification you just saw mean? Is it about a problem? Homework? A concert ticket? A weekend plan? An argument? Whatever it's about, it's not about the moment you're in.

If a phone is in sight while two people talk, it means there's a third (or a fourth if they both have phones) "person" there—one who is liable to interrupt at any minute. And that, whether subliminally or consciously, diverts your attention.

Think of it this way. Let's say you're having a conversation underneath a six-foot-long icicle. Even if the temperature was way below freezing, even if it looked like the icicle wasn't going to drop, wouldn't it be hard for you to focus exclusively on the person you're with? Or what if there's a grizzly bear 100 yards away? He looks content, munching on berries, but at any moment he might start charging in your direction. Or what if you're at a café and somebody at a nearby table keeps staring at you? Wouldn't that disturb your ability to focus on the person you're with? Or what if—

What if you stop with these analogies.

So, the first and most essential step in having good conversations is to hide and silence your phone. Seriously.

Secret #2: Ask questions.

This is a sure-fire way to feel more comfortable and get an offline conversation going. It works because most people's favorite subject is themselves. If you ask questions to get them talking, they'll have a grand ol' time and will associate that with your conversational skills. The key is to ask open-ended rather than one-word-answer questions, since longer answers mean you don't have to work as hard to keep the conversation going. Sometimes, though, a quick question is necessary to open the door to a longer discussion. For example:

"Do you play sports?"

"Yeah."

Hmmm, seems like this person could use a few conversation tips. But don't be discouraged. Follow up.

"What do you play?"

"Soccer, tennis, bocce, volleyball, varsity checkers, and ski jumping, which is my favorite."

This looks promising.

"Ski jumping?!? I'd be TERRIFIED to do that. Where'd you learn?"

You should, unless the person is conversationally constipated, have them engaged by now. If need be, you can follow up with additional questions:

"How did you prepare for your first jump without breaking every bone in your body?"
"Have you had wipeouts?" "Do you compete?"

And, at some point, unless your conversational partner has reached their word quota for the day, they'll say, "How about you? Do you play a sport?"

Questions work with anyone. The context for the conversation and your relationship to the person will suggest what types of questions to ask. Whether you're going for a job interview, talking to a college admissions officer, visiting your grandparents, meeting a new friend, or speaking to a seatmate on a bus, train, or airplane, take a minute to think up some questions ahead of time.

Secret #3: Be an active listener.

We tend to think of conversation as *speaking*. But great conversationalists are great listeners. Listening—giving your full attention to somebody—is an act of respect and validation.

Here are **seven** tips for being a world-class listener:

1. **Show you're paying attention.** Look at the person. Don't fidget, tap, drum, bounce, squirm, stare at the ceiling, doodle, or pick a scab. Oh yeah, and don't check your phone.

2. **Show you're listening with visual clues.** Nod, lean in, let tears fall, shake your head, bug out your eyes, drop your jaw—as long as your reaction is appropriate and natural, of course. You wouldn't respond to a friend who tells you her dog died by crossing your eyes, sticking out your tongue, and putting on a goofy face.

3. **Show you're listening with audible clues.** Gasp, sigh, snicker, laugh, howl, chuckle, chortle, giggle, and guffaw as the spirit moves you.

4. **Show you're listening with verbal clues.** The above tips show you're paying attention and *hearing* what the person says. This tip shows you're *listening*. At the most basic level, you do this by saying such things as, *"What?" "Really?" "No way!" "Huh?" "Oh no!"* This encourages the person to keep talking.

   At a deeper level, you show you're listening by reflecting the substance or emotion of their remarks back to them. How you do this depends on what they're saying. If it's something light-hearted, newsy, or gossipy, you can respond to the *informational* content:

   > Drew: *"Lance mooned the principal at morning assembly."*
   > You: *"That was cheeky."*
   > Drew: *"Yeah. I thought Mr. Grimm was going to have ten cows."*
   > You: *"So what happened?"*
   > Drew: *"He ended assembly and told everyone to get back to their asses. I think that's called a Freudian slip."*

   You can see how your response mirrored the *factual* content of the incident Drew described. You reacted to his comments and asked for more information. But let's say a friend reveals a powerful feeling or something that is "heavy" or upsetting:

   > Sue: *"I HATE my uncle. He's coming for Thanksgiving."*
   > You: *"You don't want to see him?"*

Sue: *"He gives me the creeps the way he looks at me and asks if I have a boyfriend."*
You: *"That's nasty."*
Sue: *"It makes me want to run away."*

Here, you zeroed in on the *feelings* behind the words. If you had responded to Sue saying, "I hate my uncle. He's coming for Thanksgiving," with "Is he bringing the stuffing?" she would have felt you weren't listening. But by reflecting the emotional content, you showed that you cared. You encouraged Sue to keep talking.

Sometimes, friends just need a warm shoulder to cry on. They need to get something out of their system. They're not asking you for advice or solutions. Other times, they may be asking for help. So, if a friend is struggling with a problem, you can say, "How can I help?" "Do you want to talk to the counselor? I'll go with you." "Have you told your mom how you feel?" If it's a problem with practical solutions, you can step up in whatever way you're able: "Let me loan you some of the money." Or "Here's a website with tons of resources for that."

5. **Follow up.** The spirit of a conversation can linger long after the words are over and you part company. Coming back to a friend, even days later, with a follow-up question *really* shows you were paying attention to what they said. For example, you could ask Sue: "How did Thanksgiving go with your uncle?"

6. **Take advantage of activities.** Some of the best conversations take place when you're not focused on the conversation. Like riding in a car. Or taking a hike. Or cooking together. So, if you're meeting someone new or seeing someone you don't know too well, consider going for a walk or taking in an exhibit—an activity that gives you something to do and to talk about so you're not staring each other in the face. Somehow, having an action or activity going on in the background makes it easier to talk. And it provides openings for conversation. You know, like, "I think I just saw Bigfoot." Or "Oops. Was that three *pounds* or three *tablespoons* of salt?"

Practice these tips and you'll be a learned listener in no time. With everyone clamoring to give you an earful, let's move on to the next secret for being a great conversationalist.

> Wait a minute. Where's tip #7? You said there were seven tips.

> Nah, I only have six.
> Just wanted to see if you were listening.

Secret #4: Say nice things.

In the rush of everyday life, you're sure to hear complaints, reminders, instructions, corrections, demands, inquisitions, and criticisms. These can make you feel stressed, nagged, demeaned, misunderstood, mistrusted, unfairly treated, and like a lab rat under the microscope. There is a global shortage of appreciation, encouragement, and niceness. A kindness drought. And it's not caused by climate change. It's caused by people too busy, stressed, or angry to think of others. (Did somebody say *narcissism*?)

When a commodity is rare, its appearance is all the more special and valued. That means a kind remark will make you stand out in the best way. People will want to be your friend. They'll want to talk with you. Your offline interactions will leave people glowing with a warm feeling.

Make a point of noticing your friends' (or anyone's) accomplishments and special qualities. Mention their fine attributes, good deeds, and triumphs. It'll be a gift to them, and people love to receive gifts. You never know when somebody is in a deep funk or at the edge of an emotional cliff. A compliment or kind remark from you may be the best thing that happens to them that day. And remember, kindness isn't just for people going through a hard time. It's for everyone all the time.

Great Ways to Boost Your Empathy Power

You'll recall, unless you've been skipping around in this book, that I have been making a big deal about empathy. That's because I see it as the foundation of decency, solidarity, justice, consideration, respect, good manners, fulfilling relationships, mental health, civilized society, the future of the planet, and you not taking the brownie I set aside for later.

As I've said, empathy is in steep decline, in significant part due to the dramatic fall in face-to-face contact that nurtures sensitivity to others' moods, feelings, needs, and intentions. So, I think we can all agree that empathy is an essential quality for healthy and rewarding relationships. Right? You agree?

> Roger that.

Good.

Here's the great thing about empathy: You want to be empathetic because it is the hallmark of being a good citizen and upstanding member of society. And, you want to be empathetic because it makes other people feel respected, loved, and valued. But there's another reason to be empathetic: It makes *you* feel good! And it makes people like you! For real. In person.

We all love to get presents. (Well, maybe not a pack of handkerchiefs from Grandma.) We all like to be on the receiving end of a compliment, a word of praise, a sweet gesture, an act of support. We all like to be the beneficiary of somebody else's empathy. But the greatest gift we can receive is the feeling inside when *we* give to somebody else. And that's what empathy is. Yes, a gift to others, but also a gift to ourselves.

According to those people who have nothing better to do than study teenagers, having greater empathy is linked with increased happiness and academic achievement, and being less likely to get bullied. Teens with strong perspective-taking skills are better able to deal with their emotions, listen, face social challenges, tolerate conflict, and achieve constructive resolutions when they have disagreements. So when you extend yourself to care for and about others, you are also caring for yourself. I think that's what they call "win-win." Or, if you were empathetic toward six people today, "win-win-win-win-win-win-win."

Given how important empathy is, I present to you some ways to become emphatically, empathically empowered—and reap the rewards.

Understand What Empathy Is

There are three aspects to empathy. They're fluid and they interrelate. One is *emotional sharing* (sometimes called *emotional contagion*).

> Don't say "contagion." It makes me want to sneeze.

> Roger that.

This is when you experience the feelings of another person. It's why you cry at movies or burst with joy at a friend's good fortune. It's not something you do; it's something that happens to you.

A second form of empathy is *perspective-taking*, or *cognitive empathy*, where you intentionally try to put yourself inside the head of someone else to understand what they are feeling or thinking. It's a conscious mental exercise.

Perspective-taking is usually the more reliable and helpful way to react. This is because if you are experiencing the same feelings as a friend—rage, fear, distress, elation—you may not have the distance, objectivity, and self-control to react in an appropriate and helpful manner. Perspective-taking engages your thought processes, creating a "time-out" that allows you to reflect, consider options, and come up with a supportive and constructive response.

Both emotional sharing and perspective-taking can trigger the third element of empathy—*empathic concern*. This motivates action: You hold the door for somebody pushing a stroller; you step up to cook dinner after seeing that your mom had a hard day; you're extra kind to your brother because he just lost a championship game.

People possess these different elements of empathy to varying degrees. Somebody who's an emotional sponge may absorb the feelings of another person (emotional sharing) but be too lazy or self-centered to help (empathic concern). Babies as young as a few months old show evidence of emotional sharing but, obviously, they are not yet cognitively able to put themselves in the mind of another person or offer somebody their seat on a bus.

As kids get older, as their prefrontal cortex develops, they are increasingly able—physically, mentally, socially, and psychologically—to incorporate perspective-taking and emotional sharing into appropriate empathic concern and action.

Value Everyone

You are a shining star, but you're not the center of the universe. Neither am I, which I still have a hard time accepting. One through-line of human development from infancy to adulthood is the growing realization that other people have needs, feelings, beliefs, and perspectives that are just as important to them as our own are to us. (The needs, feelings, beliefs, and perspectives of others may be cuckoo, but that's another story.) The extent to which a child or adolescent recognizes that they are one "star" among billions, and develops the capacity to factor the needs of others into their own orbit, is one measure of increasing maturity. Valuing others as much as ourselves is also a marker of empathy.

Think About Your Own Troubled Times

Think about how you felt when your parents got divorced, or you flunked a test, or didn't make the team, or your aunt died. What got you through those dark periods? It may have been your own strength, courage, hard work, and perseverance. But I bet in many instances, you worked it out because somebody listened; somebody gave you support and encouragement; somebody let you know they connected with your feelings or situation and understood what you were going through. They gave you the confidence that you could meet the challenge, make it to the other side. You can be that somebody for others.

There may be times when you haven't experienced exactly the same thing a friend is going through. But using your own memories can still help you imagine how your friend feels. Let's say she lost her event at a track meet. You don't play team sports so you can't relate exactly, but you do remember how it felt when you tried out for the school orchestra and were (tactfully) told to try again in a year after you'd had more practice. It was a real slap to your confidence and pride. The way you felt when you were passed over for piccolo is probably a lot like what your friend is feeling now.

Make sure you use comparable memories to guide your response. If a friend's parent died, you wouldn't want to say, "I remember when my goldfish died . . ."

> **But what if you haven't ever experienced anything like it?**

If you truly can't relate, firsthand, to what they're going through, simply be there as a friend. Hug them. Hold their hand. Ask them how they're doing. Do little things to let them know you're thinking of them. Call them. Text them. Send a card. Sneak a loving note and a candy bar into their backpack. Tell them you wish you could help but you know there's nothing you can do that will ease their pain, lessen their disappointment, relieve their sense of betrayal. Let them know you're there if they want to talk. Or if they want to *not* talk. If they do open up, use the tools of active listening to make them feel heard. Just *being there* emotionally and physically will help them and show how much you care.

Practice Empathy

Empathy, like most skills, traits, and attributes, can be nurtured and strengthened by practice. Here are some ways to:

    a. make empathy part of your identity and value system;

    b. become a certified Expert in Empathy, Identification, and Observation (E.I.E.I.O.); and

    c. earn the right to put the letters after your name.

Keep an open mind. Practice putting yourself in someone else's shoes (assuming they're not four sizes too small). Being willing to hear alternative opinions, and to let them enrich or even change your own ideas, is a mark of intelligence and humility—qualities I think are always nice to have.

Perspective-taking—the conscious engagement of empathy—is enhanced by observing human behavior and asking yourself questions. Let's say a friend gets an answer wrong in class. Try to understand how she feels. *What's she thinking now? Is she upset? Embarrassed? Couldn't care less? How would I feel if that happened to me?* If the situation has to do with a conflict between you and another person, you could ask: *Why did he do that? How does he see my actions? What is my role in this? How would he have wanted me to act?*

If a friend doesn't answer a text, before you start to feel hurt, rejected, or angry, pause and ask yourself: *Is there some reason that could explain this? Could my friend be sick, taking a test, mad at me, out of battery?* Questions can protect you from unnecessary emotional upset and your friend from unfair accusations.

Suppose a teacher explodes in front of your class (and I don't mean literally) and really lets loose with a tirade about how lazy and ungrateful students are. Of course, that's not cool, but what if, instead of feeling defensive or angry, you took a pause to ask: *Why did he say that? Was what he said true but just came out wrong? If I were a teacher and students behaved this way, how would I feel?*

Such questions can lead you to a better understanding of people, of human nature, of cause and effect, and of steps you or others might be able to take to improve any situation.

Apologize

One of the nicest ways to show empathic concern is to say you're sorry. It's so easy to do, and so powerful in its ability to right a wrong or restore a relationship, you should consider it one of the top tools in your social skills arsenal. No matter what it is you've done—damage something, reveal a secret, hurt somebody's feelings, break a promise—simply saying you're sorry will work wonders. A sincere apology is an act of empathy since it reveals that you recognized and cared about how your behavior affected somebody else. If the apology can be accompanied by an amend or act of recompense (e.g., repair or replace something you broke or lost), all the better.

An apology doesn't need to be an admission of "guilt." You may feel that your action was correct or justified. Let's say a friend has been talking for weeks about whether to dump her boyfriend. She goes on and on and on and on and on and on and round in circles and should she or shouldn't she and what if this and what if that. You are so fed up with her stupid boyfriend that, in a moment of exasperation, you say, "WILL YOU SHUT UP ABOUT IT! I AM SO SICK OF HEARING ABOUT YOUR BOYFRIEND. EITHER DUMP HIM OR DON'T DUMP HIM."

Your friend begins to cry, and she storms out, saying what a horrible person you are. And you *feel* horrible. Not because you think what you said was inaccurate or untruthful—you do wish she'd stop talking about it; you are sick of hearing about it; you do think she should either dump him or not—but because of the way you said it, and how that affected your friend. So, you can apologize for the way you expressed yourself and how that made your friend feel. To do that, you could say what you meant to say, adding, "I said it all wrong and I feel terrible about that. The last thing I would ever want to do is hurt you like that. I just wanted you to make a decision since I see how much this is upsetting you. But I didn't say it right. Can you forgive me?"

Chances are your friend will forgive you, and maybe even admit that she thought about what you said, and you were right, she does need to decide. And let's not forget, her obsession with "To dump or not to dump, that is the question" showed a lack of empathy for you and how you might feel being on the receiving end of her interminable vocal vacillations.

"I'm sorry" are magic words—just as much as "please" and "thank you" and "abracadabra." So make sure they're part of your vocabulary.

> Good advice, but I think you went on about it kind of long.

> I'm sorry. I apologize.

Empathize with Your Future Self

Anticipating your own feelings is a good way to practice anticipating the feelings of others, a skill that can help you in all kinds of situations. You need to talk to your dad about the dent you put in the car? Imagine how he is going to feel, what he is going to say. (This is perspective-taking empathy.) Then, with that in mind, think about how you will feel if he expresses anger, disappointment, or concern. Will he threaten to not let you drive anymore? Work through in your head what he might feel and say, and how that would influence what you feel and say. By thinking it through ahead of time, from both perspectives, you can be prepared with answers, apologies, and suggestions. You'll be more rational, which is always good when you have to tell your dad you dented his car.

Shower Your Parents with Empathy

No, not shower *with* your parents—that would be weird. Shower your parents with empathy. This, like apologizing, is one of those simple actions that reap amazing rewards.

Parents are often harried, hurried, and worried. A kind word or gesture—a "thank you"; "let me help"; "are things better at work?"—shows that you care, you're tuned in, you recognize all they do for you, and you want to offer support. Such empathy will make a parent appreciate you all the more, which can come in handy if you have to tell your dad something that may get you in hot water like, um . . . you put a dent in the car.

Search for What You Have in Common with Others

Studies show that we are more likely to feel empathy for someone we perceive as similar to us. You've probably recognized that you feel differently about a deadly building collapse in a country on the other side of the world than you would if the collapse happened near where you live. That's because you don't feel much in common with people in a country or culture you don't know about or identify with. That's natural. But humans all around the planet have much more in common with one another than not. We all want love and fulfillment. We all want our children to have wonderful lives. We all feel grief and longing and hope. We all fast-forward through commercials.

So, if you're feeling at odds with someone or trying to understand where they're coming from, spend some time thinking about what you have in common. To get better at this, talk to people who come from a wide range of countries, cultures, and backgrounds; who have political beliefs and other views that differ from your own; who have lived lives different from yours. Travel as much as you can, even if it's only to the next town over. Along the way, you'll discover fascinating variety, some of which may make you feel awkward or uncertain and some of which will probably thrill you. But you'll also discover that you have lots in common with lots of people, even when you don't expect it. This deeper understanding will enable deeper empathy.

Look for the Positive

We tend to think of empathy as sharing the pain, heartache, disappointments, and negative emotions of others. That's one of the best things you can do for people you care about. But empathy is about positive feelings, too. We shouldn't just support our friends and family when they're down. It's just as important to support them when they're up.

Show your joy at the triumphs, achievements, and good fortune of others. Sometimes, if you're in the doldrums and they're high in the sky, this can be hard to do. But try to set aside your own feelings. And who knows, your generous gift of kindness may be just the thing to help *you* feel better.

Know When to Back Away

There's a fine line between experiencing another person's emotional distress and *taking on their troubles.* Many teenagers are deeply empathetic, and it's easy for their friends' crises to become their crises. Empathy should be a constructive force for both giver and receiver. If it isn't, you need to take steps to protect yourself from empathy overload. In order to care for yourself, you may need to back away for a while. Backing away doesn't mean you don't care. It just means you're not going to let yourself be swamped by suffering you can't do anything about.

Care for Yourself

To help others, you have to be in a good space. Teens with strong support systems, who can count on caregivers, and who are able to deal with uncomfortable emotions are more likely to show empathic concern and help people in distress. If you're going through hard times, if you're in the stress red zone, if your self-help resources are depleted, it's difficult to extend yourself and be there for someone else. So, take care of your own needs. Get enough sleep, eat well, and exercise. Get the support you need from friends and family, take care of your responsibilities, and stay focused on your own goals.

I know, easier said than done. But you can't be there for others if you're not there for yourself.

Dear Alex,

"I thought this was a book about phones. What's with all the empathy stuff?"

You're right. This *is* a book about phones and the digital world. It's about how screen time affects teens physically, emotionally, psychologically, cognitively, and socially. The reason I spent a lot of time on social warning signs—what they are and what you can do if you feel any apply to you—is because friends, family, and social relationships are so central to the lives of teens. Good social skills (including empathy) are essential for feeling confident, understanding people, building great relationships, and being able to get what you want out of life.

But the more time teens spend online, the less practice they get relating to people offline. So this imbalance between online and offline socializing creates a negatively reinforcing loop: Offline social skills don't develop, which makes teens more uncomfortable in face-to-face settings, which makes them want to avoid or minimize those encounters, which leads to more online socializing, which leads to more offline social skills atrophying, and round and round.

Hey, that gives me an excuse for another visual:

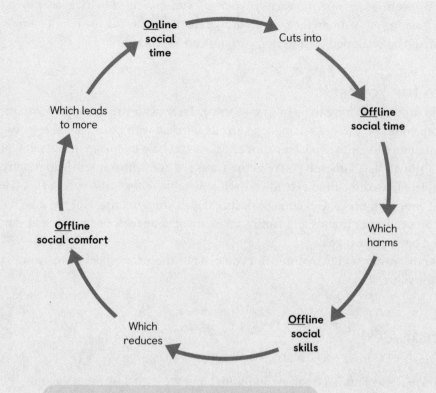

I think you're just going round in circles.

The drop in face-to-face interactions amongst teens (remember how texting is teens' preferred method of communicating?)—

You bet I do.

—and the associated drop in empathy levels are among the most distressing possible results of too much screen time.

I hear ya.

However uncomfortable you may feel with face-to-face encounters, they are still definitely the way to go if you wish to derive maximum pleasure and benefit from human interaction.

So true.

Since so many teens feel uncomfortable relating in person, that's why I included all the "empathy stuff." And the "listening stuff." And the "talking stuff." And, I bet, if teens feel more confident about their offline social skills, they'll do more offline socializing. Which brings us full circle back to phones and screen time.

Right-o.

Bottom line? Great social skills and confidence come down to just a few simple truths and behaviors: Honesty, kindness, empathy, asking questions, listening, and practicing.

I'm with ya.

What's with all the texts?

Just being an active reader!

7

PROTECT YOUR PRIVACY, SAFETY, AND REPUTATION

How Big Tech Steals Your Data and Puts You at Risk

Imagine if this were your life: Every time you leave your room, a squad of unidentified, masked agents sneaks in. They rummage through your desk and chest of drawers. Under your bed. Between the mattresses. Inside your closet. They pull out your clothes and turn your pockets inside out. They go through your backpack and put a bug in it to track you. They take thousands of photos. They play your music, examine your books, determine which you use the most. They look through all your school notebooks, your letters and journals, photos you keep in your wallet or purse, private papers, memorabilia you store in shoeboxes.

Another squad follows you whenever you leave home. They record where you go, what you do, who you see, what you eat, where you look, how much time you spend somewhere or doing something, how often you rest, what you say. When you're in school and they can't follow you through the halls, the bug they put in your backpack tells them everything they need to know.

When you get back to your room, the hidden cameras and microphones they planted monitor your movements, your posture, where you sit, where you lie, how long you spend in any position, what you do in bed, conversations you have. They make assumptions about your moods, friends, interests, ideas, politics, sexuality, academic performance, and relationships with siblings and adults. They make predictions about what you think, how you feel, how you behave, what will capture your time and attention, what makes you spend money. They compare you with millions of other teens you don't know and on whom they are also spying, and they use that information to make even more assumptions about you.

They compile a profile—tens of thousands of pages, pictures, receipts, recordings—documenting everything about you from the most inconsequential to the most private and personal. And then they offer it all to anyone willing to pay for it. You have no idea what's in your profile, what assumptions they've made, or who has bought and seen it. But as long as you want to continue to use your bedroom, you can't do anything about this secret surveillance stakeout.

> HOLY SH—

> Hey! This is a family book.

This isn't far-fetched. Or even near-fetched. It's exactly what apps and websites do to anyone who uses the internet. They spy on you. In exchange for spying on you, they give you free access to their app. (Which isn't to say that apps you pay for aren't *also* spying on you.) And what do they do with all the data they collect about you? They sell it. That's how they make money. See, you're not the customer. You're the *product.* The real customers—the people or entities truly valued by Big Tech—are the companies that buy access to the data collected about you and millions of others, so they can, in turn, use it to create and target ads and products based upon what they learn about you and people with similar online habits.

Your data has real, tangible value. Online companies, sites, and apps aren't charities. They spend billions of dollars providing their "free" services. And they make many more billions of dollars selling the fruits of their surveillance.

Why would information about what you do online be so valuable? Because it tells companies what you'll buy. When you're most likely to buy. How much you'll spend. It tells them what you like. Who you'll vote for when you're old enough. What grabs your attention. What to put in your feeds. How they can get you to spend more time on their site so they can sell more and more of your data.

You may be thinking . . .

So What?

> You read my mind. Do enlighten me.

The reason all this matters is that the more your behavior and emotions can be predicted, the easier it is for tech companies, advertisers, and special interests to manipulate and control you, get you to buy a particular product, vote for a particular candidate, or hold a certain belief. By allowing companies to know so much about us, we are giving them awesome power. We're allowing them to feed us ads and posts that shape, manipulate, and/or reinforce our beliefs, stoke our emotions, and change our attitudes and behaviors. And we're not even *really* allowing it, since these companies bury their surveillance and any possibility of opting out under layers and layers of clicks and legalese that can take hours to navigate. And who has time for that?

> Not me.

Never before have so few companies held so much power over us. As I sit at my desk writing this book, risking Tech Neck to bring you the latest info, Facebook has approximately 2.7 *billion* monthly users. There are 7.8 billion people on the whole planet. Subtract infants and young children and people who, for various reasons, have no ability or wish to access the internet, and Facebook reaches into the minds and lives of over half the global online population of approximately 4.6 billion people.

Don't use Facebook? How about Google, Amazon, Siri, or Windows? Approximately 90 percent of all searches go through Google. Amazon controls roughly 40 percent of the market of all products sold online. Siri gets 25 billion requests a month, and Apple was the first company ever valued at over a trillion dollars. A billion devices use Windows 10. The reach and power of these companies to penetrate and influence our lives is unprecedented. Without adequate safeguards (which do not currently exist), digital technology and social media can be used to poison discourse, eviscerate democracies, and destroy pillars of civilized society such as truth, respect, compassion, shared facts, trust in science, open-mindedness, and intelligent debate.

If the idea of being spied on for commercial purposes doesn't bother you or seems like a fair deal for all the "free" stuff you get, consider other ways your information can be used. What if that data is used by an authoritarian government to spread false propaganda, jail enemies, frame you for fake crimes, prevent certain people from voting, or imprison individuals based on what is learned online about their religion, ethnicity, sexuality, or beliefs? Internet surveillance is how dissidents get locked up in Russia, how Muslims get thrown into concentration camps in China, and how some countries, where homosexuality is punishable by death, entrap and arrest individuals who visit LGBTQ+ websites. If you look across the United States and the rest of the world, the loss in recent years of civil liberties and the growing abuses of power committed by governments have largely been made possible and spread more and more widely by social media and the internet.

If you think I'm making this up, it is all happening as I write this. Some of it may even be taking place in the country where you live.

> **This is getting kinda heavy.**

I know that this may seem over-the-top if you—like many teens—mainly use your devices to do homework and Snap and text and listen to music and watch videos and have a jolly old time. But it's all part of the same system. And I know that many of you *do* think and worry about "heavy" things like climate change, gun violence, racism, and political repression. Some of you are out there protesting, resisting, and making your voices heard.

But let's face it. Whether you genuinely care about big issues and making the world a better place doesn't matter much to Big Tech. To them, we're all just numbers now. Millions of data points. Ready to be manipulated. Way back in 1637, René Descartes, a French philosopher, famously wrote, "I think, therefore I am."

Today—if Big Tech has its way—that would be, "I click, therefore I am."

You are the sum total of your clicks, captures, links, likes, friends, favorites, followers, tweets, texts, tags, posts, pages, searches, and purchases. Oh, I know you're way more than that. But the companies don't care. To them, you are an algorithmic plaything they can measure, manipulate, and monetize.

This means that the trail you leave online will be used to define you. For better or worse. So you need to take steps to protect your privacy, safety, and reputation. You can resist Big Tech's snooping and minimize the chances that anything you do online will harm you now or in the future. And you'll discover how to do exactly that later in this chapter.

Signs that Big Tech Has Affected Your Privacy, Safety, or Reputation

Here are some warning signs that your privacy, safety, and reputation may be at risk.

 You Post Things You Later Regret.

You sometimes say things you wish you could take back. Angry or sarcastic comments. Jokes about drinking or illegal drugs. You say things meant to be funny, but which others take as mean, offensive, or bigoted. You post provocative or revealing photos, get into online fights, express controversial opinions just to get a reaction. You swear a lot, and you are sometimes embarrassed by spelling and grammar errors you didn't catch.

 You Don't Use Privacy Settings as Much as You Should.

You don't take the time to control what people can see and who can see it. It's too much of a pain. Every time you install a new app, you think you'll do it later, but "later" never comes. Besides, you figure, you're not doing anything you're ashamed of. Private. Public. It's all the same to you. Besides, nothing's really private anyway. So why bother?

 You Reveal Too Much Personal Information.

You give out your real name, phone number, birthday, age, address, or account numbers too freely. You share photos of yourself on public sites or with people you don't know that could identify where you live or go to school, where you are at that moment, where you're travelling. You give out personal information about friends and family members that they might want kept private. You've given a friend your password to certain accounts.

You Rarely Think About the Trail You Leave Online.
You know you should be careful, and nothing is really private, but life's too short to take time to stop and analyze every time you send a Snap, text a friend, or post a pic. You haven't really thought about your online trail or "brand," who might see it, or how it might be viewed by such people as family members, teachers, potential employers, school admissions officers, or even law enforcement agents.

 You Get Sucked into Negative Emotions.
You come across a lot of dark stuff on your feeds, on blogs, in chat groups. So much anger and hatred. So much unkindness. Conspiracy theories. Extremist groups. Lies and "fake news." It really bums you out—all this stuff that floods your mind and inflames your feelings. You try not to get caught up in it, but sometimes you do. You lash out. You say something and get trolled or cyberbullied for it, putting your well-being, online safety, and reputation at risk.

 You Respond to Emails or Messages from Strangers Without Exercising Caution.
You get curious and reply to people you don't know. You click on links in emails and texts without considering whether it's safe to do so. You reply to emails from companies that tell you your account has been frozen or will be canceled if you don't provide them with detailed information. You go by yourself in real life to meet people you "met" online.

I have a feeling that many of you will read those warning signs, sigh, roll your eyeballs, and wonder:

> **How dumb do you think I am? I would never do those things.**

Hey, I don't think *you* would do them! But somebody else might. Like your friends, siblings, or cyber-clueless great-grandmother who's never seen a link she won't click on. So it's important for *you* to know all of Big Tech's tricks so you can warn others about the potential pitfalls of life online.

The Devilish Ways Big Tech Grabs Your Attention and Your Data

So, let's look at how the internet and Big Tech operate, and the kind of threats they pose to your privacy, safety, and reputation.

Agree or Get Lost

Have you ever gone to a web page or installed new software or a new app, and found a screen that asks you to agree to the Terms of Service? Of course you have. And if you're like me, or I'm like you, we click "Accept." What other choice is there? If you don't "accept," you can't use that app or visit that site. Or, in some cases, if you "X" the pop-up or navigate the site, it means, by default, you accepted the terms of service. So it's not really a choice. They control the options.

Those terms of service enshrine your consent to being tracked and having your data collected and shared. They also explain the many privacy and legal rights you are giving up. So let's call those "Terms of Service" what they really are . . .

Terms of ownership.

. . . because, in reality, the app or site "owns" you. Well, they own your identity on that site, within that app, and, in many cases, after you leave that platform. They own what they learn about you. They track you, collect your data (or let their "partners" collect the data), and sell it. If you've ever searched for, say, a car or a city or a beauty product, and then been flooded for days, weeks, or months with ads for cars, travel, or beauty products, that's tracking and data selling in action.

Read the terms (ha, ha).

All these sites invite you to read their Terms of Service. But they know you won't. Why not? Because you don't have the time. You don't want to plow through pages of dreary legalese. Besides, why bother? You can't object to any of the terms. You can't say, "Excuse me, I will agree to Terms 1.A through 1.P, but not 1.Q, and 1.R is okay except for clause 3.6a." No, the only way you can object to any of the terms is by not using the site at all. But even that isn't a sure thing. Because even if you never use it again, the site most likely has already infected your device with a tracking gremlin or two (or twenty).

There's another reason you're unlikely to read the "Terms" and the "Privacy Policies." They take forever to read. Visual Capitalist, an online publisher that uses visuals to explore complex topics such as technology, energy, and financial markets, analyzed the word count and reading levels of Terms of Service contracts. Based on an average adult reading speed of 240 words per minute, they found that it would take 63.5 minutes to read Microsoft's terms of service! (Although Microsoft probably has a lot of products to talk about.) It would take a little over 31 minutes for TikTok, and almost 21 minutes for Snapchat (after which I bet the terms disappear). Twitter's terms of service contain 5,633 words. That's unfair. They should be limited to 280 characters.

Of course, while trying to peruse any of these you'd probably fall asleep after a few minutes of reading about "mutual arbitration clauses," "indemnity for non-personal use," and "analytics and research." I can think of a lot better things to do for 30 minutes than learning "some of the ways that our services, including our various websites, SMS, APIs, email notifications, applications, buttons, widgets, and ads, use these technologies." (That's Twitter speaking.)

Companies intentionally make their terms of service as incomprehensible and user-*unfriendly* as possible. They do this to discourage you from reading them. They don't want you to know that you may not be able to delete your account; that they own any creative work you post; that they keep your content even if you delete it; that you grant them access to your browser history; that they can change the terms whenever they feel like it. And if they do change the terms, they don't tell you what they changed—you'd have to reread the terms to see if you can find the new policies.

Not only does it take forever to review these terms, it takes advanced reading abilities. When Visual Capitalist assessed the readability scores of various terms of service, they found that such sites as YouTube, Spotify, TikTok, Twitter, Zoom, Apple Media, and even Pokémon Go were written at a college reading level. Many others (Facebook, Google, Instagram, Snapchat), required a tenth- to twelfth-grade reading level.

Well, hold onto your hashtag, because only 12 percent of Americans 16 years and older read at a ninth- or tenth-grade level or higher. So, by throwing a half-hour's worth of advanced-reading-level, legal mumbo-jumbo at busy site visitors, tech companies guarantee that few people will ever read the terms of service. Which I'm sure is the whole idea.

But what if you did read them? What would you find? You'd find a lot about "cookies."

Have a Cookie

You've probably heard about cookies. These are small files that websites place on your computer as you browse the internet. There are all sorts of cookies: session cookies, persistent cookies, third-party cookies (often known as tracking cookies), super cookies, zombie cookies,* oatmeal raisin cookies.

*Just in case you think I'm making them up, "zombie cookies" really exist. The term was coined by an attorney who filed a lawsuit against major tech companies that were secretly planting these cookies on users' computers or websites they visited. What makes these cookies so devious is that they "come back from the dead" (hence the name). You can "delete all cookies" from your computer or opt out of receiving cookies, but zombie cookies are stored in such a way that they breach your browser's security protections and defy deletion.

Some cookies are harmless; they are functionally necessary for you to navigate the site. They remember such things as your log-in information, what you have in your shopping cart, preferences you've set (such as language or privacy options). Other cookies are much snoopier. They track your browsing history: your searches, purchases, and locations; ads you've seen, links you've clicked on. They record information about your devices.

I could spend the next nine pages writing all about cookies. But I won't. That's because doing so would make me hungry. And because the technical aspects are not the point. The point is that many cookies are *not* harmless. They are the lifeblood, the cells, the active agents of tracking your online life, creating a data profile of you, and turning you into a product.

 **THINK ABOUT IT** Warm, fuzzy names and phrases have often been used to obscure the true motivation and purpose of a regulation, idea, policy, process, service, or piece of technology. For example:

Warm and Fuzzy Terms You'll Hear	Positive Associations Tech Companies Want You to Make	More Accurate Terms for What's Really Going On
Cookies	Cute, sweet, delightful, delicious, confectionary	Spybots, snoopers, snitches
Alternative facts	Creativity, thinking outside the box, individualism	Lies, falsehoods, propaganda
Privacy policy	Looking out for you, protecting your rights, being transparent	Cookies infestation plan, device invasion strategies, disingenuous data-mining deceptions
Social media	Friends, community, connection, information	Addiction generators, psyche invaders, emotion puppeteers
Search engines	Helpful, powerful, problem-solving, knowledge	Undercover spy agencies, stakeout operators, informers
Partners	Buddies, friends, helpers, allies, companions	Fellow data thieves, tracking accomplices
Advertisers	(Sorry, I keep getting this message: Error 404, positive associations not found)	Purloined data purchasers, manipulators
Improving your customer experience	Respectful, caring, giving, concerned about your needs	You're about to get fleeced, lose more privacy, or have more consumer rights taken away

Howdy, Pardner

It gets worse. It's bad enough that so many websites place cookies on your devices to track and collect data. (It's important to point out that not all websites do this. More on that later.) But another way sites make money is by letting "partners" or "third parties" load their own cookies. You'd read about this in the websites' privacy policies and terms of use—except, of course, who's reading? For example, one site says:

*"This website uses cookies and similar tracking technologies. By clicking "Accept Cookies" or **closing this banner**, you agree to the use of all such technologies, **including by select partners** for targeted ads, per our Cookie Policy."* (The emphasis is mine.)

See how, even if you don't click "Accept Cookies," you agree to be tracked simply by closing the banner? Here's an example from Snapchat:

"We use these cookies to deliver advertisements, to make them more relevant and meaningful to consumers, and to track the efficiency of our advertising campaigns, both on our services and on other sites or mobile apps. Our third-party advertising partners may use these cookies to build a profile of your interests and deliver relevant advertising **on other sites***."* (If I may be so **bold**.)

I got curious about these "partners," so I actually followed links to the terms of service, privacy policies, and partners of sites I use. What I discovered blew my socks off all the way to the other side of the room. Many of these sites had HUNDREDS of partners! On one I counted over 700. So you may go to a lovely little website, not concerned if they collect your data, without realizing that that website has a bazillion partners planting their own cookies and collecting their own data. While you won't have heard of 99 percent of these partners (I hadn't), you'll almost always find the big monster tech companies in the list. You can't escape them. Even if you've never used Facebook or Google or Amazon in your life, they'll find you through partnering with other websites and cookie up your devices.

Fortunately, on many websites you can choose which third-party cookies to accept. Oh, wait—I spoke too soon. The default is that you accepted them all. All 9,687,451,283 of them. You can't just click "none." So, if you don't want third party cookies, you have to *individually* toggle off every single one of the hundreds of companies whose cookies you don't want to accept. Oh, nope, hang on. That's just on the helpful sites. On others, the only way to block tracking by partner cookies is to *go to each individual partner website* and refuse to accept the cookies through *their* privacy options.

Think about it. Let's say there are 600 partners. That means you'd have to go to 600 websites to turn off their tracking. And each of those sites, the moment you visit, has *their* partners who start to track you. It's exponential. Never-ending. Who in their right mind, wrong mind, or any other kind of mind has the time or inclination to do that? Plus, you have to trust that the websites will actually follow your directives. (Which I, for one, do not.) So, you can see that cookies are like a plague you can't escape. Go to any website and your goose is cookied, er, cooked.

You Are Being Profiled

What do you click on?

Whom do you follow?

What do you "like"?

How much time do you spend on a site?

How did you get to that site?

What site did you go to next?

What do you buy?

What were you doing right before you bought something?

Who are your friends?

What videos do you watch?

Which do you watch all the way through, and which do you bail on?

How many do you watch in a row?

What time on what days do you do what?

What are your searches?

What do you ask Google or Siri or Alexa?

Where are you?

From all this covert tracking, a profile of you emerges. These companies know your gender, habits, and health concerns. They know how old you are, where you live, and how much money your family has. They "read" your texts and emails. They "listen" to your calls. They know where you are physically—within a few feet. They know whether you're happy, sad, scared, lonely, angry, worried, or depressed. They know whether you're gay, straight, both, none, in-between, or questioning. They know what time you go to bed and get up in the morning. They know every site you visit online, every click you click, every video you watch, every news story you read, how fast you read, where you linger, what you check daily or hourly or every three minutes. They know which teams you follow, which songs you like, which colors draw your attention. They know your political leanings, your circle of friends, your popularity, your fitness, your movements, your purchases, your emotions, your face.

They know you googled "suicide hotline." They don't know whether it was for you or a friend. They know you googled "sexual abuse." They don't know if it was for you or a friend or a paper for school. They know you googled "can you masturbate too much?" They don't know whether it was for you or—well, of course they know it was for you.

Some of the information about you may be misleading or wrong. For example, you may google something to help a friend; or search a travel destination for a social studies paper; or look up an illness because your brother has it. Profiling makes assumptions, and those assumptions can be wrong. Since the surveillance never stops, companies keep learning more about you, and that improves their ability to predict your moods, attitudes, preferences, and behavior.

But that's not the end of it. At the same time they're tracking you, they are tracking and profiling millions upon millions of other people. By knowing what millions of people *like you* also do, think, feel, buy, click, and avoid, companies can use that information to fill in the blanks, to make assumptions about you. So, your profile is created not just by knowing things about you, but by knowing things about millions of people with similar data profiles to yours. And that further determines what you're shown, how you're manipulated.

Loopy Feedback Loops

The more companies learn about you, the more that shapes what you are shown. Think of it as an endless feedback loop. They spy on you. They learn who you are and how you operate. That affects what you see; what "rewards" you're given; what products you're pitched; what prices you're offered; what news, videos, and posts you're shown; what's on your feeds, what emotions are triggered. Your reactions provide more data which is then used to refine further manipulations.

The result is a narrowing of experience, not a broadening. You're not exposed to ideas that might expand your knowledge or change your opinion. Nor are you exposed to ideas and information that people with different perspectives, values, and lives see. Everyone is placed in their own box, category, and column. This obstructs discourse, hinders intellectual growth, reinforces biases, and thwarts empathy. People on one side of an issue—say, climate change, abortion, gun rights, mask-wearing during a pandemic—don't get any sense of what people with different viewpoints are seeing and experiencing.

If these companies know that you tend to be angry on Mondays, they will use that information to send you divisive posts on Mondays to get your attention. If they know you are getting your period and are more likely to buy music at that time, you can count on receiving ads and clickbait for music you like. If they know that you spend more time on social media when you're sad, algorithms will try to stimulate that sadness.

If this sounds creepy, callous, and materialistic, that's because IT IS. Why would companies engage in such invasive, chilling surveillance?

PROFITS and POWER

It's that simple. Much of human behavior can be, and always has been, explained by greed. Big Tech collects endless amounts of data on you. Companies, special interest groups, political parties, foreign intelligence agencies—in short, anyone with an agenda (hidden or obvious)—can purchase access to the data to push their products, fake news, or propaganda at the very audiences who will be most receptive or susceptible to them. On Facebook, for example, an advertiser could pay for access to college-educated fathers in the United States between the ages of 40 and 45 who own homes, work for the government, live with teenage children, have gym memberships, dine out, and donate to environmental causes—or any other combination of a mind-blowing number of demographics, behaviors, spending patterns, interests, and life situations.

This is the snoop-loop: you engage online; Big Tech watches you; they sell what they learn; the buyers target you with ads, posts, and provocations; your engagement generates more data—and round and round it goes. Your "file" gets bigger and more detailed, providing more points of contact for Big Tech to get its claws into you.

Blowing Negativity Bubbles

For most people, negative emotions—anger, resentment, jealousy, contempt, suspicion, hatred—are more accessible and easily triggered than positive emotions. Bad news is more attention grabbing than good news.

I mean, which headline are you more likely to click on:

BREAKING NEWS: 87,000 flights take off and land safely today.

BREAKING NEWS: Jumbo jet carrying 265 passengers crashes into Mount Rushmore.

Social media algorithms are designed to capitalize on conflict, conspiracy, negative feedback, and polarizing issues. News feeds know that the best way to get your attention is to get you angry, emotional, upset, agitated—to push the buttons that they know or believe (from everything they've learned about you) will raise your blood pressure. Their goal is your *engagement*—your "eyeballs"—because that's what advertisers are paying for. You're not going to buy their products or services unless you see their ads. So Big Tech feeds you content they know will keep you engaged. The longer you're engaged, the more ads you'll see. And more ads = more money.

Problem is, you don't know how that selection was made; how the content was altered; how it's different from what your friends are seeing; how, by whom, and for what purpose you are being manipulated. It was tailored to your data points. You're shown stuff you'll like—and stuff that'll rile you up, because it's your attention they're after, not your agreement. So, if you're an animal rights activist, you'll be shown content that supports and reinforces your values, activism, and interest. But you'll *also* be shown content depicting barbaric slaughterhouses, alligator boots, $100,000 sable fur coats, hormone-bloated chickens packed wing-to-wing, and rich trophy hunters bragging about rare animals they killed.

Big Tech wants you to experience the internet in a bubble—a bubble they and others can manipulate for their own purposes. You can see how this narrows experience, vision, understanding, empathy, compassion, and discussion. How it can reinforce racism, tribalism, and feelings of "us" versus "them." You begin to feel that "good" people think like you. If the algorithms present you with contrary opinions and world views, it's done to inflame you, not to educate you. In the bubble placed around you, you don't see other people's realities, and they don't see yours. You are invisible to each other, except as a mass of "others." At its extreme, this can lead to bigotry, discrimination, violence, and war. People characterized as "others" are no longer seen as fully human or as individuals with wants, needs, fears, and dreams. So it becomes easy to lock them up, shoot them, put them in cages, slaughter them. The greatest genocides and atrocities in history have always begun by defining "others" as subhuman.

It's not hard to imagine characteristics Big Tech can identify—race, gun ownership, magazine subscriptions, religion, education level, sexual orientation, age, charitable donations, geographic location, campaign contributions, fondness for kale—that would accurately predict people's social, sexual, religious, cultural, economic and/or political leanings. Whether they're pro-choice or anti-abortion. How they feel about immigration, marijuana laws, same-sex marriage. Once such things are known, Big Tech can target specific groups with hateful messages, rumors, lies, "fake news," "fake videos," and conspiracy theories to shape opinion, divide and inflame, and suppress (or increase) the turnout of certain voters. Governments, foreign countries, political candidates, social movements, fringe groups, white supremacists, and "bad actors" have done this and more. To make matters even worse, studies show that fake (false) news—because it is designed to incite an emotional response—spreads roughly six times faster on social media than does truthful, factually based news.

Facebook's algorithms for what gets amplified and shown to millions of people, regardless of its truth, have been rightly criticized and blamed for much of the increase in polarization, hatred, and misinformation online. This, of course, then bleeds into offline behaviors and politics.

YouTube is another major offender. Now, we all love our YouTube. It kind of feels like infinity—video-style. But YouTube is also where many people, especially young men, get radicalized. This is the result of recommendations that push users toward more extreme content and radical movements if they venture in certain directions. YouTube's algorithms and recommendations are responsible for over 70 percent of the time users spend on the platform. Combine that with the fact that 94 percent of all Americans ages 18 to 24 use YouTube, and, well, you get the picture.

So, let's say after living for 15 years on a desert island with no WiFi you move to a city and connect to the internet for the first time in your life. Big Tech knows nothing about you or your brand-new laptop. You're writing a paper on Black Lives Matter, so you go to YouTube and run a search. (You're a very quick study with the internet.) Some of the top results are pro-BLM and others are anti-BLM. You see a video called "Peaceful BLM Protesters Get Creative," and another called "Study Shows BLM Movement Is Linked to 91% of Riots." Hmmm. "Peaceful" versus "riots." "Riots" sounds more exciting, so you click on that video, not knowing that it was put there by a mysterious, far-right, conspiracy-theory-spreading, discredited propaganda machine. Nevertheless, the fact that you clicked on that video tells YouTube to suggest others like it.

Continuing to click on those types of videos tells YouTube to keep suggesting *anti*-BLM videos and more extreme recommendations that, in turn, could lead to white supremacist videos. And if somebody were susceptible to radicalization—if they had prejudices waiting to be reinforced or biases they hadn't acknowledged; if they believed they had been rejected, sidelined, or victimized; if they were looking for belonging and purpose—they might be attracted to a movement or set of beliefs they didn't consciously set out to join or adopt.

Remember how I said earlier that Big Tech knows not only what *you* do online, but what people *like* you do?

> **Of course! You've got my eyeballs.**

Well, that means that if YouTube's algorithms know that people who are anti-BLM also tend to believe other false conspiracy theories such as climate change is a hoax, election fraud is rampant, immigrants spread disease, or Elvis is alive and living on Pluto, then those algorithms will push videos with related extremist views once you've clicked on one of them.

So you can see how the malignant use of surveillance and data collection has a dark side that goes way beyond trying to get you to buy an album or a pair of sneakers you might like. It can be (and has been) used to deny reality, destroy truth, shatter trust, identify and kill protesters, sway elections, weaken democracies, and strengthen corrupt leaders.

"Reading" the Internet

I'm sure you've heard the term *media literacy*. You may have had a unit on it in school. It's a valuable skill for sifting through the fakery and falsehoods you'll find online. How do you know what's honest, fact-based, and legitimate, and what's dishonest, untrue, and unreliable? Well, you could ask me, but I'm not always around. So here are some things to keep in mind so you won't be bamboozled by biased brain barrages.

Be a skeptical consumer of information.

Anything online was put there by somebody for some reason. The reason could be to sell a product, promote someone or something, perform a public service, provide information, or influence public opinion or behavior. The reason could be altruistic or self-serving, inspirational or malignant, pro-social or criminal—or just because someone felt like sharing, creating, entertaining, educating, or letting off steam.

With some content, like a video of a parakeet-python jazz band, it's pretty clear what it is. There's probably no hidden agenda; they're just trying to sell albums. Other content, like that on blogs, feeds, Facebook, Twitter, or supposed "news" sites, is at higher risk of truth and accuracy tampering.

For anything you see online, always ask:

- Who posted, shared, or published this?

- Who is behind this?

- Who paid for this?

- Who benefits from this?

- Who is hurt by this?

- What is the purpose of the material?

- What are they trying to get me to do? (Buy something? Sign a petition? Provide contact information? Join a cause? Vote for a particular candidate?)

- How are they trying to influence me?

- What techniques are they using?

- What emotions are they trying to incite? (Fear? Anger? Envy? Compassion? Jealousy? Sadness?)

- How old is the information?

- Is the material's type or category (advertisement, editorial, opinion piece, blog, news story, press release) clearly identified and/or represented?

As you answer these questions, you should be able to say what your evidence is. How do you know the answer to any one of the questions? If you don't have evidence beyond "because the site said so"—if you don't know who wrote it, who's behind it, who benefits from it—those are red flags. They suggest there may be a hidden purpose behind the information.

To get to the truth, you need to be an investigative reporter—a detective—and learn to scrutinize content you find online for bias, deception, falsehoods, and hidden motivations. This is especially important if you're using that content for assignments or making critical decisions. But don't worry. This doesn't mean you have to spend hours investigating every site you visit. Over time you'll get to know, from your own browsing and recommendations from people you trust, which sites can be believed.

Get your news and quotes directly from the original source whenever possible.

The people whose blogs and online feeds you follow decide what to show you. That means they also decide what *not* to show you. Don't let others decide for you. Read news directly from a trustworthy source to make sure you're getting the whole story.

Let's say you come across a review on a Hollywood blog that quotes a well-known film critic saying the latest superhero movie is "a masterpiece." That could make you want to see the movie. But would you change your mind if you saw the entire sentence?

"~~This terrible film could have been~~ **a masterpiece,** ~~if only it had a plot, a director who could direct, actors who could act, and a music score that didn't sound like 1,000 screaming baby hyenas.~~"

You can see how "quote mining"—taking words out of context and/or selectively deleting others—can completely change the meaning of somebody's words. Going to the source of a quote, article, or study will help you avoid being tricked by malicious misrepresentations and distortions of meaning.

Don't be deceived by "official"-sounding names.

Some of the biggest spreaders of lies, fake news, and conspiracy theories try to sound like reliable news sources. They'll use names like "Boston Tribune" or "Denver Guardian" to make you think they're legitimate newspapers. They'll mix real news stories with fake news so the lies get a bit of camouflage. They'll create URLs just slightly different from trustworthy sites—washingtonpost.com.co (fake) versus washingtonpost.com (real); breaking-CNN.com (fake) versus cnn.com (real)—to make you think you're reading news from the genuine paper or cable channel. But you're not. You're being deceived.

Distinguish between satire and false news.

Satire is a form of writing that uses humor, exaggeration, parody, or caricature to criticize or ridicule the behavior, stupidity, vices, hypocrisy, or ideas of people and institutions. Satire poking fun at political leaders and current events often takes the form of a news story with outrageous headlines. The *Onion* and the *Borowitz Report* are established satirical "news" sources. Some fake news websites that push conspiracy theories pretend, deceptively, that their content is satire, parody, fiction, opinion, and/or for "entertainment purposes." But this is just for greater legal protection against lawsuits, since, under the First Amendment of the US Constitution, these uses are held to a lower standard of truthfulness than "legitimate news." Most of the readers devouring posts on these sites take everything they're seeing there as the truth, the whole truth, and nothing but the truth. But truth it ain't.

Sometimes it can be difficult to tell fake news from satire. So you need to engage your full media literacy smarts. Keep in mind that the purpose of fake news is to deceive you. To make you believe things that are not true. The purpose of satire is to use humor and exaggeration to comment upon and ridicule cultural trends, current events, and public figures. Satire is not meant to be believed or taken literally; it assumes you are in on the joke. Sometimes, just doing a search on "satire" or "fake news" and the name of the website, article, or author you're viewing can quickly reveal whether the site is known for satirical humor or fake news and conspiracy theories.

Ask what you're *not* being shown.

Let's say there are protests in a city. Five thousand protesters are peaceful. But someone sets a car on fire. A few people loot a store. Conflict erupts with the police. Police and federal troops shoot tear gas into the crowd. Some officers shoot and beat some peaceful protesters.

Reporters descend upon the city. One cable news network focuses on the rare incidents of violence and damage to property. The network gets dramatic videos of tear gas being deployed, protesters running through the streets, and the burning car. The network describes the situation as a city out of control—violent mobs rampaging through the streets, destroying buildings, businesses, human life, and the rule of law. It doesn't show officers beating or teargassing peaceful protesters. They broadcast comments from residents who say they are fearful for their lives and their city.

Meanwhile, another cable news network focuses on the violence committed against protesters by police and federal forces. The reporter explains that the protests only occupy a couple blocks, and the rest of the city is calm, quiet, and safe. Their videos show thousands of peaceful protesters as well as views of city life going on as usual. The protesters they interview say that law enforcement is using excessively aggressive tactics.

By focusing on certain elements and ignoring others, by selecting certain comments and ignoring others, by using certain visuals and ignoring others, different media can create different stories leading viewers to wildly different conclusions as to what happened. As a media-literate person, your job is to find the truth. If you identify trustworthy news sources (which pretty much rules out social media), you don't have to investigate every single story you see. But if in doubt, the next tips will help you to verify accuracy.

Cross-check.

Is the information available on other sites? Is it quoted elsewhere? Can you find corroborating stories from reliable news sources? Take a few keywords from the post and run a search.

Fact-check.

A number of organizations (often nonprofit) are dedicated to checking the accuracy of news stories, conspiracy theories, trending tweets and posts, talk-radio rants, and media exposés. If you want to verify something you heard or read, go to factcheck .org; politifact.com; truthorfiction.com; or propublica.org. Another great source for the truth on urban legends, rumors, or scams making the rounds is snopes.com.

> **Why should I trust these sites? Maybe they're fake fact-check sites.**

> **I like the way you think!**

You *should* be skeptical until you can confirm their legitimacy. Run searches to find out: Have the sites won awards? Are they quoted and/or described as trustworthy by legitimate institutions and news sources? Do they fact-check issues, public figures, claims, and theories across all political and ideological spectrums? "Yes" answers to these questions will bolster the trustworthiness of any fact-checking site.

For the above sites you'll find that some have won Pulitzer Prizes and other awards, and they're all recommended by respected institutions and news sources for their accuracy and lack of bias. Plus, you know they can be trusted because I recommended them to you.

> **Now I'm definitely skeptical.**

Check before you post.

I can't tell you how many times I've gotten messages from friends that strike me as bizarre or too good to be true (the messages, not my friends). I think: Did the president *really* say that? Is Bill Gates *really* giving away $5,000 to everyone who clicks on this link? So I always run a search of key words relating to the message, along with "fact check," to see if it's true. And, as often as not, it turns out to be some viral scam or fake news story making the rounds. So, before you like, retweet, repost, or forward, make sure it's true. You'll avoid getting suckered, snookered, and snickered at.

Your Refrigerator Is Listening

Your TV, car, washing machine, thermostat, alarm clock, lamp, garbage can, and home security system may be listening if you have smart versions in your home. (Which I, most certainly, do not. When A.I. takes over and the appliances revolt, I don't want to wake up to my vacuum cleaner sucking my nose off.) Oh, and don't forget Alexa. More and more companies are developing voice-activated control systems and products. To work, these systems are always "on." They may require a spoken phrase or spoken keyword to be activated (like "Yo, Alexa baby, the eagle has landed"), but that means they have to always be listening to hear the keyword. You have to trust that the device isn't recording your conversations. The companies pinkie-swear that they aren't eavesdropping, though. So I guess you have no worries. Heh, heh.

Since these devices are connected to the internet, they can all be hacked. In fact, there are reports of baby monitors that were hacked, with threatening statements made through the device. Fortunately, the baby wasn't disturbed, but you can bet your sippy cup the parents were. While I don't have a baby to monitor, I can tell you that I would be mighty peeved if my icemaker started talking to me in the middle of the night. So, voice-controlled systems and products are another technology that can invade your privacy.

Now, I grant you that some of these devices offer incredible convenience. For people who have disabilities that limit mobility or communication, they can be indispensable and life-changing. But for other people, wouldn't you like, just once, to hear Alexa respond to a request to turn up the thermostat by saying, "Get off your butt and do it yourself!"

Whether you use these devices is largely up to you (or your parents). But be mindful, if they're listening *for* you, they could be listening *to* you. In fact, scientists conducted a study to determine if smart speakers are listening to you. They broadcast 268 hours of Netflix to their sample of smart speakers (I know, you gotta love researchers). While they found no evidence to suggest the devices were recording, they did discover that speakers such as Amazon Echo, Apple HomePod, and Google Home got falsely "woken up" as many as 19 times a day by dialogue on the Netflix shows. This happened when the voice assistant misinterpreted something it heard for the "wake word." So, Siri sprang to attention upon hearing "seriously" and "I'm sorry"; Alexa fell for "exclamation"; Cortana was tricked by "Colorado."

Amazon, Apple, and Google all use human reviewers to listen to random samples of voice recordings. They say this is to improve the device's operation, the voice assistant's understanding of human speech, and/or to see if the outcome matches the initial request. Such monitoring, the companies attest, adheres to strict technical and operational safeguards, does not reveal your identity (although each Amazon recording was associated with that device's serial number, a first name, and an account number) . . . is treated with high confidentiality . . . yadda, yadda . . . restricted access . . . multi-factor authentication . . . user privacy respected . . . encryption . . . blah, blah, blah, blah, blah. Big Tech's promises always sound reassuring until you learn about the big loophole, the security breach, or the violations of their own policies that seem to inevitably come to light.

For example, an Oregon couple's conversation was unknowingly recorded and sent to one of their contacts due to Alexa sequentially misconstruing background conversation as an activation command, a "send message" request, a contact, and a confirmation. Another man had a conversation sent to his insurance agent without his knowledge. And then there was the six-year-old girl who managed to get Alexa to order a $170 dollhouse simply by saying she wanted one.

You or your family may decide the convenience of these devices is worth any risk of privacy loss. But there are steps you can take to protect yourself.

- Switch off the smart speaker if you're having a super-private conversation.
- Access the device settings and disable the collection or recording of data and conversations.
- Set the device to respond to only one voice.
- Listen to recordings to see if you find instances of conversations being captured.
- Delete all recordings in the account.

TV or not TV: That is the question.

Your TV is watching you. If your family has a newer "smart TV" connected to the internet, it tracks everything that crosses its screen: cable TV shows, streaming apps, games, even DVDs you play. Most American televisions are set to do this by default. It's a good bet that whoever set up the TV didn't knowingly agree to having their pixels pilfered. Instead, each set-up screen asked you to click "accept" or "OK," and somewhere in the process you bypassed "Terms and Conditions" and gave the television manufacturer, cable company, streaming apps, and/or satellite service provider permission to invade your viewing habits.

If you have one of these smart TVs, your TV viewing history is harvested as often as once per second, and then transmitted to data firms that can link it to what you do on your phone, tablet, or laptop. They then resell the data to marketers and advertisers. Since a TV may be watched by many people in the same household, you might think it doesn't reveal much about any single viewer since all devices used in that home share the same IP address. But data tracking can be so sophisticated that it figures out which occupants are watching which shows or using which apps by combining viewing data with "real world" tracking. For example, if they know *your* IP address regularly changes to your school's during weekdays, it's a safe assumption that it's not you watching a soap opera at one in the afternoon.

Snooping TVs are just one more way Big Tech invades your privacy. Ultimately, marketers will learn enough about a family's household viewing patterns to target ads and product placements to those specific viewers. One household may get commercials for infant diapers. Another may get commercials for adult diapers. Let's say a film has a scene in a restaurant. Evolving digital technology will allow advertisers to pay to place cans of beer on the table for one household, while another sees cans of soda. A car manufacturer could have its newest SUV parked in the background for some viewers, while other viewers see a compact electric vehicle.

This is "show and tell" for the digital age. You watch a show. And *they* tell.

Who's Watching Whom?

Let's Face It

You've probably heard all about facial recognition. Until recently, it meant that if, say, a security camera picked up your image, that image could be compared with other photos on existing databases such as driver's licenses, passports, visas, or arrest records. The largest of these databases, compiled from many smaller ones, was the FBI's, which contained 641 million people.

Recently, though, a facial recognition company called Clearview AI announced that it had scraped photos off of public websites, especially social media sites like Facebook and Twitter. It created a database of 3 billion people. Clearview AI sells access to its software and face-base to other companies, law enforcement agencies, and governments.

What that means is that, if you have photos of yourself online, it's almost certain that your picture and identity is now, without your permission, in a database. Let's say you march in a protest, or go to a concert, or walk into a store. If a photo of you is taken there, anyone who buys the Clearview AI software can seek to identify you by comparing that image with the database. Someone could even use "augmented reality" eyeglasses in conjunction with the software to determine, real-time, the identity of anyone they see.

Yes, it's possible that a wanted serial killer might be identified and captured by this technology. Or that a kidnapped child might be located. But it's far more likely that millions and millions of people will have their privacy invaded by individuals, corporations, and government agencies that may or may not have their best interests in mind. You've seen videos of police or federal troops bashing or tear-gassing protesters exercising their right to protest. How would you feel if the government filmed and photographed all the protesters, identified them, and then put their names and photos in a giant database of people who hold certain opinions?

Corrupt, fascist, and/or dictatorial leaders and governments around the world are already using this technology to identify dissenters, protesters, and members of opposition organizations. People disappear off the streets. They get imprisoned and executed. The potential for abusing facial recognition software is real and frightening.

It's easy to think that such abuse could never happen where you live. But facial recognition technology is used by hundreds of police departments and law enforcement agencies in many nations. In the US, it's used by agencies including ICE (Immigration and Customs Enforcement), US Customs and Border Protection, and DHS (Department of Homeland Security). Schools use it. Businesses use it. Your online privacy is already virtually non-existent. (Hmmm, "virtually." Is that a pun?) Facial recognition technology, combined with cell phone location tracking, means your "in real life" privacy might also become non-existent.

What's more, facial recognition technology makes lots of mistakes. According to one study, Black and Asian people were 100 times more likely than White men to be misidentified. Native Americans were even more frequently misidentified. Given the injustices already committed against people of color by law enforcement, you can imagine how many accusations, assaults, arrests, and/or jailings of innocent people might occur due to erroneous identifications.

After the announcement of this huge new database, there was a backlash. The computer giant IBM said it would no longer develop or sell facial recognition technology due to the potential for abuse. Other huge tech companies such as Amazon and Microsoft announced that they would stop selling their facial recognition technology to local and state law enforcement departments "pending federal regulation" (which is a loophole big enough to drive a SWAT vehicle through).

It's possible that, by the time you're reading this, laws and regulations will have been enacted to limit the use of facial recognition technology and protect your rights. But it's also possible that the outrage will have died down, and that Big Tech will continue to be making Big Money selling companies and governments the tools to identify you wherever you go, whatever you do. So, even if there isn't a pandemic, you might want to keep wearing a face mask!

> You're sounding a bit paranoid.

> As the saying goes, "Just because you're paranoid doesn't mean they're not after you."

If you really want to thwart facial recognition technology, though, even a mask might not be enough. Instead, you need to mess with the face patterns their algorithms are designed to look for. They're scanning the spatial relationships between features such as your eyes and nose. Here are some tricks you could try if you're committed to tripping up facial recognition software.

Make your face asymmetrical. The algorithms are looking for symmetry. So use an eye patch, strands of hair, clusters of piercings, feathers, streamers—whatever—to make one side of your face look different from the other.

Cover the bridge of your nose. Algorithms scan the space between your eyes and the bridge of your nose as markers for detection. Use jewelry, glitter, face paint, and hair stylings to obscure that area. If you wear glasses, you can attach little sculptures or colorful cardboard cutouts to the bridge.

Use contrasting hair and makeup colors. Facial recognition algorithms make assumptions about human skin tones and textures. Mess with that and you mess with the technology. Use colors on your face that *contrast* with your skin tone. That means dark colors if your skin tone is light, and light colors if your skin tone is dark. Apply makeup and face paint in wild patterns and tones that are not found on faces.

I know. It all sounds kind of out there. And you can be sure the facial recognition masterminds are working night and day to try to outwit the outwitters. But until then, at the very least you can make a grand fashion statement. And if a teacher asks, "What have you done to your face?" you can reply, "I am using tonal inverse strategies, asymmetrical algorithmic avoidance adumbration, and nose bridge camouflage to foil facial recognition." How cool would that be?

Now that we've gotten totally covered in the mud and the muck of Big Brother Tech and CCTV—closed-circuit television, or the surveillance cameras you see everywhere on buildings, at airports, in banks and stores, and more—let's turn to steps you can take to protect your person, privacy, and online "brand."

How to Protect Your Privacy

There are three main ways to address the privacy and security of your devices:

1. Adjust settings on your hardware—your computer, tablet, and/or phone

2. Adjust settings on your internet browser

3. Select your desired privacy settings on the individual apps you use and websites you visit

You can achieve maximum privacy by setting preferences in all three of these areas. I'd love to tell you precisely how to do this. But that would require—wait a sec, I'm doing a quick calculation in my head—an infinity-squared number of instructions, given that you, my dear readers, represent multiple devices, models, operating systems, and browsers, and access hundreds of thousands of different apps and websites, all with different site mappings, layers, and privacy policies.

So I'm afraid you're on your own. Think of it as a treasure hunt for greater privacy. You'll need to find the menus on hardware, browsers, apps, and websites where you can select your privacy options for data collection and sharing, information stored, and who can see what. Clues that might lead you to the treasure are terms such as "preferences," "settings," "privacy," "your account," "profile," "cookies," and similar. If you get stuck, ask a tech-savvy friend. Almost everyone has one. Or ask a parent (although they probably come to *you* for tech advice). Or do a search on the specific question you have.

Always Use Protection

Here are some things you can do to keep the privacy vultures from ravaging your devices.

Don't feed the cookie monster.

Many websites greet you with a screen informing you that they use cookies. You'll be asked to "accept." There should be other options such as "manage cookies" or "privacy settings." Click on that. It's a bit like following a trail of (cookie) crumbs. Keep clicking on what seems likely to bring you to privacy or cookie options. You should eventually see a description of the types of cookies the site uses. Some are required. You can't disallow them. But others are optional. Turn off all the cookies you can.

Throw out stale cookies.

Even if you block cookies, new ones will appear from sites you visit for the first time. So, every day, use your browser settings to get rid of cookies. This will help prevent the Cookie Monster from devouring your privacy. You can delete them individually, but that's not practical if you have thousands of cookies. Keep in mind that when you clear all cookies, some of the "functional" ones that perform useful tasks, like remembering you for log-ins, will also be deleted. Your browser doesn't distinguish between helpful cookies and narc-y cookies. So you may need to re-enter your log-in information when you next visit those sites.

You'll learn over time which cookies you want to allow and keep. You can eliminate all the others, using broad brushstrokes of "select" and "delete." You can also configure your browser to automatically delete cookies every time you close it. But remember, when you return to the sites whose cookies you deleted (or new sites), you'll get re-cookied. Sorry, but that's the way the cookie crumbles.

Adjust your device settings.

Go to "preferences" or "settings" on your phone, computer, and other devices. You'll find privacy and security choices for your hardware. These will include options for such things as screen locks, disk access, data encryption, back-ups, camera and microphone status, location detection, and more. Select the settings that give you the desired level of privacy. Maximizing the privacy of your device will help minimize tracking and data collection.

Enable "do not track."

Your browser should have a toggle to turn this feature on. This tells websites you visit not to track you. Some sites will honor your requests. Others will ignore them. (And tell you they're doing so in their privacy policies. How obnoxious is *that*?!?) They can do that since nobody enforces compliance or holds companies accountable for ignoring you. But disabling tracking for as many sites as you can will still provide you with *some* protection. Remember, though, that even if individual sites and their partners are not tracking you, your phone carrier (such as Verizon, AT&T, or T-Mobile), your ISP (internet service provider), and the companies that provide WiFi where you live, work, shop, or attend school, are.

Install an anti-tracking browser extension.

Your device browser may offer a "private browsing" option. It's fine to use, but this only deletes your data locally, that is, so your trail can't be seen *on the device*. It doesn't block tracking from the internet. To do that, there are lots of options, many of them free, for blocking ads and tracking cookies. Some of the best known are Privacy Badger, Disconnect, Ghostery, and Adblock Plus. Run some searches, look at their features, see which are most highly rated, and then choose the best fit for your device, browser, and needs. A bonus will be that your devices should run faster if they're not bogged down by thousands of third-party cookies.

Personalize privacy settings on websites.

It's a pain, but it's worth the effort to go into the privacy settings for any app or website you use frequently—especially social media sites. You'll see various options for data collection, sharing, third parties, marketing, and more. Keep in mind that the site is determining the choices you can make. They'll only let you opt out of what they're willing to let you opt out of. Based on your needs and comfort level, opt out of as much as you can.

Go Undercover

Here's a set of strategies for hiding your identity and side-stepping surveillance online.

Use a VPN.

VPN stands for virtual private network. A VPN hides your IP address. This is the unique "address" the internet assigns to your device to allow it to communicate with other devices. The address is based on your location. So, if you're accessing the web from your home, your IP address is different than if you're browsing via your school's WiFi, even if you do both on the same device. Your browsing history, therefore, may be associated with different IP addresses. But, believe me, tracking algorithms are so sophisticated that they can often identify you as the same person.

A VPN encrypts your internet traffic and routes it through other servers in the VPN's network. This means that your data trail is hidden, and "your" IP address is that of the VPN's server, which is also being used by dozens, hundreds, or thousands of other users.

Some VPNs are free for a basic level of protection. You can get greater protection by purchasing an annual subscription. Given that most subscriptions allow installation across multiple devices, the prices are modest on a per-device basis. For some reason, I'm hearing in my head, *"Dad, I really think our family would benefit from a virtual private network to protect everyone's data, privacy, and security."*

VPNs are cool because you can select the server location you'd like to use. I have a VPN, and I enjoy deciding whether I'm in the mood for routing my browsing through Bangkok, San Francisco, Berlin, Peoria, or a hundred other places. Of course, be prepared to get weather updates for Thailand and to learn that your "local" Walmart is in Peoria.

Use encryption.

Encryption is like using a secret code. It turns your data into gobbledygook that nobody else can understand. For example, many messaging apps encrypt the DMs you send. Shopping websites encrypt credit card information buyers provide. While Big Tech may not be trying to sneak a peek at your hard drive, these and other companies can be hacked. Major data breaches have occurred at hundreds of corporations including eBay, Yahoo, Fortnite, WhatsApp, Zynga, Adobe, Facebook, Instagram, TikTok, Uber, Verizon, YouTube, Ancestry.com, CVS, Dropbox, and dozens of hotel chains, banks, credit agencies, hospitals, universities, and dating and hook-up apps. Oh, and let's not forget the Bulgarian Revenue Agency. These hacks resulted in billions of records and accounts being breached, revealing personal information such as phone, credit card, and social security numbers, as well as home and email addresses and passwords. With this information, hackers may be able to get to your accounts and hard drive. Unless you're an undercover spy, you may not feel a need at this time to go this far in protecting your data and hard drive. But should you ever wish to, you can encrypt your hard drive with BitLocker (Microsoft) or FileVault (Apple). There are also encryption programs for chatting, cloud storage, email, web browsing, and VoIP (internet voice calling). But keep in mind that encryption only goes so far. It can prevent "outsiders" from seeing the contents of emails you send, but the "to" and "from" addresses must be visible for email to be sent. Similarly, you can encrypt messages and voice calls, but the phone numbers have to remain unencrypted. Plus, the platform doing the encryption, whether it's Gmail or a social media site, would have the "keys" to the encryption, so they could unlock the data.

Use Tor.

Tor is free, open-source software that increases your ability to conceal your location and online usage from surveillance or analysis. It makes it much harder to track your online posts, browsing, and communication. Tor's purpose is to protect your privacy. And you *should* be able to have confidential communications and use the internet without being monitored. But, as with so much technology, Tor can be used for good or bad purposes. There's a "dark web" aspect of Tor, with people using it for scams, financial fraud, hoaxes, hacking, and all sorts of crimes and conspiracies. Of course, you won't use it for anything like that, and you aren't likely to see any of that. Tor is just a tool, like an automobile. Just because people have used cars to rob banks, commit murders, and have demolition derbies doesn't mean you're never going to drive.

Tor is available for Windows, macOS, and Linux computers. You can download it from torproject.org. For Chrome OS computers, you'd have to use the Tor browser for Android, which Tor says has limitations and is not yet fully audited for that application. For phones, you can find Tor Browser for Android on Google Play store. Keep in mind that, no matter what device you're using, Tor only protects you when you're accessing the internet *through* the Tor browser. For additional protection on your phone when using the internet outside the Tor browser, they have a free proxy called Orbot that allows you to send data from other apps (email, instant messaging, etc.) through the Tor network. While Tor isn't available at this time for iOS phones, they recommend an open-source app called Onion Browser that uses Tor for routing your internet traffic.

Be forewarned: Ensuring you are getting maximum protection through Tor can get kind of complicated. If you install Tor, you're going to feel like a spy going through the set-up process. But if you're an investigative reporter working on an explosive story, an inventor on the cusp of a major discovery, a citizen of a country that censors internet traffic, or just somebody who doesn't want Big Tech following your every move, you might be glad you have it.

Use DuckDuckGo instead of Google.

This is a free search engine that protects your privacy. Their home page states: "We don't store your personal info. We don't follow you around with ads. We don't track you. Ever." That says it all.

> Why should I trust what they say? Aren't they just like the other companies?

Great question—again! Skepticism is essential to protecting your privacy. And to being an educated person with an enquiring mind. Here's why I think you can trust them. DuckDuckGo (DDG) has built its business around not logging users' IP address, not using cookies, not collecting any personal information, and not bombarding users with sponsored ads as search results. Their brand is privacy. If they were lying and got found out, they would be done for. Moved to trash. Kaput. Finito. It would be as if a vegetarian restaurant were discovered to be putting beef stock in its recipes. Bye-bye beetroot. Plus, many reputable websites that review tech companies and products give DuckDuckGo a thumbs up for being on the level.

That said, there's one important catch. DuckDuckGo may not be tracking you and storing personal information about your searches, but your device's "history" is. To test this, I just searched for "potato pancakes" on DuckDuckGo. (It was the first thing that popped into my mind.) And, sure enough, when I checked my "history," it said "potato pancakes at DuckDuckGo." So, anyone with *access* to your device can see your searches. And if it's there in your history, and it went through your browser, Google and other Big Tech cookie monsters can see it and track you anyway.

No single thing you do to protect your privacy will solve the whole problem. But *every* single thing you do will make a difference. Do enough "single things" and it'll make a big difference in keeping Big Tech guessing about who the real you is. (Another benefit of DDG is you can say, as if you are a tech insider, "I don't use Google. *Such* a silly name. I only use DuckDuckGo.")

Turn off location services.

Of course, if you're using your phone for directions, traffic alerts, or "best pizza near me," you'll need to enable location tracking. But if you're doing other things, turn it off. Here's how. (You may need to tweak these instructions depending on what model of phone you have.)

On iPhones, go to *Settings* ➔ *Privacy* ➔ *Location Services.* For each app you use, select whether to share location data. You can also disable your mobile ad ID. This number, created by your phone, is used by advertisers and app makers to merge what you do online with where you go in the physical world. To turn it off, go to *Settings* ➔ *Privacy* and look for *Advertising* or *Apple Advertising.*

For Android phones, go to *Settings* and look for *Security, Privacy, Location,* and *App-level Permissions* to disable location tracking for selected apps (the exact clicks may vary with your phone's model).

Be ready: If you toggle off location tracking, you'll probably get a message saying the sky will fall and your app may not work properly. Ignore it. Many apps work just fine with location tracking turned off. (And if not, you can always turn it back on.) A weather app doesn't need to know which park bench you're sitting on. It just needs to know your town or city or pasture.

To block your mobile ad ID on Android, go to *Settings* ➜ *Google* ➜ *Ads* and click on *Opt Out of Ads Personalization.*

Block your device cameras.

One school district near Philadelphia lent laptops to students. Spyware allowed the school to record students' online activities, communications, and behaviors. They were even able to take photos of students in their bedrooms through the laptop cameras! The surveillance was *supposed* to occur only in the event a computer was missing or stolen. But the rules were laxly followed, and the spying occurred in unjustifiable ways, with over 58,000 photos taken. How was this discovered? An assistant principal accused a student of using drugs, claiming he had photos of it. It turned out the popped pills were candy. But, you might be wondering, how on earth did the school get photos of this student at home? Exactly. And that led to a successful lawsuit by the student and his family.

Even if your school would never do something like this, hackers can gain access to your device cameras. They can disable the warning light that tells you the camera is activated so you won't even know it. But, more commonly, your greatest risk is the invasion of your privacy every time you give an app permission to access your camera. The app can:

- Take videos and pictures of you, and "by you" without your knowledge (think about that the next time you're using your phone on the toilet)
- Upload or livestream pics and videos to the internet without telling you
- Record you anytime you're using the app
- Use facial recognition software to identify you by making a match with your existing online photos

To protect yourself against the world knowing you have pink toilet paper with playful bunnies, take these precautions:

- Use your device settings to turn off your camera and microphone.
- Revoke camera access for all apps unless essential to their functioning.
- Use tape or a sticker/sticky note to block your webcam and/or front and back phone cameras.

- If you want to be really cool (as I do), you can buy (as I just did this very second) inexpensive "camera covers." These are thin, nifty, little self-sticking rectangles with a sliding cover. So you place it over your camera lens, and then, when you want to use the camera, you just slide the cover. Easy-peasy.

- When you're feeling paranoid about this, remember that Mark Zuckerberg, the head of Facebook; James Comey, the former FBI director; and tons of internet security experts all use camera covers.

Obfuscate.

Besides being a great word, *obfuscate* means to confuse, bewilder, or render unclear. Confound surveillance. Swap shopper loyalty cards with friends. Conduct random searches on things you have no use for or interest in. Use outlandish walks when you're out in public. This'll make it less likely you can be identified by "gait recognition" software. Paint your face to confound CCTV cameras. (See page 172 for more tips on avoiding facial recognition.)

Okay. I get it. Some of these are kind of extreme. But it's worth mentioning them to give you an idea of how far-reaching surveillance has become. And if you don't end up using any of these tips, they may at least give you some ideas for a great crime novel about getting away with the perfect murder.

Create a junk email address.

When setting this up, don't use your real name or anything traceable to you. Use this address for online purchases, websites that require an email address for activation or confirmation, and any other internet activity where you want to create a barrier between your public and private life.

Give false information on forms and templates.

Many websites require you to register to get beyond their welcome page. To confound trackers and protect yourself from identity theft, be a phony. Use your junk email address. Give a phony name. Give a phony telephone number. Give a phony birthday. Give a phony address, like 13 Yellow Brick Road, Emerald City, OZ. Of course, you do have to be careful with giving out phony information. In some instances, like voter registration, applying for a driver's license, or other official business, it would be a crime to give out false information. But in most cases, the entity asking for personal details has no right or need to know. And if it's helpful for you to be "in their system," all that matters is that you remember the info you gave them. So use a standard, easy-to-remember data set, or keep a list of who you are for various purposes.

Challenge requests for personal information.

If you're at a store and they ask for your birthday, zip code, address, or phone number, tell them, "I prefer not to disclose that." Often that's enough to put an end to the discussion. If they press, ask them why they are asking for the information. Always be polite. It's not the cashier's fault that the store has nosy policies. You can also ask to speak to a manager. The store is probably just trying to get identifying info on you to assist with their tracking, data collection, marketing, and data selling. As you might guess, I always refuse (politely) to provide this sort of information. And it's never been a problem.

Don't share.

From birth we're taught that it's nice to share. But sometimes it's not a good idea. Like when nosy apps want you to give them access to every nook and cranny on your phone. In some cases, this is necessary for the app to function. For example, a GPS app needs to know your location to give you directions. A photo app needs access to your camera. But often, apps are simply greedy; they're trying to get their hands on unrelated data and functions. Be careful what permissions you give. Sharing your contact list may be helpful for messaging apps, but you're also giving that app access to names, phone numbers, email and physical addresses, and other personal information for every one of your contacts. A good guideline for knowing what permissions to grant is to ask yourself why the app needs that information. If you can't figure it out, don't share. If that prevents the app from working, it will prompt you and you can then choose to allow that access—or to delete the app.

Don't use social media.

Shocking? Unthinkable? Maybe. But it doesn't mean you have to give up communicating with your friends. Call them. Use encrypted chat and messaging apps. Email them—but use an email provider that doesn't scan your email. (Bye-bye, Gmail.) Here's the best idea of them all: see your friends in person.

Don't sign in through Facebook or Google.

Instead, cut them out of the loop. Sign in to sites directly, and you may cut down on snooping. Of course, it's possible (likely?) that Facebook or Google will cookie you up anyway once you're on the site, but why make it easy for them?

Pick Your Privacy Protection

As you think about which strategies you might use to protect your privacy, keep in mind that technology is always changing. Companies come and go. Products appear and disappear. Privacy policies improve and weaken. Big Tech seems to be feeling increasing heat as:

- Huge databases get hacked
- Social media is increasingly tied to election interference, societal polarization, and ruptures in truth, decency, and democracy
- Consumers are becoming more aware of the breadth and depth of surveillance
- Investigative reporters and congressional committees drill down on the role and responsibility of social media in today's world
- So much power is vested in so few companies
- People make a whole lot of jokes about Mark Zuckerberg's haircut

Check out the digital landscape and decide what protection you want to use. No protection is 100 percent effective. But every little bit helps. Each strategy will have a positive impact on hiding your data and keeping it private. The more strategies you use, the better. But you are still going to be watched and followed. We live in a surveillance society—bus passes, electronic toll systems, drones, photographing of mail, CCTV cameras, facial recognition, tracking cookies, online and offline monitoring of citizens by companies and governments. It's not going away.

How to Protect Your Reputation

You *will* be "out there." Unless you're a CIA super-spy, greatest-internet-security-expert-in-the-world sort of person, you can't totally eliminate tracking and hide your identity. What you can do is ensure that the online trail you leave is one of flowers, not turds.

Yup. Flowers.

Friendship

Love

Originality

Warmth

Empathy

Respect

Support

Not turds.

Trolling

Unkindness

Rage

Discrimination

Swearing

Corny.

I know. But it was fun to come up with.

What's with no swearing?

It leaves a bad taste in my mouth. But I'll allow it for genuine creative or artistic expression.

For people who know you, your reputation is a reflection of who you are in real life and who you are online. For people who don't know you, your reputation is largely shaped by your internet trail. What you post and put out there. What anyone—friends, relatives, employers, teachers, admissions officers, strangers—would see if they googled you or looked for you on social media. Your trail could be anything: photos, awards, blog posts, kind comments, school paper articles, videos, playlists, arrest records, vulgar tweets, art, writing—you name it. Plus, it's not just what *you* post. It's also what your friends post that identifies you. What you're tagged in. What's posted in groups or chats you're part of.

In essence, your online reputation is your brand. (See page 214 for more on this idea.) Think of any company. You probably have a gut reaction based on personal experience with their products, things you've read or seen, what people say about them. Their brand may be one of innovation, elegance, quality design, and good customer relations or one of poor service, cheap products, and terrible reliability. Or take a country. Its "brand" may be gorgeous beaches, great food, beautiful scenery, and friendly people. Or civil unrest, dictatorship, racism, crimes against humanity, and crumbling society. Virtually anything that intersects with the public has a brand. Celebrities. Cable news networks. Cars. Hotel chains. Department stores. I could go on and on, but for your sake I won't.

> **Good. I only have time for the bare minimum of examples today.**

The point is to think of your internet presence as *your* brand. Or if that seems too "commercial," think of it as a museum exhibit you are curating: "Me, Myself, and I—and My World." What would you want in the exhibit? What would you *not* want in it?

Here are some things you can do to create and define your online presence and reputation—in a way that you control.

Don't Think of Grandma, Think of Your Values

I bet you've heard that you should never post anything that you wouldn't want your grandmother to see. Well, my grandmother's dead. Does that get me off the hook? Can I post anything I want? Of course not. Some people would then say, "Don't post anything you wouldn't want your mother, sister, dad, coach, teacher, priest, scout leader, astrologer, trainer, yoga teacher, future employer, or plumber to see."

Well, I'm sorry. That seems too simplistic. Teens live in many different worlds—both online and off. It's perfectly reasonable to behave one way in one world (like with your friends) and another way in another world (like at my grandmother's funeral). You should be able to text a friend with sentiments and language that you might not use in an email to your school principal.

The problem is, you can't guarantee that things you post in one world will not find their way into other worlds. Even if you are using private messaging and private accounts, or messages that "disappear," people can take screenshots or forward communications to others. That's why you'll keep hearing that *nothing online is truly private*. And it's true.

So the challenge is to find a way to be "real," to have fun, to be silly, jokey, gossipy, unguarded, pensive, provocative, and honest, without the risk of laying turds that people will step on and think the less of you for.

The key to doing that is not to worry about your grandmother. No, the key is to know your values. Know the kind of person you want to be. Ask yourself:

- Is what I am about to post consistent with my values?

- Does it represent the person I want to be?

- Will it hurt, anger, or embarrass anyone?

- Am I intentionally trying to upset someone with this post?

- Could it hurt me if certain people see it?

- Does it reveal personal information (my own or somebody else's)?

- Does it enhance or harm my reputation and brand?

If you answer those questions, you'll always know whether a post is appropriate or not.

So, before you post something, run it through your values harmonization meter, confirm that it enhances your brand, and double check you're putting it out to the intended audience.

Prevent Ghost Posts

Ghost posts are *posts that come back to haunt you.* If you've never heard of them, it's because I just made up the definition. These are the posts people have in mind when they say "Watch-what-you-post-nothing's-private-everything-stays-online-forever." These are the posts you don't want future bosses, coaches, teachers, school admissions officers, landlords, lenders, girlfriends' parents, or boyfriends' grandparents to see.

You've probably heard tons of stories about celebrities, politicians, business leaders, private citizens, and people nominated for important positions who get into hot water when embarrassing, bigoted, or just plain stupid tweets, photos, videos, sexts, and comments are revealed. Some of these posts may be 20 or more years old. People end up humiliated, investigated, ridiculed, scorned, "canceled." Some lose their jobs or endorsement contracts. Some have personal relationships destroyed. Some have college acceptances rescinded. Depending on the nature of the post, we can debate whether it's fair that one thoughtless tweet can destroy your life.

Haunted by Ghost Posts

We can. But let's not.

Right. Let's not. The important thing is for *you* to avoid putting anything online that might harm your reputation—your brand—and come back to haunt you. What might those things be? It varies with the audience. But certainly cyberbullying, oversharing, embarrassing photos, hateful or vulgar language, emotional drama, revealing pics or videos, and anything featuring illegal drinking or drug-taking would qualify.

According to one survey, 93 percent of hiring managers check out the social media accounts of anyone applying for a job. The things that turn off a majority of recruiters are:

- Posts about guns
- Posts that are sexual in nature
- Swearing and foul language
- Joking or talking about illegal drugs
- Errors in spelling and grammar

Forty-four percent of the recruiters also turned thumbs down on posts involving alcohol. You can imagine other turn-offs such as cruelty, hatred, racial or ethnic slurs, other discriminatory language, or political rants.

Picture who else might be viewing your online trail. College admissions officers can have 100 qualified applicants for five slots. How do they choose from so many good candidates? For one thing, they check out social media. If they see a student whose comments are foul-mouthed, whose photos are alcohol-related, whose online portrait reflects bad judgment, well, that student is not going to be invited to join that university community.

Rejection letters from schools and employers aren't the only way ghost posts can boomerang and conk your aspirations on the head. What if you want to babysit? Be an intern? Volunteer to work with children? Take music lessons from a highly sought-after teacher? Date somebody's daughter? Rent an apartment? You can be sure parents, landlords, potential romantic partners—anyone deciding whether to get involved with you—is going to check you out before trusting you with important responsibilities, privileges, or *their* reputation.

So, be a GhostPostBuster. Make sure nothing you post will ever come back to haunt you.

Define Your Accounts

You may have many different social media accounts. Some may be public, private, identifiable, anonymous, searchable—or a combination of those variables. Public means anyone can see it. Private means it's restricted to only those people you allow to see it. Identifiable means it's clear that the account is yours. Anonymous means your identity is hidden. Some accounts will turn up in searches; others exist behind a search firewall. The variables that apply to your accounts will be a function of the platform's policies and choices you are allowed to make. Your account may have to be public, but you can have an anonymous handle or username. Some platforms require you to be known and visible; others permit users to be anonymous.

It's important to be aware of the privacy options that apply to your accounts. In general, the strictest levels of privacy and anonymity will protect you the best. But you may want people to be able to find you by searching. You may want a public account for your lawnmowing, dog-walking, t-shirt making, or babysitting business. You may want a newsy account for a broad circle of friends and relatives on a photo-sharing site, and a private account for closest friends.

Mix and match in a way that best suits your needs. But keep in mind that . . .
There is no such thing as 100 percent private or anonymous accounts.
Even "ephemeral" accounts such as Snapchat, where messages and stories "disappear," do not guarantee privacy. People can take screenshots. Apps have been developed to capture ephemeral posts. And law enforcement can breach privacy walls in response to circumstances such as threats of violence, criminal activity,

child pornography, videos of crimes taking place, or someone talking about planning a school shooting.

Some companies and social media platforms have resisted breaching the privacy of their users in response to legal demands. Depending on the nature of the post and the demand, we can debate whether companies should have to turn over data and/or reveal identities to courts, law enforcement, and/or the government.

> **We can. But let's not.**

> Got it.

On some sites, you can delete posts if you have second thoughts. But they, too, may have already been archived or passed along by viewers. So, it's much better to have "first" thoughts. Before you post anything:

- Think—before you click, tap, or send
- Sync—with your values
- Link—to the right account. How do you do that? First, consider the content of your post or message. Who's the recipient or audience? Is there anything personal being revealed? Do you want the post to be anonymous or identifiable as yours? Is it something you intend to be "permanent" or ephemeral? Answering such questions can point you toward the appropriate account.

Make a Pact with Friends

Your online trail isn't just a matter of what *you* put online. Your friends have photos and videos of you. They have a trove of messages from you. They have viewing access to your private accounts. They might think it's a hoot to post on their Instagram the photo they took of you drooling in dreamland. Or when you were drunk. Or to forward to another person a private email you wrote. They're your friends, so they wouldn't intentionally want to harm you. But, like everyone, they are capable of being thoughtless, rushed, hurt, or angry. And that can lead to their posting something that stains your online reputation.

Talk about the issue with your friends. Tell them that you guard your online reputation ferociously. Let them know your boundaries for what and how they can share things that involve you. And reassure them that you will treat their online reputation with equal care.

Use Brand Sanitizer

Let's say you have an online trail that you fear is a little heavy on the turd count. What can you do? First, google yourself. That's what somebody else would be doing. See what turds up. I mean, turns up. Maybe it will just reveal a bountiful trail of flowers. But if not, if you start seeing posts that would be harmful to your brand, it's time to sanitize your online reputation. Here's how.

- Delete everything you can that would reflect poorly on you: photos, tweets, raunchy comments, unkind remarks. I know it's tedious, but it's worth the effort.

- Conduct an *image* search under your name. This may reveal tagged photos of you that are not on your sites or under your control. You could then ask the site owners, who may be people you know, to please remove the photos.

- If your turd-to-flowers ratio is too pungent, think about deleting the account entirely. You can launch a new one with more care.

- Don't tag others in posts and photos, and don't allow *yourself* to be tagged, if you can avoid it. Also try to remove tags of yourself when possible. Tagging is one of the major ways you can lose control over where your posts and photos go.

- Make all your accounts—unless they are specifically intended for public consumption—private.

- Delete offensive comments from others. We're judged by the company we keep. If somebody goes to your social media and sees a lot of comments that turn them off, that reflects poorly on you. You should not only delete off-putting past comments, but consider blocking comments in the future if there's a good chance people will continue to lay their own turds on your sweet-smelling social media lawn.

- Post tons of positive photos. If there are embarrassing photos of you out there that a search would turn up, and you can't remove them, adding lots of newer, great photos will push them down in search results.

- Explore SEO strategies. *SEO* stands for search engine optimization. It can get pretty technical, but the basic idea is that you can take steps to boost some items so that they appear first when people search for you online, and obscure others, or push them further down in the search results. Since people who check you out online don't usually go beyond the first few pages, this is a good way to make it less likely they will stumble upon old turds. Run a search for "SEO strategies" and you'll find some good resources for doing online housecleaning.

- Finally, in extreme circumstances, you may need to consider engaging a service to help clean up your reputation. These can cost money, but if your turds add up to real deep doo-doo, it may be worth it to wipe the slate as clean as you can, and start over.

THINK ABOUT IT

I once had a good friend who said something I've never forgotten. "Some friendships," she said, "have an expiration date." I didn't think about it much at the time, but then, many years later, our friendship just faded away. Contact got less and less frequent, and then stopped entirely. It made me think about her comment and how true it was. You may have experienced friendships where you just drifted apart. Sometimes that happens for practical reasons—you move away or transfer to a different school. Sometimes it happens because your interests or social circles change.

And sometimes the "expiration" happens abruptly. There may have been an incident or a betrayal (whether real or perceived). There may have been a romantic relationship that went horribly wrong. One way or another, the friendship is over. Expired. And sometimes, all that remains are powerful feelings such as resentment, jealousy, anger, or hurt. These might lead to a desire for revenge.

It's not a good feeling if you know someone's mad at you and they have a lot of "ammo" in the form of compromising texts or photos, or confidences you entrusted them with. There may, sad to say, be nothing you can do about that other than keep your fingers crossed and decide to be more cautious in the future about what you reveal.

If you think there's a chance of at least a truce, you can try to defuse the situation. Assuming a face-to-face meeting isn't possible or advisable, send them an email or a real letter, or try calling them or leaving a voicemail. (These types of emotional issues aren't suitable for messaging.) Don't blame or accuse. Express your sadness and regret for the broken relationship. Acknowledge your awareness of the hurt or anger that exists. If you know that your actions caused the rift, apologize. Make or offer amends if you can. Reflect on the wonderful times you shared. Let them know you will always remember and be grateful for their friendship, even if, sadly, it ended this way. Conclude by wishing them well. With any luck, this will take the edge off any fury or desire for revenge they may be harboring.

How to Protect Your Personal Safety

We've looked at how to protect your online privacy and reputation. Now let's look at a few ways to protect your offline safety from things that might happen as a result of online activity.

Know the Risks of Sexting

Sexting is the sending or receiving of sexually explicit messages, photos, or videos using a digital device. Depending on the when, where, what, how, and with whom, we can debate whether sexting is ever okay.

> We can. But let's not.

> Wait. I'd actually like to hear that debate.

Sorry. There's no universal answer. It would be like asking if it's okay for teens to have sex. It depends on their age, experience, personality, values, morals, and religious beliefs. It depends on how they were raised. It depends on the nature of the relationship, the maturity and trustworthiness of the participants, the context in which it might happen, the precautions they would take. This isn't a "one answer fits all" question.

The fact that some teens sext should not cause anyone to swoon with surprise. Humans are sexual beings, and adolescence is a prime time for exploring and understanding one's sexuality. And if there's a relationship to be found between sex and technology, people will find it. I'm sure, before cars were invented, teen couples in the 1800s borrowed Dad's horse and buggy on Friday nights to make out on the prairie. Polaroids, video cameras, DVD players, and, of course, the internet spawned new possibilities for dating, hooking up, making and viewing pornography, and expressing or acting upon sexual interests and feelings.

So, of course, it didn't take long for people to realize that if they could text, they could sext. Should you ever face this issue, it's important to consider the possible consequences of sending or receiving sexts. Because there are risks.

First, no sext is 100 percent private. Even those that are supposed to "disappear" in seconds can be captured and saved. One in 10 teens who receive sexts forward them without consent, according to a study of over 10,000 teens published in *JAMA Pediatrics.* You may send a sext to your crush, who then shares it in secret with just one friend. That one friend then forwards it to another friend. Pretty soon it could be on a public website, with the original sender having never even considered that the person they sent it to would forward it to somebody else.

Then there's "revenge porn." You may have heard that term. It's when a relationship goes bad and one of the partners posts sexual texts, photos, or videos to shame and get back at the other. This has happened frequently enough—you may have read stories about politicians, business leaders, celebrities, and couples to whom it has happened—that there are now laws in some states that make it a crime. But that hasn't put an end to it.

If intimate photos of you appear online, the consequences can be significant and long-term. Once posts go up, they almost never come down. As soon as you might get one site to delete them, they're already on 100 more. You know how quickly things spread across the internet. Those consequences would include the humiliation and shame you'd likely feel, plus the effect on your relationships with parents, siblings, friends, teachers, and other people you know. Just somebody having photos of you, even if they do nothing with them, keeps open the possibility of sextortion, blackmail, school discipline, possible criminal charges, getting on a sex offender list, and damage to your reputation.

Take all these potential pitfalls and "it depends" factors and you can see why sexting is a complex issue that triggers so much debate.

> ### Oh, good. Can we debate it now?

No. But if you're debating it in your head or thinking about sending a sext, here are essential safety tips to follow.

Never give in to pressure.

If somebody is pressuring you to send a revealing photo, that should be a conversation stopper. Period. End of story. Pressure means you have doubts—otherwise why would they need to pressure you? Honor your doubts. Your gut is telling you the right answer. In a caring, equal relationship, one partner should not be pressuring the other. So, if there's coercion, that's a flashing warning sign not to do it.

Never show your face.

If an intimate photo of you should go public, not being identifiable at least helps protect your privacy. Remember that some social media sites use facial recognition to tag and identify people. If your face isn't shown, you thwart facial recognition. You can deny it's you and nobody can prove otherwise—unless there are things in the photo that people would recognize.

Never include identifiable features.

Hiding your face doesn't protect your privacy if the photo reveals tattoos, scars, piercings, birthmarks, or jewelry that people who know you might recognize. Same thing with your bedroom or home. Posters, furniture, bookshelves, bedspreads, stuffed animals, cars—you name it—could all be clues to your identity.

Hide your location.

Some social media apps automatically tag your photos with identifying markers such as location or username. Make sure you know exactly what privacy settings are in effect and what they might reveal about you. If any photo you send would pierce your anonymity, it's better to know that *before*, rather than after you send a sext.

Be aware of legal issues.

Sending and/or receiving sexts can be a crime. If any of the participants are minors, charges could include distribution and possession of child pornography, sexual exploitation of a minor, and/or nonconsensual sharing of pornography. These are felonies. Even if both teens are dating each other, even if the photos are consensual, even if the teens are the only people who ever saw them, they can be prosecuted. That's exactly what happened to two North Carolina 16-year-olds whose nude sexts were discovered by law enforcement. You can imagine the legal nightmare they went through. Child pornography laws were never intended to address sexting by minors, and many states are now seeking to rewrite them to protect teens from having their lives destroyed by sending a sext. But for now, it's a mess, and you could get into serious trouble simply by having such photos on your phone or sending them, solicited or not, to somebody else.

Don't store explicit images on your phone or other internet-connected devices.

If they're not on your devices, they can't be hacked, and they're also much less likely to be discovered or accidentally seen.

Use "disappearing" messages.

While you can't guarantee that somebody won't take a screenshot of an image before it disappears, the use of message apps that offer this feature will at least reduce the chances of a sext going public.

Never send a sext to somebody you don't know or haven't met.

If you don't know the person, they could be anybody—an undercover cop, a predator, your uncle. That's the thing about people you don't know—they could be *anybody*. And they're always *somebody's* uncle, teacher, coach, priest, waiter, or repairman. You don't want to be sending private photos or sexual communications to anybody whose identity and motives are hidden. If you've ever created a "pretend" profile, or if you know friends who have, clearly there are millions of other people doing the same thing.

Safe Sexts

Me in the Shower

Me Streaking in the Backyard

Be Careful When Meeting New People Online

Of surveyed teens, 57 percent say they've made a new friend online. That makes sense since the digital world facilitates social interaction. Some of those friendships may remain virtual and never result in face-to-face encounters. They'll be enjoyed via messaging, correspondence, and video calls. Others may blossom into "real world" meetings, wonderful lasting friendships, or even marriages and baby carriages.

When meeting someone in person for the first time, you need to be initially cautious. With online relationships, there's always a possibility that the person you're meeting isn't who you think they are. Sure, you've seen their social media, they seem "authentic," you've gotten good vibes from your online encounters. But, especially with "sexting," there's a possibility that the person has created a phony profile, collecting photos from the web to make a social media account. They can pretend to be anybody.

Now, you can't lead a life where you assume everyone online is actually a vampire waiting to lure hapless teens to a dungeon and attack them, vacuum pack them in shrink-wrap, and put them through a paper shredder. (I mean, seriously, what are the odds?) But still, you need to be careful.

If you were introduced to somebody via a group Zoom chat where friends brought friends and it's clear the person in the upper left corner is known to people you know, and you want to meet for a coffee, that's fine. But if it's somebody who doesn't come with ironclad, trustworthy "references," follow these safety rules for a first meeting:

- Never go alone to meet in person someone you've met online.
- Meet in a public place.
- Never go to somebody's house for a first meeting.
- Don't get in their car.
- Tell a friend or parent where you'll be and when you'll be back.
- Keep your phone and location tracking on. (This is one case where it's a good idea.)
- If you feel embarrassed about taking precautions, blame it on your parents.

Be on the Alert for Online Predators

Among the many wonderful people you come into contact with online, there may be some dangerous duds. Among them are sexual predators. These are people who use social media to meet young people for their sexual purposes or fantasies, whether online or in real life. Here's how they prey, and how you can protect yourself.

You may strike up a warm friendship with somebody online. It may be on a site teens visit, and/or a chat room for people who share certain interests. The person you meet might value your opinion, they make you feel special, they may say they're your age. At some point, as the relationship proceeds, the person may bring up sexual topics, pose personal questions, and/or ask you to send a sexually explicit photo. He—statistically it's more likely to be a "he"—may even first send you one of himself (purportedly), to show you he trusts you. Don't fall for it. This could be an online predator who wants to get nude photos of teens. It could also be an older person who hopes to eventually set up a face-to-face meeting. Think of online predators as a 21st-century addition to the advice of never getting in a car with a stranger.

Here's how online predators groom young people, either to send photos, perform sexual acts on camera, or meet up in person. Depending on a groomer's ultimate goal, they may use some or all of these tactics:

- They validate your feelings and choices.
- They are attentive and supportive and willing to take time to chat.
- They compliment you and may offer gifts.
- They express sympathy for your problems.
- They make you feel valued and listened to.

- They portray your friendship as special, rare, and something to be kept secret.
- They seem to share many of your interests and experiences, as if they already know you (possibly from having studied your social media accounts or those of your friends).
- They appeal to your desire for approval, closeness, and companionship.
- They encourage you to listen only to them, and may try to drive a wedge between you and your parents, teachers, and/or friends by saying your parents don't understand you, your teachers don't know what they're talking about, and your friends will be jealous if you tell them you have a special relationship.
- They hold out promises of adventures, trips, and things you can do together.
- They exploit your natural and healthy curiosity about sex.
- They slowly introduce sex into your conversations and may expose you to pornography.
- They ask you to send revealing photos or film a sex act.
- If you refuse right from the start, they will threaten to expose any secrets you've revealed or sexual communications you may have had.
- If you do send sexual photos or videos, they'll blackmail you so that you *keep* sending them.
- They push you to meet in person.
- If you do go to meet them . . . well, the truth is I have no idea what might happen, but that would be very, very dangerous.

The best way to ensure that you don't get approached by a predator is to be cautious about any new online friendship, to maintain anonymity, to guard your privacy, and to be alert to the warning signs. Of course, many people in, say, a chat group, might provide you with validation, support, and kindness. It doesn't mean they're predators. They might be wonderful souls you'd be pleased and proud to know in person. But if it's a group for people who are, say, into a certain video game, and then the person asks you what you're wearing, well, that might be a clue that something else is going on. If you begin to get creepy vibes, do the following:

- Honor your intuition. Bleep the creep.
- Document everything by taking screenshots and saving messages. This could prove essential in any investigation or prosecution, and in getting a social media site to flag or delete the person.
- Immediately tell a trusted adult. Too many teens keep what's going on a secret. That's too heavy a burden for any teen to bear.

- Get the help you need to block the person, report the person, and deal with your feelings and situation.

Also, this is really important: Even if things went too far, even if you said things you wish you hadn't, even if you sent photos or videos of yourself, none of what happened was your fault. Getting support from a trusted adult will help. Promise.

Other Online Predators and Fakery

There's another type of online predator you should look out for—bots pretending to be real people. They repeat lies, amplify misinformation, and spread false rumors and conspiracy theories, fracturing our sense of what's real and what isn't. Once people consume these misleading or untrue stories, doctored photos, and fabricated videos, *they* often become the primary spreaders of conspiracy theories and fake news.

When accepted truths and factual realities are attacked, it threatens our internal *and* external security. The hidden people, organizations, and agencies behind these hidden entities have hidden reasons for polarizing opinion, inciting chaos or violence, or promoting self-serving ends. These could be economic interests (like fossil fuel companies wanting to discredit climate change); political interests (such as spreading lies about a rival candidate to win an election); or social interests (like inflaming divisiveness over abortion with false claims). Even though the information is false and coming from shady sources, it can jump to legitimate media outlets when it is being quoted by political figures or going viral online.

A lie, repeated over and over and over again on social media until tens of millions of people believe it, is still a lie. Yet in some ways it might as well be true, since it causes real people to act in real ways with real consequences. When people believe that pandemics are fake news, that climate change is a hoax, that mail-in ballots are fraudulent, that vaccines are deep-state plots, that immigrants are to blame for job losses, that mass shootings are staged, that McDonald's restaurants in Colorado are turning children's play spaces into marijuana lounges—well, such ridiculous and untrue beliefs can provoke real death threats and real violence, prevent real legislation, influence how real people vote in real elections, and cause customers to ask for a Big Mac with a side of weed. This can lead to deaths, shortened life spans, resurgences of eradicated diseases, climate disasters, protests over events that never happened, bankruptcies, and many other real-world consequences.

Many people died of COVID-19 because they were told that it was "fake" and that mask-wearing was an unnecessary infringement upon their freedom rather than a simple act of caution and goodwill toward others. They *believed* what they heard and read, much of it online, on websites and blogs that had hidden agendas.

TRUTH DOESN'T MATTER

This is going to get dark. So, turn on the lights. Put on your headlamp. Invite a few bright friends over.

Let's ease into the darkness with a question: What makes it possible for millions of people every day to drive safely from one place to another? It's not luck. It's not police at every intersection. It's not laws. It's because all drivers recognize the same facts: Green = go. Red = stop. A solid double line means do not pass. We obey these conventions because we accept them as true, we trust that other drivers will honor them, and we know that these mutually accepted meanings are essential to the safe and orderly flow of traffic.

Now, imagine what would happen if half of all drivers came to believe that *red* = go; *green* = stop; a solid double line means *pass*; and traffic signs are fake, infringe upon their rights and freedom, and must be disobeyed. The entire system would break down. You'd have chaos. Gridlock. Accidents. Fire engines couldn't race to a burning house. Ambulances couldn't save lives. Trucks couldn't deliver food, fuel, or other goods.

> This *is* getting a little dark.

> Just wait. It gets darker.

If half the population rejected what "red" and "green" mean—rejected the norms and realities that govern the flow of traffic—commerce, infrastructure, economies, and social order would collapse. Why? Because societies are based on shared norms, values, and facts. Human societies without accepted rules, agreed-to facts, and expectations for behavior degenerate into chaos and conflict. And this brings us to the digital world. Social media, hidden algorithms, and an online tsunami of lies and false "news" stories are undermining the shared norms, facts, values, and beliefs that are essential to peaceful coexistence, social order, and democracy.

> Yep. Definitely dark now.

How is this happening? Let's connect the pixels.

We live in an *information age*. The accumulation, control, and monetizing of data has become a powerful engine of our economy, transforming cultures and human interactions. Those with the most data have the most power and wealth. To collect your data and then use it for profit, Big Tech must get you to engage. They need to get and keep your attention. They need your *eyeballs*. Their algorithms are designed to do whatever it takes to keep those eyeballs glued to their platform. And often, what it takes is lies.

Studies show that conspiracy theories, false news, and posts that arouse negative emotions travel faster, farther, and deeper online than truthful, informational posts. Since the goal is eyeball engagement, social media giants don't care whether what they're pushing to your feeds is true or false. Their algorithms are profit-driven, not truth-driven. This leads to what we are seeing today: huge proportions of the population believing lies and conspiracy theories that are demonstrably, provably false.

Once-extreme fringe elements have now become mainstream due to the megaphone social media offers to anyone with an internet connection. And the more deceitful, malevolent, angry, toxic, or outrageous their posts, the more likely they are to be retweeted, regurgitated, and believed. This means that the dominance of profit over fact is shattering the shared "truths" essential to functional governing, civilized discourse, and social progress. The societal equivalents of *red = stop* are becoming extinct.

This has created a new economy where information reigns supreme, and megatech corporations manipulate users' behavior for profit. Shoshana Zuboff, a social psychologist and professor emerita at Harvard Business School, calls this new economy "surveillance capitalism." She believes (me, too!) that surveillance capitalism and democracy cannot coexist. This is because surveillance capitalism depends on amplifying the most enraged and extreme content to capture your eyeballs. More lies = more attention = more data = more profit. As long as this remains the case, the online playing field tilts toward the erosion of shared truths, norms, and values. Divisiveness, polarization, and the inability to distinguish fact from fiction, reality from fantasy, will be the inevitable result of a surveillance capitalism business model.

> Waayyy too dark. I'm going out to get some sun.

> Don't forget to wear sunscreen.

I admit that these dire consequences may seem irrelevant, alarmist, or even ridiculous when you're using a puppy-face lens to Snap a friend. I don't want to spoil anyone's fun. But keep in mind that underneath all the great, funny, and joyful things the internet makes possible, your attention is being commandeered, your data is being collected, and somebody is making money off of you. And while you may be frolicking on the sunniest mountaintops of the digisphere, others are being sucked into the darkest trenches. And people are only now realizing the extent to which their rights have been usurped, their psyches have been hijacked, their privacy has been stolen, and their societies have been threatened.

But this can be fixed if enough people rise up and resist. So let's find some light.

Support efforts to regulate Big Tech. Recognize that these corporations and their business models need to be regulated to protect individual rights, societal values, and the foundations and future of civilization. Such regulation is not a radical idea. The pharmaceutical, banking, airline, automobile, oil and gas, and food industries, for example, are all regulated to protect consumers, competition, and the environment. Support organizations, activists, and political leaders who want to reign in Big Tech's power and abuses.

Demand your right to determine what data you share, and for what purpose. Band together with like-minded citizens. Call, write, and petition lawmakers. Boycott businesses and platforms whose business models are based on the commercialization of stolen personal data.

Fight to end tracking and data collection. Reject Big Tech's claim that they are entitled to invade and profit from your life. Data collection, if it exists at all, should be something users affirmatively opt *into* that serves the public and individual good.

Support the idea that the internet should be used to enhance lives, communities, and societies. That was the original dream—using this marvel of technology to eradicate poverty, illiteracy, famine, and disease; safeguard the climate and environment; protect individual rights; and make the world a better, safer place for future generations— rather than enrich a handful of powerful corporations, subvert societal harmony, and undermine democracy.

So don't despair, dear reset rebels. Yes, the promise of the digital age has been hijacked for profit. But if enough people rise up, demanding change, we can create a new digital world that works for everybody.

The Meteorology of Privacy Protection

No Privacy Measures   Some Privacy Measures   Many Privacy Measures

Lying in Wait

Let's face it. The digital world can be (choose your metaphor): a carnival, a barnyard full of cow-pies, a minefield. You need to step carefully to avoid the human, robotic, and algorithmic predators out to get you and your attention. With stealth, lies, and misdirection, they're tracking you, profiling you, grooming you, invading your privacy, manipulating your emotions, and commandeering your time—all in pursuit of profit, power, politics, or sexual gratification.

But . . .

There's no need to fret, and no need to mope. Please don't be upset—there's reason to hope! For sure it's a mess, a bummer supreme. You don't have to stress, you've got self-esteem. Don't ever lose heart; you know what to do. You won't fall apart, you'll always pull through. Just learn to resist—you have all the skills. And if you persist, you'll turn up new thrills.

> **AAAAGGGGGGHHHHHHHH!!!!!!!**

You're discovering how to protect yourself from the Digital Dark Side. You now have tools to turn glum into fun. Grim into grin. Turds into flowers. Cow pies into apple pies. Minefields into—

> **Hey, enough with the metaphors.**

> Glad you stopped me. I didn't have anything for the minefields to turn into.

So don't despair. Just beware. And take care.

> **Or be square.**

TALES FROM THE DIGITAL FRONTIER

You've probably picked up that I am concerned about the ways in which smartphones, social media, internet tracking, and experiencing life through a device can affect relationships, human development, civilization, and other little things like democracy, truth, peace, and acceptance. I'm concerned that, as has been the case with many habits, inventions, and technological breakthroughs, we will learn—years or decades from now—of unhealthy, unintended consequences.

> So what, exactly, is it you don't like about the internet?

It's not that I don't like the internet. I *LOVE* all the things the internet makes possible. I *LOVE* being able to say or type a few words and get answers to any question. Shop for a book or fuel filter or oximeter and have it show up at my house two days later. Pick from thousands of movies and TV shows to watch anything I want anytime I want to. I love listening to a seven-hour playlist of music I love. Chatting for free with friends on the other side of the world. I love being able to plan a trip, send snarky messages, and get a response seconds later. I love being able to check my bank balance, look up a recipe, and get the weather forecast. But here are some aspects I don't like.

I don't like being profiled and categorized by people I don't know, in ways I don't know, for purposes I don't know.

I don't like the feeling that somebody is tracking everything I do, ask, think, and feel.

I don't like asking Google about the weather in New Zealand in July and then being shown travel ads for New Zealand for the next two years.

I don't like there being so many thousands of options for anything I might buy that I feel compelled to spend hours online to make sure I get the "best deal."

I don't like seeing comments so petty, ignorant, unkind, and bigoted that it makes me feel like I need a shower to wash the filth off.

I don't like the feeling that there can be personal information about me online that I never put there or agreed to its being there, that is wrong, and that there is nothing I can do about it.

I don't like seeing ads so stroboscopic that I have to cover part of the screen with cardboard to keep from getting dizzy, throwing up, or having a seizure.

> Whoa. Sorry I asked.

That's just me. You may have completely different feelings and attitudes about these things.

The positives may vastly outweigh the negatives. That could have something to do with growing up with digital devices and the internet. You've gone to thousands of sites, posted a trillion things—and the secret police have never come in the middle of the night to throw you in prison. (At least I assume they haven't.) You may decide that this level of blocking, protection, anonymity, and/or invisibility isn't important or necessary for you. My intention is not to freak you out or make you paranoid.

One thing to keep in mind, though, is that as your life evolves, as you intersect with Big Tech in more and more ways, its invasiveness, data collection, and algorithmic assumptions about you will grow. If you get a driver's license or a car, your whereabouts will be tracked. How you drive and accelerate and brake will be tracked. If you shop in stores, they will be monitoring which displays you stop at, where your eyes focus, how much time you spend, whether you use your phone to price check, what you ultimately buy. The stores will then not only use your data for their own profit-making purposes, but sell it. (Remember, sites and platforms have hundreds of partners!) If you use a dating site, just imagine the assumptions it will be making, the data it will be collecting. If you ask a search engine a sexual question or a question about depression, it's all being tracked and recorded and stored away.

When you start making purchases with credit cards or mobile wallet apps, when you use loyalty programs to get discounts and special deals, everything you eat, drink, buy, wear, read, use, and do will fatten your data profile. That information will then be used, not just to stalk you with ads and addictive content, but to determine whether you'll get a loan or health insurance, what prices you'll see, what options you'll be shown, how long you'll have to wait—the list goes on and on.

We are all now lab rats. Billions of people undergoing mass behavior modification.

> Dude. You need to meditate. Or take a pill. Or something.

> Breathe in . . . 2, 3, 4.

> Breathe out . . . 2, 3, 4.

PROTECT YOUR PSYCHE

How Social Media Can Crush Your Heart, Seize Your Soul, And Hack Your Identity

Or not.

Social media can make you depressed, anxious, lonely, and unhappy. Or not.

Some teens LOVE social media. They see it as joyful, funny, and enriching to their lives. It helps them connect with friends and family and meet new people. It's where they go to laugh, learn, create, express themselves, and find support to get through tough times.

Some teens HATE social media. They don't like the bullying, the phoniness, the drama, the distraction, the pressure to post and respond and show everyone what a great life you have.

Still other teens see social media as just a tool, something they use, that isn't positive *or* negative.

In a survey of 13- to 17-year-olds . . .

. . . 31 percent say social media has had a "mostly positive effect" on people their own age

. . . 24 percent say social media has had a "mostly negative effect" on people their own age

. . . 45 percent say social media has had "neither a positive nor negative effect" on people their own age.

But it doesn't matter how social media affects *other* teens. What matters is how it affects YOU. And the people you're close to.

Why does social media have such power? Because, of all aspects of digital life, social media, more than any other online interaction, gets its hooks into your psyche.

> What's a psyche?

> Your psyche is *you*. It's your essence. Your soul, spirit, and emotions. Your thoughts, karma, and energy.

> How do you pronounce it?

> It.

> No! "Psyche."

> SIGH-kee. (Emphasis on the first syllable.)

> Why isn't it pronounced PEA-sitch?

> Because English language spelling is wild. Turf. Tough. Through. Bough. Bow-wow.

> And now, if you're done with all the questions, I'll get back to psyches and social media.

The first thing to recognize is that social media is not a monolith. Since "social media" includes any apps or websites that let users create and share content and/or engage in social networking, you can't treat it as one thing. It encompasses sites for texting, chatting, dating, hooking up, telling secrets, microblogging, livestreaming, and gaming. Everything from Facebook to Snapchat, Twitter to Instagram, YouTube to TikTok, Zoom to WhatsApp, Twitch to Itch, Yik Yak to Riff Raff.

Some sites are anonymous and can be a swamp of bullying, cruelty, trolling, and people's darkest behaviors. Some sites are crawling with bots. Some sites are for creating a professional presence or building a personal "brand." Some are for people who share interests or want to get support for problems. Some are for messaging and conferencing. Some are online "playgrounds" where you can post and watch wild and crazy videos, dye your hair, and change your looks. Some sites are "ephemeral" and let you send texts and pics and videos that disappear (except they don't; see page 187 for more on that).

In general, I'm avoiding focusing on specific platforms. That's for two reasons: One, who knows how long any particular platform will be around or how long it will stay popular with people your age. For years, Facebook was super popular, and now it's Snapchat, YouTube, and Instagram. Social media platforms come and go, teens shift their loyalty. So, today you may be sending tweets, Snaps, and yaks; in a year it may be peeps, raps, and quacks. The second reason is that teens have different experiences on whatever social media they use. So it's difficult to say how a specific platform will affect a specific user. When I refer to "social media," I'm counting on you to personalize it to the social media you use.

Signs That Social Media Is Negatively Affecting Your Psyche

For many teens, social media is wonderful. It can be a way to bond and share, make new friends, and talk to people around the world. It's a place where you can anonymously ask questions and get answers, talk with a supportive person, find people who share your interests or concerns, explore your sexuality, have a video party.

This connectivity, by transcending geography, can be especially helpful if you live in a remote community or go to a school or belong to a family where certain issues are off limits, where certain discussions, views, or behaviors would not be respected or tolerated. That's because with social media, you can make connections that you couldn't in "real life." Social media can be a miraculous sphere of contact, convenience, creativity, accessibility, and opportunity. If that's been your experience, I hope you continue to find it a thriving, rewarding, entertaining part of your life. But simply talking about the wonders of social media isn't very useful. If social media is great for you, you already know that. You don't need me to tell you.

> Right about that.

What's more useful is looking at the possible not-so-great aspects that you might have experienced or thought about. For some teens, social media is a door into darkness. To see what that might be like, here are some warning signs of possible negative consequences teens might experience from using social media.

 You Feel Depressed, Lonely, or Self-Hating After Being Online.
Everybody seems to be having a better life than you. You see people's posts and photos, who's seeing whom, parties you weren't invited to, clothes you wish you had, achievements you wish were yours, and in comparison, your life seems

boring and empty. You feel ugly, dumb, unpopular, uncool. Negative "self-talk" takes over and you believe that nothing will ever change. You feel that you'll never have the friends, relationships, and adventures you'd like; you'll never feel confident and successful; you'll never be happy.

 You're Quick to Anger and Get Upset About Small Things.
You feel like a loose-cannoned, hair-triggered, gasoline-soaked pyre of sticks, firecrackers, grenades, and dynamite ready to explode with one spark—*especially* after you've been on social media. The tiniest things set you off. Your mind gets stuck in rage loops against people, situations, and even objects that don't behave the way you want. You're such a tinderbox you get mad about things that haven't even happened—but might. And worst of all, you're often the target of your own fury.

 You Have Mood Swings Without Knowing Why.
You're like the pendulum on a clock, swinging from one extreme to the other. You think it must be a cuckoo clock because you feel crazy having no idea why you go from being up in the clouds to down in the dumps in a heartbeat. Was it something somebody said? Something you saw online? Something in your feed? A test grade? A friend's triumph? A parent's comment? A lost game? A memory? A wish? Who knows? You sure don't. And that makes it scary. You feel like a puppet with somebody else, or some*thing* else, pulling your strings.

 You Feel Stressed Out and Unable to Cope.
You know stress is part of life, but you feel like stress *is* your life. It never lets up. Pressure to do well in school. Pressure to look good. Pressure to post. Pressure to reply. Pressure from parents, friends, problems, fears, and secret thoughts— even secret hopes and dreams. You never have enough time, you don't get enough sleep. You perpetually feel late, lost, and rushed, like you're holding on to life by your fingernails and losing your grip. You don't see a way out. You can't imagine getting to a better place. Is it always going to be like this?

 You Feel Anxious, Empty, and/or Irritated When Away from Your Phone.
You can't imagine life without your phone. It's by your side when you sleep. It's the first thing you reach for in the morning. It's how you connect with friends and learn the latest gossip. Hours fly by when you're on social media or playing video games. If you can't use your phone, if you run out of battery, if you lose it or leave it someplace, you feel nervous, on edge, cut off, vulnerable—like a part of you is missing. And if a parent or teacher tells you to put your phone away you want to bite their head off.

⚠ **You Use the Internet to Escape Problems and Feelings.**

You just want to get away from your life and your problems: people on your back, school pressures, family conflicts. Sometimes you just hate being you. You hate the voices in your head, the feelings in your heart. So you disappear. Online. When you're playing games, checking feeds, posting photos, watching videos, streaming shows, you can escape being you. Get away from it all. Even if just for a few hours. That's why you spend so much time on your phone. It's a better world than the real one you have to live in.

You can see how these warning signs form a cluster. They reinforce each other. If you feel stressed, if problems in real life overwhelm you, it's natural to want to escape online. And if you can't be online, if you're separated from your phone, it's natural to feel anxious, angry, or irritated. You'll want to get back online as soon as possible.

Of course, all teens (and adults) feel stressed, trapped, sad, or anxious on occasion or go through low periods. In fact, feeling and working your way through stress, disappointments, failures, setbacks, embarrassments, and worries can be of value in helping build the strongest, most confident, and most interesting "you."

So, when I talk about emotional warning signs, I'm looking at the frequency, chronicity, and severity of the feelings. In other words, how often, for how long, and at what level of distress do you experience those feelings? It's the difference between occasionally feeling a pang of loneliness (and doing something constructive about it) and feeling that way all the time, to the extent that you want to crawl into bed, sob, and feel hopeless.

The Diabolical Ways "Like Me" Gets into Your Psyche

> Bet you're proud of that rhyme.

> You noticed! Yes, very proud. In today's world, one has to find joy wherever one can.

Let's look at some of the negative ways social media can grab hold of your psyche.

Ha-Ha, You're Not Invited

Social media can make you feel excluded. You see photos on Instagram of class-mates at a party, or shopping, or at the beach or a park. You think, *why didn't they invite me?* You and a friend had plans to go to a movie Saturday night. At the last minute she cancels, saying she has to stay home and babysit. Later that night you see the photo she posted of her and her boyfriend at the food court. By seeing what you're missing, what you didn't get invited to do, being "connected" can make you feel lonelier.

Dumping a Load of Happiness Crappiness on You

Social media forces "happiness" on users. The real you, with fears, worries, goofs, gaffes, and blemishes, must stay hidden. In a survey of college students, nearly three out of four (73 percent) said: "I try always to appear positive/happy with anything attached to my real name."

Happiness becomes a badge. A level achieved. It's a "thing" to show off. Social media is a happiness competition in which everyone presents their upbeat, smiling, brave, and beautiful façade to the world. Meanwhile, you may be feeling stressed, disappointed, unloved, and downright *un*happy. But you can't show it. Because everyone you see on social media is posting the "greatest hits" of their lives. "Here I am having a *fabulous* time at the bonfire! #bestsmores." "Here I am with my *gorgeous* boyfriend! #sosexy." "Here's the *amazing* taco I had! #chilichowdown." "Here's me and my brother sailing on my dad's *superfast* sailboat #soblessed."

And here's you stuck at home on Saturday night eating a bowl of cold cereal, bored to tears, while your little brother keeps shooting rubber bands at you and your mom tells you to stop being so glum and find something to do.

You can't help comparing your seemingly dreary life to theirs. You know in your head that your friends' real lives aren't like their posts. You know that they, too, have bad hair days and periods of sadness, anger, and self-doubt. You know that they must have spent three hours trying on different clothes and poses and taking 400 photos to get the perfect selfie they just posted, hoping to get lots of likes. You *know* that, but still, it doesn't *feel* like that.

It's not as though comparing yourself to others hasn't been part of human nature since long before the internet ever existed. I'm sure early humans checked out who had the biggest club and who looked best in a bison-skin bathing suit.

Comparing is natural human behavior. But with the ever-present specter of social media, the "happy face" imperative has never been so *in your face*, so public, so quantifiable, so everlasting. You can't avoid comparisons if you use social media. Social media *amplifies* them. And the platforms design it this way, since looking for the dopamine hit of approval is what keeps you coming back.

Creating Unrealistically Great Expectations

Just as social media turns happiness into a commodity to rank, it makes it hard not to compare your accomplishments with the apparently awesome accomplishments of others. The "air-brushed" lives people post can make you feel you're not smart enough, popular enough, sexy enough, or good enough. You're constantly making— you're constantly *feeling*—comparisons between your existence and achievements and those of other people. You compare grades, looks, clothes, weekend plans, vacations, purchases, and more. There's always going to be somebody who did it better, scored higher, got luckier, looked cooler.

Upsetting as these types of comparisons can be, it gets worse. That's because social media *numerically* ranks, scores, and judges you.

Giving You a Social Media Report Card

On social media, your worth gets measured in friends, followers, views, likes, tags, comments, retweets, shares, hearts, thumbs up, thumbs down, whether your post stays at the top of a feed or disappears into oblivion. This quantifiable ranking forces you into a state of never-ending comparison with friends and other people online. You can't escape the metrics. If your photo gets 10 likes, and somebody else's gets 100 likes, they got 10 times as many likes as you did. The numbers don't lie. So you judge yourself by the extent to which others "like" and affirm you—or not. You feel as though your popularity and public image is under constant scrutiny. And it is, since everybody can see your "grades."

Social media platforms use human nature to draw you into an endless loop. They know that these processes (and, yes, you can call them "loopy") will keep you coming back:

1. **Engagement.** This is the hands-on activity—posting, viewing, tweeting, Snapping, communicating—that sets you up for being judged, for judging others, and for seeing how others are being judged.

2. **Anticipation.** This is the suspenseful period after you put something out there— waiting, wondering, hoping, checking to see what the response is.

3. **Rumination.** This is where your psyche considers, speculates, interprets, fumes, worries, or jumps for joy at the response you got (or didn't). If the "likes" or hearts or cuddly koalas or whatever pour in, you're happy and may make a

mental note to post more things like that. If the response is not what you hoped for, there's going to be doubt, regret, and/or second-guessing. Do you delete the post, ask friends to boost it, wait longer, shrug it off, spiral into bummerland? Whatever you decide, whether your motivation is joy or disappointment, the natural reaction is . . .

4. Re-engagement. (See step 1 above.)

This cycle repeats itself ad nauseum—emphasis on *nausea*—since social media is a never-ending stream of information and judgment. You're never "finished" since it's open 24/7—counting, liking, sharing, judging—even when you're offline or asleep.

SUBJECT	GRADE	SELF-ESTEEM
1. Biology	A-	☺
2. # of Likes	👍	☺
3. # of Friends	👭	☹
4. Spanish	C+	😐
5. # of Retweets	👏	☺
6. Great Selfie Comments	🤳	☹
7. Invited to Enuf Parties	😢	☹
8. Whose Vacation Was Best?	🌴	☺
9. Snap Streak Length	😠	☹
10. Texts from BF	💔	☹

One way to tell if social media is hacking your self-esteem is to ask yourself:

- Have I ever deleted a post because it didn't get enough likes?
- Have I ever posted at a certain time of day because I think it'll get more likes?
- Have I ever asked somebody to like one of my posts?
- Have I ever asked somebody why they *didn't* like one of my posts?
- Have I ever changed a profile pic because it didn't get enough likes?
- Have I ever posted a revealing photo just to get likes?

- Have I ever noticed that the more likes I get the better I feel?

- Have I ever felt bad about caring so much whether people "like" my posts?

- Have I ever accepted a friend request from somebody who's not really a friend just to increase my number of friends?

If you answered "yes" to any of these, it could mean that social media has invaded that part of your psyche where comparison, validation, self-esteem, jealousy, envy, and aspiration hang out.

These numerical comparisons are especially insidious because they force you to keep engaging with the platform. Social media uses your own curiosity and desire for approval—powerful psychological forces that affect all of us—to compel you to constantly post, Snap, respond, view your feeds, check your stats, post some more, view some more, check some more, respond some more.

But as manipulative and acidic as these types of comparisons are, there is another way social media can devour your psyche. This one attacks the core of who you are.

Squashing the Real You

Social media confronts every user with an "authenticity dilemma." If everybody is putting their "Happy Face" out there, do you? That seems so fake. But it's not as though the answer to "Happy Face" pressure is to start posting your low or awkward moments, your troubling thoughts and feelings. That could cause a different set of problems such as being ridiculed, cyberbullied, or told to lighten up and stop being such a drama queen.

You can see the conflict here. On the one hand, many people are fake on social media, putting up only their "best" moments and images. On the other hand, being "authentic" could reflect badly on you in the eyes of others—even if there's nothing bad or shameful about what you post—because you're going against the norm.

So you get a mixed message. Social media should be a place to connect, be real, express yourself. But you'd better monitor every single thing you put up.

Letting your guard down—being goofy, dumb, careless, gross—no longer exists for teens, even in your bedroom or basement. You never know who has silently pressed "record." Most likely, it's always been this way for you and your friends. Your phones are rarely out of reach, so the ability to capture and reveal private moments is omnipresent. Since it's always been that way, you may not have any concerns about it. But had you ever experienced the freedom of being able to exist—to, say, accidentally fart in front of your friends—without the fear of it being revealed to the world, you might feel different about it. Hmmm, maybe there's a better example. But you get my point.

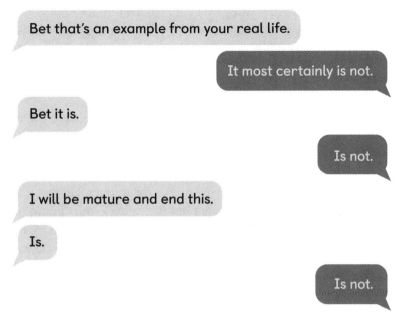

Social media creates a "being fake" versus "being real" dilemma that all teens need to resolve for themselves. There's also a difference between "being fake" and being discreet. Keeping things to yourself. You don't have to reveal everything. It's a bit like honesty. We all agree that being honest is a good thing. Right? Agreed?

But there are times when being honest serves no purpose other than to hurt somebody's feelings or create unnecessary conflict. So, you might not say to a friend on her way to prom: "I think you look terrible, your dress makes you look like a hot air balloon and your hair looks like two ferrets mated and died mid-coitus on your head." (It would, though, be okay to tell your friend she has spinach stuck in her teeth.)

The opposite of being fake isn't letting everything hang out. It's finding the sweet spot between authenticity and discretion where you can feel good about what you put out for the world to see—not too fake and not too real. And still *you*.

Branding Yourself

I am not referring to having "Joey P." burned on your butt with a red-hot iron. I'm referring to the reality that every social media account is a "brand." Everything you post is a choice you make. Every photo, video, Snap, or tweet is the result of a conscious action you take. You may agonize over what you post. Or you may not give it much thought. It may be impulsive or reflexive at times. However it gets out there, your posts are your brand. Creating (and recreating) your "brand" can be a joyful and rewarding way to reach into yourself and out to others. On the other hand, if maintaining your online presence and identity begins to feel like a chore, a pressure, or an act of phoniness, the stress of self-branding can scorch your serenity, torch your confidence, and set your psyche ablaze.

For some teens who become "influencers," who have hundreds of thousands or millions of followers, their branding becomes a sophisticated, hyper-orchestrated performance, often with corporations, agents, and branding specialists advising and shaping them. And sometimes you see how one insensitive, thoughtless, or bigoted post can damage the brand, causing that YouTube or Instagram "star" to lose followers and advertisers.

For most teens, though, that's not a problem they have to worry about.

> Finally! A problem I don't have to worry about.

What you do have to think about is *your* brand. What messages are you putting out there for others to see? You've probably heard 10,000 times that the things you post can last forever, and you have no real control over who sees them or what they do with them—forwarding, tagging, retweeting, taking screenshots. Well, now you can hear it for the 10,001st time: College admissions officers, employers, teachers, principals, coaches, your boyfriend or girlfriend's parents, law enforcement agents—all of them can, do, and WILL check out your social media accounts. There are countless stories of teens who have had college admissions rescinded, job applications denied, arrest warrants issued, and school expulsions triggered by things they posted.

For 99.9 percent of the history of civilization and teendom, teens didn't have to worry about "branding." Oh, sure, if they took a galleon for a joyride, tripped Michelangelo while carrying a sculpture, or tore pages out of the Gutenberg Bible, they could get a bad reputation in their neighborhood. But they could reform, make amends, maybe move from Florence to Sicily, and start over.

Sorry, Mike. I'll glue the arm back on.

More recently, but still before social media, if teens wore a T-shirt with a message or drawing, if they paid $100 for a pair of torn jeans, if they dyed their hair purple, you could say it was their "brand." Same thing if they affected a certain way of speaking, exuded kindness, or got straight A's. If they had a chirpy, hilarious personality, it was their "brand." But it could be changed from day to day with no eternal aftertaste. It was something that only a close circle of friends, family, or community might see. There was no way for strangers to see it. No way for the director of the camp where they're applying to be a counselor to see it. No way that it would hang around their neck forever.

With the advent and ubiquity of social media, that's no longer the case. Your social media presence is now a brand that people assume is a reflection of you. This can place enormous pressure on teens to present a certain image, to constantly create new content, to monitor everything lest one photo of you drinking or one joke that comes across in a way you never intended could be Google-able for the rest of your life—and dramatically alter the rest of your life.

FOMO

I don't have to tell you what a powerful force FOMO is.

> But you will anyway.

FOMO (Fear Of Missing Out) is where curiosity, rumor, gossip, drama, intrigue, scandal, friendship, sociability, and information all converge. It's the fear that exciting things are happening and you're not part of them. The worry that if you don't jump to reply, friends will be upset or concerned. Who with what when why where—WHOA! Knowledge is power, so it's natural to want to know the latest at the earliest.

FOMO is a big part of why so many teens don't want to let their phone out of their sight. Why they take it to bed with them. Why they check it first thing in the morning. There's nothing wrong with wanting to be up-to-date, in the know. But when it distorts your life, when it becomes a pressure or even an obsession you can't resist, it can lead to the emotional imbalances and psyche invasions described in the warning signs on page 206.

Social media platforms love FOMO. It's one of the main things that keeps people hooked. But there's another fear that should be at least as important for teens glued to social media:

FOMOOARLLAFTFCWIAVM (Fear of Missing Out On Actual, Real-Live Life And Face-To-Face Contact Which Is Also Very Meaningful).

POOP

While you've probably been aware of FOMO for a long time, I'm pretty sure you don't know about POOP: **P**reoccupation **O**ver **O**nline **P**osting.

POOP?

With so many people posting and messaging dozens or hundreds of times a day, showing how great their life is, how "happy" they are, you may feel that you have to keep up with the Joneses (or whoever is doing all that posting). It's a competition. There you are at a food truck? Here I am at the taco stand #chimichanga. There you are on your new 3-speed? Here I am with my new 27-speed #gearingup. There you are with your new T-shirt? Here I am with my new Tie-Dye Ultra-Air Infinity-Rebel Gluten-Free High Tops! #sneakerhead.

I'm not saying that all teens are consciously trying to one-up each other on social media. Some are. Some aren't. Most just want to be in the arena. To be visible and responsive. To share and connect. To be sociable. And that means posting. Constantly posting. Which can be exhausting.

And once you've identified an image or experience you want to post, do you take a selfie? Do you make a video? Six seconds? Fifteen? Five minutes? Does it go on YouTube? TikTok? Instagram? How many platforms do you post it to? Do you edit the photo or video? Change how you look? Use special effects? Add music? Is it something you want to stay up or have "disappear"? Are there certain people you *don't* want to see it? Which social media accounts should you use? Decisions, decisions, decisions.

Have you ever been with friends where all they seem to want to do is *document* that they did something, saw something, went someplace? The point seems to be getting the selfie, taking the photo, rather than experiencing the moment. It's as if *experiencing* the moment is secondary to putting it up on social media. All that documenting can get in the way of your enjoying the actual moment *in* the moment.

This pressure to post, to come up with new "content," can push some teens to filter their lives through the lenses of their social media accounts. They don't lead their lives so much as "package" them. They become curators. They put together an "exhibit" of what they do, what they experience. They are what they post. They live through their posts. Posting becomes a form of "people pleasing." Their friends expect it. They have to keep doing it so their friends don't feel ignored, rejected, or concerned about them.

Not everything needs to be photographed and shared. Your experiences exist. They're like the tree falling in the forest; does it make a sound if nobody is there to hear it? Of course it does. It's just nobody was there to hear it. Everything you do makes a sound, leaves a trail, imprints a memory, even if it isn't posted to social media. Memorializing every event online can mean you're documenting your life, not living it.

Of course, it's great to have photographs and other mementos to look back on as a way of revisiting experiences. And it's wonderful to share your adventures, discoveries, and "self" with others. But that sharing should not be the reason you do something. It should be a lovely by-product of having done something.

I'm not saying it was better in the good old, pre-POOP days. "Good old days" were never as good as people who experienced them think. Other times had other problems. I'm just saying that it was different. Those differences, looked at in retrospect, have their pros and cons.

In the days before social media (and all the way back to Michelangelo's time and beyond), teens shared their lives with others, captured memories, and socialized with friends. They just did it in different ways. There was nothing "superior" about The Time Before Social Media. But the one thing that does strike me, having experienced both eras, is I don't think teens' social lives *pre*-social media were as difficult, stressful, or all-consuming as they are today—*post*-social media. Pre–social media, you could get away from your social life, from all the intrigue and gossip, when you needed some space. It wasn't 24/7. It wasn't broadcast to the world for eternity. You didn't get 100 notifications an hour. You weren't ranked and scored for every little thing you did or shared. Just being a teen has always been hard enough. Having to document it only adds to the pressure.

The nature of social media today means you can't ever really get away from school, socializing, drama, the pressure to respond, the pressure to post, or the pressure of being judged and ranked. Social media invades your psyche. It creates FOMO. (And POOP!)

POOP?

THINK ABOUT IT I sometimes play a game on buses and subways, in airport waiting areas, in lines to order coffee, at tourist sites. I look to see how many people are experiencing their surroundings, versus how many are buried in their phones. Once you begin to look for this, it is AMAZING how the vast majority of people in public settings are looking at their phones, oblivious to the teeming humanity around them, the small magical moments, the magnificent buildings, natural beauty, creativity, history—oblivious to possibility.

I've watched so many people—maybe you have, too—who visit a famous tourist destination or stand in front of an iconic painting, snap a selfie, and then are on their way. They don't take 10 seconds, let alone several minutes, to look with their own eyes, soak up the atmosphere, feel the depth of what they're experiencing. It's as if, now that they can post the photo that shows they were there, that's all that matters. Time to move on to the next selfie station. Instead of being in the moment, they're inhabiting social media. Everyday moments get lost as well. People so immersed in their phones they don't notice the rainbow above them. Teens sharing a pizza while too engaged with their phones to talk to each other. Tiny toddlers radiating such laughter and joy it would fill you with warmth and hope—if only you looked up to see it.

I wonder what it means for human societies now that so many of us are alone together. A hundred people may be in the same space, in the same moment, but they are apart. Each is in their own bubble, someplace else, through their phone.

What does it mean when "presence" has turned into "absence"?

Selfie Saturation

How Does Social Media Affect YOU?

It's pretty clear that social media use—especially compulsive, constant use—can invade and manipulate your psyche. It can do this with a sucker punch or slowly like emotional acid. Whether it will do YOU any harm is hard to predict. Non-stop comparing, ranking, and "grading" gets to some kids, causing negative emotions, but not to others. The 24/7 pressure to post and check and respond and make sure you're not "missing out" can cause imbalances in some teens' lives, but not others'.

Research offers some clues as to which teens are more likely to experience some of the emotional warning signs social media use can trigger:

- A study of eighth graders who spent 10 or more hours a week on social media found that they were much more likely to say they were unhappy than were peers who spent less time.

- The more invested teens are in social media, and the more important they say it is to them, the higher their reported levels of anxiety.

- While, in general, more teens see social media as something positive rather than negative in their lives, teens with *low* social and emotional well-being experience more negative effects from social media than do teens with *high* social and emotional well-being. Social and emotional well-being was assessed by measuring such attributes as loneliness, depression, happiness, confidence, self-esteem, and relationships with parents. In other words, the more unhappy, depressed, lonely, or insecure teens feel, the more likely they are to feel left out or excluded when using social media, to delete posts because they get too few "likes," and to feel bad about themselves if no one comments on or likes their posts.

When you think about these statistics during your free time, like when you're sitting on the toilet, keep in mind that a lot of the findings of social-psychological research are unclear, inconsistent, or open to debate.

> Farts. POOP. Toilets.

> I think you've got an issue.

> Thank you for noticing. I am blessed to have *many* issues.

This ambiguity is called causation versus correlation. I'll give you an example.

Let's say a study finds that the more time teens spend on social media the more likely they are to be depressed. That's a *correlation*: more time = more depression. Now, we might conclude that the *time* spent on social media is *causing* the depression. That would be *causation*. But making that conclusion could be wrong. Why? Because maybe it's not more time that is *causing* more depression, but that kids who are *already* depressed spend more time on social media (because they're depressed).

It's kind of a chicken-egg thing. Or maybe it's a chicken crossing the road thing? Let's see, if the more chickens cross the road, the more likely they are to be depressed, is crossing the road making them depressed, or are depressed chickens more likely in the first place to want to cross roads? And what do chickens have to be depressed about, anyway? Oh yeah. Chicken fricassee.

> **Maybe they're the grown-up chickens that got all those phone calls as eggs.**

So you have to be very careful when looking at correlations and research findings before making assumptions about what causes what.

Getting back to these teens with low social and emotional well-being who were more likely to experience negative emotions from social media: They also reported that social media made them feel *less* depressed or lonely. That suggests that some teens who don't feel good about themselves or their lives benefit from being on social media. You could picture a lonely, unhappy teen who goes online and connects with people, posts videos that people like, shows artwork, says funny things, and begins to feel more confident and liked. That might cross over and improve one's offline life, or at least make it feel more bearable.

You can see that research about teens and social media is all over the map. So, when you think about all the studies and variables and teens in the world and all the different ways they use social media and all the advances in technology and changes in culture—keep in mind that to say researchers know how social media will affect any particular teen (like you, for instance) is, to use the scientific term, idiotic.

So, if scientists don't know, and I don't know, how do *you* know? By being honest with yourself. Do some of the warning signs apply to you? Did you identify any concerns while filling out the challenges and gathering intel on your screen scene? Did you recognize yourself in some of the descriptions of negative effects of social media? If so, that's all you need to know. Forget the research. But do read the next tips and begin to think about pressing the reset button on your digital life. (You'll find out even more about how to do that in chapters 10 and 11.)

Tips for Practicing Safe Social Media

So, what's the key to protecting *your* psyche from social media?

FINDING BALANCE

The best way to make social media work for you, and not the other way around, is to find the sweet spot between . . .

> . . . being fake and being real
>
> . . . being public and being private
>
> . . . being visible and being anonymous
>
> . . . sharing accomplishments and showing off
>
> . . . liking "likes" and living for "likes"
>
> . . . expressing strong or controversial opinions and offending people you care about
>
> . . . wanting affirmation and being controlled by it
>
> . . . being thoughtful about what you post and thinking too much about what you post
>
> . . . sharing goofy, funny, or gross moments and scaring off a college or employer
>
> . . . trying on identities and leaving a cringeworthy trail you come to regret
>
> . . . being spontaneous or fun-loving and turning off future mentors or romantic partners
>
> . . . using social media to make deeper connections and using it to avoid them
>
> . . . using social media as a healthy escape and using it to avoid dealing with problems
>
> . . . using social media as a tool and becoming its tool.

Here are some ways to find *your* healthy balance.

Avoid Toxic Sites

If you ate something you absolutely hated that made you feel like puking, you wouldn't eat it again. (Unless you're a masochist.) Do the same thing with social media. If you use a certain platform, and you often or always feel worse after using it, don't use it anymore. It's really that simple. (If you *can't* stay away, that's a different issue, and you'll find tips in chapter 11 for how to dump a social media platform.)

> **How do you know if a site is toxic?**

Toxic platforms make you feel lousy. They may make you feel lousy about *yourself*. It might be the result of the pressures, comparisons, and rankings social media imposes on users, or you might feel guilty about how much time you spend (or waste) on it or ashamed about some of the things you do or say there.

Some platforms may make you feel lousy about *other people.* These platforms, often ones where people are anonymous, can be cesspools for humanity's worst impulses: cyberbullying and shaming; scoring people on looks and sexual behavior; making threats and rude, nasty comments; spewing racist, homophobic, divisive rants. On these apps and websites, you see ignorance, ugliness, and hatred. For some, such platforms may be a joke. They go there for a laugh. They can't believe what they're seeing. They may not even post. They're just lurkers. But if you keep visiting a site or using an app to see cruelty and caustic mental sewage, is that really how you want to spend your time?

It's hard to predict how a particular social media platform will affect somebody. What's a hoot to some is a horror to others. When it comes to cruelty, hatred, divisiveness, unkind comments, feelings of exclusion, pangs of jealousy, or "thumbs down" ratings, some teens can shrug them off while other teens are hurt to the core. Some laugh, others cry. Some couldn't care less, others are devastated.

Look at the apps quiz you filled out on page 37. Did you identify sites or apps that trigger negative feelings? That are a concern for you? If yes, they may be toxic for you, and you can choose to cut back or no longer use those apps. And if that seems impossible, you'll find strategies in chapter 11 to help you do it.

Develop a Thick(er) Skin

Big Tech's invasion of your psyche commandeers your emotions. If you watch a funny video, get a warm glow from a friend's Snap, or experience a shard of rage when you read a hateful comment, that's social media rummaging around inside your feelings.

Big Tech also gets inside your thoughts. Those thoughts can become a haranguing inner voice. It's like there's some nasty person with a bullhorn inside your head shouting: *"You're such a loser. What an idiot! Why can't you do better?"* This bully with a bullhorn predicts your future: *"You'll never graduate." "You'll never have any friends." "You'll never be popular."* The more you have certain thoughts, the more likely you are to continue to have them. The neural pathways those thoughts forge in your brain become "ruts," just like repeated rainfall creates ruts in a field.

Given that thoughts are self-reinforcing, we want them to be positive and life-affirming rather than negative and deflating. But there is a tendency, especially for teens, to gravitate toward negativity. Why? Because we are biologically primed to perceive our environment in terms of potential threats. That's why, if you sit down at a cafeteria table and two kids glance your way and laugh, you'll think they're laughing at you (even though it was about something else). That's why, if you don't get a response to a text, your mind, your "self-talk," immediately goes to the darkest, most judgmental places: They're ignoring you (rather than maybe just being busy); they've ghosted you (rather than their phone died). This tendency to think the worst is called *negative bias*. Evolutionarily speaking, it's safer to see a lion and believe it's getting ready to attack you (negative bias) than to assume it's just lying out in the sun to get a tan.

Do lions really tan?

No. But they do wear sunscreen. Just to be safe.

Social media is for people with thick skins, who can stand up to negative thoughts and feelings. It reveals who's in, who's out. Who went to what party. Who didn't. Every visit to Social Media Land lets you know, at least by other people's standards, whether you're cool or not, liked or not, attractive or not.

To a large extent, your ability to resist evaluating yourself based on the opinion of others reflects who you are in real life. If you're confident and feel good about yourself, you aren't likely to be brought down by the scrutiny and comparisons. While your psyche may register your social media "scores," you won't care (too much) one way or another. If you see friends promoting their "happy" lives, it won't make you like your life any less. You'll take their posts in stride—be they genuine or phony—with a smile. You're secure in your identity, so you're not going to be sucked into the "game" and superficialities of social media.

But what if your self-confidence isn't super-charged? What if your self-esteem isn't off the charts? What if jealousy, self-doubt, and regret creep unbidden into your consciousness? What if you *do* base your self-worth on what others think? Well, join the club. You're like many, many teens. (And adults.)

Some of how social media affects you has to do with your emotional pain tolerance. Think of physical pain tolerance. Doctors sometimes ask patients to rate their pain on a scale of 0 to 10, where "0" is no pain and "10" is unbearable, worst possible, makes-you-pass-out pain. It's not an objective rating since one person's "4" could be another person's "9." All it tells the doctor is how mild or excruciating the pain is from *that* patient's perspective.

I once knew somebody who never took novocaine when she went to the dentist. "But what about drilling? Isn't it painful?" I asked. "No," she said. "I just meditate." YIKES! I need novocaine just to *think* about going to the dentist. In fact, I once fainted in the dentist's office. But that's another story.

> Do tell.

> Sorry. That'll be for another book: "Tales from the Dental Frontier."

The same way people have different tolerances for physical pain, they have different tolerances for emotional pain. Fortunately, as your life experiences bolster your self-esteem, you will naturally develop more "emotional pain tolerance," as well as new perspectives that put social media in its proper place—a practical tool for you to use, rather than a manipulative force designed to invade your psyche. You can also increase your emotional pain tolerance by learning how to challenge negative thoughts and feelings. The key is to "thicken" your skin just enough to withstand the turbulent tumults of social media, but not so much that you lose your emotional openness and vulnerability. In order to experience joy, you have to be able to experience pain. Fortunately, by changing your thoughts, you can change your feelings. Here are some things you can do to resist negative thinking triggered by social media, and find greater truth, balance, and serenity.

Talk to yourself the way you'd talk to a good friend.
No matter what goes on in your life, you can ALWAYS have a kind, compassionate voice to buck you up, to be on your side. That voice is YOU. Talk to yourself the way you'd talk to a best friend. Be *your* best friend.

Let's say you posted a photo and nobody liked it. You're hurt and upset.

Now imagine that this had happened to a friend. What would you say to her? Talk to yourself with the same kindness you would extend to your friend. You can "self-talk" aloud or just in your head.

"That sucks. It's no fun feeling that way. You really wanted lots of likes. But, hey, it's just a photo. It's not a big deal. You don't have to let it bother you. Everyone feels this way from time to time. Just 'cause other people didn't like it, it doesn't mean it wasn't a great photo. You like it. That's what counts."

Have some positive, feel-good reminders handy.

For those times when negative self-talk runs wild, keep a stock of handy phrases in your head that calm you down and make you feel valued and loved. Phrases you'd like someone to whisper in your ear.

Sound hokey? Well, do the hokey. Do the hokey pokey. Nobody will hear or see you. This is just for you.

Keep a realistic perspective.

Counter that critical inner voice with a voice of reason. Don't torture yourself because you're not perfect. Nobody is. You have strengths and weaknesses, like all of us. And you have far more strengths than weaknesses. Remind yourself that social media, as a means to an end, can be fabulous. But much of what you see there paints a false reality that nobody can live up to.

Know that you're not alone.

Negative thought loops can make you feel alone. Like you're the only person who has these thoughts. Believing that can make you feel even worse. Like, "What's wrong with me for thinking this way?" "Why can't I stop these feelings?" "I'm such a loser."

It's normal to have those types of thoughts. But you are NOT the only person who rants at yourself once in a while. *Everyone* has negative feelings and makes critical judgments about themselves. Don't add to your self-dumping by believing that you're the only person who feels that way.

Drown out the negative noise.

The minute you feel yourself slipping into self-criticism, block the thoughts. Don't let the negativity ruts get deeper. Engage in full-strength counterprogramming: Sing a favorite song. Do 20 jumping jacks. Make a smoothie while pretending you're a TV chef doing a show. Put your books in alphabetical order by title. Count backwards from 100. Recite a poem 10 times in 10 different voices. Cluck like a chicken. Moo like a cow. Roll down a hill. The trick is to do something—anything—that will muffle your reproachful mental mutiny.

Challenge Distorted Thinking

Social media, with its relentless demands for putting yourself out there for all to see, acts like fertilizer, or should I say manure, for an anxiety garden. When your critical inner voice starts to behave like a runaway train, you can resist it by recognizing different types of distorted thinking and talking back to it. Here are some of the ways teens dump on themselves—along with some ways you can turn those negative thoughts into positive ones.

Distortion	Example	Negative Thinking	Positive Thinking
Worst-Case Thinking This is when your mind leaps to a single (worst-case) interpretation of an event, without considering all the possibilities.	You send your boyfriend a long, heartfelt message. His reply is brief and not what you hoped for.	"I can't believe he blew me off! What, he couldn't write more than two sentences??? Is he mad at me? What did I do wrong? Oh, gawd, I think he wants to break up with me."	"I hope everything's okay. Maybe he didn't have much time to reply. I did send a pretty long message. And he doesn't like writing. We've been getting along great. I have no reason to think he'd want to break up."

CONTINUED ›

Distortion	Example	Negative Thinking	Positive Thinking
Musturbating ✱ This is when you take reasonable desires—such as for love, money, success, fairness, friendship— and turn them into absolute "musts" and "shoulds." "I *must* be popular." "I *must* get likes." "People *should* respond to me right away." "The world *should* be fair."	You post a new video. You're waiting to see what the response is.	"I *have to* get likes." "Everybody *must* like it." "I *must* get more likes than Tasha." "No one has liked it yet—I should take it down."	"Take it easy. Maybe I'll get some likes, maybe I won't. I hope I'll get some, but it doesn't matter. It's just a video. I had fun shooting it. I'm not going to let myself be sucked into an insidious, super- ficial, Pavlovian, dopamine-hit system designed by greedy tech companies to addict me to their site." ✱ ✱
Awfulizing ✱ ✱ ✱ This is when you proj- ect the worst possible consequences of not having your "musts" met.	Somebody takes an unflattering pic of you asleep at a slumber party and posts it.	"HOW COULD SHE DO THAT?!? I look HORRIBLE!! I can't STAND it!!! If people see it, I'M GOING TO DIE! I won't have any friends anymore. I'm going to change schools."	"Okay. Deep breath. Calm down. That was not cool of Amira to post it. I'll tell her how I feel and ask her to take it down. I think she will. And if not, it's just me asleep and in a few days, everyone will move on and nobody will even remember the pic."
Self-Critical Comparing This is when you look at your friends' posts of their "incredible" and "happy" lives and feel inferior about yourself and your life. You forget that people are putting their "greatest hits" online, not their bloopers.	You look at Rami's Instagram and he's so smart and handsome and popular and great at sports and goes on cool vaca- tions and has the best clothes and the coolest bedroom and tons of friends.	"I HATE my life! I'm terrible at sports, I look terrible, my clothes are terrible, my room is terrible, I don't have any friends, nobody likes me, I don't go anywhere, everything I post is dumb, I never do anything exciting."	"That's not true. I do have some good friends. I'm good at track—I just don't like team sports. That's okay. I'm sure Rami has bad days and worries. I don't have to be like him. I can be me. I really don't care that much about clothes or having a cool room. There are other things I care about and am good at."

CONTINUED ›

Distortion	Example	Negative Thinking	Positive Thinking
Labeling Yourself This is when you condemn your entire being with a label that suggests nothing can ever change. The label keeps you stuck, preventing you from believing you can improve things.	You were in a bad mood and made some comments that maybe were a bit mean, so some people you thought were online friends blocked you; now they're saying nasty lies about you that people are starting to believe.	"How could I be so dumb? I'm so STUPID!!! What a LOSER! A total FAILURE! I can't do anything right. I deserve the lies they're telling. I'll never have any friends again. Nothing will ever change. I'm such an IDIOT!!!"	"Hang on. Yeah, I goofed up. I wish I could take those comments back. Marco didn't block me. I'll let him know how sorry I am and ask him to let the others know. Maybe that'll at least stop the lies. And if they don't take me back, I have other friends. I made a mistake, but I learned a valuable lesson."
Perfectionizing This is when, yup, you got it, your mind holds you to some ridiculously high standard that can never be achieved.	You post a photo of yourself after a basketball tournament.	"Oh no! I look so sweaty and gross. My knees are so knobby. The hoop in the background looks like horns are growing out of my head. What's that shadow? Makes me look like I have a snake wrapped around my leg." That actually sounds like a GREAT photo to me. I'd like it!	"I suppose I could have edited the photo, but I was about to join my teammates on the bus and I wanted to send it. Besides, I yam what I yam. I'm not going to waste time creating an air-brushed me. It's a happy photo and I look fine. If anybody gives me grief, I'll say I'm a *cinema verité* photographer. I seek artistic truth and reject artificiality."

* The idea that feelings are caused more by our *thoughts* about life rather than by life itself is at the heart of a method of psychotherapy developed by Albert Ellis called Rational Emotive Behavior Therapy. He coined the term *musturbating*.

** You can tell this teen read chapter 7 on how tech companies design their social media platforms.

*** Albert Ellis also came up with *awfulizing*.

The problem with distorted thinking is that our "musts" can never be fully satisfied. The world doesn't work that way. So, we are in a perpetual state of having unmet desires (musturbating), and fearing terrible consequences if we don't get what we want ("awfulizing"). This causes stress, anger, and worry. And because most of us tend to think the worst about ourselves—or have a negative bias—we conclude that we're at fault. Something must be wrong with us for not having our (irrational) wishes met. So, it's a triple whammy where we are: 1) plagued by unrealistic expectations; 2) stressed by predictions of dire consequences when our "musts" are not met; and 3) mad at ourselves for being dumb and worthless, and mad at the world for being cruel and unfair.

But if you practice recognizing those distorted thoughts and turning them into more helpful, realistic, positive thoughts, you will get better at it. You can do that by protecting yourself from STDs.

> STDs? Wait—what—huh??

You heard that right. STDs (Self-defeating Thought Distortions) are all those types of distorted thinking you just read about on the table on pages 226–228. They are invisible enemies, ready to infect you the moment you let down your guard. But you can protect yourself. When a particular negative thought appears, whether it's perfectionizing, labeling, comparing, or awfulizing, submit it to your mind lab for analysis. This will lead to the best treatment plan. You can use the form on page 230 to run the necessary tests. Here's an example of how someone might fill out the form:

Protecting Yourself from STDs (Self-Defeating Thought Distortions)

Identify the negative thought. (Isolate and record the distorted thinking so you can examine it.)
I'm a total failure.

Identify the nature of the distortion (such as awfulizing or perfectionizing).
Labeling myself. Worst-case thinking. Jumping to an extreme conclusion.

Check for emotional symptoms.
Makes me feel depressed. Ashamed. Hopeless.

Check for truth. Scan for reality. (Is there any factual basis for accepting or disputing the thought?)
I'm not a TOTAL failure. Maybe just a partial failure. Sometimes I fail at things.

Treat the thought distortion with a strong dose of positivity.

Just because I don't always succeed the way I want, that doesn't make ME a failure. Making mistakes doesn't mean I'm a mistake. I'm good at some things like soccer and science and helping my dad. And I do have some friends who wouldn't hang out with me if I were a total failure.

Test for triggers.

Instagram. When I see all the cool things people are doing.

Preventive steps I can take in the future to avoid STDs.
Don't go to Instagram. Use other apps. Use positive thinking.

Now, give it a try yourself. This form is also available for download at freespirit .com/dragons.

Protecting Yourself from STDs (Self-Defeating Thought Distortions)

Identify the negative thought. (Isolate and record the distorted thinking so you can examine it.)

Identify the nature of the distortion (such as awfulizing or perfectionizing).

Check for emotional symptoms.

Check for truth. Scan for reality. (Is there any factual basis for accepting or disputing the thought?)

Treat the thought distortion with a strong dose of positivity.

CONTINUED ›

Test for triggers.

Preventive steps I can take in the future to avoid STDs.

TALES FROM THE NON-DIGITAL FRONTIER

Negative thinking. I can relate. Whenever I get stuck in a loop of anger, negative thinking, or self-pity, I say, "Alex, don't listen to that voice. You know it's not true. Count your blessings." And then I go through an exercise in my head, thinking of my various good fortunes and reminding myself how lucky I am that I am not a refugee living in a war zone, or sick or persecuted or homeless or hungry or suffering from any number of other afflictions. At the end of this attitude adjustment, I have a new outlook on my life. I am able to find and maintain a more mature perspective and feel better. (For at least 30 seconds before I slip back into my default anger or self-pity.)

So I know it can be difficult when your mind is telling you one thing and your emotions are telling you another. But social media is an emotional arena, not an intellectual one. That's why its hold on your psyche is so strong—and devilish. Social media—interacting with other people—pushes more buttons and triggers more feelings than anything else you can do online. I mean, I don't think looking up the capital of Slovenia for your history paper has the same emotional impact.

When the negative thought loops go round and round, challenge them with positive thinking. Question your assumptions. Look for facts. Seek truth. Recognize the distortions in your thinking.

Remember, negative thinking is self-reinforcing. It creates ruts in your brain which get deeper with every negative thought. Soon, negative thinking becomes your mind's default state. The thoughts just pop into your head without any trigger. That's the bad news. The good news is that positive thinking is equally self-reinforcing.

Give yourself a values tune-up.

Social media can distort what's important in life. It's so easy to get drawn into the 24/7 online amusement park of never-ending thrills, laughs, dramas, and feeds. Social media can seem like it *is* your life. To keep a healthy balance between social media and what kind of person you want to be, check in with your values. Are they in harmony with how you use social media? Ask yourself:

- What is most important to me in life?
- What makes me happiest?
- What kind of a person do I want to be?
- What do I like most about myself?
- What traits would I like to acquire more of?
- What impact would I like to have in the world?
- If I have children, what kind of people would I like them to grow up to be?
- What three words do I hope people would use to describe me?
- Who best supports me in becoming the person I'd like to be?
- Who thwarts me from becoming the person I'd like to be?
- What best supports me in becoming the person I'd like to be?
- What thwarts me from becoming the person I'd like to be?
- What do I value most about the people I admire?

Okay. Did you ask yourself the questions?

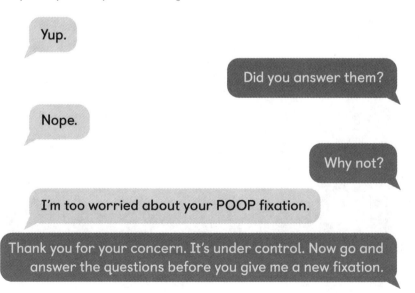

Yup.

Did you answer them?

Nope.

Why not?

I'm too worried about your POOP fixation.

Thank you for your concern. It's under control. Now go and answer the questions before you give me a new fixation.

Many of these questions require deep thinking. But remember, it's the *examined* life that's worth living.

After you've gotten in touch with your core values—your *psyche*—ask yourself one last question:

How does my use of social media nourish or hinder living according to my values?

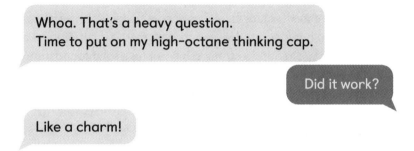

> Whoa. That's a heavy question.
> Time to put on my high-octane thinking cap.

> Did it work?

> Like a charm!

Let it go.

When negative thoughts just won't go away, imagine you're holding a balloon. Place the negative thought—the anger, the regret, the harsh self-criticism—in the balloon. Let it go. Watch it float away, higher and higher into the sky, getting smaller and smaller, until it's a tiny dot, until it disappears.

But WAIT!

Before you put the thought in a balloon, check to see if your inner voice is telling you something you *should* hear. You don't want to throw the baby out with the thought water. While our thoughts can bully us, they can also provide sound advice. Maybe you did do something "dumb." Maybe you did hurt a friend's feelings or disappoint a parent. Maybe you did blow off studying for a test. In cases such as these, "self-critical" thoughts can serve a valuable purpose. You can learn from them and follow your own advice to do better in the future.

It's a bit of a cliché (but clichés are often clichés *because* they contain at least a little bit of truth) that mistakes are the best teachers we have. So, you don't want to ignore critical thoughts you have after posting something hurtful, making a mistake, or failing to achieve a goal. Your inner voice, as long as it addresses you politely, may be worth listening to. It may be guiding you toward becoming a better person.

Try this: Before you let a thought go, examine it for anything useful. Is there a valuable lesson to learn? Maybe something not to do again? Something you might try in the future? Something you can change in yourself? If so, grab the value out of the thought, and then, with kindness, tell yourself what you want to take away from the experience.

And now . . . let it go.

Don't base your self-worth on the opinions of others.

The problem with social media's judgmental essence is that your sense of worth is not coming from inside you but is controlled by outside forces. It is conditional on what others think. It's like trying to build a strong cabin not on a solid foundation but on shifting, changing blocks that other people keep giving you and taking away from you.

I once asked teens what they do to keep their mind on their side (and I included their answers in my book *How Rude!*). Here are some of the ways they tell their mind to shape up and stop dumping on them:

"I compliment myself."

"I value myself for who I am."

"I encourage myself."

"I respect myself."

"I meditate."

"I set aside time to relax and think."

"I keep my confidence and self-esteem high."

"I judge myself fairly."

"I try to be calm and take things step-by-step, because if I do things in a hurry I'll mess up."

"I try not to swear in my thoughts."

"I think positive."

"I try not to believe in things I know aren't true (about me)."

"I avoid putting myself down."

"I love myself."

"I smile at myself in the mirror."

Say No Mo' to FOMO

So much of the pressure of being on social media comes from the feeling that you'll miss out on something if you're not constantly checking your phone. Here's the truth: You WILL. Absolutely, if you don't check for an hour, an afternoon, a day, or a week, there will be posts, tweets, updates, gossip, photos, and all sorts of social media confetti that you won't see. Social media content can come in so fast and furiously that, if you don't check for a day or two, you'll be overwhelmed if you try to go back and catch up on everything you missed.

The question is: Did you miss anything *important*? Anything that in a few hours, days, or weeks will have any meaningful impact?

When **REALLY** important things happen, you'll learn about them in other ways. You can decide where your most comfortable balance is between feeling the pressure to be in the know as quickly as possible, and feeling the freedom to focus your attention on other people and activities. You can choose to resist FOMO.

Scoop the POOP

Preoccupation Over Online Posting is a close cousin to FOMO. FOMO has to do with other people's messages and posts. POOP has to do with your own. They're both stressful. POOP is the pressure to be visible, to respond quickly. You have to constantly be producing "content."

Think about the things you post; how you engage with your various social media accounts. Do you mainly respond to other people's posts? Do you post because you have something you really want to express? Or do you do it because you're full of POOP and feel pressured to respond to everything and put things out there for others to see?

To turn POOP into POP (Positive Online Posting), keep the following do's and don'ts in mind.

Do share what is uniquely you.

People appreciate seeing and hearing the things that make you special. Your talents, music, art, and stories; your wry, twisted sense of humor; your insightful commentary on current events; your accomplishments and interesting activities.

Don't be a drama llama.

Life is emotional. Teenage life is emotions on steroids. There's no end of social drama. And why should there be? Social life is the lifeblood of, well, life. Hopes, joys, dreams, desires, love, longing, jealousy, and betrayal are driving forces of humanity's greatest creations and worst evils. I'm not against drama. I'm just saying there's a time and place for it. And, generally speaking, that's not social media. Certainly not *public* social media. Feuds, arguments, and torrents of torments are best handled in private. Think of overpowering emotions as you would dirty laundry. Perfectly normal and natural, but not something to display to the world.

Do disable "likes."

Some apps allow you to hide or disable their little dopamine hits. You may also be able to choose who gets to see them. As more and more teens resist the creepy clutches tech companies use to keep them glued to their sites, you can expect to see greater privacy controls. The best thing to do is to explore the privacy setting of any apps whose "rewards" you'd like to shut down or hide. You can also find instructions for changing your settings by running a search with the app's name and what you want to do, such as "Instagram hide likes."

Don't share personal details about others.

You may learn that a friend's parents are getting divorced or that somebody lost their job or won the lottery or was diagnosed with cancer. Whether and to whom to disclose it is for them to decide, and nobody else.

Do match content to the right platform and device.

When you want to share something, you have many options. You can Snap it, tweet it, text it, post it on a public or private account, and on and on. Much of this you do automatically, the result of habit or a gut sense of where it belongs. Sometimes, though, you may need to be more deliberate about which platform is best for conveying certain information, especially if it is dramatic, personal, embarrassing, raunchy, or potentially upsetting. Your friends, followers, group recipients, and contact lists vary from platform to platform, so take a moment to be sure that your post or message is appropriate for all recipients, from your grandparents to your teammates.

For some content, social media—and indeed all digital communication—should be avoided if at all possible. The more serious, emotional, or confrontational an issue, the less appropriate it is for digital dissemination. Use in-person communication. If that isn't possible—say, you're not in the same city—next best would be a phone call. Sometimes, like in an emergency, it might be necessary to send a text if you can't reach somebody right away. But if you do, recognize that for things like news of deaths, tragedies, illnesses, hardships, or family or relational upheavals, the brevity and impersonality of a text is something to avoid whenever possible.

Don't flood people with links.

People are busy. There are only so many cute dogs, skateboard wipeouts, music videos, and funny memes a person can consume per day. Be selective.

Do get permission.

Let's say you want to forward, retweet, or otherwise share a photo, post, or message sent to you privately. Or maybe you want to tag somebody. With your closest friends, you may already have an understanding about the boundaries for that sort of thing. But, unless you're sure, better to be safe than sorry. Take the few seconds needed to check that they're okay with it.

Don't be unkind.

I know you're not going to be cyberbullying anyone or putting out hate-filled screeds on your social media accounts. But sometimes, a hasty reply or post or something said in the heat of the moment can come across, intentionally or not, as nasty, hurtfully sarcastic, and unkind. Before you hit "send" or post anything, ask yourself: Will it hurt someone's feelings? Will it embarrass, betray, or anger anyone? Will it reveal a secret? Will it get somebody in trouble? If yes, then, NO. Don't post it. Make your social media presence infuse the online ether with the sweet fragrance of spring, the freshness of an ocean breeze, and not the dank stench of an open sewer.

Do aim for quality over quantity.

Some people's social media activity is like water pouring out of an open faucet. It never ends. It's a gushing torrent of "Yoo-hoo, it's me. I'm here."

👤 Ugh. Hard-boiled eggs again. #eggs #breakfast

👤 Math test today. #gofigure

👤 Late for school bus. #dog #ate #alarm #clock

👤 Snug in my knit cap. #thanks #grandma

👤 Another rainy day. #rain

While we're all glad you're here, you don't need to remind us quite so frequently. Even if we don't hear from you for an hour, we know you still exist. We all have object permanence. Be known for the quality, rather than the quantity, of your posts. When people see you turn up in their feed, their reaction should be, "Oh boy, another tasty treat from Trish," and not, "I'm so stuffed, I can't eat another bite."

Bonus Tip: Remember, it's not just how *much* you share. It's also the nature of *what* you share. TMI (Too Much Information) can make people uncomfortable. They don't need or want to know that you had another argument with your dad or threw up all night.

Don't let anonymity change who you are.

You may have some accounts where you're amonymous, er, anomynous, er— ANONYMOUS! There's a freedom in being able to express yourself without having your posts linked to "the real you." Personal anonymity can be beneficial on sites where you ask questions, seek help, find support, or deal with certain issues; where you participate in interesting debates without worrying about your ideas being traced to you; where you can be more jokey, risqué, uncensored, or direct than what you'd put up on your public posts; or where you can try on and have fun with playful identities to see how they fit. There's nothing wrong with that.

But some people take anonymity as permission to be their worst self. They can be racist, xenophobic, homophobic, and/or sexist. They taunt, troll, and trash. They show their hatred and scorn for women, gay people, trans people, Muslims, Jews, Black people, immigrants, people with disabilities—you name it. Some trolls truly embrace their bigotry and caustic beliefs. Others are just in it for the "fun" of causing pain and getting a rise out of others. They enjoy igniting flame wars. Whether trolls believe what they're saying or not, the hateful, hurtful language is still out there, causing harm and poisoning discourse. And, yes, they'll likely get away with it. That doesn't mean it's cool to do these things. Don't use anonymity to say, do, or be things that go against your values or that would get you in deep trouble if you were identified. And remember that even if your poison is aimed at somebody else, it has to flow through you first. Make sure you never allow any poison to flow through you. **＊**

＊ Keep in mind that anonymity is not impenetrable. If posts threaten violence (like a school shooting or bomb threat) or reveal a suicide plan or an intention to commit a crime, someone may report them. Authorities would then be able to compel the website or app to reveal information that could track the person down.

Do make people smile.

Dullness and downers run rampant on social media. Trivia and trolling are constant
background noises. There's overposting and underthinking. Bad news and badder
news. Repetition and regurgitation. Algorithms blasting content designed to enrage
and divide. What's harder to find are posts that brighten your day, put a bounce in
your step. Share things that will make people smile.

Others Viewing Your Posts

Don't be a rumor tumor.

Lots of rumors get passed around via social media. The lines between news,
rumors, and gossip can be blurry at times. But I think you have excellent eyesight.
You can tell the difference between responsible news sharing and careless libel.
Rumors and false accusations can cause great harm. People see them and spread
them. Later, when it's discovered they're untrue, the damage is already done. You
can see this in the public forum of politics. If lies are repeated often enough, huge
proportions of the population will believe them, even when they are provably false.

Do get help.

If your psyche is really hurting, if thoughts and feelings are causing distress, affecting relationships, or interfering with your ability to function, reach out to somebody you trust—a friend, parent, counselor, coach. They can serve as a sounding
board, offer advice, provide comfort, and/or point you toward further resources
and support. The worst pains and problems are the ones you may feel compelled
to keep to yourself. Share them. You won't be burdening anybody. You'll be giving
them a gift—your trust.

When are you most authentic, most like yourself?

On social media?

Having dinner with your family?

Playing sports?

Late at night talking with a friend who's sleeping over?

How do you define "the real you"?

What is the difference between being phony and being playful? Being phony and pretending? Being phony and trying on identities?

Are you more authentic when you can be anonymous, or less?

Do likes and shares influence you to post what gets the best response, rather than be who you are?

Do you ever feel like you're keeping up a façade on social media?

If social media disappeared, how would you feel? How would your life change?

Keeping up a façade takes energy. Feeling you have to be fake is stressful. It's fine to be a playful extension of yourself online. Being a "different you" online than in real life doesn't mean you're being fake any more than being aggressive in a football game when you wouldn't be that way in a classroom means you're being fake. You adapt to different environments.

But if being anonymous is the only way you feel comfortable being the real you and expressing yourself honestly, it's worth asking yourself why.

Give Yourself Lots of Likes

Social media can be great, terrible, amazing, devastating. Some teens thrive, some get hurt. Some can take it or leave it, others get sucked in. There's no way of telling for any particular teen whether it's going to become a wonderful addition or a woeful addiction. The only person who can tell if it's a positive or a negative in *your* life is *you*.

The best way to protect your psyche is to know it. Understand it. Cherish it. Know your values and limits. Know what pushes your buttons. Know what energizes you and what weakens you.

By knowing who YOU are, and how the complex and unique machinery of your soul, spirit, emotions, and mind work, you can preserve and protect your online and offline identities and integrity. You may modify your identity a bit online. You may emphasize some aspects of your self and your life and de-emphasize others. You may give expression to some thoughts and feelings and not others. This can be a sign of mature social skills and empathy—just as you might modify your behavior, dress, and language for a job interview, visiting a parent's place of work, attending a funeral, or going out to eat with your grandparents.

The key, though, is that any editing of your self should be in service of your health and happiness. Your psyche. Without losing your compassion, empathy, kindness, and concern for others, look out for your own best interests. *Protect* your psyche. Don't let yourself be contorted or molded into something you're not. Social media should serve YOU. You should not serve IT.

That's deep.

Self-doubt is paralyzing. Self-kindness is empowering.

Just because you have a thought, it doesn't mean it's true.

Most of the things you worry about will never come to pass.

If you believe everybody is thinking about you—what you said or did or posted—they're not. They're too busy worrying about what they said or did or posted.

Now, if you absent-mindedly showed up at school without any clothes or won a worldwide talent show, I admit, they might be thinking about you for a bit longer. But don't worry. Soon enough, someone will throw up in the cafeteria or wipe out in the hallway, and your escapades will be forgotten.

CHAPTER 9

PROTECT YOUR LIFE BALANCE

How Big Tech Hijacks Your Attention, Your Autonomy, and Your Time

Life balance means maintaining healthy proportions between the various activities, events, and elements of your life—online/offline; family/friends; work/play; solitary/social; physical/mental; salt/pepper. "Balance" is important because it keeps people and machinery running in optimal condition. Too hot, too cold, too stressed, too lonely, too much oil, too many red blood cells—when systems, whether human or mechanical, get out of balance, that's when trouble occurs. If you lose your balance on your bike—CRASH. If you lose your balance in a canoe—SPLASH. If you lose your balance in a relationship—CLASH. I don't want to get too cosmic on you, but balance is an essential force of life, nature, movement, physics. It applies to everything and everyone. Seesaws. Airplanes. Athletes and dancers. Surfers and skateboarders. We're in a climate crisis because we've let elements in our environment and atmosphere get out of balance. When you're sick, your body is out of balance. In school there needs to be a balance of critical feedback and encouragement. In a job there needs to be a balance of challenge and reward. In relationships, there needs to be a balance of needs, roles, and responsibilities. I bet you can't think of anything where balance doesn't come into play.

A rock.

Try carrying that rock without it being aligned with your body.

A tree.

If you don't want it crashing through your roof, it better not be leaning too far to one side.

An ice cream sundae.

The hot fudge has to be in perfect proportion with the number of scoops and the whipped cream can't be falling off the side and the nuts need to be sprinkled evenly for aesthetic perfection and the—

I'm just messing with you, man. I get the point.

Life balance is threatened once any element crowds out, for a sustained period of time, other essential elements.

Fortunately, human software and hardware have a great deal of built-in resilience. For example, let's say you're a parent who has to put in 18-hour workdays to complete an important project (like, say, creating a vaccine). That will surely imbalance your life. During that period, your relationships will suffer, and you won't be able to exercise or enjoy hobbies or tuck your kids into bed. You may have to skip meals, cancel plans, postpone other projects. But if it's a temporary imbalance, and if you discuss your shift in priorities with anybody who will be affected, explain the reasons for and value of the imbalance, and take steps to minimize any negative consequences, you and the people and things you care about should come out on the other side in good shape. You may even look back upon that period with pride and appreciation.

By the same token, let's say somebody (certainly not *you*) spends from 5:00 p.m. to midnight every day after work going to bars to drink. By the time he gets home, he's drunk, and his family is asleep. Obviously, this sort of imbalance will cause serious problems for his health, family relationships, job, finances, and future.

So, imbalance can be a tricky thing. It's not all or nothing. (And being suspicious of "all-or-nothing" thinking is a good trait to have.) Some types of life imbalance can be devastating; others can be empowering. Some can cause permanent damage; others can cause little or no damage. Some destroy; some create. We'll look at this more deeply later in this chapter. But for now . . .

Here's a quick quiz. There are thirteen statements. (Hmmm, is that bad luck?) If the statement applies to you more often than not, put a check mark in the "YUP" box. If it really doesn't describe you at all, check the "NOPE" box. And if it sometimes applies, or you don't want to commit, or you're totally indecisive today, or it's really "YUP" but you're not yet ready to admit it, check "MEH."

This quiz is also available for download at freespirit.com/dragons.

Life Balance Quiz

	YUP *Sounds Like Me*	MEH *Kinda, Yeah, No, Oh, I Dunno*	NOPE *Not Me at All*
When I'm offline I can't wait to get back online.			
I keep spending more and more time online.			
I've tried to cut back on screen time but haven't been able to.			
When I'm bored I grab my phone.			
I use my phone even when I know it's unsafe or against the rules.			
When I see or hear a notification, I check right away even if it interrupts something else.			
I keep using my phone even though I know it causes problems for me.			
People I care about have expressed concerns about my phone use.			
I have posted, shared, or bought things online impulsively.			
I'm secretive about my online time.			
I wish I could spend less time online.			
When I'm offline I think about what I'm missing.			
I feel like being online—or *not* being online—is a major factor in my moods.			

Add up how many "Yups," "Mehs" and "Nopes" you have. This will give you your "Yumenopes Score" (a famous diagnostic measurement instrument).

Signs That Screen Time May Be Affecting Your Life Balance

If you're solidly in the "Nopes" camp (and you're not in denial), it's likely that you're the master of your phone. If you're mainly "Meh," you're either feeling very wishy-washy today or you're teetering atop the fence of life balance. It could go either way over time, but if you take steps now (see more about this in chapters 10 and 11), you can tell your phone that you're the boss and to stop bugging you! And if you have a *bunch* (I'm using the scientific term, here) of "Yups," your life balance may be *out of whack* (another scientific term) due to excessive screen time.

Here are some warning signs suggesting digital life-balance "out-of-whack-i-tudity":

 You Have a Wonderful Feeling of Well-Being or Euphoria While on Your Devices—and Feel the Opposite Afterward.
You get lost in whatever you're doing. Adrenaline flows, you're on top of the world. Worries vanish. Problems hibernate. Deadlines and demands disappear. It's as if you're in a safe zone. When you separate from your phone, the high continues—but only for a short time. Soon, without your device, you feel empty, depressed, and irritable.

 You Constantly Think About Being Online.
When you're not online, *not being online* is all you can think about. You wonder what you're missing. You want to check your feeds, Snap your friends. You can't wait to get back to your video game. And even when you can't use your phone, you check it constantly. Sneak a peek. Just to see. It's as if your phone speaks to you from your purse, your pocket, your backpack. "Hey. Hey, you. Check me. NOW."

 Your Screen Time Keeps Increasing.
You crave more time. It never seems to be enough. You spend way more time online than you used to. Sometimes you think you're addicted to your phone. You've tried to cut back but weren't able to. You can't imagine life without your phone, but you also can't imagine things continuing the way they are now that your screen time has taken over your life. You feel trapped.

You Do Things Online That You Know Are Against Your Values or Best Interests. But you don't seem able to change. Which makes you feel guilty. So you keep dumping on yourself. You've started lying to others about your use. Hiding what you do. Deleting your browser history. You're ashamed of some of your online activities, the sites you go to, the things you say and search for. It's like you become a different person when you get behind the wheel of your device.

 You Neglect Your Family and Friends and Responsibilities. You used to enjoy spending time with your family. You used to shoot hoops with your dad, play catch with your sister. You used to invite friends to your house and go exploring with them. You used to play on school teams and join after-school activities. Now, your mom is constantly after you about your room and chores and cleaning up after yourself. But you just want to stay in your room and go online. You wish everybody would just leave you alone.

 You Keep Using Your Phone Despite Negative Consequences. Your schoolwork has suffered. Your teachers are on your back. You may lose your afterschool job if your boss catches you on your phone one more time. You get into arguments with your dad about screen time. Some of your friends have dropped you because you're no longer "there" for them. It's all bumming you out. You get angry and depressed about it. You wish things would change, but you don't see how they will. That makes you feel hopeless.

 You Have Unhealthy Physical Symptoms and Personal Habits. You frequently have dry eyes and headaches. Your back, neck, shoulders, fingers, and/or wrists ache. You eat tons of junk food and sometimes skip meals entirely. You've gained or lost a lot of weight. You stay up too late and sometimes even use your phone during the night. You never get enough sleep and feel tired all day. Your personal hygiene gets a failing grade. Physically, you're a mess.

These are all signs of possible smartphone addiction.

I debated whether to use the word *addiction* in this book. It's a powerful and controversial term with lots of associations. People hear it and think of heroin, opioids, cigarettes, and alcohol. Many experts in the field of addiction and substance abuse prevention prefer *use*, *abuse*, and *dependency* when referring to the continuum of a person's possible relationship to substances and/or behaviors.

Some social researchers even question the premise that teens can be "addicted" to devices, arguing that the passionate way teens use their phones simply reflects healthy priorities and developmental tasks that have always been typical of adolescence. These include bonding with friends (social media), connecting with others (multi-player gaming, chat rooms), exploring identity and sexuality (creating avatars, role-playing, posting photos, making videos, sexting, viewing pornography), and separating from parents (inhabiting private online worlds removed from adult supervision). To these researchers, adults who freak out over teens being "addicted" to their devices are no different than moralistic adults in the past who predicted doom for teens who were "addicted" to rock and roll, comic books, TV, hanging out at the mall, or talking for hours at night with friends, tying up the one landline in the house so nobody else could make or receive calls.

I don't want to get into an argument over whether *addiction* can be applied to something like screen use. (I firmly believe it can.) What ultimately made me decide to use the term and concept of addiction here is that teens recognize it. A survey conducted by Common Sense Media revealed that 39 percent of teens say they "feel addicted" to their mobile devices. Imagine that! Thirty-nine teens out of 100, also known as 19.5 teens out of 50! I figured, if so many teens themselves say they "feel addicted," it's not going to stir up any trouble to use that word. In another survey that didn't use the "a-word," but asked teens if they believe they spend too much time on their cell phone, over half (54 percent) said yes. So teens recognize a problem, whether it's called *addiction*, *abuse*, *dependence*, *problematic use*, or *too much time*.

Even more teens, roughly nine out of ten, see too much screen time as a problem for people their age. Sixty percent say it is a *major* problem. And, in what I see as an encouraging sign, over half of all teens (52 percent) have cut back on the time they spend on their phone, with video games and social media remaining the biggest attention thieves. So, wherever you fall along the continuum from "healthy use" to "smartphone itchy-itis," you have lots of company.

> Smartphone itchy-it is? Is there, like, a cream you can get for that?

> There is. It's called cortiphone.

Why Screens, Devices, and the Internet Are Addictive

When we think of addiction, it's typically about substances: alcohol, tobacco, caffeine, cocaine, and other drugs. But people can also be addicted to behaviors such as gambling, eating, sex, work, jogging, and, yes, screen time and technology.

To cut through all the controversy, here's my definition of "addiction" for you to think about:

The psychological and/or physical inability to stop compulsive behaviors despite harmful consequences.

So, it doesn't matter whether the behavior is drinking, cigarette smoking, watching TV, gambling, gaming, using social media, or building superhero models out of sugar cubes. If you keep doing it, and are unable to stop doing it, even though it's causing harm to you (or others), it's an addiction.

> **Yeah, but don't addictions have withdrawal symptoms?**

Many addictions have physical withdrawal symptoms such as shaking, sweating, and vomiting, or having tremors, headaches, insomnia, heart palpitations, or seizures. But withdrawal can also take the form of anxiety, depression, anger, irritability, agitation, mood swings, and FOMO. Many teens say they experience these responses if they are separated from their phones for any length of time. And since these symptoms, which you might call emotional or psychological, involve your brain, nervous system, and chemicals in your body, I consider them physical as well. So as far as I'm concerned, the distinction between physical and psychological doesn't amount to a hill of caffeine-copious coffee beans.

TALES FROM THE NON-DIGITAL FRONTIER

My name is Alex, and I am an ice creamaholic.

If I have it in my house, it calls to me from the freezer. "Yoo-hoo, it's me, Chocolate Chip Cookie Dough. I know you're craving me. I know you're salivating. I know you can't get me out of your head. What are you waiting for? Just a little taste. So sweet. So soft. Just a spoonful, and then you can put me back. I promise!"

I can't resist. I pull out three or four huge containers of different

The Author When He Was an Active Ice Creamaholic

flavors, take off the lids, and start eating. I don't even bother to put it in a bowl. What's the point? I know I'd just keep refilling the bowl. Once I start, I can't stop.

I *also* know there are people who can have a small amount, say, "Yum, yum," and put it away until next time. Like my sister. She could nurse a pint of Rocky Road for three weeks. Not me. Even if I'm getting brain freeze, even if I've had a gallon, even if I feel my stomach bloating to the size of a watermelon about to explode, I can't stop.

So, the only solution for me is to avoid all ice cream. I know that might sound like a penalty worse than death, but it is much easier for me to have none than to try to have just a little. I thought about going to Ice Creamaholics Anonymous, but, fortunately, I was able to go cold turkey on my own, and it's been many years since ice cream has entered my house. Or stomach. (Hmmm, cold turkey and cranberry ice cream. That sounds good!)

> Way to go, dude. I'm proud of ya.

What's Bad About Screen Addiction

Different addictions pose different threats to your health and well-being. As long as you don't take your eyes off the road, driving while consuming your sixth diet soda of the morning is not as big a physical threat to your safety and that of others as driving drunk. Smoking three packs of cigarettes a day is far more dangerous an addiction than having 60 breath mints a day. (As long as they don't eventually discover that breath mints cause your brain to leak out your ears.)

The effects of any particular addiction can be measured in terms of its impact on your:

- Physical health (both short- and long-term)
- Family health (levels of conflict, quality of relationships)
- Psychological health (confidence, self-image, self-talk, coping skills, sexuality)
- Emotional health (mood, levels of stress, depression)
- Cognitive health (ability to focus, think deeply, complete tasks, retain information)
- Social health (quality of friendships, sense of belonging, social skills)
- Future well-being (impact on life options, school and job performance, career choices, legal jeopardy)

The potential risk of any addiction, therefore, can be assessed by asking a number of questions:

- Which health domains (physical, emotional, social) are most vulnerable to harm?
- What is the range of severity of possible consequences (e.g., headache, cancer, overdose, death)?
- How reversible or permanent could any harm be?
- Are certain demographics (such as age, race, gender, economic level) at greater risk of developing this addiction?
- How much harm might a particular addiction cause to others?

If you think of various addictions in this context, it becomes clearer what risks they pose and what negative consequences they can cause. Some substances, such as wine or coffee, in moderate amounts, can be pleasurable and may even be beneficial to your health. But an *addiction* to alcohol could lead to serious damage in every single health domain and could even result in death. An *addiction* to coffee might pose physical risks (anxiety, insomnia, heartburn) or cognitive risks (you forget how to say "small," "medium," and "large"), but is unlikely to harm your family relationships or get you in trouble with the law (unless you start dashing out of cafés without paying for your latte).

An addiction to technology, video gaming, or social media, while unlikely to cause death (although there have been instances of people dying from blood clots from sitting too long and from taking dangerous selfies), could put one's physical, family, psychological, emotional, cognitive, and social health at risk.

Why would these devices be addictive? They're just "things." Tools. A collection of parts. You can name them:

- CPU
- GPU
- PU
- RAM
- EWE
- Motherboard
- Fatherboard
- Optical Drive (DVD, RW, LOL)
- Storage Device (SSD, HDD, STD)
- Monitor

- Keyboard
- Mouse
- Squirrel

I could go on, but I don't want to show off. The point is, the addictive pull of these devices doesn't come from their hardware. I mean, I've never heard of anyone snorting a video card or chug-a-lugging a trackpad. No, the addictive behavior is triggered by some of the things you *do* on your devices. So why would certain uses lead to addiction?

Because . . .

Tech Companies Design Their Products to Be Addictive

Let that sink in. Companies that create online games, social media platforms, shopping sites, entertainment streaming services—you name it—intentionally design their sites, platforms, and products to keep you watching, playing, posting, and buying. Nothing you interact with online happens by accident. It's not as though algorithms, lines of code, and eye-popping images just happened to wander by when those sites and pages were being put together and snuck in while the designer took a bathroom break.

No, addicting the user is a *goal* of these sites and platforms. And if that seems like a harsh thing to say, I will say it more gently: Given that profit is the motivating force behind most businesses (including online ones), making money requires them to constantly increase viewership, clicks, attention, consumer spending, and advertising revenue. That means they have to get you to visit as often as possible for as long as possible, they have to make you believe their site is essential to your life, they have to sink their claws into your psyche. And that means they have to get you addicted.

There, was that gentler?

You may not have heard of Sean Parker. But you have heard of Facebook. Sean Parker was the founding president of Facebook and became a billionaire "insider" of the tech world. One of the emperors of the empire. What's interesting is that he left Facebook and turned into what he calls "something of a conscientious objector" about social media. Listen to what he said in an interview with Axios:

When Facebook was getting going, I had these people who would come up to me and they would say, "I'm not on social media." And I would say . . . "You will be." And then they would say, "No, no, no. I value my real-life inter- actions. I value the moment. I value presence. I value intimacy." And I would say . . . "We'll get you eventually."

. . . The thought process that went into building these applications . . . was all about: How do we consume as much of your time and conscious attention as possible? And that means that we need to sort of give you a little dopamine hit every once in a while, because someone liked or commented on a photo or a post or whatever. And that's going to get you to contribute more content, and that's going to get you . . . more likes and comments. It's a social-valida- tion feedback loop . . . exactly the kind of thing that a hacker like myself would come up with, because you're exploiting a vulnerability in human psychology.

The inventors, creators . . . understood this consciously. And we did it anyway.

There you have it. Straight from the source's mouth. The creators of social media consciously exploited human psychology to "consume as much of your time and conscious attention as possible." To them, "likes" are "dopamine hits" that will keep you in their clutches. It's the same principle used in video games where kills, saves, wins, and conquering more difficult levels are seen as dopamine rewards. And humans crave these rushes of pleasure.

Teens aren't blind to this. A whopping 72 percent believe that tech companies manipulate them to spend more time on their devices. Yet the manipulation and dopamine hits seem to be more powerful than many teens' ability to resist.

How They Do It: Tools for Addiction

To be fair (which I occasionally feel compelled to be), virtually all brick-and-mortar companies design their products, ads, and stores to "entice" you. Food manufactur- ers pay supermarkets to place their products at eye level where you are more likely to see (and buy) them. And, similarly to Big Tech, Big Food uses scientific knowl- edge about the brain and body (plus lots of salt, sugar, and fats) to addict you to their super-poppy-puffy-munchy-snappy-crackly-dopamine-releasing snacks. Some stores use music or fragrance to create environments that will keep customers there longer. Dairy and pharmacy items, the most frequent reasons for entering a store, are usually placed at the rear so you have to walk through the aisles, which increases the chances of your seeing something else to buy. There's nothing sinister about this as long as the companies aren't making false claims or secretly trying to brainwash you. It's reasonable that in a capitalistic society, people and companies with a product to sell will try to make theirs stand out so you'll buy it. And it's unlikely you'll get addicted to, say, buying milk or anti-smartphone-itchy-itis cream because, frankly, there's nothing too rewarding about spending nine hours a day in a super-market or drug store.

But it's different with the digital world. It's inescapable. Virtually every human activity and need has an online interface. No technology in the history of the world has ever made so many connections with, or invasions into, human existence. Your phone talks to you. Makes you laugh. Gives you news. It teaches, answers questions, finds the best route, summons rides. It connects you with friends and family. Online, people can do everything from shopping to banking, creating to learning, dreaming to playing, hooking up to viewing pornography. They can steal, scam, blackmail, impersonate, commit fraud, and hold data for ransom.

In fact, it's hard to think of a single human behavior, interest, passion, or goal; a single social, emotional, psychological, cognitive, or physical need, that doesn't have a digital doppleganger. **＊**

＊ I love that word! It means a double, a counterpart, a spirit of a living person.

Your devices and the online world have a virtually unlimited number of tunnels that can be used to exploit and burrow into your life. Many are wonderful. Many are not. But it's the totality of what screen time has come to represent that makes it so powerful, and so hard to resist.

The technology and internet industries know that. And they want to get you hooked. Here's how they do it. (Get a blanket to wrap around yourself. Because your blood is about to run cold.)

In-Your-Face Addiction Methods

Many strategies for addiction hide in plain sight. They may masquerade as user-friendly interfaces or helpful suggestions for customers. While they have a "helpful" veneer, under the surface, these design choices are meant to keep you on that site longer and make it harder for you to leave.

Just one more scroll.

The bottomless site. You can keep scrolling from now to the day after eternity. Facebook has an endless feed. Instagram, Pinterest, Twitter—you can't get to the bottom of a page, because there is no bottom. One more photo. One more tweet. One more post. One more scroll. Something great is always just below the bottom of the screen. It's gotta be. Almost there. You just have to keep scrolling . . . and scroll-ing . . . and scrolling . . .

DITCH THE DOOMSCROLLING

Doomscrolling is a special type of toxicity. It's when you gorge on bad news despite it being sad, troubling, or depressing. Endlessly scrolling your feeds, consuming one upsetting post after another, is bad for your mental and emotional health. You wouldn't stay in a garage, breathing deeply, if it were filling with exhaust fumes.

So why would you continue to breathe in noxious feed fumes of doom and gloom if they make you feel bad?

Doomscrolling, like worry, is self-destructive unless it can be a catalyst for action, change, or self-awareness. Don't get sucked into bottomless bummers. When you confront bad news, ask yourself: Is there anything positive I can take from this? Is there anything I can do to help? If yes, act. If no, read a post or two to be an informed citizen, and then move your psyche to a more comfortable space.

Just one more video.

Most streaming sites automatically play the next video. Netflix, YouTube, Amazon Prime Video, Hulu—these types of platforms present new videos and next episodes within seconds after the one you're watching ends. It wasn't always this way. Netflix, for one, used to always require viewers to choose to play the next episode. Then they changed their settings so that was no longer the default. Binge watching soared! Now, you have to choose *not* to autoplay the next episode. And your reflexes better be fast because by the time you locate your hand to reach for the remote or trackpad, the next video is already on—and you're hooked.

Imagine if, instead of autoplay, you always saw a screen with a choice: *"Would you like to see the next video/episode?"* And then you had to click Yes or No. That would give your mind a pause. You'd be more likely to think: *I really should do my homework; I promised Dad I'd wash the dog.* But you don't get to make that choice. They make it for you. (Check the settings for those sites. It is usually possible to drill down and turn off autoplay.)

Just one more Snap.

Let's face it. Snapchat streaks are brilliant. Just in case you've been grounded for years, and your parents took away your phone, and therefore you don't know what a Snapchat streak is, it's when two people Snap back and forth within a 24-hour period. The streak gets longer with every consecutive day you Snap each other. If you break the streak, you start all over at zero. The longer the streak, the more pressure many teens feel to continue it. When you hit certain milestones, like 100 days or 1,000 days, you get to unlock a Snapchat reward. Streaks capitalize on teens' desires to maintain friendships and to express that commitment.

There can be competitive elements, too, as teens compare who's got the longest streak. For teens really invested in maintaining a streak, imagine how upsetting it would be to break a streak after 60, 200, or 857 days. What if somebody's battery died right before midnight and they missed Snapping that day? What if you broke your leg and had to go to the hospital and couldn't get on your phone? The pressure to keep a streak going can be so intense that some teens, if, say, their parents take away their phone or they go on a camping trip, ask their friends to maintain the streaks.

Snapchat also developed a "Snapchat score" which, according to their website *"is determined by a super-secret, special equation that combines the number of Snaps you've sent and received, the Stories you've posted, and a couple other factors."*

Sure, everything you do on Snapchat can be a riot of fun, friendship, and closeness, but the brilliance of the streak concept is that it makes you the agent of your own daily "addiction." If you don't Snap every day, you break the streak. And since the friend with whom you have a long streak is equally invested in keeping it going, she might be mighty peeved if you got busy and broke the streak.

You got to hand it to Snapchat for coming up with such a clever, in-your-face device for making teens use the app every single day.

Recommendations for YOU.

Go to any shopping site. Chances are, no matter what you're in the market for, you'll see "similar items," "must-haves," "most-loved items," "deals of the day," "things you might like," "products other customers buy," and "recommendations just for you" (because the site cares so much about you).

Now, don't get me wrong. Such "assistance" can be helpful. I often learn of new music or books from these recommendations, and I'm glad to know of them. If I'm searching for "face masks leopard pattern," I am *overjoyed* to be shown a face mask with a zebra pattern. (Gee, I might never have thought of that . . .) But, along with the selfless kindness of the site, there's another motive: keeping you there for as long as possible. The more time you spend, the more you click. The more you click, the more advertisers pay. And, ultimately, the longer you're there, the more likely you are to buy something.

Links, links, and more links.

Imagine you're driving through a tunnel. You're barreling along, making good progress, but with every mile you drive, another mile is added to the far end of the tunnel. You're in constant motion, but you're not getting any closer to the end. And you never will. That's how websites are designed. Let's say somebody sends you a link to a YouTube video. You land on the site, watch the video, and see there's a bottomless sidebar of links to more videos. Since they are algorithmically related to the one you just watched (which has already been replaced by a new autoplayed video), you're likely to find something of interest. So you click, and there's a new video and yet another list, and this goes on from now to 1,000 years beyond the end of time unless you can tear yourself away.

Free association.

$$ FREE $$

[For 7 days, and then just $19.99 a month conveniently billed to your credit card.]

Lots of online companies and services—like streaming sites, digital publications, and product subscriptions with automatic refills—use free or discounted trial periods to lure you in. They know that you'll be thinking, *Hey, it's free! I'll be sure to cancel before the 30 days are up.* And maybe you will. But Big Tech is hoping you won't, either because you love their product or service or because you just forget. And if you're their most dreaded customer, someone who remembers to cancel, they will do everything possible to make it a difficult, annoying, time-consuming, and shaming process.

Are you sure? No, really—are you SURE?

Have you ever tried to unsubscribe from a newsletter? Close an account? Cancel notifications? Stop getting 100 emails a day from a website where you once bought something?

These sites don't want to lose you. So they make it as difficult as possible to disengage. The cancel/unsubscribe/opt-out buttons are often tiny, hard to find, low contrast, buried in text, and made to look inactive. And once you do find them, the site forces you to repeat your request multiple times. You'll see a screen: "We're sorry to see you go. Are you sure?"

They use what's called *confirm-shaming* to try to guilt you into staying. This is one of many "dark patterns" platforms employ to trick or shame you into doing their bidding and to make it as difficult as possible for you to opt out, exit, cancel, and end your relationship with the company. I mean, just *try* to cancel an Amazon account. There are so many hoops to click through—multiple emails, warnings, recitations of unimaginable, irreversible doom and gloom that will befall you—it's amazing they don't just send a hundred drones to tie you to your bed with silly string.

But you really do want to sever ties. So you persist. You click "Yes." The app still won't let you go. They want to know your reasons. (None of their business.) They try to find a middle ground, offering you choices for receiving less frequent notices or more narrowly-defined topics. Anything but a total break-up. Each option warns you that you'll miss their best deals or scoops. But you persist.

Now there are new boxes to check before you can opt out: "I don't want to receive hot tips." "I don't care about hearing the latest news." "I'm not interested in saving money."

Or, you can check: "I want to stay informed." "I want to be in the know." "I want to be the coolest person on the block." Check those and your mission has been thwarted. They won.

But you persist. Now the heavy-duty shaming begins. That's when you have to agree that "I am willing to miss out on the best gossip." "I am willing to lose all my data." "I don't want free delivery." "I am willing to disappear into a cave and hide from the world." "I agree that I am a total loser who is about to make the worst mistake of my life."

Finally, once you confirm that evolutionarily speaking, you are little better than a primordial slug, the site will let you go. But don't be surprised if you receive endless streams of emails with offers and enticements aiming to get you back.

TALES FROM THE DIGITAL FRONTIER

I once had a digital subscription to an expensive online publication. It cost over $200 a year! (It was quite a publication.) Then I learned that a library I belonged to offered free digital access to it. The only catch was that each time you wanted to read it, you had to log in with a bunch of codes, and your access was only good for three days. And then you'd have to log in again. Still . . . free versus a couple hundred dollars? A no-brainer, and having to log in every three days wasn't that big a deal. So I decided to cancel.

I went to the publication's website. The site where it's so easy to sign up to subscribe to the digital edition, the even-more-expensive print edition, and all sorts of other offerings. They make spending money a breeze. I finally made my way to my account, and clicked on "Manage Subscription." There I found, in the smallest, hardest-to-read font, "Cancel Subscription." I followed the link and kept clicking to the point where I thought I was done. But, NOOOOOOOO. In order to finalize the cancellation, I was instructed that I had to call the company and speak to one of their customer service representatives! CALL?!? Like, to an actual person? Unheard of.

Give them money? Easy as pie to do online. Cancel? Impossible to do online.

So, in a very annoyed mood, I called. Naturally, they wanted to know my reasons. That annoyed me even more. I am always very polite to service reps because I understand that the person with whom I am speaking did not create the rules and policies. But I explained in no uncertain terms that my reasons are my own, that my time is valuable, that I resent being forced to jump through all these hoops to cancel, and that if I want hoops, I get out my hula hoop.

The representative then offered me a special offer of $52 a year for one year (as opposed to $200+). Because I was so irritated, I refused it. (But I can tell you, if it had been offered as part of a cancellation process on the website, I would have taken it. Their mistake.)

The service rep said she understood. "So," I asked, "is that it? Is my subscription canceled?" Silly me. I had to be passed to the supervisor, who would finalize the cancellation. Can you believe it? TWO PEOPLE? Just to cancel one subscription. Anyway, I was transferred to the supervisor, to whom I gave a further piece of my mind (politely, and only to the point where I didn't want to lose any further mind), and the subscription was canceled.

EPILOGUE

For the next six months, I continued to receive weekly emails with the $52/year offer. I deleted them without even looking. Finally, I got an email with "Last Chance" in the subject line. I opened it. The special rate was expiring the next day, never to be repeated. And you know what? I took it. I signed up. The combination of persistence and "urgency" (which is what marketers use to make you jump at a deal) pierced my resistance. They got me. They won.

It's all tiny and inconsequential in the grand scheme of things. But when you start to multiply one experience such as that by all your accounts, subscriptions, messages, push notifications, and pushier notifications, you realize that using the internet makes you (and me) into a puppet, with huge, monopolizing corporations pulling invisible strings of coercion, psychological manipulation, and hidden engineered choices. The good news? Now that you know this, you can start rebelling against the puppeteers.

Sneaky, Slimy, Tricky, Trappy Addiction Methods

While the methods I've mentioned so far for keeping you glued to a website are plenty manipulative, at least they are *also* self-evident. The sites keep presenting you with options, recommendations, and links to click; they ever-so-helpfully play the next video so you don't have to perform the Herculean physical task of tapping a key or clicking on a selection. You might even appreciate some of these features. You discover new things, you get a laugh, you find a product you didn't know about.

But there's another, much sneakier way Big Tech tries to addict you. This method is more insidious. Site and game designers understand psychology and how the brain functions. They know exactly how to design their games, sites, and apps to hook you. They are intentionally messing with your mind. Hacking your brain. Taking advantage of human needs, impulses, and vulnerabilities.

They do this based on principles of human nature and neurochemistry (the chemistry of the nervous system). *Human nature* refers to traits that virtually all humans share. These can be:

- Social (wanting to mate, have friends, or belong to a group)
- Emotional (wanting to love and be loved)
- Psychological (wanting approval, rewards, competence, success—wanting MORE)
- Cognitive (wanting mental stimulation and challenges)

Site designers know that people crave:

- Being mentally engaged
- Mastering a skill (getting better at something)
- Connecting and bonding socially
- Reaching goals (winning)
- Completing tasks (pride of accomplishment)
- Receiving praise and positive feedback
- Resolving tensions (just *try* singing an eight-note scale and stopping on the seventh note; your whole being will want to finish the scale)

I just tried that.

Did you resist?

I couldn't hold out.

Here are some of the sneaky tricks Big Tech uses to get inside your head.

Pain and gain.

Addiction satisfies something. It may relieve pain, stress, or loneliness. It may create a feeling of belonging. It may provide comfort, support, excitement, escape, pleasure, or thrills. The satisfaction you're getting—the reward, the gain, the release—is so compelling you repeat the action that triggers it. The early stages of addiction seem positive, so it's easy to ignore, deny, or not even notice any harmful effects. But, sooner or later the negative effects emerge as the addiction takes over. It commandeers your time, relationships, and responsibilities, becoming the tail wagging the dog of your life. You're no longer in charge. The addictive behavior is. Personally, I don't think it's an accident that people who take drugs and people who visit apps and websites are both called "users."

Pleasurable experiences activate the reward center in your brain. Whether that experience comes from a drug or a behavior makes no difference to how your brain operates (although the intensity of the stimulus and reaction can vary). The brain patterns of somebody addicted to cocaine, gambling, or video games are all similar since the same reward center in the brain—the dopamine system—is activated. And if you think video game addiction can't happen, consider the fact that 44 percent of *World of Warcraft* players say they feel addicted to the game. There's even an online support group called Wowaholics Anonymous for people who want to quit.

WOW!

What's happening is that certain online activities stimulate your brain to release a chemical called dopamine. This produces a profound feeling of pleasure. Humans are programmed to want to seek and repeat pleasurable experiences. But something interesting happens over time. Your brain develops what's called tolerance, where it produces less and less dopamine in response to the same stimulation. The only way to achieve the same "high" is to increase the "dose." So, where an hour of gaming or social media used to give you a glow, now it takes two hours. And then three. And then six. And more and more.

Platform designers know that early rewards keep you going. Have you tried a new game and gained a higher level, scored a kill, or reached a goal quickly? That's by design. "Beginner's luck" is built into the game since it's a powerful motivator. So you keep playing. But it will take you longer to reach the next level. And longer still to reach the next. These designers know exactly when to give you a reward, when to offer an in-app purchase option. If you get too frustrated, you might (horrors!) leave the site or quit the game. The key is to increase the difficulty of the challenges, while keeping them within reach.

I just tried singing *almost* all of the scale again.

What happened?

I couldn't hold out. Again. :(

You're being watched.

Designers often run hidden experiments on their sites and apps to find out which elements keep you playing, clicking, swiping, and Snapping. Which colors, fonts, sounds, names, and reward systems maximize your attention and engagement, and which minimize the likelihood of your getting frustrated and leaving.

Let's say developers have created a game that has millions of players. Those developers can tag different elements and track which ones players spend the most time on, which ones are most popular. They can discover whether "kill" missions are more compelling than "save" missions. (Sadly, they are.) They can see to what extent small bursts of positive feedback influence players and which sound effects are most appealing. In other words, they can identify exactly which dimensions are most enticing, pleasurable, engaging—and addictive.

And it's not just gaming sites that do this. Instagram conducted experiments to see if hiding or eliminating "likes" *increased* engagement and time spent on the site. They became concerned that the pursuit of likes, and the bummer of not getting enough likes, was causing some users to turn off. By the time you read this, Instagram, and possibly other sites, may have made changes to such fundamental aspects of their design. Keep in mind, though, that their concern for your emotional health is secondary to maximizing users and attention.

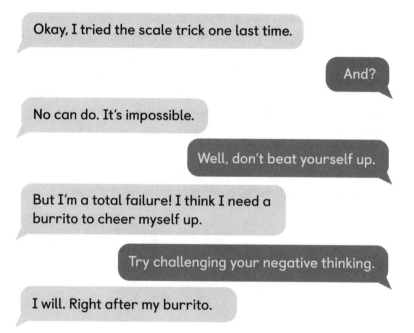

Okay, I tried the scale trick one last time.

And?

No can do. It's impossible.

Well, don't beat yourself up.

But I'm a total failure! I think I need a burrito to cheer myself up.

Try challenging your negative thinking.

I will. Right after my burrito.

You are under our control.

Gaming sites manipulate you to relinquish self-control. They know you're more likely to keep playing if the tasks are just beyond your abilities, but ultimately reachable. Once you attain a new skill level, you are even more motivated to increase your mastery yet again. There's a delicate balance between feeling anxious if your abilities aren't up to the task and feeling bored if the task isn't challenging enough. If you hit the sweet spot in between—if you're *in the zone*, if you're experiencing *flow*—you can feel an intense, intoxicating euphoria. You lose track of time, the "outside" world disappears, you are immersed in the game, the mission, the challenge.

This profound pleasure, based on how the human brain and psyche work, makes it a potentially addicting experience. Combine this with the fact that so many games never end. They don't have "open and closed hours"; they're always open. Even bars and liquor stores close at some point. But these infinite-format games just go on and on and on. Sessions don't start and stop; levels don't begin and end.

Some games now display messages to warn you to take a break if you've been playing for a long time. But that's a joke. Do they really expect (or want) somebody who's been at the screen for hours, who may be flowing along the zone in a pleasurable canoe of rapture, to step away? I don't think so. If they were serious about it, they could block the game for that player for 15 minutes or institute a daily limit. It's more that game manufacturers are beginning to "feel the heat," and they want to *appear* to be looking out for young players.

To be fair (there I go again), there are some designers and companies that recognize, and are opposed to, addict-grooming. Their games and sessions conclude. Players must consciously re-engage. These designers, who have explicitly gone in the opposite direction, shine a light on the way *most* designers and corporations are out to steal your time, attention, and willpower.

The quest for likes.

Like gaming and other highly addictive apps, social media platforms are designed to take advantage of the same inherent human needs and desires. You want to connect with people (belonging). You want to get likes and shares and followers (rewards). You want to be retweeted (approval). Every time you post a photo or video, you want to see what the reaction is. It's like buying a lottery ticket or pulling the lever on a slot machine. (And slot machines are the most addictive form of gambling.) If you get lots of likes, you hit the JACKPOT of rewards, approval, and mental stimulation.

Naturally, having won the jackpot, you're going to want to repeat the action—pulling the lever again/posting another photo—to get more rewards. It's human nature. But let's say this time you didn't get as many likes as you wanted. You'll continue to post (pull the lever) in the hope that the *next* photo or video will hit the jackpot. So, "losing" doesn't deter you from trying again. You feel it as "*almost winning*," and that *motivates* you to post (or play or gamble or buy) again. And again. And again.

Of course, if you keep losing over and over and over, you can end up with serious problems. For a gambler, that could be financial ruin or a destroyed marriage. For a social media user, it could be depression, low self-esteem, self-critical thoughts, or an addictive relationship to the platform.

But it gets even trickier.

The variable rewards hook.

There's one type of reward that is the most addictive of them all: intermittent, variable rewards. Here's how they work.

Think of yourself as a lab rat in a cage.

> **I beg your pardon???**

> Sorry. But it's necessary.

To get food you have to press a lever. If food appears every time you press the lever, you'll think (being a clever rat), *Okay, when I'm hungry I'll press the lever to get food.* Your frequency of pressing the lever is moderated by the expectation that "you press, you eat." This is known as "continuous reinforcement." Since there's no "suspense" as to whether you'll get the reward, your engagement with the lever is occasional—it only happens when you want food. Should the reward be withdrawn, so you press the lever and nothing happens, you will quickly give up on the lever.

But let's say you press the lever and sometimes you get food, and sometimes you don't. This is "variable reinforcement." The lack of a consistent, predictable reward will make you press the lever compulsively to compensate for not knowing whether you'll get food on any given try. In other words, the unpredictability compels you to keep pressing the lever, and to not give up, since sometimes—maybe the very next time!—you'll get the reward.

Okay. You can go back to being a person again. This was an actual experiment, one of the most famous ever conducted, by B.F. Skinner, a psychologist and social philosopher. He was interested in the effect of rewards and punishments on behavior, so he studied rats. Unfortunately, Skinner never carried out any experiments with rats posting to Instagram to see how getting "likes" consistently or unpredictably affected their posting. Too bad. Would have been interesting. But you can guess what the results would have been.

What this has to do with you and your phone is this: You may not have thought of it this way before, but much of your online time and energy is spent responding to hidden, variable-reward systems created by the app designers. Think about it. Every time you play a video game with wins, new powers, losses, obstacles, and higher levels, you've been drawn into a variable-rewards matrix. Every time you check your social media account (press the lever), you may find "food" (rewards), or you may not. The variability of whether you'll get a reward—likes, great pics, funny memes, invitations, messages from friends—keeps you checking over and over again.

Let's say you get a notification. You check it (pressing the lever), and sometimes it's a great message that makes you happy you got it (reward). Other times, it's a real downer or something of no use or interest. But that just motivates you to keep responding to notifications, since you never know—the next one could be another great one.

Inducing FOMO in visitors and users is the grand prize for designers. The fear of missing out on a "reward"—a social drama at school, a new video, a daily deal, a 50-percent-off "today-only" sale—is a powerful force for getting people to read texts, stay longer, keep scrolling, keep clicking, keep posting, and keep coming back.

When users check their phones (the average person checks 150 times a day)—pressing, tapping, clicking, scrolling, and swiping in pursuit of rewards—the platforms know they have successfully implanted the addiction bug.

Now that you're aware of this addictive behavior modification model, you can see it at work when you open emails, scroll down a feed, respond to notifications, swipe left or right, or check your phone. Resist it. Don't let anyone turn you into a lab rat.

Your choice. (Not!)

Just about everything you see and do online involves making choices. That's what "menus" are. Interfaces for making choices. It can feel empowering to be able to view lots of options and to Make a Choice! WOW—so many possibilities! Click, send, post, select, submit, agree, buy, save, this video, that video, him, her, now, later. Never forget, though, that every menu you see, every choice you're offered, is predetermined by the website or platform. They control the menu. They've already decided what you can (and can't) choose.

It's like a parent who says to a young child, "It's bedtime. Do you want your blue pajamas or red pajamas?" There is no choice about whether it's bedtime or not. Just pajamas. Little kids will be delighted at being given a choice. It won't occur to them (until they're older) that the choice of *not* going to bed was never offered.

The choices you're offered online are designed to keep you on a particular site. Attention is the currency. When you perform a search, the items (options) you see are the result of that site's hidden algorithms. Your results will be different from somebody else's based on what the site knows about you. Many of the choices you're given aren't really choices at all, since the site has already determined the framework, excluding choices they don't want you to have.

Let's say you're looking at a news feed. Social media sites are famous for using algorithms that highlight divisive material. They know what'll push your buttons, keep you reading, keep you engaged (and enraged), so that's what you'll be shown. If you've ever been presented with "articles you may like," you'll notice how they relate to your interests, politics, gender, age, and previous choices. The platform (the algorithms) decides what to bring to your attention and what not to.

When you're on a website or an app, remember that the choices you see are edited based on the goals, needs, and profit motives of that website. Facebook wants you to stay on Facebook. It doesn't care if the news you get is truthful or a lie or balanced or biased.

Ask yourself:

- Do the choices respond fully to my request, or did the website put its own spin on my question?

- What choices might I NOT be seeing?

- Why might the site be presenting me with these options and not others?

- Which choices are sponsored by advertisers?

TALES FROM THE DIGITAL FRONTIER

During the pandemic, an airline (which shall remain nameless) canceled a flight I had booked many months earlier. Because *they* canceled the flight, I was entitled to a refund. (If *I* had canceled it, I would have only been entitled to a voucher for future travel.) When I called the airline, the service rep said I needed to go to their website to file my claim for a refund.

So I dutifully went to the site and was greeted with the flashy, colorful "Book Travel" screen, just waiting for me to enter my destination. Their choice. Since it wasn't *my* choice, I finally found the button for "Refunds" in tiny print in a long column of options at the bottom of the page. Funny, it was much harder to find the "Refunds" button than the "Buy Ticket" button. So I clicked on "Refunds." I had to "X" a bunch of pop-ups, and then got to the template for entering my ticket number and last name. I clicked "Submit" and got . . .

. . . a screen offering a voucher for future travel. Prominently displayed was a button for "Accept Voucher." Huh? The site was initially presenting me with one choice: to accept a voucher rather than the refund. I can understand their desire to do so, since it would mean they could hold onto my money. But being an informed, suspicious, cynical consumer aware of the tricks websites play, I scoured that screen and eventually found a tiny button for "Other Options." That led me to a more detailed template to fill in for my original request, a refund. After entering additional information, I clicked "Submit" and got . . .

. . . a screen offering a voucher for future travel with a BONUS of 20 percent increased value! See how they're controlling the choices to make it as difficult as possible to receive the refund? Now, I admit I was tempted. Twenty percent was a lot of money, but then I thought, *Who knows when I'll be able to travel again? What if the airline goes* bankrupt *by then? Plus, vouchers give you only a year to book your new ticket.* So I didn't succumb to the temptation. I got out my magnifying glass to see if there was a "No thanks, proceed to refund" button, and finally found it. I clicked and got . . .

. . . a screen informing me that my refund application had been submitted. And to the airline's credit, I received my refund about a week later. But I'll never forget the choices they kept presenting to try to dissuade me from getting it.

Butting in line.

Of all online communications, texts and messages get the most immediate response from users. This is because they butt in on whatever you're doing, interrupting you with a notification. Sometimes, receiving a notification right away—say, from a friend who's going to be late—is desirable. But make no mistake, tech companies intend for notifications to be a key component in their variable-rewards, addiction-inducement system. You see the icon, you hear the sound, and you just *have* to check it out (because it might be a reward).

You can see how disruptive and addictive these interruptions can be for an individual user. They force you to switch tasks every few seconds or minutes. They mess with your attention span and prevent you from concentrating. With phones ever-present, notifications are constantly butting in and compromising the quality of face-to-face interactions.

Now, multiply the impact of these pushy notifications on one person—you— by millions of people. Think of millions of people being interrupted every day by billions of pings of potential rewards. You have to wonder what that does on a global scale to creativity, decision-making, person-to-person contact, productivity, mood, and relationships. I'll let you wonder while I go on to the next paragraph.

Some messaging apps let senders know that their message was read. This creates further pressure on recipients to respond quickly. Apps that barge into your consciousness, and let senders know they have done so, are most likely to keep you pressing the lever and coming back.

We've been conditioned to think of all the things technology does *for* us. But it's just as important to think of all the things it does *to* us.

Dear Alex,

I think I'm addicted to my phone. I've tried to stop but I can't. I have friends who use the same apps, but they aren't addicted. Am I just weak or do I have no willpower or something?

If you're addicted to your phone, it's not your fault. It's the logical result of spending time engaging with websites and apps that are designed to be addictive. That's the whole point. They're trying to get you hooked.

You ask an interesting question, though: Why is it that *you* haven't been able to control your screen use, no matter how hard you try, but people you know who use the same apps don't have the same problem? You'd think that if these apps were designed to pulverize your self-control, everyone would get hooked. You could ask the same question about alcohol use. How come some people can have a beer or a glass of wine, no problem, but others, once they start, can't stop, even though they realize how much harm it is causing?

For some people, this may have to do with their unique body and brain chemistry. They metabolize, process, or respond to the chemicals produced by certain substances and behaviors differently based on their particular body and neurochemistry. Again, thinking of alcohol, one person may get "tipsy" or fall asleep after one drink; another may have four drinks without showing any obvious signs of having been drinking; and another will keep drinking until they pass out with a dangerously high blood alcohol level.

In your case, maybe there's a particular game you play that you just can't stop. The excitement, missions, hits, and close calls are all sending signals to your brain that cause it to produce dopamine. That may create a force so powerful in your particular brain and body that you feel as if you are helpless to resist. (But you *can* resist, and you'll learn more about how in chapters 10 and 11.) For another person, it may not trigger such a strong reaction, and they can take it or leave it.

Remember the idea that addiction satisfies some need? That need may be social, emotional, psychological, cognitive, or physical. For most teens who feel addicted to their phones, it's not really the phones themselves they're addicted to. It's usually certain sites or activities they feel most powerless to control. Could be social media, gaming, texting, watching videos—anything. If the addiction is to certain sites and behaviors over others, that could provide clues as to the need being satisfied. Maybe it's a need for friendship, social connection, and group bonding (social media); or a need to feel powerful, capable, or destructive (gaming); or a need to escape from loneliness, depression, or real-life problems (watching tons of video clips); or a need to find help or support for stress or a particular worry or fear (chat rooms). Could be anything.

I don't know what needs your screen time might be satisfying. If you haven't thought about it from that perspective, try it. (The triggers and temptations challenge on page 44, as well as the exercises in chapters 10 and 11, will provide you with clues for figuring out these needs.) Maybe you'll have a strong sense of what they are. Maybe not. But identifying the "payoff" can be a route to breaking the addiction. If you know what need you're satisfying, you can find other, healthier ways to satisfy it.

Most important, don't beat yourself up over this. You've taken the hardest step: Admitting to yourself that there's a problem. That, in and of itself, is courageous and puts you closer to finding a solution. Read chapters 10 and 11 for strategies for reducing screen time. Those may help. And if you're still struggling, you'll find additional suggestions there for getting support.

Balancing on the Seesaw of Life

Here's the challenge when it comes to screens and life balance: Screens are almost impossible to avoid in today's world. Say a person has a drinking problem or simply doesn't wish to drink for religious or health reasons. They can avoid going into bars or clubs or liquor stores. They can maintain an alcohol-free home. They can go to support groups. Approximately one third of adults in the US choose not to drink at all, and nearly half of the world's population over the age of 15 have never consumed alcohol at any time during their entire life. Not drinking won't affect their ability to travel, buy things, do their banking, communicate with friends, work in an office, or attend classes.

Similarly, if—heaven forbid—you have an ice cream addiction, you can ban ice cream from your freezer, avoid going into ice cream parlors, and, with incredible mindfulness, willpower, diversionary activities, and mental re-training, you can keep at bay all thoughts of ice cream cones, ice cream sandwiches, ice cream bars, ice cream cakes, ice cream pies, banana splits, hot fudge sundaes, and giant tubs of coconut, mint chip, rum raisin, and strawberry cheesecake ice cream covered with walnuts, whipped cream, and chocolate sprinkles. Except at night when they invade your dreams.

> Um . . . maybe you should see somebody about this?

With addictive screen-time behavior, it's different. This is because screens hook into every aspect of our lives. In today's digital world, abstaining from devices seems virtually impossible since *everything*—schools, businesses, commerce, communication, relationships, entertainment—increasingly relies on screens in one way or another. If it seems "everyone" is on social media, it's hard for you not to be. If a lot of your friends rely on social media to stay in touch, make plans, and keep up with the latest gossip, it makes it awfully tough for you not to do the same. If school assignments are on the internet, if a teacher asks you to do online research, how can you not use a computer?

There are tons of stories of teens whose lives got so out of balance from addictions to gaming (most likely for boys) or social media (most likely for girls) that they had to go to extreme measures, at least at first—such as joining support groups, attending cell phone addiction treatment programs, or throwing their phone down the toilet—to restore balance. But it can be done, and there are many teens who decide to give up online gaming and social media entirely, while still using their devices for other purposes.

In chapters 10 and 11, you'll find a guided process to help you reset your digital life based on your specific use patterns and life-balance goals. But, before we go there, let's briefly focus on two areas where teens most frequently get hooked: video game playing and social media.

Are You a Video Gaming Fan—or Fanatic?

While video games are "pretend," the emotions they trigger are real. You feel powerful and in control. You feel skillful, triumphant, and proud. And if you connect with other players, you feel a sense of belonging. These good feelings stimulate the reward centers in your brain, releasing that feel-good chemical called dopamine. And it's human nature to want to repeat doing things that make you feel good. So, the more video games you play, the more you want to play. Your brain's reward center keeps saying, "More, please." Game designers know this, and they construct their games to keep you on the dopamine path. (Designers of educational software also know this, which is why they often model their online learning products on video games.)

One study of 14-year-olds found that the part of the brain associated with rewards was larger in teens who played nine or more hours of video games a week than it was in teens who played fewer than nine hours a week. This enlargement in the brain is similar to that found in people with substance abuse or gambling disorders, leading scientists to see a possible connection between excessive video gaming and other behavioral addictions. In fact, the World Health Organization (WHO)—

WHO?

Yes, "WHO"—says it's possible to become addicted to gaming, and added "Gaming Disorder" to its *International Classification of Diseases.* (The American Psychiatric Association also added "Internet Gaming Disorder" to the *DSM-5*, the manual used by mental health professionals to make diagnoses.)

Of course, most people who play video games aren't addicted to them. In fact, in moderation, video gaming may even be good for you. (I said "in moderation," so don't use this to justify the six hours a day you spend gaming!) Studies suggest that if you play co-op games, you're more likely to help others in the real world. If you value gaming and see it as part of your identity, your successes in that world can translate into feelings of confidence in this world. Gamers, as opposed to non-gamers, have better hand-eye coordination, spatial awareness, and real-world navigating skills. Gaming can foster creativity, train you to notice visual details, sharpen certain cognitive skills, and keep your brain purring like a well-tuned engine.

If you play video games and would like to reassure yourself that your video gaming is healthy, or if you've ever worried about how much you play, run it through the challenge on page 48. That will help you figure it out.

Are You a Social Media Maestro— or Maniac?

Given the importance of human connection, and what you now know about the strategies Big Tech uses to hook you on their platforms, it should come as no surprise that social media is a big addiction magnet for teens (and adults). It's zany, funny, and full of emotion. It connects you with people

you care about. It's a forum for self-expression and creativity. And it's designed to be a digital, dopamine-dispensing slot machine that provides enough rewards to keep you posting, keep you scrolling, and keep you pressing the lever in the hope of getting social reward candy. If you're not sure whether social media is a plus or minus for you, use the challenge on page 48 to gather some intel.

Dear Alex,

What's with this life balance stuff? You make it sound like we should be robots, every-body in perfect balance. Isn't having different balances what makes people interesting?

To answer your question, I'd like you to think about healthy eating habits and "balanced diets." That means certain foods, in certain proportions, eaten in certain ways, at certain times, will best keep your systems in tip-top shape. So nutrition experts recommend consuming fruit, vegetables, fish, grains, dairy, protein, meats, poultry, fats, carbohydrates, oils, sugars, and luscious, delectable, creamy ice cream in greater or lesser amounts. While some categories might be expendable (like meats or spinach), others would be more essential (like luscious, delectable, ice cream).

A vegetarian could maintain a healthy diet, but a tortillatarian could not.

Healthy eating means keeping the different categories in proportion to each other (that is, not eating six cheeseburgers and ten pickles as your daily diet), eating throughout the day rather than one pig-out meal at midnight, and so on. You might be able to binge on one type of food to the exclusion of others for a period of time without doing lasting harm to yourself. An infant might not. The possibilities are endless for accommodating personal likes and dislikes—while still maintaining a healthy balance of foods. One person can avoid red meat while another indulges in rutabaga. One person can go wild over sushi, while another is hot for hummus.

And so it is with "life balance." Certain behaviors, experiences, and elements of existence need to coalesce in certain proportions in certain ways at certain times during certain stages of development to support optimal physical, social, emotional, and intellectual growth. These elements include such things as exercise, nutrition, shelter, love, protection, healthcare, parenting, education, play, exploration, mental stimulation, socializing, language acquisition, and ice cream.

> **Don't take this the wrong way, but I think ice cream is affecting your life balance. You really need to see somebody.**

As with balanced diets, there's wiggle room for what constitutes a balanced, healthy life. You can bulk up on one area without doing damage to another. You can even get imbalanced for a period of time (like if you have to pull an all-nighter to finish a paper) without it being a problem. But if imbalance lasts long enough during a "ripe" period for learning and development,* that's when lasting damage could be done.

*See page 93 for more on "ripe periods."

So, the key question to always be asking yourself is: *Does my screen time imbalance my life in ways that inhibit or prevent my healthy development and important life experiences?*

Dear Alex,

What's the difference between an interest and an addiction? I play guitar and have a band. I'm always on my computer writing songs, mixing, sound editing, you know. I spend every minute I can doing that. Does that mean I'm "addicted" to my music?

I like your question. Let me recharacterize your deep and consuming interest in making and performing music as a "passion." So the question becomes, what's the difference between a passion and an addiction?

I'm a firm believer in having passions. I think of passions as wonderful, powerful interests and activities that you can't wait to do, that you feel compelled to do, that you think about all the time, that crowd out other activities. Passions fill some intellectual, creative, artistic, physical, interpersonal, or spiritual need—a desire to express, explore, change, invent, save, master.

Think of kids who want to be Olympic skiers, soccer strikers, or skateboarding stars; or kids who have business or volunteer missions that occupy them from sunup to sundown. Or kids who can't get enough of running cross-country, working on cars, designing clothes, writing stories—or playing and composing music.

Spending lots of time doing things you love isn't necessarily harmful as long as those interests, *in balance,* affect you in *positive* ways. You recognize that if you're going to be a great skier, artist, dancer, musician, or entrepreneur, you need to train and practice now. You make a *conscious* choice to give up certain activities and create imbalance in your life in pursuit of a passion and a goal. *You're* making the choice. The activity (or Big Tech) isn't choosing *for* you.

Someone might say, "What's the difference between spending six hours a day playing video games, and spending six hours a day practicing cello, making sculptures, ice skating, or being a mentor to younger kids? It's six hours either way."

The difference is who's in charge, and what the passion (the imbalance) offers. Ask yourself:

- Why am I doing this?
- Is it my choice?
- What do I get out of doing this?
- What need or desire does the passion fill?
- How does pursuing this passion affect my life balance?
- What am I giving up?
- Is the imbalance manageable, or does it threaten my development?
- Am I gaining useful or important skills from this passion?
- Does this passion open or close opportunities for me in the future?
- If in one, five, or ten years I stopped doing this, would I have gained something from pursuing the passion or would it seem like a waste of time I might regret?

You can see how the answers to these questions can lead in positive or negative directions. Passions may display "addiction-like" elements, but, in general, their context, motivations, and outcomes tend in positive directions, whereas addictions tend in negative directions.

You can also think of the differences between passions and addictions in terms of active versus passive engagement. Think of the difference between a teen who spends hours a day *playing* video games, and a teen who spends the same time learning coding and graphics to design her own video games. Or the difference between a teen who watches music videos all day and a teen who uses his screen time to create his own music (if you can imagine such a teen). It's the difference between being an active *creator* of content and being a passive *consumer* of content.

Don't get me wrong. I'm not saying that everything teens do should be productive, constructive, goal-oriented, and aimed at getting better grades, getting into college, getting a job, or saving the world. Au contraire. I'm all for *proportional*, life-balanced vegging out, goofing off, and doing things simply because you want to, for no other reason than they're fun, silly, and/ or totally useless. But . . .

As you think about your own life balance, if it seems out of whack, ask yourself the above questions. Try to figure out whether, overall, your interest in—your passion for—music is healthy or unhealthy out-of-whackedness.

If your answers to the questions point in positive directions, if you have friends, if you spend time with your family, if school is going okay, if you get exercise, if you're not neglecting your responsibilities, it sounds to me like your music is a wonderful part of your life to cherish and pursue. And that is music to my ears.

(And please forgive me for going on for so long in answering your question. It's just that I have a passion for passions.)

Now What?

Only you know if any of the addiction warning signs are flashing red for you, if excessive screen time has turned your life balance out-of-whack-a-doodle.

Keep in mind that a common characteristic of people with addictions is that they deny the addiction. As far as they're concerned, there's nothing wrong. They don't have a problem. Everyone else has the problem. *I'd be fine if they'd just get off my back and stop bugging me. That's the real problem.* So the person closest to the addiction may be the last person able to recognize and admit it.

That places a lot of pressure on you as you consider these warning signs. Getting back to the quiz at the beginning of this section, you may be a "Noper," someone who simply doesn't exhibit any of the warning signs. That could be because you truly don't have any. Or it could be because you are in denial. Your dependency, as an active force, prevents you from that self-awareness—in which case you need to reach deep inside yourself to find a place of stillness and honesty that lets you take a brave look at your relationship to the digital world.

Same thing if most of your answers were "Meh." Go back and look at them again. Were you really solidly in the "Sometimes Zone," or did you just not want to acknowledge that maybe you experience that warning sign more frequently than you'd care to admit, and you have less control over your screen time than you'd like?

And what if you had a lot of "Yups"? That would suggest that you may have a dependent or addictive relationship to your devices—and you have an inkling (or more than an inkling) that it's messing up your balance. You're able to see how those warning signs indicate that your ability to control how much time you spend online and what you do is under attack.

A good question to ask yourself is:

Am I on screens because I want to be, or because I can't NOT be?

Whether your screen time is harmonious with the rest of your life, a *little* off-key, or jarringly, Discord-antly out of tune, you'll find steps in chapters 10 and 11 for resetting your relationship to digital devices to a place of perfect life balance. Oh, all right, let's settle for pretty darn good life balance. (After all, I think every teen has the right to get their life out of balance on at least a few occasions.)

PART III

RESET

LIFE IN THE FAST LANE

Refreshing Your Digital Spirit

You may want to sit down. Wrap yourself in a fuzzy blanket. Get some smelling salts handy. For I'm about to propose that you consider going on a digital fast. This means not using your phone and other devices for a period of time.

I know, I know. Stay calm. Open a window. Breathe in some fresh air. And hear me out. A digital fast gives your brain a time-out by disengaging from digital drama, texting turbulence, and the raucous racket of social media. It allows you to restore your systems to their healthy default settings. You can do a fast as a "stand-alone" activity. Or you can include a fast as part of your App-endectomy—your screen scene reset—which you'll read about in the next chapter. *Or* you can do an App-endectomy without a fast. There's no hard-and-fast fast rule. But no matter how you view your phone use, a brief or extended fast could be life-changing. For the better!

Hitting Fast Forward

You can do a phone phast by yourself or with a phriend or phamily member. You'll phind a phreedom you've never phelt before. This isn't phorever. It's just for phifteen minutes, or for a day, or maybe for a phew days. My filosofy is: Phorget what other people might think. Phollow your fonetic bliss.

> Did you get that out of your system?

> Phor now.

How long do you do a fast?

It could be for a morning, a day, a week, a month, or—summer vacation.

I think I'm going to faint.

Take some deep breaths.

Chances are a lot of "buts" are flying through your head just thinking about a fast. Fear not. For each anxiety-filled "but," I bet you can come up with some powerful, positive rejoinders. For example:

Negative "But"	Positive Pushback
But my phone is my life.	My phone is just a gadget I use.
I won't be able to function.	There might be a few things I can't do, but of course I'll be able to "function."
I'll be a freak.	Lots of people do occasional phone fasts or use their phones much less than I do. They're not freaks.
I won't have any friends.	Some friends may feel the same way about their phone use as me. Either way, my real friends will support me.
I LIKE spending time online.	And I have my whole life to enjoy it. A break doesn't change that.
People will think I'm holier than thou.	I don't have any more holes than the next person.
I'll be so bored.	I can turn being bored into a chance to do something new and interesting.
I won't be able to do it.	It might be tough. I don't know yet. Either way, I want to find out if I can do it.
If I'm not on my phone I won't have anything to talk about.	I have all sorts of interests and experiences I can talk about. Like what NOT being on my phone is like. I can ask people questions about themselves.

Going "cold turkey" may seem a bit like diving into a frigid lake. Unimaginable! Freezing! But people do it every winter. You *can* take the plunge—and if you power through the initial shock, it's wonderful. Refreshing. Invigorating. You feel terrifically alive. I believe the same is true of a phone fast. If you dive into it, if you stick with it, you'll almost certainly experience the relief that comes from not having to worry about likes, pressures to post and respond, or "happy face" photos of people's amazing, spectacular, photoshopped lives. And if the fast goes on for a while, you'll discover oodles of newfound time which you can use to see friends, study, indulge in hobbies, and pursue passions.

Don't worry about how your friends will react. And remember, you don't *have* to tell them. But if you do let them know about your plan, you can just say you need to do a digital detox for a bit. Own it as something you need to do for *yourself.* To avoid sounding "superior" or triggering a defensive reaction, don't describe your decision as an across-the-board condemnation of social media or screen time that your friends might take as a personal attack. If your friends are true friends, they will accept, be interested in, applaud, and maybe even be a bit jealous of your decision to unplug from social media. That's because, in a Common Sense Media survey on social media and "How Teens View Their Digital Lives," 43 percent of teens wished they could sometimes "unplug" from their phones.

Want to guess where millions of teens go to unplug?

> **The North Pole?**

Summer camp. More and more camps don't allow cell phones, believing they're a distraction that interferes with becoming more independent, making friends, having new adventures, and fully experiencing the joys of nature. Campers may experience a few days of "withdrawal," but after that they report many benefits from

Raccoon Robbers

a summer phone fast. It seems "no cell phones" at camp may be harder for parents, who have been known to evade camper arrival inspections by smuggling their child's phone inside a teddy bear or by giving their child two phones so, after letting one be confiscated, their child still has another. *Really, parents?*

One study followed preteens at a sleepaway camp. After only five days, campers who had no access to screens improved at interpersonal communication cues such as interpreting different tones of voice, making eye contact, reading body language, and correctly identifying facial expressions. It makes sense. More in-person "people time" usually makes for more in-person "people skills."

I'm not asking you to go away to camp *or* give up your phone. But my phantasy—

> Dude . . .

> Sorry. Phorgive me.

—is that you'll be curious and brave enough to experiment with a phone fast.

Pulling a Fast One

Let's look more closely at the different types of fasts.

Intermittent Fasts

These are fasts you program into your daily or weekly schedule on a regular basis. They can be structured in a number of ways. You can even mix and match by combining, say, a location fast with a time fast. You'll see what I mean below. Here are several different ways to structure a phone fast:

- **By physical location.** Designate phone-free *zones*. This could be your bedroom or bathroom, the library or gym—places you go to regularly. Associating digital downtime with certain locations creates a simple structure on which to hang your hiatus.

- **By context.** Here, you let a behavior, responsibility, interaction, or social setting be your cue for a phone break. This could be an afterschool job, dinner with your family, bus rides to track meets, lunch with friends. The idea is to improve the quality of the experience, to notice more, to give your brain a break from phone-hectic stimuli. You might even try to engage others in your phone phade-out: "What if we put our phones away during dinner and talk?" "Wanna have a phone-free coffee with me?"

- **By time.** This one's straightforward. Decide to abstain totally from your phone during a consistent time slot. Could be every Saturday morning; or for an hour after school; or between 10:00 p.m. and bedtime (which you should already be doing to get the best night's sleep). Certain times may seem more "natural" than others. Look for them.

- **By type of activity.** This involves limiting a particular *category* of device use in some way. For example, no shopping platforms during the week. No social media between dinner and 9:00 p.m. (good time to do homework!). No video gaming for five years—

> Ha, ha.

App Fasts

An app fast is characterized not by turning off your phone, but by fasting, according to rules you set, from a specific app or behavior. You might decide to *Kik* the habit and give yourself a "Snap Stop," a "Discord Detox," a "TikTok Time-out," an "Insta Intermission," a "Video Void," a "Pinterest Pause," a—

> Okay. Enough already.

> Oh, and just so you know, I don't know anyone who uses Pinterest.

> I know. I just needed a "P."

Purge Fasts

These are high-powered total fasts for flushing out your digital system. When doing this type of fast, you give up *all* phone use for a set period of time. It's the ultimate reset for cleaning out any accumulated online stress, noise, drama, and time suckers. Think of it as an electronic enema. No, on second thought, don't. But still: whether it lasts for a day, a weekend, a month, or longer, a purge fast is a great cleanse for restoring life balance.

Choosing the Fast That's Right for You

Phone fasts are powerful super-tools for maintaining or restoring your digital health. But how do you know which fast to do?

Imagine you live in a big, crowded city (you can skip the imagining if you *do* live in a big, crowded city). Imagined or not, you love the excitement and stimulation and amazing things you can do. But sometimes it gets to be **TOO MUCH!** Rude people, sidewalk hogs, nasty cashiers, rush hour traffic, litter on the streets, nonstop noise. It stresses you out, jangles your nerves, puts you in a bad mood. So you decide you need an escape. Something that will counter the chaos and let you exist without getting worn down by the urban jungle. Maybe an early morning walk in a park does the trick. You might take a long bike ride every Saturday on a traffic-free trail. Or maybe you save up to spend a week with friends in July at the beach or camping in a state park to rebalance your system. Maybe you even decide you can't stand it anymore, and consider moving to a new—quieter—place. And, of course, the opposite holds true, too. If you live in a cabin in the middle of Birnam Wood and the cicadas are driving you to distraction, a trek to the big city might be just the ticket for restoring your balance.

Now, substitute your phone for a noisy city. And a phone fast for an escape to natural beauty and peaceful surroundings. The goal is to use a fast as a tool to resist any imbalances *before* they cause you stress or problems.

That might mean fasting for an hour every day. Or for one weekend a month. Or dropping a particular app for a while (or longer). More "extreme" fasting for weeks or months may be needed if you feel addicted to your devices, if you've tried to stop and can't, if your screen time is a source of conflict with adults and a source of guilt or shame for you, if you feel like your life is going down the tubes, if you beat yourself up over your use.

I'll be honest with you. Doing a fast for a few days, or maybe even a few weeks, may not be enough if your screen scene is causing serious problems for you. Think of it as a digital diet. If you only do it for a few days or weeks, you won't see the results you'd like. That's simply not enough time to develop and solidify the new habits needed to sustain such major changes in your digital life. A total purge of your system for an extended period of time may be necessary. And then, with caution and careful monitoring, you can bring back the healthy interactions and useful, non-toxic apps, bit by bit. And make no mistake: **THAT IS GOING TO BE HARD TO DO.**

> Why are you shouting?

> I'm not shouting. I'm EMPHASIZING.

So, whatever your relationship to your screens, I recommend phone fasts—whether mini or mega—as prime tools for maintaining or resetting screen scene health.

Brief, intermittent fasts are great for keeping your balance on the high wire of online life. They're like the adjustments a tightrope walker makes with his balance pole to stay above the wire, rather than belowwwwwww_w.

And longer purge fasts are a great way to restore digital balance or kick off an App-endectomy.

Whatever you decide, you have your work cut out for you. But I believe in you, and I'm confident that if you set your mind and motivation to it, and follow the tips in this book, you'll succeed.

Fasting Tip 1

You may initially think about and experience a fast as *doing without. Being deprived.* That's natural. But if you think of it that way, you create a mindset of *absence.* That can make it harder to complete the fast.

So here's a mind trick. Try not to think of a fast as a sacrifice. Instead, think of it as a gift—a lovely recess—to refresh your spirit, clear your head, calm your nerves, and improve your mood. Instead of focusing on what you are "giving up," think of what you are *gaining*: serenity, inner strength, psychic space, power over Big Tech, free time. You may just find that the things you are getting outweigh anything you are going without.

Fasting Tip 2

Habits (and addictions) are powerful forces. They don't like being messed with. One of the ways they express their displeasure with anyone (such as you), who dares to confront them is by messing with your mind. Let's say you decide to fast for a month. (Don't faint. There are circumstances where that might be needed to regain digital life balance.) If you think of going without your phone for a month, it'll seem IMPOSSIBLE. *No way I can do that!*

The key to success is to *not* think about doing it for a month. Get that out of your head. Instead, think of doing it for just one day. No phone for one day just might be doable. That's all you have to do. One day. Today. You can do that.

Then, tomorrow comes. You have a new "today." Can you do without your phone for just that one day? You succeeded the day before, so you can succeed today. Forget about a month. Just do it for one day. Thirty times. And if a day seems like an unimaginably long interval, reduce it to two hours, or even one hour. Then, all you have to do is fast for an hour. At the end of that hour, all you have to do is fast for an hour. Keep that up, and the day will go by.

I've used this "mind trick" many times in my own life for achieving seemingly insurmountable goals. Writing a book is a good example. If I think of writing a 408-page book, my first reaction is: *No way! I can't write a book that long!* But could I write a few pages—maybe three, four, or five—today? Yup. I can do that. Then, when *tomorrow* is *today,* can I write a few pages? Should be able to. So I don't have to write a 408-page book after all. I just have to write a few pages "today." And after I've done that for 100 or so "todays," what do you know? I've written a 408-page book. One day at a time.

Fasting Tips 3, 4, 5, 6, 7, 8, 9, 10, 11, 12, and 13

- Before starting your fast, fill out the "My Fasting Matrix" form on the next page. This will place your fast in context—why you're doing it, what you hope to achieve, what steps you need to take to do it responsibly.

- If you have friends who will call 911 if they don't hear from you within 10 seconds of sending a text or Snap, tell them you're going offline.

- Alert others who need to know you won't be available in the usual way.

- See if you can enlist some fellow fasters—maybe friends or siblings who have bemoaned how "addicted" they are to their devices.

- Plan in advance how you'll use extra time generated by being offline. Otherwise, the void of unstructured free time could create feelings of stress or boredom that tempt you back into the arms of your phone.

- Set up auto responses for emails and texts.

- Forward calls to your home landline (that's not cheating) if you have one.

- Do your friends' phone numbers exist offline? If not, jot them down so you can call them from a landline without your contact list.

- Strike up conversations with somebody you normally wouldn't.

- Each day (or hour for short fasts), write down how you're feeling, what you're noticing.

- When re-engaging with your screens, take it easy. After a food fast, you wouldn't resume eating by gorging yourself. Your system would rebel. Same thing with a phone fast. Take small bites of your apps.

Not So Fast

Planning is key to a successful fast. It's not something you can just "wing." When you're ready to try a fast or include one in your reset, fill out the following table to structure your success.

You can also download this matrix at freespirit.com/dragons.

My Fasting Matrix	
Type of fast (example: Intermittent, App, Purge)	
If Intermittent Fast, list your framework (example: phone off between 8 and 9 p.m.; no phone every Saturday morning, phone off in carpool)	
If App Fast, list the app, your rule, and timeframe (example: no Insta for one week starting Monday)	
If Purge Fast, list start and stop time and day (example: Begin 5/12 at noon; end 5/15 at noon)	
Lifeline person(s) (People you can count on to help you succeed)	
Lifeline behavior(s) (Things you'll do if the going gets tough)	
Reward (How you'll celebrate after finishing a successful fast)	

Dear Alex,

I want to try a three-day fast. But my mom is going to have a fit if she can't reach me whenever she wants. Do you have any suggestions for this?

Is the earth round? Of *course* I have suggestions.

Good for you for wanting to try a fast. This is a sticky issue, but a common one with parents who have grown up expecting instant, 24/7 access to their kids. You're going to have to disabuse your mom of that notion—at least for a three-day period. Think of it as a teachable moment that will help her grow.

You'll need, of course, to approach your mom to resolve this. But first, you have to prepare.

1. Think about why you need or want to try a fast. The reasons are bound to be compelling and will show your mom that it's something you feel is in your best interest. Surely she wouldn't want to stand in the way of such a responsible, mature act on your part.

2. Anticipate your mom's objections. Are they emotional? (*"I'll worry if I can't reach you."*) Practical? (*"I have to be able to reach you if I'm going to be late picking you up."*)

3. Come up with solutions and workarounds that will address her concerns.

Once you've thought things through, find a calm time when your mom is relaxed and in a good mood. Approach her with something like this:

"Mom [or Mother, Mama, Mater, Maw, Mummy, Mommie Dearest, or whatever you call her], *do you have a minute? I'd like to talk with you about a challenge I've set for myself. I'm going to need your help to do it."*

She's bound to be intrigued. Tell her about the fast. Explain your reasons for wanting to do it. Then, acknowledge the issue of her being able to reach you. This shows you've considered her wishes and feelings. That's called empathy. Parents love seeing empathy in their kids. For each concern or objection she might have, offer a solution.

"I know you like to be able to text me, but if I keep my phone on for that, I don't think I can stick to the fast. So I thought of other ways you can contact me. If you need to reach me during the day, here's the number for the school office. They can get a message to me. And if…"

And so on and so forth. Anticipating your schedule during the three-day fast period—knowing when you'll be at practice, or at the library, or with friends (it's okay to give out a friend's number, but be sure you give them a heads-up first)—will help you come up with workarounds. Chances are good that, between your considerate attitude and your mom's desire for her child to be healthy and successful, she will get behind your effort. And if she doesn't, you can always try throwing your phone out the window and telling her you wish you'd never been born.

Dear Alex,

If you do a fast, is it okay to watch TV or Netflix? Or is that cheating?

Great question! And a difficult one to answer given how many variables there are. Let's start with the easiest part of the answer:

It is forbidden during a fast to stream movies or TV on your phone, tablet, or lap- or desktop computer.

Who forbids it? I do. That's because an important reason for fasting—and I'm talking about a purge fast—is to give yourself a total break from screens. *Especially* small screens where, with one click, you can jump from Netflix to your social or to the very video game causing problems. It's just too tempting. The idea behind a purge fast is to experience new sensations and moments, to get your brain and body and social relationships active in different ways, to break patterns of screen time causing negative consequences.

Now, if you're a crafty reader, you may have read the above rule and noticed that I specifically mentioned watching on a phone, tablet, or computer as being forbidden. You may have been champing at the bit ever since, wondering if maybe watching on a bigger screen is okay. Well, champ no more. I do allow use of a television if:

- Those activities were not problematic uses for you on your smaller devices (i.e., what caused you to fast in the first place)
- You've fulfilled your responsibilities for the day (homework, chores, etc.)
- You're not using the full-size TV as you would your device (for example, watching YouTube or TikTok videos through the TV)
- You aren't hidden away in your bedroom (see, you get bonus points if your viewing becomes a social activity with other household members)

Now, of course, if you're doing an intermittent or app fast, whose purpose is to limit use during specific times and/or to cut out certain apps, it's okay to watch TV or movies on your small devices as long as they're not "problem" uses for you and you're observing the limits you've set for yourself.

Dear Alex,

I don't need a whole fast. My problem is three apps I can't stop using. I don't think I can quit them all at once. Is it okay to pick one for starters? How do I decide which one?

It's not only okay, it's *great* to pick just one app as the initial target of your fast. To decide which one, it makes sense to identify which app is causing you the most problems or discomfort. It's like, if your roof is leaking, you should put the bucket where the most water is pouring in. You may already have a good sense of which app is most troublesome. If, however, you're not sure, ask yourself:

- Which app is causing me the most harm?
- Which app is hardest for me to control?
- Which app makes me feel the worst after using it?

These questions will help you get a sense of the "weight" of the consequences, how much they bother you. Once you have that, you'll know which app to zap. And if you truly can't decide—if they all seem equally in need of a fast—flip a three-sided coin.

Dear Alex,

Can you listen to music during a fast?

If you're asking about listening via radio, vinyl, Sonos speakers in your home, a CD player, or an audio channel on a TV, I would say it's fine. But I assume you're asking about listening through your device. In that case, the issue is not music, it's temptation. If you're just accessing a playlist that goes on for hours, that's different than frequent clicking, tapping, scrolling, selecting music videos, and buying tunes—all things that require active engagement with your phone. The question, then, is whether you can operate your phone to play music without violating the intentions of your fast.

That depends on you—and the nature of the fast. If it's an intermittent or app fast, and you can stick to your rules or schedule without being tempted to peek at a feed, check your messages, or watch "just one" TikTok, listening to music on your phone is fine. If, however, it's a purge fast, my guess is that turning on the phone, tapping the screen, and putting in your earbuds would be a risky temptation.

There are a couple other things to consider. One is what I'll call "purity." Part of the value of a fast is to experience life directly, and not through a device. Think how ingrained in your existence your phone is. It's implanted in your being. Even your hands and posture are physically imprinted by phone use. Listening to music through your device—even if you successfully resist the other temptations it presents—deprives you of the full value of being phone free for a period of time. It's a bit like swearing off playing tennis for a week, but still hitting balls against the garage wall.

The other thing to think about is bandwidth. Music takes up brain bandwidth. If you're trying to experience life for a period of time without electronic stimuli blazing straight into your head through your eyes and ears, listening through your phone would compromise that. If, however, music is playing from a different device into the room, that is less intense and intrusive (unless you have it turned up to 4,000 decibels).

So, conclusion: music through a non-screen audio source, no problem. Music through any device with a screen, be cautious. After all, there was a famous Motown band called the Temptations.

Dear Alex,

What if you're doing a fast and there's an emergency and you don't have a phone?

One of the best things about having a phone is that you can make a call or be reached in the event of an emergency. But people dealt with emergencies long before cell phones were ever invented. If you're on a total fast and leave your phone at home so as not to be tempted, wherever you go, unless you're on a solo trek in the wilderness with no cell reception, there are bound to be other people with phones. In an emergency, you can borrow a phone or the phone's owner can make a call for you.

Bear with Me

If you can safely keep your phone with you and not be tempted to use it, you can always turn it on to make a call if you have to. An emergency overrules a fast. (But it has to be a real life-and-limb emergency and not that you desperately need to check the football scores.)

As for people being able to reach you, it's usually parents who are most anxious about that. Again, if you can safely keep your phone with you and on, you can modify settings to allow calls and texts from certain people/numbers, like parents, while blocking everyone else. If, however, this would sabotage your fast, ask your parents to support you by agreeing to suspend instant access for the duration of your fast. (For more on how to do that, see page 289.)

Dear Alex,

I think I need to do a long fast. But I have to use a computer at school and for homework. How is a fast going to be possible?

This is another tricky one, since—once again—there are many variables at play. For example, how much, and what sort of screen time is required at school? Do you go online to take tests? Receive individualized lessons? Flip through flashcards? Do you use your own laptop (which gives you access to all of its contents and installed platforms, including those which may be problems for you), or do you use school-furnished devices? What type of screen time is necessary to complete homework? Can you work offline to write a paper? Or do you need to visit websites to do research and read digital textbooks? Are you expected to connect online with classmates to complete collaborative projects? How do *teachers* use the internet? Is there a school portal through which all assignments are handed out and turned in? How flexible is the school in responding to student needs? How individualized is its approach to teaching and learning? And finally, how long a fast are you considering? There's a difference between a week and a month (or longer). Since I don't know any of those answers, I'll give you some guidelines.

Consider in-class computer use as an allowable exception. If your screen time in school is on school-issued devices, and strictly limited to keep students from straying, it may be okay to exempt that time from your fast. If, however, you can go to Insta or Minecraft while everyone else is looking at the Periodic Table of Elements, that won't work. So, the advisability of excepting in-school screen time depends on the nature and technology of your school's internet access, and the strength of your commitment to a fast. But the easiest initial path, if you feel you can safely be on screen in school, is to try that. It may just work without compromising your fast.

Do homework in the kitchen. The use of the internet for assignments is the other big school-related issue to resolve when fasting. As with classroom screen time, it may be possible for you to use your devices for homework without compromising your fast. To give this the best chance of working, do your homework in a public spot in your home—the dining room, kitchen, family room—someplace where other people come and go. That can act as a deterrent for doing anything other than schoolwork. Look, I'm the first to recognize that's not ideal. There may be distractions, and you'd probably rather be in a quieter, more private setting. But we're talking about your *health*. You wouldn't be doing a long fast if you didn't feel it was necessary. So, to support your goal, adjustments will have to be made.

If you know these exceptions won't work for you, or you tried them and they made it difficult or impossible to maintain your overall fast, you'll need to talk to your teachers whose classes require screen time, whether in school or for doing homework.

Negotiate with your teachers. Explain what you're doing and why you need to do it. Ask if they can support your fast by making accommodations regarding in-class and at-home screen time. Unless you've been a total goof-off for half a year, most teachers will respect you for your initiative and will want to help. Now that I think of it, if you *have* been a goof-off, they will still want to help since maybe your screen time is the culprit. Work out a plan with them for handling in-class computer time and completing assignments. Remember, billions of students went to school for centuries before computers were invented. And they managed to learn, finish homework, and do wonderful things in life.

Get someone to go to bat for you. I hope that most if not all of your teachers will readily make accommodations. If some don't, you will need to strengthen your case. If you are experiencing serious negative consequences from screen time, that is a *medical* condition. Being on screens is causing you physical, mental, emotional, and/or social harm. So you may need to get a parent, doctor, or therapist involved. Your mom or dad can speak with the principal or counselor. A doctor or therapist can write a letter saying that abstention from screens for a period of time is a "medical necessity" for you. If you broke your leg, there'd be no question you'd be excused from gym. And if screen time broke your psyche, you should be excused from digital devices while recovering from that injury.

And if all else fails, if your teachers refuse to cooperate, you send them to me. I'll give them a piece of my mind!

> **Are you sure you can spare one?**

Putting Yourself on the Fast Track

If you asked teens who decided to do a fast why they did it, I'm sure this is what they would tell you:

I felt addicted to my phone.

I was obsessed with video games.

Too much stress.

All I cared about was likes.

Pressure to check my phone all the time.

Pressure to respond.

Pressure to put on a happy face.

Fights with my parents.

My phone was taking over my life.

Bad grades.

Too little sleep.

I hated wasting so much time.

Everybody online is so judgmental.

Bullying. People can be so mean.

My phone controlled my mood.

I felt like I was living my life for social media, not for me.

And if you asked teens what changed after their fast, this is what I know they would say:

I felt more relaxed.

I did things I hadn't done in ages and it was great.

At first, I kept thinking about what I was missing. But then I thought about what everyone else was missing.

I felt like I was living more in the moment.

I didn't worry about a lot of things.

I liked being able to focus on me.

It was great not having to be "on call" all the time, having to meet everybody's expectations to respond instantly.

It was nice not feeling controlled by my phone. It's like I was controlling me.

I liked seeing the world around me. I noticed a lot of things I never had before.

I wasn't thinking so much about what everybody else was doing. I was thinking about what I was doing.

I felt free.

I know. You're probably skeptical. Sounds too good to be true. And even if it were possible, you're thinking *"No way I could cut back or give up my phone."* At the same time, you may also be thinking that there's no way things can keep going the way they are.

Look, I know cutting way back on your phone use, or even giving it up completely for a period of time, seems unthinkable. Impossible. Like losing a huge part of yourself and your life.

And it would be a gigantic change. No question.

But there's also no question that you *can* do it. Of course you can! If you want to. If you *truly* want to. It may be the hardest thing you've ever done. But you *can* do it.

So, now's the time to think about doing a digital reset, and what it might look like. A phone fast can be just one of many tools you use, or it can be the whole enchilada if you think that's all you need to maintain or restore the balance between your life and your screens.

> **I love enchiladas. And burritos!**

How do you figure out if a fast is right for you? And whether to do one all by itself or as part of a more complete and multi-faceted reset plan? You turn to the next chapter, that's how, where you'll learn everything you need to know about giving yourself an App-endectomy.

CHAPTER 11

GIVE YOURSELF AN APP-ENDECTOMY

Taking Charge of Your Digital Life

All right! Start your engines. This is where the pedal hits the metal. The screen meets the wean. Put on your scrubs and PPE. It's time to operate. To give yourself an App-endectomy.

> Say again, what's an App-endectomy?

It's a custom plan you're going to create to reset your relationship to your phone. Custom, because you are you, and nobody else. (And, yes, you can quote me on that.) You will identify a single element of your digital life that you want to change or improve, whether that means cutting back on an Achilles heel app, reducing screen time overall, changing your emotional relationship to social media, or even spending *more* time on something. I'll be coaching you through how to choose your goal and make a detailed plan for attaining that goal.

As you prepare for surgery, keep in mind these four key points:

Key Point 1: Nothing you're going to do is irreversible. You're trying out some new behaviors and possibilities. It's an adventure. You can always go back to the way things were. Or you may end up in places you never dreamed of, and never look back.

Key Point 2: In the grand scheme of things, the slice of civilization that has lived in the digital world is infinitesimal. For 99.9% of the time homo sapiens have walked the planet, the internet didn't exist. Some of the greatest achievements and ecstasies of humanity took place in the millennia before digital technology. So, the full bounty of life exists no matter how much or how little you use digital devices.

Key Point 3: While you might decide as this adventure unfolds that you need to go "cold turkey" and give up your phone for an extended period, we're not talking about that right now. It's very tough to do in today's world, and you'd miss out on a lot of the genuine benefits of smartphones. For now, we're talking about setting limits, being in charge, making your phone work for you.

Key Point 4: Every day of your life is an opportunity. Some of what happens is beyond your control. School beckons. People make demands. You have appointments and responsibilities. But other parts of the day are yours to command. You decide what to do, where to go, how to spend that time. You may choose to play a sport, write for the school paper, get together with friends, spend time with your family, play with a pet, go for a jog, pursue a passion, indulge in a hobby, or spend 10 hours a day on screens. As each day passes, that day and that time can never be replayed. It may be archived as a wonderful memory and life-enhancing experience. It may go down as totally rotten. It might fall somewhere in between. Whatever the case, there's no reset button to do yesterday over. But there *is* a reset button for tomorrow. So . . .

Ready. Reset. Go!

To create your plan, you're going to use the intel you gathered in chapter 3 about your screen scene, as well as the brain-bursting knowledge you've acquired on possible negative effects of excessive screen time, to come up with a digital-health strategy that:

- Strengthens your Big-Tech-fighting immune system
- Surgically removes any elements of your device use that may be infecting your psyche and life balance

At this point, based on the chapters you've read and the challenges you've completed, you should have a gut (that's near your app-endix) sense of your relationship to screens. Depending on your concerns and scores, you may be thinking, *PHEW! My phone use is okay.* Or maybe you're a little worried. Or maybe you discovered (or confirmed a suspicion) that your screen time is creating negative consequences for you. Or maybe you're in a state of total 12-alarm, whirling-dervish freak-out, feeling you're being sucked into the muck of digital quicksand, drowning under an avalanche of rowdy posts, pics, and pixels. (I think that counts as five mixed metaphors in one sentence, quite possibly a world record. A little trivia for you language buffs.)

The good news is that no matter where you find yourself, there are steps you can take to improve your digital health.

You may be wondering what the steps are.

All right, simmer down. I'll tell you what's in this chapter and how it's going to work:

1. **Choosing Your Goal.** This is the key to your App-endectomy: Identifying *one* specific element in your digital life that you would like to change. It could be cutting back on a particular activity. Or using your social in a different way. Or turning your phone off an hour before bedtime. If you have several (or more) things you want to change, you're still going to choose just one to start with. After you've achieved that goal, you can always tackle a new one.

2. **Preparing for the Operation.** This is the groundwork you'll need to do to maximize your chances for a successful outcome—things like building a support team, green-lighting a counter-threat plan, and ensuring FOMO will be a no-show.

3. **Choosing Your Tools.** You need and deserve the best tools, tips, and strategies for carrying out your App-endectomy and ensuring the most favorable prognosis. You can look through the list of tools later in this chapter (starting on page 318) and choose the right ones to turbocharge your motivation and provide practical and moral support for your reset.

4. **Performing the Operation.** Here's where you take your goal and create a personal "App-endectomy Reset Plan" that will serve as your guide throughout the operation. You'll enter your goal, the tools you'll use to achieve it, the pitfalls you may encounter, and the measures and milestones that you'll use to monitor your progress. And then, it's off to the races!—I mean, off to the App-endectomy!—as you carry out your plan.

5. **Troubleshooting.** It's possible you'll encounter some problems or glitches carrying out your plan and achieving your goals. This sometimes happens, which explains the phrase, "If at first you don't succeed, try, try, again." Or you might have met your initial goals, and then find that you're backsliding into old behaviors. This can occur with any changes requiring personal discipline (exercising, healthy eating, studying, controlling your temper). Don't give up. The chapter ends with ideas for troubleshooting your plan, making course corrections, and/or maintaining your success.

If you bring your courage, creativity, perseverance, and knowledge-stuffed little gray cells to these five steps, you will meet a new digital you (whom I think you will like!).

THINK ABOUT IT

Most of you, my dear readers, have never known a time without smartphones and the internet. From tiny toddlerhood when your mom stuck a tablet in your hands to shut you up—I mean, to delight, entertain, and educate you—to tangled teenage-hood when phones are a vital organ, their use as natural as breathing, you have never experienced life without screens. I don't mean that as a criticism; it's just the truth.

But it does make me wonder, would it be a disservice to a teen if they never had an opportunity to experience life *without* screens, to make a personal decision about their role and value? Imagine if you were born with, say, constant music playing in your head. You'd have a soundtrack accompanying you wherever you go. Some of the tunes are peppy and pleasant, some are blues-y and mellow, and some are screechy and ear-shattering. Some make you cry. Some make you dance. Occasionally, you can pick the music you want to hear. Often you can't. But it's always there. Nonstop. Reverberating through your body. You've never questioned it because you've never known anything different.

And then, one day, somebody says, "You know, you can turn that off whenever you want."

And you say, "No way! I can't imagine that. It's always been on."

And they say, "You don't have to imagine it. Try it."

You have the right to set your own digital boundaries, to do what is best for your own happiness, peace, confidence, and self-esteem. Cutting back on screen time or quitting a toxic app doesn't have to be forever. It could be just for a day, a week, a summer. Even a short respite can give you a new perspective, a breather, a feeling of freedom and renewal.

1. Choosing Your Goal

Identifying your goal is the most important step in creating an App-endectomy plan. No goal, no plan. What keeps App-endectomies simple is that the process will be the same no matter where you find yourself along the "no problem" to "total freakout" screen-scene continuum.

If you're in peak digital condition with few or no concerns about your screen time, you'll pick a goal that helps you to maintain your already smart smartphone habits. Think of it as digital brushing and flossing.

Or, you may have identified a few screen-related behaviors, feelings, or life imbalances that concern you—anything from time-sucking apps to digital don'ts. No aggressive intervention required; just some precise incisions with a screen-time scalpel. Even if you have a number of things you'd like to change, you'll still start with just one goal.

And some of you may feel that your digital well-being is flashing code red. You're worried about or feel overwhelmed by real-life problems related to your screen use. You show symptoms of App-endicitis such as swollen social media, upset Insta, loss of self-control, and/or severe pain in the app domain. Major surgery is needed to prevent a burst digititis. But you'll still face your challenges one goal at a time, one step at a time.

So any reset, whether mini or major, begins with identifying your goal. You may already know what it is: You want to do homework without being distracted by your phone. You want to stop spending hours a day on Instagram or YouTube. You want to cut back on a certain video game. You want to spend *more* time moderating Zoom meetings for a particular cause.

If you're clear about your goal, you can leapfrog to "Preparing for the Operation" (page 310). But be forewarned: You'll miss out on a lot of brilliant ideas and sparkling witticisms between here and there.

> What if you don't know your goal yet? What if you don't even know if your screen time is a problem?

> You can create a Screen Scene Profile.

> A what? What's that? How's that gonna help me?

> Hold your horses. Did you wake up on the impatient side of the bed today?

A Screen Scene Profile is a diagnostic template to bring together the intel you collected in chapters 2 and 3 and create a clear picture of your screen scene. Gathering that information in one place will help you decide whether your screen time is problematic and point you toward your first goal.

So put on your surgical gloves, sterilize your pen, and fill out the following forms. Your answers will guide you to the best treatment plan for your screen scene.

Tip: The Screen Scene Profile asks you to gather and transfer certain intel from the challenges you completed in chapters 2 and 3. If you've been reading this book in order, a lot of knowledge has poured into your head since then. Hopefully, more has poured in than drained out. Some of that information may have altered how you think about your screen time. You may now recognize in yourself certain consequences of device use that you hadn't noticed or thought about before. This might make you want to reconsider some of your earlier answers or concerns. *So as you transfer your intel, feel free to update your answers in chapters 2 and 3 to represent your latest thinking.*

Create Your Screen Scene Profile

These questions will help you summarize your adventures in the Land of Screen Time. You'll need to refer back to the harrowing, life-threatening challenges in chapters 2 and 3 which you heroically conquered with courage and poison-tipped No. 2 pencils. Some of these you'll be able to answer right off the bat. Others may require more thought. If that's the case, you can come back to them later.

The Screen Scene Profile is also available for download at freespirit.com /dragons.

My Screen Scene Profile

Go back to **Challenge 1: What's *Your* Screen Scene?** (chapter 2, page 17). Please.	
Write down your total points in the box to the right.	
Look at any statement(s) you circled and identified as a concern. Select the three that worry you the most. Write them down here.	1. 2. 3.
If you had no concerns, go on to the next section.	

CONTINUED ›

Hang a U-ey and go back to **Challenge 3: How Much Time Do I _Think_ I Spend?** (chapter 3, page 30).

Look in the "Actual Time Per Day" column. Enter the **total number of hours** you spend (the sum at the bottom) in the box to the right.

Don't freak out note: The total number of hours doesn't necessarily indicate a problem since it depends on how you spend that time. You'll be able to adjust for that later when creating your plan.

In the box to the right, enter the total number of activity categories you marked as a concern.
If you marked any categories of screen time as a concern, pick the three that worry you most. Write them down here.

1.

2.

3.

Retrace your steps to **Challenge 3: Bonus Question** (chapter 3, page 30).

In the box to the right, record the actual number of times you unlock or pick up your phone each day, on average.

If you marked this as a concern, place a check-mark in the space to the right.

Return to **Challenge 5: How 'Appy Am I?** (chapter 3, page 37).

Record your total number of frowny faces in the box to the right.

List the three apps that leave you feeling the frowniest after using them. For each app, explain why you gave it a frowny face.

Ex.: Ask.fm · too much bullying
Insta · hate my photos, waste time

APP   REASON

1.

2.

3.

CONTINUED ›

Do the moonwalk back to **Challenge 6: Am I Under Attack?** (chapter 3, page 41).

In the box to the right, record the total number of apps whose notifications are a concern for you.

List the names of the three apps whose notifications concern you the most.

1.

2.

3.

Take a meandering stroll to revisit **Challenge 7: What Are My Phone Habits and Triggers?** (chapter 3, page 44).

Count up the number of "Yes" answers you gave and record it in the box to the right. (Ignore the question about the dog. He's sleeping.)

Now look at the different triggers you identified for picking up your phone. Write down up to three triggers that lead to device use *that is a concern for you*. For example, if you worry about social media use, select the trigger(s) that lead to that use. (For example: Boredom, loneliness, FOMO.) Then list the apps or activities that you tend to use as a result of those triggers. (For example, Instagram, Snapchat, Twitter.)

TRIGGER	LEADS TO	ACTIVITY
Ex. Hunger		Uber Eats
1.		
2.		
3.		

Follow the Yellow Brick Road to **Challenge 8: Do I Have an Achilles Heel?** (chapter 3, page 48).

Record in the boxes to the right your scores for any screen activities you ran through the Achilles Heel challenge. Below each score, list the app/activity that gave you that score.

1.

2.

3.

CONTINUED ›

Walk backward until you bump into **Challenge 9: Am I At Risk?** (chapter 3, page 52).

You should see anywhere between 0 and 36 "Yeses" indicating statements you identify as a concern. Record your total number of concerns in the box to the right.	
If you had no concerns, you've finished your screen scene profile questions.	
From among the concerns you identified, pick the three that trouble you the most, and list them here.	1. 2. 3.
If a particular *category* of warning signs worries you (for example, "social," "physical," "emotional"), record it in the space to the right.	

Now, add up all the numbers you've just entered in all the boxes on this form to give you a mathematical sense of your screen scene.

Oh, man. That's a lot of math.

I'll make it easy as pi.

So, quit yer beefin' and get out your pencil. You can enter your numbers below for easy addition.

My Screen Scene Profile: Scoring Sheet

Screen Scene Profile Section	Number to Add
Challenge 1: What's *Your* Screen Scene? (page 17)	
Challenge 3: How Much Time Do I *Think* I Spend? (page 30)	
Challenge 3: Bonus Question (page 30)	

CONTINUED ›

Challenge 5: How 'Appy am I? (page 37)	
Challenge 6: Am I Under Attack? (page 41)	
Challenge 7: What Are My Phone Habits and Triggers? (page 44)	
Challenge 8: Do I Have an Achilles Heel? (page 48)	
Additional Achilles Heel (optional)	
Additional Achilles Heel (optional)	
Challenge 9: Am I At Risk? (page 52)	
TOTAL	

Whew! If you want to take a rest after that mental exertion, be my guest.

Interpret Your Score

Now that you've got your total, let's see what it says about your screen time.

0 – 120   Looks like you're in good shape. Maybe you just need a few tweaks and tools to maintain and strengthen your already excellent screen habits. Or maybe you want to *increase* your screen time. (Can you believe I actually said that?) Perhaps you want to use your devices to support a cause, pursue a creative project, or acquire a new set of skills or knowledge.

121 – 220   Your score suggests you sometimes experience negative consequences from your screen activity. You may find it difficult at times to control what you do and how much time you spend on your phone. An App-endectomy should help you correct any imbalances or unhealthy uses and get you back on top of your device use.

221 and up   If your total is 221 or higher, your screen time is likely causing significant problems, concerns, and negative consequences. You saw yourself in quite a few warning signs. You may feel unable to control your screen time and may have even wondered if you're addicted to your phone. An App-endectomy is just the ticket to restore your life balance and put you back in charge. You may need to work on a number of goals—one at a time—over time.

So now you have your "mathematical" screen scene score. But there's also the "score" in your gut. That's just as important. In filling out your Screen Scene Profile, you selected your most troubling concerns. Now think about them. Weigh them. Turn them inside out and upside down. Listen to them.

Which concern pops to the surface as the *most* troubling, the highest priority? *That* should be your initial GOAL. It may be a general goal like, "I want to spend less time on my phone." That's fine for now. Later in this chapter you'll see how to turn a general goal into a specific one that is clear, realistic, and achievable.

TIP: Earlier I advised you not to freak out (necessarily) about the total number of hours you spend on screens. Hours alone can be misleading in reflecting the health of your screen scene. You may be spending very few hours, but what you're doing is harmful to your psyche or safety. You may be spending many hours a day, but you're creating art or music; editing a film; managing a network of volunteers; "traveling" 'round the world by visiting the websites of museums, wildlife refuges, or artisanal ice cream makers to pursue a passionate interest—all things that nourish your growth and spirit. Or you may spend many hours playing unchallenging games, fretting over posts and likes, compulsively checking feeds, or lurking on websites where bullying, hatred, and darkness reign—activities that leave you feeling empty, angry, or ashamed. So, when assessing your screen scene, be sure to think not just about the amount of time, but also about the *nature* of the time you spend.

So, Brave Resistance Fighter. You have a decision to make. Do you want to give yourself an App-endectomy?

> **Why do I get the feeling I'm supposed to say yes?**

Or are you such a paragon of pixel perfection, such a master of megabytes, such a sovereign of social media sanity, that you can't imagine a single area where your digital life could be improved?

> **I definitely think I'm supposed to say yes.**

I jest. Of course there are people—you may be one of them—whose screen time is safe, fun, healthy, important to them, and in excellent balance with other aspects of their life. You may decide that no surgery is required at this time. But it's still helpful to familiarize yourself with the elements of an App-endectomy. For one thing, many teens are concerned about friends or family members with unhealthy digital habits. Being familiar with the reset process could put you in a position to help someone else. Plus, you never know when, down the road, you might feel the need to give your own digital life a therapeutic tune-up.

So . . . drum roll please . . .

Add up your numerical score and your "gut" score, factor in the *nature* of your screen time, and decide which of the following statements best reflects your screen scene:

I have no concerns about my screen scene.	Accept	**DECLINE**
I have minor concerns about my screen scene.	Accept	**DECLINE**
I have major concerns about my screen scene.	**ACCEPT**	Decline
I intend to give myself an App-endectomy.	**ACCEPT**	Decline
My first goal is:		
I'll decide later, thanks.		
Are you sure?	Yes	No
Would you like to update your decision now or:		
Try in an hour		
Try tonight		
Remind me tomorrow		
Turn on Auto Update		

Why does that sound familiar?

I'm channeling Big Tech and trying to control your choices.

Did you make a decision? Did you identify your goal? Congratulations! No matter what you decided, I hope you feel good about having examined your digital life with such honesty and fortitude.

If you did decide to perform an App-endectomy and you've chosen a goal to start with, here are the next steps you will need to take to help ensure your success.

2. Preparing for the Operation

This section talks about the action steps you'll need to take to prepare for the App-endectomy. Once you're done with these, you'll be ready to craft your personal plan. With that plan in hand, you'll then select the tips, tools, and strategies you feel will best serve your goals. (And if you choose not to perform an App-endectomy at this time, don't worry! I will pop up on your screen every 24 hours to ask if you want to restart your mind to install an updated decision.)

So, let's get started!

You may have noticed that the right preparation makes work go more quickly and smoothly and leads to better results.

> Nope. Never noticed.

Well, it does. Problem is, preparation isn't always the most exciting thing to do. You're so eager to get to the part of the project that shows results, it's easy to skip over the prep work. For example, I need to paint a fence. I want to just start painting right away so I can quickly see how nice it will look with a fresh coat. But I know that if I don't first scrape it and wash it, the paint won't adhere properly, and in a few months it will look terrible and I'll kick myself in the butt (a difficult contortion) for not having done the prep work. Whether preparation involves sharpening tools, making an outline, digging deep inside your feelings, or reaching out to people, it can often make the difference between an efficient, successful process and a frustrating, mucked-up mess.

The same principle applies to giving yourself an App-endectomy. Getting your ducks in a row (hopefully they all have medical degrees) will make the operation easier to perform, and more likely to be successful. Quack, quack.

Here are the important steps to take. Fill out each template (please), so you'll have the information handy to insert in your App-endectomy plan.

Build Your Team

Have you ever noticed how people who achieve an important goal or win an award often thank their "team"?

> That, I've noticed.

Well, the team *should* be thanked, because their contributions can be essential to meeting challenges. Whether it's a pitcher who throws a no-hitter, a mountain climber who conquers a summit, or a teen who conducts an App-endectomy, a support team can make the goal more reachable and the journey less lonely.

A digital reset can be hard to do. If you're lucky, you may find a friend or a sibling or even a parent—we *know* how addicted some of them are to their phones—who learns what you have in mind and wants to do it with you. Or you may be on a solitary journey. But that doesn't mean you're all alone. Even solo travelers often receive kindness and support from people they meet along the way. Prior to undertaking any of the App-endectomies, you need to identify your "team"—people who will understand what you're doing, encourage you, ask how it's going, and be available to lend their assistance.

When you ask someone for their help, you're not burdening them. You're giving them a gift—the warm feeling they'll get from being trusted and having a chance to lend their support. Never hesitate to:

- **Say the magic words.** The most powerful, courageous words anyone can say are: "I need help."

- **Ask a parent for help.** Think of what your mom or dad can do to support your App-endectomy. Make them earn their keep. Maybe they can hold onto your devices overnight. Or offer an incentive for successfully completing your App-endectomy. Or temporarily change the WiFi password so you can't log on.

- **Ask a sibling for help.** You may feel more comfortable turning to a brother or sister, if you have siblings who live with you. Maybe you'd like them to not text you for a while. Or to not game in front of you. Or not stick their phone in your face saying "You gotta see this." Your sib should be able to do many of the things you'd ask of a parent. Just make sure you don't place them in an unfair position where, say, you give them your phone to hold overnight, and then browbeat them into returning it before morning.

- **Ask friends for help.** They can provide emotional support if you feel like tearing your hair out, kicking a hole in the wall, or sobbing on your bed. They can keep a Snap streak going for you (assuming Snapchat isn't one of the issues you're trying to fix) or meet up if you feel at risk of a Reddit relapse. They can check portals for notices you might need to know (team meetings, school assignments) or promise to tell you if anything *really* important happens on Instagram. They can even send DMs on your behalf:
  Dear Mr. Liszt,
  I am Cindy Allegro's personal assistant. She asked me to inform you that, regrettably, she is not able to make her piano lesson this Thursday.

You might feel embarrassed at first to tell friends, parents, coaches, or teachers that you're doing a reset or to admit that you got in over your head with certain online activities. But if you do share what you're trying to do or what you've been through, you're likely to find that most people will admire you for realizing there's a problem and taking steps to solve it. Enlist their help. If you hid your use in the past, it doesn't have to be a secret anymore. That alone will reduce stress and make you feel freer.

Some of your support squad can be in the wings. They're there if you need them. Others may be essential for moral or practical support or for aiding you in filling newly-found free time. You'll want to formalize or schedule the support they'll be providing. For example, you might ask a friend to check in with you at certain times when you think you might feel most at risk of a digital relapse. You might ask a school counselor if you could see her once a week while you're doing your App-endectomy. You might ask a neighbor with a pottery studio if she would have time to teach you how to make ceramic vases.

While having support is important, don't feel you have to tell the whole world what you're doing. You're making a personal choice, for personal reasons. If people notice you're not on your phone or responding to messages, you could just say you lost your phone, or your mom confiscated it, or it's being repaired. (Sometimes a white lie is okay.) If you do decide your reset is nobody's business but your own, make sure you still have at least one person who will know about it and be there for you. Having a "cheerleader" will give you an extra oomph of motivation since you'll want them to witness your success.

My Support Squad

Identify your team. The more, the merrier. List the people you can count on to help you achieve your goal. If there's a specific way you want them to help, write that below each name.	1.
	2.
If you feel you don't need or want an entire crew, make sure you have at least one person who knows what you've set out to do. You need someone with whom you can share your joyful success and digital unshackling—and who will *also* be there to encourage you when you say, "I can't do it. I'm losing my mind. This is too hard!"	3.
	4.
	5.

Issue App-Endectomy Alerts

There may be some people—friends, coaches, teachers, parents, teammates, band members, your co-editor of the student yearbook—who aren't on your support squad, but who still need to know what you're doing if it might affect or worry them. This mainly applies if your reset involves cutting out or cutting back on certain apps, being less accessible or responsive, or even going "dark" for a period of time.

Friends who expect you to be available 24/7, parents who expect you to respond to texts right away, or online friends who count on your showing up to chat, message, or game may feel hurt, rejected, irritated, or worried if your digital habits change. In some cases, you can give them a heads-up with a group text or auto-response that lets them know you're offline or not checking messages for a while. In other cases, you'll need to tell them in advance.

My Alerts List

Write down any people or groups you need to notify to set expectations and prevent trouble. For each, list the recipient(s) of the alert, the method you'll use to alert them (text, phone call, check-in before gym class, telegraph), and any necessary workarounds (for example, a teacher will print out and hand you assignments; friends will call your landline; your mom will get messages to you through your sister). Use additional paper if needed.	Issue alert to: Method: Workaround: Issue alert to: Method: Workaround: Issue alert to: Method: Workaround: Issue alert to: Method: Workaround: Issue alert to: Method: Workaround:

Plan Alternative Activities

A digital reset changes your habits, routines, moods, and schedule. If you used to spend four hours a day on social media or YouTube and decide to reduce it to two hours, that means you'll have two extra hours to fill (told you I was a whiz at math). Two extra hours is like finding a treasure—but if you don't have a concrete plan for how to fill the time, you might get bored, nervous, depressed, or lonely. That could threaten your success. So you need to identify tasks, projects, activities, and "love-to-do's" that you can plug in to your newfound time. Ideally, they should be offline activities.

I'm so bored. There's nothing to do.

FOMO

The possibilities are endless. The best are often physical, social, and/or creative, where you get energized, connect with others, and express yourself. Think of how good you feel after a workout or meeting up with friends. Think of the satisfaction you feel after creating something. Here are some suggestions for brainstorming your own list of alternative activities:

- things you love to do
- things you've always wanted to try
- things you've always wanted to learn
- things you've always wanted to make
- tasks hanging over your head that you'd feel soooo good to be rid of

- acts of kindness, mentoring, volunteering
- people to see or reconnect with; people who would be thrilled to hear from you
- self-care (meditation, exercise, journaling)
- cleaning, organizing, seeing if you have things to donate, recycle, or throw out

By the way, getting more sleep counts as an alternative way to fill newfound time. If you used to spend the last hour before going to bed on your phone, and your reset eliminates that pattern, getting an extra hour's sleep is a fine way to use that time. Pleasant dreams.

My Alternative Activities Brainstorm

Brainstorm things you can do to enjoy your newfound time, resist triggers and temptations, be good to yourself, and fill your being with positive life forces. Some activities may require research, materials, signing up, etc. So below each activity, write down any preparation steps you need to take. I recommend doing these *before* you start your reset, so you're rarin' to go on Day One.

Since this is so important, I'm giving you lots of space for lots of ideas. But feel free to use even more paper if you need it.

1.

2.

3.

4.

5.

6.

7.

8.

9.

10.

11.

12.

13.

14.

15.

Make a Countermeasures Plan

Challenge 7 asked you to identify behaviors, feelings, situations, people, and/or events that lead you to pick up your phone (see "What Are My Phone Habits and Triggers?" on page 42). Some of these triggers are perfectly fine and do not threaten your time, self-control, resolve, or well-being. For example, your phone rings, you pick it up; you check the weather every morning before getting dressed; your mom said she'd text you with the time of your dentist appointment; you have warm thoughts about somebody and want to say hello. Other triggers are more insidious, more likely to provoke the screen behavior you want to resist. So it's essential that you anticipate how you will counter those triggers when they occur—and believe me, they will.

A countermeasure might be one of the alternative activities you just brainstormed. It could be talking to somebody on your support team. It could be a positive thinking exercise, a meditation, listening to a song, cuddling with your pet porcupine. As long as your countermeasure is a healthy activity that doesn't harm you or others, it doesn't matter what it is. What matters is that you're prepared for when that "Uh-oh-I'm-feeling-tempted" sensation seeps into your psyche.

My Phone Habits, Triggers, and Temptations—and Countermeasures

Think of the triggers, temptations, and habits that are most likely to threaten the success of your App-endectomy. For each trigger, write down one or more specific things you can do to vanquish it.		TRIGGER	COUNTERMEASURE
	Ex.:	Loneliness	Talk to mom, call Tracy
	Ex.:	Boredom UGH!	Build shelves for my room

Give Yourself a Reward

We all know the satisfaction of a job well done. It can be a sense of accomplishment, a feeling of pride, a jolt of confidence. It can be praise or approval from somebody who cares about you. Often, those are the best rewards. But that doesn't mean you can't give yourself a tangible reward. If you reached a goal or got yourself through a tough time, you deserve to do something good for yourself. Something you enjoy. It could be taking a favorite run, attending a free concert, hosting a sleepover, cutting your neighbor's lawn (yes, that's a gift to yourself, too), baking cookies, going canoeing, or buying yourself an item of clothing, a book, a bracelet, a belt, a hot-fudge sundae with mint chip, coconut, and chocolate brownie ice cream smothered with whipped cream and walnuts, a pedicure, or a pet turtle (I had one I named Pokey). And I have no objections if you want to negotiate a deal with a parent—especially a parent who has been bugging you to change your digital habits—to see if they will cough up a reward.

My Rewards

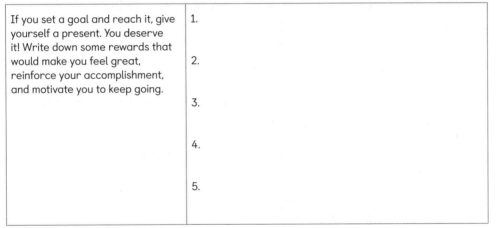

If you set a goal and reach it, give yourself a present. You deserve it! Write down some rewards that would make you feel great, reinforce your accomplishment, and motivate you to keep going.	1. 2. 3. 4. 5.

No-Go for FOMO

FOMO is real. It's human nature to be curious and not want to miss out on the latest news and gossip. So you need to be prepared, if cutting back on social media, for FOMO to be a threat to your resolve. It's a powerful trigger. It'll be easier to forgo FOMO if you anticipate what you're afraid you'll miss and identify ways to deal with it. The following table will help you to make FOMO a no-show.

My FOMOs

In the first column, identify your FOMO concern—your MOF (Missing-Out Fear). In the second column, write down how you can assuage or deal with your concern.	My Specific MOF (Missing-Out Fear) Ex.: I'm afraid everyone will be talking about someone's post and I'll be left out.	How I'll Deal with It Ex.: Donnie and Marie promise they'll tell me anything I need to know at lunch.
	1.	1.
	2.	2.
	3.	3.

Once you begin the App-endectomy operation, you'll need to refer to the information you entered in these preparation templates. So keep them handy.

And now, with your goal set and your preparation done, it's time to select the tools and strategies that will best help you to score a bullseye on your reset target.

3. Choosing Your Tools

Have you ever seen an operating room? Maybe on one of those doctor TV shows? There's always a trolley stocked with surgical tools so when the doctor says, "Scalpel," or "suction," or "chainsaw," it's right there. The medical team knows which tools are needed for the operation, which might be necessary in an emergency, and which will help the patient have a good recovery and prognosis.

The same goes for an App-endectomy. Some tools will be essential. For example, if you're concerned about notifications interrupting your concentration, tools for controlling notifications would be essential. Other tools are there in case you need them. To select the best tools for your specific plan:

- **Look over the list of tools beginning on the next page.** The tools are arranged in categories to help you find what you're looking for.

- **Come up with your own ideas.** You may think of something that I haven't included. Don't be modest. If you think it'll help, use it!
- **Check out the RESIST chapters of this book (chapters 4–9).** They describe ways in which Big Tech may be harming your body, brain, psyche, relationships, and reputation—and how you can protect yourself. There's a good chance that your App-endectomy is motivated by concerns that fall into one or more of those areas. For example, maybe you have tech neck. Or difficulty focusing in school. Or you see a connection between your social and feeling down on yourself. If so, re-read the "tips" section of the relevant chapter. Then select any of the tips you'd like to use as tools to support your reset.

The more tools you use, the greater your chances for a successful App-endectomy. That's because healthy habits reinforce each other. If, say, you exercise, sleep well, and eat nutritious meals, you'll be more energetic, focused, and productive—which will motivate you to continue those healthy habits.

*Un*healthy habits also reinforce themselves. *Not* exercising or eating or sleeping well can make you tired and stressed, unmotivated and unproductive. You'll find it hard to focus or stay awake; you'll crave sugar and caffeine, which will make you jumpy. You'll feel lousy and trash talk yourself, which will make you feel even worse.

It's the same with screen time. If you can take charge of your digital life so that it creates positive energy and experiences for you—whether online or offline—you'll find that will reinforce your motivation to maintain those screen scene changes.

As you select tools and strategies, remember, you're focusing on just one goal at a time. Select the tools that will help you achieve that specific goal. If you see some tools that make you think, *"Gee, that would be nice to try,"* feel free to add them as well. For example, if you like the idea of giving yourself a private, peaceful moment every morning before turning on your phone, it's fine to do it even if it doesn't relate directly to your goal. Any of the tools will add to your overall screen-scene health. Just don't let yourself get distracted from your primary goal.

So, browse the hardware store I've built for you in the pages that follow. See which tools might help you to best achieve your reset goal. When you're done, you'll be ready to create your App-endectomy Reset Plan and start filling your toolbox.

And while you're doing that, I think I'll take a break and do some neck stretches.

Pulling a Fast One

As you saw in the previous chapter, fasts are like multi-tool pocketknives where you can use the big blade to slice a salami and the smaller tools to open a bottle, turn a screw, cut paper, or maybe even dislodge a piece of celery from between your teeth.

Fasts are just as versatile. An intermittent fast or app fast, for example, can be part of a gentle screen-time tweak where you just want to reapportion how you spend your time. Or a purge fast could be the foundation of a major screen-scene reset—the kick-off to a life-changing, shock-to-the-system App-endectomy. Fasts can be done as part of an App-endectomy or all by themselves as a little booster shot from time to time. Since fasts are so handy and powerful, be sure to keep them in mind as you examine the rest of the tools in this chapter. You just may want to put yourself in fast motion.

What if smartphones suddenly ceased to exist? How would your life change? Does the whole idea seem unimaginable? Try to picture it.

What would you miss most? Texting? Games? Videos? GPS? Social media? Instant access to friends and information?

What would you be happy to be rid of? Texting? Games? Videos? GPS? Social media? Instant access to friends and information?

What are your happiest, most pleasurable moments of the day? When do you feel most connected, joyful, productive, fulfilled? Is your phone part of, or essential to, those times?

For many teens, smartphones are a double-edged sword, offering both the best and the worst. How would you compensate for the extinction of your phone? How would it change you as a person?

If you could design a phone and a digital life for yourself that would keep the best and get rid of the worst, what would that look like?

Tools to Stay Serene and Reduce Stress

A reset means you're trying on new behaviors and emotions. This may produce feelings of agitation, worry, loss, or doubt (before the positive feelings overtake them). Calming your mind can help you manage any anxiety or uncomfortable feelings you might initially feel during a reset.

Start the day with a moment for yourself.

Many teens check their phone first thing in the morning. Maybe even before getting out of bed. If you're one of them, try this instead. Take some personal "me time" before you look at your phone. This could be a five-minute meditation. A run around the block. A quiet moment with a cup of milk or coffee. A review of the day that lies ahead. Clear your head from the night's dreams and cobwebs. Center yourself. Fill your being with positive thoughts and feelings. Then, and only then, turn on your phone and let the drama, notifications, requests, demands, reminders, and obligations pour in.

End the day with a moment for yourself.

Bookend your day with a bedtime ritual offscreen. Practice the tips for getting a good night's sleep from chapter 4 (page 72). Pay special attention to reducing blue light and phone-generated drama during your final waking hour(s) of the evening. Slide into sleep with serenity. Congratulate yourself and feel your gratitude for the good things that happened that day. Comfort yourself for the not-so-good things. Pamper your mind, body, and spirit with something relaxing and restorative.

Go for the gray.

Color affects your mood, body, feelings, and attitudes. Different colors can make you feel sad, angry, energized, wary, warmer, colder, and even hungry. There's a whole psychology to color, and you can bet your bitcoin that app designers use it to keep you engaged.

A powerful resistance tool is to set your phone to gray scale. This is because color is seductive. Enticing. It rewards your brain. Gray, by contrast, is neutral. Bland. Ugh!-ly, even. It eliminates much of the visual glitter and chaos that stimulates your brain. And that's the whole point. It turns your device into a tool, not a fireworks display. To do this, go to your settings and look for "accessibility." You should find toggles for "color filters" or "gray scale."

Be kind to your mind.

The mind works nonstop, constantly whirring away. Sometimes it needs a time-out. Consider using apps that create moments of meditative serenity for yourself. It may seem strange to use an app to counter the effects of other apps. But *Stranger Things* have happened. Search for "meditation apps," or start by checking out the apps Headspace and Smiling Mind. These resources can help you bring meditation and mindfulness into your life.

Check in with yourself.

Pay attention to how you feel while using your device. Does your mood change depending on what you're doing? Do certain photos or comments produce certain emotions? Be your own ultra-sounding board. It's not that all negative feelings should be avoided. They can be useful guideposts and natural, healthy reactions to things that are sad or enraging. But recognizing big-picture patterns in your use—seeing how some platforms consistently bring you down, while others regularly cheer you up—can be helpful for fine-tuning your screen time. There are even mood-tracking apps that allow you to stay in touch with your feelings.

Tools to Resist Temptation

Triggers and temptations can threaten your resolve and the success of your App-endectomy. The following tools will help you to reduce them in the first place and to fight back if they occur.

Tuck your phone in for the night.

Remember the three cardinal rules to ensure your phone behaves itself during the night, and you get a good night's sleep:

1. Turn it off.

2. Charge it outside your room.

3. Use a physical alarm clock.

Put all your devices in a different room before going to bed.

This goes a long way toward reducing temptation. Stow them in a different room, or hand them to a parent or sibling for even safer "keeping." Relinquish your phone, tablet, laptop, iPhone, iPad, iPod, iPud, or iPoodle. Also give up your gaming console—anything with a screen. The only screen you can keep is sunscreen.

Plan ahead for overcoming "temptation moments."

Let's say you're trying to stop gaming. If your habit was to start gaming at 9:00 p.m. and continue for hours on end, that's when you need to be on guard to avoid the circumstances that would tempt you. If you let yourself be bored or at loose ends so you *feel* the absence of gaming, you'll be at risk. So make a schedule—in your head if not on a calendar—for exactly what your alternative activity is going to be. It may be talking to a parent, being with a supportive friend, taking the dog for a walk, writing in a journal, watching an episode of a favorite series. This "planning ahead" is essential for breaking any habit.

Delete the app.

You'll still have your account, but you'll have to reinstall the app or go to the website each time you want to use it. Make the apps that are your Achilles heels hard to get to. It's like, if you were addicted to ice cream (crazy, I know), you could put your ice cream in a freezer with a time lock in the attic of a 30-story building with no elevator surrounded by an alligator-filled moat that's a three-mile hike from home along a path of glass shards. You *could* still get to it, but it'll be a lot harder.

Organize your apps, limiting your home screen to tools only.

This is another, somewhat gentler way to make it more difficult to access platforms whose use you want to limit or avoid. Think of it as creating a moat filled with nibble fish instead of alligators. Move your time-sucking apps off the first page of your home screen. Either move them several swipes away, or, even better, banish them to separate folders requiring as many clicks and swipes to get to as possible. That way, all you'll see when you unlock your phone are utilities: maps, camera, clock, settings, weather, traffic, ride-hailing, etc. Instead of automatically opening an app just because you see the icon, you'll have to take multiple steps and make a conscious decision.

Organizing your apps into folders can help you to resist temptation and reduce reflexive checking since you'll have to intentionally seek them out. Give each folder a name that reminds you why you put the app in it or what reset rule you're following. So, you might have a "Danger" folder for time-sucking apps. A "Do Not Enter" folder for an app you're fasting from.

The right label—"10 Minutes Only"; "Are You Sure?"; "Brings Me Down"; "Junk"—can create just enough of a pause for you to be sure you want to open it. It would be as if an ice cream addict (if you can even imagine such a thing) hid ice cream behind three rows of frozen peas in a box within a box within a box with a label saying: "Are you sure you want to open this when you know eating ice cream is going to make you feel bloated, unhealthy, guilty, and ashamed?"

Use your support squad.

Unless you're doing just a minor touch-up to your screen scene, you can expect to experience periods where temptation shrieks, resolve weakens, and you think about resetting your reset to OFF. This is *exactly* the moment when you need to reach out to somebody and talk through your thoughts and feelings. Often, all it takes to keep you on your path is a caring, supportive listener.

Tools for Staying Motivated

While triggers and temptations are often external forces, the most powerful motivation comes from within. Motivation can be threatened by negative self-talk, doubt, losing sight of goals, and natural tendencies to lower stress or seek the path of least resistance. In those moments, you need tools to remember why you're doing a reset and keep your motivation high.

Do it with a friend.

Challenging tasks—whether studying, working out, or eating better—can be easier and more fun if you form a mutual support unit. Statistically, there's a good chance that one or more of your friends has had feelings similar to yours about wanting to reset their digital diet. You may have even talked with a friend about your phone worries and/or theirs.

Work on your App-endectomies together. You'll likely have different goals, triggers, and methods for measuring success. So you should each fill out your own App-endectomy Reset template for an action plan. If there's overlap, great! You can use similar techniques and measures. But that's not essential. What's important is that you can support and encourage each other.

Start on the same day. Check in with each other for motivation and pep talks. Plan activities to help you fill your newfound time and to power through temptation zones. Have reward ceremonies where you celebrate your milestones and accomplishments.

Do a streak for success.

You've heard of Snap streaks. You may have even participated in some. If so, you know how addictive they can be. Turn the powerful psychology of a streak to your advantage. If you have an App-endectomy partner, give yourselves an App Clap. This is a daily congratulations—a "neat-feat streak"—for sticking to your plan.

Create a daily ritual for your App Clap. Maybe it's a six-second video that you make and send one day, and which your partner reciprocates the next. Maybe it's a phone call every night to congratulate each other. Maybe it's a secret talisman—a marble, coin, ring, shell, pine cone—that you pass back and forth to signify another day of success. Come up with something fun and meaningful. See how many days you can keep it going.

Make sure the ritual you choose doesn't compromise anyone's plan. For example, if one of you is trying to text less, texting wouldn't be a good format for your App Clap. If you have a "relapse" in sticking to your plan or somebody breaks the streak, the App Clap goes back to zero. Sorry.

If you like this idea but you're doing the reset on your own, you can still do an App Clap with somebody on your support team. You let them know each day you triumphed, and they send back their kudos.

Create a "burdens and benefits" card.

To keep your motivation strong, make a list of the top three to five problems, concerns, or negative consequences that led to your App-endectomy, and write them down on an index card or small piece of paper. Then list the top three to five bene-fits you'll receive from staying true to your commitment. When you feel tempted to break one of your reset rules, look at the card to remind yourself why you're doing a reset and all the positive changes it will bring. You can make multiple cards. Tape one to the mirror you look at each morning; tape one to the back of your phone; tape another inside the flap of your school bag or inside your locker.

Create a "losses and loves" card.

This is similar to the "burdens and benefits" card, but with a different focus. Make a list of the top three to five things you have lost, neglected, or cut back on due to your screen scene. This could be parental trust, self-respect, health, friendships, participation in group activities, a hobby you used to enjoy. Then list the activities, qualities, feelings, relationships, and/or behaviors you wish to rekindle. Keep the card handy where you'll see it each day. Here, too, you can make multiple copies so the reminders will always be "in your face" (politely, of course).

Create a lock screen message.

No, not "Put down your phone, you jerk." Something that, when you unlock your phone, makes you feel empowered and motivated: "I'm on top of my reset." "Just five minutes." "Are you sure?" "I'm in charge." "I'm doing it!" "Success is mine."

Tools for Keeping the Blood Pumping

In the same way that a calm mind and spirit improve the prognosis for your App-endectomy, so do high energy levels. Be sure you take steps to stay alert, peppy, and refreshed. After all, whenever possible, people having operations are encouraged to improve their health and strength before undergoing surgery. Same thing applies when conducting an App-endectomy. It's a good idea to get and stay physically fit before and during the operation. Doing this will help you maintain your energy and keep motivation-sapping sludge from pooling in your veins. So, whenever you're on any device for an extended period of time (and I consider that anything more than 45 minutes), take a few minutes to break, rattle, and roll. Try the following ideas for locomotion:

- Go for a run or bike ride, even for just five minutes.
- If you can't tear yourself away from what you're doing, stand up. Stretch. Spin. Yodel. Touch your toes. Run in place. Dance it out.
- Windmill your arms like whirligigs.

- Do 20 jumping jacks. Get your blood circulating.

- If you can't do any of these—if you can't stand up or move around because you're in class; if you're soooo close to the next level; if you've got to keep your hands on your device—at least rotate your neck in circles, bounce your legs up and down on your toes, and knock your knees together.

Remember, spending hours sitting in the same position is hazardous to your health. For further ideas, check out the tips in chapter 4.

Tools to Protect Your Time and Reduce Distractions

If reducing overall screen time or limiting certain activities is part of your action plan, tech tools can help you do it. Of course, there's an irony in using one's device to resist the negative consequences of using one's device. But I've never been anti-device (although I am pro-irony). I'm just opposed to devices that invade your body, brain, psyche, privacy, and life balance.

Consider some of the following tools and strategies for monitoring, controlling, and customizing your screen time.

Track your screen time. Many App-endectomies involve cutting back on the use of certain platforms. A screen-time tracker is essential for helping you to do that. (For some of you, an old-fashioned timer or the stopwatch on your phone may be all you'll need to maintain your digital time-limits discipline. But a screen-time tracker is more foolproof.)

> I hope you're not suggesting I'm a—

> Wouldn't dream of it.

We've talked a lot about trackers. You may have already used one to come up with your screen-scene "actual use" figures (page 32). If your App-endectomy goal is to block or reduce use of a particular app or website, enter your time or access criteria in the tracker. You should also be able to set "on and off" periods for specific apps. Screen Time for iOS and Digital Wellbeing for Android should be pre-installed on recent devices. You can also check out Moment, RescueTime, and Freedom. Some of these are free; some are not; some work on most operating system(s), some don't; some can sync across all your devices, some can't. Do a bit of research. You may find other options. Just think, a few seconds of installation time can save you from minutes, hours, days, weeks, and months of vaporized time.

Schedule posts. While you may wish to tweet or post certain things immediately, lots of posts are not time sensitive. Whether they appear right now, this afternoon, tomorrow, or later in the week doesn't matter. Many social media apps and extensions allow you to create posts in advance and then schedule when they appear. This means you can maintain a presence on social media without having to be present. If you feel pressured to post, Snap, tweet, bleat, gleet, or skeet (I'm anticipating there will soon be new social media apps called Blitter, Glitter, and Skitter), plan a time when you create content, and then schedule when it will appear to free you from hourly or daily POOP.

TALES FROM THE DIGITAL FRONTIER

When I was active on Twitter (I'm currently taking a brief six-year hiatus), I always felt this pressure to tweet. And, of course, each tweet had to be perfect—witty, clever, original, error-free, timely—and brief. Brief, as you may have noticed, is not one of my defining characteristics.

> I noticed.

Every morning, upon awakening, as the birds tweeted outside my window, I felt this pressure to join them. Once I sent a tweet, the pressure went away, but it was soon replaced by a new *"I really should send another tweet"* pressure. Soon, I discovered that I could create a batch of tweets, and schedule when I wanted them to go out. That meant I just needed to be witty, clever, and original once a week (which I could usually manage), but it would look as if I were on Twitter every day. And, of course, if I were moved to send out a real-time tweet, nothing prevented me from doing so.

Schedule _when_ you receive content. In the same way you can schedule posts, you can control how content flows to you. You can program, either on an app itself or using your tracker, when to receive notifications, email, messages, and feedback on posts.

Unsubscribe from everything. So many things you do online—email, shopping, visiting websites—can sign you up, without your approval, for an endless barrage of follow-up emails, texts, notifications, and messages. And it's only going to get worse over time. Wherever you can, unsubscribe, opt out, and deny permission. Otherwise, a huge proportion of "incoming" to your phone will distract you and waste your time.

Use auto responders. You may feel pressure to reply immediately to texts, emails, or other messages. Yes, it can be polite to do so. But, if you receive dozens or hundreds of messages a day, it's not fair or realistic to expect you to jump every time someone says "Boo." Use an auto-response reply to let people know you got their message and they don't need to worry. You can tell them you're unable to respond, tied up at the moment, or off the grid. You can make your auto-response warm, funny, accurate, vague—whatever you want. Most senders will be grateful for the (auto) reply, and you will have protected your time—for studying, meditating, being with a friend— from interruption.

Make a schedule. The more specific your reset plan, the more likely you are to succeed. If your goal is even a little bit "fuzzy," like "Reduce screen time from seven to four hours a day," that can make it harder to achieve. That's because you may use your device throughout the day and then discover it's 5 p.m., you've used up your four-hour daily limit, but there's still stuff you need/want to do. One of the ways to avoid this is to schedule your screen time in advance. If, say, you've set a general time limit, create time slots for social media, gaming, streaming, messaging—the main categories of your device use—and enter them on your daily and weekly calendars. This type of time management will provide signposts that let you know you're honoring your App-endectomy goals.

Study and do homework with your phone off and outside your room. Remember the research on how the mere presence of a phone, even if it's off, reduces your available cognitive capacity? Of course you do. When you need to focus, lose the phone. Having it on and within reach is the worst. Having it silenced in a bag or backpack is better. Having it off and in another room is best. Put it out of sight and sound and you'll be as focused as a falcon with binoculars. (For more on how the presence of phones can affect thinking, concentration, and human interactions, see pages 106 and 133.)

Notify your notifications to shut up. Turn off all notifications except from real people. Why? Because when you see those red dots—and red is a "warning" color apps use to get your attention—it pulls your psychological strings. Curiosity and FOMO trigger a reflex to check. And that puts you at the mercy of Big Tech. Most notifications are machine generated. They're not coming from a live human being. Go into your device and app settings. You can decide you don't want to be disturbed at all or that only certain people or types of notifications can get through. A good rule of thumb is that real people get through. Robots, algorithms, Big Tech, and Russian bots don't. (For more on notifications, see page 104.)

Remember, Big Tech wants to break your self-discipline and keep you engaged for as long as possible. Seek out apps and extensions that block "features" seeking to overrule your self-control. Here are a few. You can find more by checking the "Help" pages of the particular platform whose functioning you want to modify, and by doing a general search on the feature or feedback you want to block or change.

- **Install DF YouTube** (the "DF" stands for "distraction-free). This is a plugin that blocks the bottomless suggestion list that sucks you into watching 100 videos besides the one you came to see. It's available for Chrome, Firefox, IE, and earlier versions of Safari.

- **Turn off autoplay.** A friend sends you a link to a video or you watch one episode of a TV series, and autoplay takes command, presenting you with a new video or the next episode before you even realize the one you were watching has ended. Wherever you can, whether on YouTube, Netflix, or another site, disable autoplay.

- **Use News Feed Eradicator for Facebook.** Do you go to Facebook to do something simple and get sucked into your endless news feed? This plugin will prevent that from happening by removing the newsfeed and substituting an inspirational quote. You can ignore it, or you can let yourself be inspired. The Eradicator is also available for Twitter.

Tools to Protect Your Psyche

Social media can be like a tapeworm. It gets inside your psyche. You may not feel any symptoms at first. But bit by bit, it grows until it is 50 feet long. Yes, you may have a 50-foot-long tapeworm in your psyche (or intestine). Here are some tools for resisting some of the potentially toxic effects of a social media overdose.

Resist being emotionally manipulated. Turn off toxic metrics. You saw in "Protect Your Psyche" that many social media sites are designed to encourage users to fixate on the "scores" they receive, such as likes and retweets. This feedback distorts the positive aspects of social media and lies behind many of its negative consequences. Check the settings and privacy controls for any platforms you use. They may provide ways to hide certain metrics from public view or from your view. Wherever you have that option, take it.

Use Twitter Demetricator. This extension removes likes, retweets, and follower numbers from your Twitter.

Try out Facebook Demetricator. This extension performs a similar gatekeeping task by hiding metrics such as likes, comments, shares, and numbers of friends from your Facebook. Facebook and Instagram have been experimenting with eliminating some of these metrics, recognizing that they may be harmful to users' mental and emotional health or, more accurately, that users may be leaving platforms because of them. So, who knows? By the time you read this, some social media sites may have taken helpful measures on their own.

Unfollow or block people who make you feel bad about yourself. Go through your various lists. If you see a name that doesn't cause your heart to light up with joy or your mind to spark with delight, unfollow them. Unfriend them. Block them. Show them to the digital door. Protect yourself from people whose posts or messages bring you down.

Bet-You-Didn't-Think-of-Them Manners Tools for a Successful Reset

Using good phone manners will reinforce your App-endectomy. If you follow the guidelines below for digital etiquette, you'll naturally reduce screen time. And, as a bonus, you will be seen as a respectful, considerate, attentive, and charming person. Such people are so rare that you will shine as a bright star in the otherwise dark, expanding universe of incivility. Your friends will appreciate that you give them your full attention. Adults will shower you with admiration, approval, and extra perks and privileges. That will give you a good feeling and increase your confidence about your social skills. And the better you feel offline, the greater the chance your online life will be in a healthy balance.

Here are a few key principles of phonetiquette that will support your App-endectomy, effortlessly reduce screen time, *and* bring you offline benefits. ✱

✱ For even more netiquette tips, as well as pointers for navigating teen life with aplomb (but not a plum), check out my book *How Rude! The Teen Guide to Good Manners, Proper Behavior, and Not Grossing People Out*. If you like *Slaying Digital Dragons,* you'll love *How Rude!* And if you hate *Slaying Digital Dragons,* you'll still love *How Rude!*

- Lose the phone when you're in face-to-face social settings. Be with the one you're with. (Remember, just the presence of a phone reduces the quality of human interaction.)
- Turn off or silence your phone in places where people are trying to concentrate (such as in class, at the library, or during a monastic retreat where people have taken a vow of silence).

- Don't use your phone in places where quiet, respect, or attention is required or expected or where ringtones, alerts, or light from your screen would annoy or offend others, such as darkened movie theaters, live performances, or religious services.

- Ditch the devices when eating with others. Apart from the risk of accidentally buttering your browser or dropping your tablet in the tamales, it's rude to be more attuned to your phone than the people around you.

- Follow the rules of polite social media behavior. Don't overshare. Stay away from drama and rumors. Don't post mean comments or impersonate anyone. Call people instead of always messaging. You will naturally reduce your screen time.

- Choose the right tool, platform, and method for communicating. For emotional, difficult, or "heavy" situations, that often means a phone call or, ideally, face-to-face interaction.

Tools for Extra Support

You may feel *really* up against the wall if your device use has become the driving force in your life and it's taking you to dark, uncomfortable, scary, dysfunctional, or conflicted places. Fear not. There are people and groups that can make you feel less alone and offer valuable support.

Consider 12-step programs and other support groups. I mentioned earlier in this book that scientists have observed similarities in how drugs and screen activities affect the brain. A number of 12-step programs have emerged for "internet addicts" that use the same principles shown to be effective in helping alcoholics and other drug addicts recover from their addictions. Encouragement from others who know exactly what you're going through, who have been there themselves, can be a powerful motivator and support system for resetting your digital life.

Support groups and programs focused on problematic tech use recognize that some screen time may be essential for realizing one's potential and operating in today's world. So abstinence is not presented as the only acceptable or worthy goal. Check out Computer Gaming Addicts Anonymous (CGAA) and Internet and Technology Addicts Anonymous (ITAA). Members of such programs are often teens, just like yourself.

Seek professional help. The counselor at your school may have helpful resources. There are also counselors who specialize in internet dependencies, as well as treatment programs for teens whose screen time has imbalanced their lives. Search online for "teens, internet, addiction," and where you live. Also try "internet, addiction, counselor." Well, you get the idea. You know far better than I how to do a good search for what *you* need.

Okay! Got your goal set?

> Check.

Got your support team lined up?

> Check.

Got your triggers and temptations identified?

> Check.

> When do we start?

> NOW!!!!!

WAIT! HOLD THE PRESSES!

> Now what?

> I want to give all you App-endectomologists a proper send-off.

> This better be worth the wait.

A Note to All App-endectomologists

In choosing to give yourself an App-endectomy, you are making a vivid and valiant choice. You may look back on it as one of the best and bravest things you ever did. For it means that you are taking a stand, declaring your worth, protecting your psyche and future, and giving Big Tech the finger.

If you have no concerns about your screen scene, congratulations for being on top of your devices and using them as nifty tools to help you accomplish your goals, stay connected, be creative, have some laughs, and add to the world's quotient of goodness. But you can still perform an App-endectomy to reinforce your already excellent self-regulation, strengthen your resolve and resistance, and maybe even bring a bit *more* balance, serenity, joy, and satisfaction into your life.

If you acknowledged having minor concerns about your screen scene, that level of honesty and self-awareness is a rare and wondrous trait to possess. You are to be commended! By me.

> Me, too!

If you have major concerns about your screen scene, three cheers for you! No, make that four.

> I'd make it 10.

You've done one of the hardest things a person can do: recognize and admit to having a problem. Just doing that means you're over the most difficult hurdle when it comes to a reset. By acknowledging a problem, you're reaching out to *yourself* for help.

And to all brave App-endectomologists, my hat is off to you.

> Mine, too.

Teens who perform an App-endectomy can expect to see many short- and long-term benefits. You're likely to feel less anxious, stressed, moody, or depressed. More even-keeled, in the moment, and in control. There's an excellent chance you'll sleep better, have more energy, improve your school performance, revisit activities you enjoyed doing, find new interests, and be more responsible and trustworthy (and be seen that way!).

If you have more offline time, your activities and interests should expand, bringing you in contact with more people and opportunities. You'll become more socially confident, more open to meeting new people, and more aware of other teens who don't seem that involved with their devices. All these benefits will lead to feeling better about yourself, knowing who *you* are, and having better relationships with people you care about. You'll have more time to daydream, imagine, and create. And you'll win a Nobel Prize, receive the Presidential Medal of Freedom, and achieve sainthood by the time you're 21. Well, I'm not totally sure about the sainthood thing, but *definitely* the other two.

I know you'll be able to pull this off and successfully reset your digital life to one that nurtures and nourishes your personhood. But promise me one thing. If the going gets tough, if the feelings get too intense, if you're not hitting the goals you set—reach out. There are people who want to help.

4. Performing the Operation

Time to administer the anesthesia. Oh wait, if you're unconscious, you can't give yourself an App-endectomy. Never mind. I'm sure the pain will be minimal.

We're going to go step-by-step to come up with a clear, workable, attainable plan. Most important of all, remember that you are going to focus on **JUST ONE GOAL.** Trying to do too much can lead to reset failure. You, however, are headed for success. So . . .

Just.

One.

Goal.

Later, after you've achieved your goal, after you realize how empowered you are to manage your digital life, you can always choose another goal to pursue.

Sometimes the hardest things to do are the things that are best for you. Strange, isn't it? Working on this book, I'd sit at my laptop for five, six hours straight. My eyes would get blurry, my wrists would hurt, my neck would ache. And I'd just keep typing.

I'd get a notification and instantly grab my phone to look. And then I'd send a text or three. And check email. And scope out the weather forecast. Hmm, did Amazon deliver my package yet? Better check. Any important news I'm missing? Better check. Finally, I'd get back to the book, with my concentration broken. I'd hear this negative voice in my head saying, "Alex, you dummy, get up, take a break, do some exercises for your eyes and your neck. What is wrong with you? Turn off your notifications. How do you expect anyone else to follow your advice if you can't do it yourself? You DUMMY!"

And then, I'd challenge those negative loops with positive thinking: "Alex, you really are a dummy." Oh wait. Positive thinking. "Alex, you're a fine fellow. You deserve to take good care of yourself. Now, take a break and turn off your %@#! phone."

My point is, I know firsthand how difficult it can be at times to maintain healthy habits. Stress, deadlines, laziness, being in a rush, pressure from friends, even feeling down on yourself can all interfere with doing the very things that will make you feel better.

So as you embark on this reset of your digital life, go easy on yourself. But also be tough on yourself. I think you know what I mean. Be tough in demanding the best for yourself. In summoning your honesty, self-awareness, and commitment. In holding yourself to a high standard for how you want to be, be seen, and behave. At the same time, go easy on yourself. Recognize that a reset can be hard, that your efforts and process may feel wobbly at first, that the path of a resistance fighter will be strewn with obstacles, and that others (yes, Big Tech, I'm talking about you) will want you to fail. Don't let them outsmart you. Now you know what they're up to.

How to Plan Your App-endectomy

This sample, annotated App-endectomy template shows you what a finished one will look like, plus it has my comments and feedback. It's for a teen who wants to cut back on Fortnite. Later in this chapter you'll find a blank version of this form for you to use for *your* specific reset goal.

My App-Endectomy Reset Plan: Sample

I would like to do an App-endectomy because: This can be a hope, concern, warning sign, consequence, or "mission" statement about how you want to use or relate to your devices. Try to state it positively, in a way that puts you in charge. Positive phrasing makes you the boss. For example, instead of saying, "I'm addicted to Insta," say, "I want to be in charge of my time on Insta." Instead of, "I can't stop texting," you could say, "I want to socialize offline more." It's a subtle but important difference. Being positive gives you the power, not Big Tech. Think about why you decided to do a reset and what you want to get out of it. Your reason doesn't necessarily have to be a problem. It could be you want to spend more time writing a blog, learning something, or participating in a club, chatroom, or other group.	*I hate all the time I waste on my phone.* *It's great that you recognize that feeling. Can you turn it into a positive statement?* *I want to control my phone use.* *Perfect.*
My *specific* goal is: Set a goal that is specific, realistic, attainable, and measurable. This is the key to a successful reset. For example, "I don't want to be distracted by my phone so much," is a fine overall goal. But it's not specific enough for a reset. It doesn't suggest a solution. If, however, you say, "I want to be able to do my homework without getting distracted by my phone," that gives you a specific target and timeframe to shoot for. You'll be able to consider the best tools for achieving that goal and measuring your success. The goal also needs to be realistic, attainable, and measurable. For example, wanting to lose 50 pounds in a week is not a realistic or attainable goal, whereas losing two pounds a week for 25 weeks would be.	*I want to cut back on screen time.* *That's a good general goal. Can you make it more specific?* *I want to cut back on Fortnite.* *Great. But you need to make it even more specific so it gives you a clear target.* *I want to cut back on Fortnite from five hours to one hour a day.* *You got it! That's a clear goal. Now, check that it's realistic. You want a target you can reach. Would it be more realistic to set the goal at two hours? Or would a TOTAL Fortnite fast be easier than trying to limit your time? Consider lots of possibilities in setting your goal.* *I want to limit Fortnite to no more than two hours a day.* *You are a quick study!*

CONTINUED ›

My reasons for setting this goal are: List the concerns, consequences, problems, hopes, dreams, or "mission" motivating you to set this goal. Why did you pick this *particular* goal as opposed to a different one? For example, if your reason for doing an App-endectomy is to cut back on screen time, there might be several goals you could have set to achieve that. Why did you select this one?	I spend more time on Fortnite than anything else. My friends are mad 'cause I don't see them anymore. *Uh-oh. Nobody wants their friends to be mad at them.* My grades are bad 'cause I rush through homework to get back to Fortnite. My mom and stepdad are on my back. *Ouch. Seems like a lot of good could come from achieving your reset goal.*
My action plan for achieving this goal is: List the steps you need to take, the rules you need to follow, the habits and behaviors you need to change. Be specific. For example, depending on your goal, you might say: "I will disable all social media notifications." "Give phone to mom to hold overnight." "Uninstall Insta." "I'll turn off my phone and put it in another room when doing homework."	Finish homework before playing Fortnite. *That's a nice, clear rule. You'll know exactly how you're doing in following it.* Set my screen-time tracker to block Fortnite after two hours a day. *Great use of technology to control your use of technology!* See my friends more. *That's not specific enough. Try again.* Grab a coffee with Cassie after school twice a week. Hang out Saturday nites like before with Tasha and Nick. *Perfecto!*
I will use the following tools and strategies to support and carry out my plan: Refer to the tips, tools, and strategies in chapters 4 through 9 and beginning on page 318. Come up with your own ideas for helpful tools. Be specific.	Use screen-time tracker to limit Fortnite. Tell Cassie why I backed away and about my reset, and that I miss her, and ask if we can make a plan to meet up twice a week. *Superb strategy!* Do the same thing with Tasha and Nick. Text Nick on Thurs or Fri to make a plan.
I will be doing the following Phone Fast as part of my App-endectomy: If a fast is one of your tools, list the type of fast you'll be doing here (it could be an intermittent fast, an app fast, or a purge fast). Be sure to complete My Fasting Matrix on page 288 and include it as part of your App-endectomy reset plan.	Not doing a fast. Just reducing time on Fortnite. *Trying to reduce time on Fortnite makes sense as a specific, realistic, and measurable starting point for your reset. You can keep a fast in mind as a backup tool.*

CONTINUED ›

My timeframe for this plan is:	Start Friday. Do it for one week. If I'm not going crazy, do another week. And so on. If it's working, goal is to keep going with two hours or less forever (?)
List all time-related elements that are part of your plan. Include as many specific dates as you can.	*You've got a strong, clear plan. You know why you're doing it. So I'm betting you won't go crazy! We can check in after forever to see how you're doing.*
For example, is your plan for a day, a week, a month, or until further notice (that is, you hope it will be a permanent change in your screen scene)?	<u>Tonight (Oct. 10)</u> Tell Nick and Cassie about my plan. Ask if they'll help.
Enter such things as: • start and end dates and times (if applicable)	*I'm sure they will. They sound like good friends.*
• when you'll alert people	Tell Dad. Ask him about an incentive. (Better word for him than reward.)
• when you'll ask people to be on your support team	*Anticipating how your dad will react is a nice use of perspective-taking empathy. Bravo!*
• when you'll install apps, activate features, and/or change settings if part of your plan	Notify Fortnite squad.
• when you'll gather items or materials for alternative activities	<u>Tomorrow nite before bed!!!</u> Enter Fortnite 2-hour time limit in tracking app
	Friday—begin *Too bad I can't sound a trumpet fanfare to herald the start of your App-endectomy. But I will send some powerful encouragement vibes your way on Friday!*
The threats that might undermine my action plan are:	Turning off the screen-time tracker.
List any people, habits, actions, feelings, temptations, or triggers (emotional, social, or practical) that might threaten the success of your App-endectomy.	Spending the time I'm not on Fortnite on YouTube. *Identifying these potential threats gives you a leg up on resisting them.*
Ex.: "Being bored." "Feeling lonely." "The bus ride home." "Sleeping with my phone on." "Missy sending me 4,000 texts a day."	Isolating. Getting depressed. *We don't want that. In the next box you can come up with a strategy for overcoming these threats.*
Refer to your Screen Scene Profile on page 303 for Habits, Triggers, and Temptations.	My Fortnite squad bugging me. *Might want to get a can of bug spray handy.*
	Being too dumb to do my homework. *Self-dumping not allowed.*
	Getting frustrated about Spanish. *Mucho mejor.*

CONTINUED ›

I will counter these threats by: **List the actions and countermeasures you can take to overcome these challenges. Be specific.** ☺ Examples: "I'll call someone on my support team." "I'll go for a bike ride." "I'll bake cookies." "I'll remind myself I can do this." "I'll take a bath and read a book before bed." "I'll look at my "Burdens and Benefits" card." (See page 324.) For ideas, refer to My Alternative Activities Brainstorm (page 315) and My Phone Habits, Triggers, and Temptations—and Countermeasures (page 316).	Call Jamie if I'm tempted to turn off the tracker. *You may want to give Jamie a heads up.* Block YouTube with the tracker if I watch more than 45 minutes. *I'm picking up that YouTube may be a strong temptation for you. It's great that you've identified it. Forewarned is forearmed.* Ask Nick to message or FaceTime me every night at 8:00. *Having a good friend check in with you is a solid support strategy.* Tell my Fortnite squad ahead of time that I'm cutting back. *Providing them with an alert should minimize the chance of their bugging you.* Ask Sue if we can do Spanish homework together. If I get bored, lift weights, ride my bike, clean my room. *You could also lift weights while riding your bike in your room. Or clean your weights while lifting your bike. Lots of possibilities!*
I will measure my progress or success by: **Write down how you will know that your reset is going according to plan.** This could be: • Data from a tech tool (monitoring number of phone pickups; sticking to a time limit) • Meeting a quantifiable goal (spending more hours offline with friends; re-joining a school club) • Following a reset rule you make (turning your phone off an hour before bedtime, not posting reputation-harming photos) • Recognizing an emotional change (feeling less stressed, having more confidence) • Using a self-care strategy (challenging negative thinking; going to bed earlier)	Using the tracker to limit my time on Fortnite. Sticking to it. Finishing my homework better. *More specific, please.* Finishing all my Spanish homework before dinner every day. *¡Excelente!* Getting together with my friends according to my plan. *This is important. Friends are the best for providing encouragement and emotional support.*

CONTINUED ›

My support team consists of: **Choose the people who best match your needs for this specific plan, and write down how they can be helpful and how you're going to count on them.** Refer to the list (page 312) you made of people you'll turn to for practical and emotional support for your App-endectomy.	Nick or Cassie—call if I'm feeling down. *You bet! Here's another idea: Also call Nick and Cassie if you're feeling "up." Let them share in the "high" of your success.* Mom—ask her to keep my phone overnight. *Something tells me she'll be happy to oblige.* Nick will text me every night to check in. *Just in the nick of time.*
People or groups I need to alert about my plan are: Refer to the list (page 313) you made of anybody you need to notify, and how you'll do it.	My Fortnite squad. Jamie, Nick, Cassie, Mom, Dad—talk to them tonite
My reward(s) for reaching my goal(s) are: **This needs no explanation.** ☺	Go fishing with Uncle Ben. *I bet Uncle Ben will love doing that.* From Dad—new backpack if I keep it up for a month. LED string light after two months (Have to ask him!)

My Progress Checklist: Sample

List the measures you'll monitor to know if you're sticking to your plan, using your tools, and achieving your goals. Place checkmarks to indicate how things are going for each measure.

The following checklist is designed to measure your progress each day. It's important to do this so you can feel a sense of pride and empowerment at your achievement. Plus, if you've strayed from the plan, a daily evaluation will give you early warning so you can correct your course. If some elements of your plan don't occur daily—let's say you're doing a phone fast every Saturday morning for a month or meeting a friend twice a week—just adapt the column for that measure so that it matches up with its timeframe.

Depending on your reset plan, your measures may be:
• quantifiable (number of phone pickups, sticking to a time limit)

• behavioral (spending more time with friends, re-joining a club, not bringing your phone to dinner)

• emotional (feeling more cheerful, more confident, less irritable)

• relational (getting along better with a parent, positive feedback from others)

Place a checkmark to indicate how things are going for each measure. Feel free to write notes, create a ratings scale (like 1 to 10), or invent icons to represent your measurement tools. You can use any system that makes sense to you.

CONTINUED ›

Day	Measure Stick to 2-hour daily Fortnite limit	Measure Have coffee with Cassie 2x week	Measure See Nick & Tasha every weekend	Measure Give Mom my phone every nite	Measure Good job on my Spanish homework	Measure Didn't veg out on YouTube
1	✔			✔	✔	✔
2	✔	✔		✔	✔	
3	✔			✔	No homework	
4	✔			✔	✔	Uh-oh. Gotta use tracker.
5	✔	✔		✔	✔	Ditto.
6	✔			oops	✔	✔
7 YAY!!!	✔		✔	✔	✔	✔
8	✔			✔	✔	✔
9	✔	✔		✔	No homework	✔
. . . 31						

That concludes our sample App-endectomy reset plan. I hope you enjoyed the ride.

> Not bad.

> Could you be a little more enthusiastic?

> Not bad!

> Thank you.

And now, my friend, it's time for you to create your own plan. Good luck.

> Could you be a little more enthusiastic?

> Good luck!!!

> Thank you.

To design your personal App-endectomy and fill in your own reset plan template, be sure to have these handy:

- the intel you gathered from the challenges in chapters 2 and 3
- your Screen Scene Profile from earlier in this chapter (pages 303–307), if you created one
- the preparations you just completed
- your gut, head, and heart

No problem if your answers to one question overlap with another. This isn't a test. So you also don't need to worry about grammar, punctuation, complete sentences, or coloring outside the lines. Feel free to jot down words, phrases, or full thoughts. All that matters is that your answers make sense to you.

You can also download the App-Endectomy Reset Plan at freespirit.com /dragons. Feel free to refer to the Sample App-Endectomy Reset Plan for refresher coaching.

My App-Endectomy Reset Plan

I would like to do an App-endectomy because: This can be a hope, concern, warning sign, consequence, or "mission" statement about how you want to use or relate to your devices. Try to state it positively, in a way that puts you in charge.	
My *specific* goal is: Set a goal that is specific, realistic, attainable, and measurable.	

CONTINUED >

My reasons for setting this goal are: List the concerns, consequences, problems, hopes, dreams, or "mission" motivating you to set this goal.	
My action plan for achieving this goal is: List the steps you need to take, the rules you need to follow, the habits and behaviors you need to change.	
I will use the following tools and strategies to support and carry out my plan: Refer to the tips, tools, and strategies in chapters 4 through 9 and beginning on page 318. Come up with your own ideas for helpful tools. Be specific.	
I will be doing the following Phone Fast as part of my App-endectomy: If a fast is one of your tools, list the type of fast you'll be doing here (it could be an intermittent fast, an app fast, or a purge fast). Be sure to complete "My Fasting Matrix" on page 288 and include it as part of your App-endectomy reset plan.	
My timeframe for this plan is: List all time-related elements that are part of your plan. Include as many specific dates as you can.	
The threats that might undermine my action plan are: List any people, habits, actions, feelings, temptations, or triggers (emotional, social, or practical) that might threaten the success of your App-endectomy.	
I will counter these threats by: List the actions and countermeasures you can take to overcome these challenges. Be specific. ☺	

CONTINUED ›

I will measure my progress or success by: Write down how you will know that your reset is going according to plan.	
My support team consists of: Choose the people who best match your needs for this specific plan, and write down how they can be helpful and how you're going to count on them.	
People or groups I need to alert about my plan are: Refer to the list (page 313) you made of anybody you need to notify, and write how you'll do it.	
My reward(s) for reaching my goal(s) are: This needs no explanation. ☺	

Celebrating with
Your Support Team

My Progress Checklist

List the measures you'll monitor to know if you're sticking to your plan, using your tools, and achieving your goals. Place checkmarks to indicate how things are going for each measure.

Day	Measure	Measure	Measure	Measure	Measure	Measure	Measure
1							
2							
3							
4							
5							
6							
7							
8							
9							
10							
11							
12							
13							
14							
15							
16							
17							
18							
19							
20							
21							
22							

CONTINUED ›

23							
24							
25							
26							
27							
28							
29							
30							
31							

5. Troubleshooting

Well, here you are. (Me, too.)

Me three.

Whether you've completed your App-endectomy or are still in the middle of it, the advice in this section will help you troubleshoot any problems you've encountered. Maybe you're making minor tweaks to your screen scene. Or you might be attempting a major reset involving fasts and life balance issues you want to address. No matter what your goal, it's different from anyone else's. So if you're experiencing some glitches, you'll need to create a custom plan for surmounting them.

The best way to make a mid-course correction, or even restart your App-endectomy, is to look through the following troubleshooting table. Locate the problem you're having, see if any of the possible causes ring true, and then implement the suggested solution(s). Since many problems have similar causes, and many solutions can apply to more than one problem, it's a good idea to read *all* the possible causes and solutions. That way, even if your problem isn't listed, you may still recognize your situation in a particular cause and solution.

Problem: Gave up. Couldn't do it. Too hard.

Possible Cause	Solution
Trying to do too much all at once.	Simplify the plan. Make sure you're targeting just one goal.
Unrealistic goal.	Make sure your goal makes sense in relation to your starting point. Better to succeed at going from seven to six hours than fail at trying to go from seven to two hours. (And once you hit six hours, you can do another reset to go from six to five.)
Goal not specific enough.	Revisit your goal. Make it as precise, actionable, attainable, and measurable as you can.
Not enough support. Too much reliance on willpower.	Make sure you have your support team or person in place. Ask them for help and encouragement. Find a friend to do a reset with you.
Insufficient tools.	Review the tools in this chapter (beginning on page 318), as well as those in the RESIST chapters that relate to your goal. The right tools can reduce temptation, bolster your willpower, and support your efforts.
Not motivated. Ambivalent about wanting to do a reset.	Take a pause and give it some more time. You may not be ready to do a reset. Some people need to feel deeper levels of imbalance—even pain—and experience greater negative consequences before being motivated to take action. If you wait a while and try again, you may have more success.

Problem: Didn't work. Did the reset. Followed plan. Achieved the goal. Nothing changed.

Possible Cause	Solution
Initial reset intervention "dose" too low.	It's important to set an attainable goal. But the goal also needs to be in proportion to the scale of the problem, concern, or consequence you want to address. If a particular app is toxic for you, cutting your use from six hours to five hours may not be enough to make a change in the symptoms you feel. You may need to cut back to two hours, or even no hours, to mitigate the negative consequences.
	If you met your initial goal without seeing the change you hoped for, "up" the dose. Address the issue with stronger "medicine." If you reduced screen time by an hour, reduce it more. If you blocked some notifications, block more. If you turned your phone off 30 minutes before bed, try an hour.
	You've already succeeded in meeting your initial goal. That's a wonderful base from which to set a new goal, strengthen your plan, and bring additional tools to the task.
Reset target misidentified.	If you achieved your goal and nothing changed, revisit your plan. Think of it this way: If a car won't start, and you change the battery and it *still* won't start, something else must be causing the problem. If you're still experiencing the "symptoms," your diagnosis as to what's causing them may be wrong. It's time to try a different intervention.

CONTINUED ›

Problem: Cheated by borrowing a phone; played at a friend's house; used a friend's tablet.

Possible Cause	Solution
Rationalizing; thinking it's not really cheating if it isn't your screen.	Remind yourself of the reasons for your reset. The type of person you want to be. The change you want to make. The control you wish to have. Tell your friend you're doing a reset. Ask her to not let you use her device. No matter how much you beg, whine, or threaten. ☺ (This needs to be a really close friend who will understand what you're doing and what you need and won't take anything personally. You don't want to risk harming a wonderful relationship.)

Problem: Felt lonely. Depressed. Anxious. Irritable. Angry. Tired.

Possible Cause	Solution
Insufficient support system.	Build up your support team—and give yourself permission to call on them when you need to.
Abrupt change in screen habits, and a corresponding loss of certain activities, interactions, and/or rewards.	What is missing or changed as a result of your reset? What did your screen time provide that you're not getting? Try to identify triggers for the feelings. Then look for other ways to satisfy those needs or desires. See page 316 for doing that.
Failure to identify emotional triggers.	Try to identify the source of the feelings. If you know what's causing them, you can "counterprogram" by doing your best to avoid the triggering person, behavior, setting, or interaction.
Natural response to disruption of habits, daily rhythms, and emotional disequilibrium.	In the first few hours or days, a reset may create voids in your daily schedule and in your sense of self. Painful emotions may fill those empty spaces. Don't let yourself be at loose ends. Engage in alternative activities. Surround yourself with people. Use tools and tips to get a good night's sleep.
FOMO.	Identify specific things you're afraid you'll miss out on. Come up with other ways of getting that information or interaction. These could include reaching out, increased face-to-face socializing, or asking friends to be communication conduits.
Loss of "rewards" from online stimuli to the brain.	Your brain is reacting to the change in stimuli. It may take a number of days for it to readjust. Power through those days with lots of friends, support, and other rewarding activities.
Fear of change. Fear of uncomfortable emotions.	People naturally resist change. They don't like unpleasant emotions. There's even a trend to shield kids and young adults from ideas and feelings that might upset them. This, however, keeps them from learning how to process distressing feelings, and inhibits growth, learning, and self-confidence. Most painful feelings pass. But while they are present, use the discomfort to build your self-awareness and emotional fortitude. "Bad" feelings aren't like sticking your hand in a fire. They won't burn you. You can touch them, weigh them, look inside them. And often, when you get to the other side, you'll be in a better place.

CONTINUED ›

| Distorted thinking. Negative self-talk. | Reach out—especially if you're struggling with dark feelings that just won't leave you alone. Talk to a friend, parent, counselor, therapist, or other trusted adult. |
| | The new feelings and temporary disorientation that might result from a reset may trigger a rash of discomforting or self-critical thoughts and feelings. See page 224 for tips on how to combat negative thinking. |

Problem: Couldn't stick to a fast.

Possible Cause	Solution
Wrong time to do one.	Fasting has practical and emotional ramifications. If you're super-stressed or in a period where using your device is especially critical for certain reasons, it may not be a good time to start a fast. Wait, and plan to do it at a more conducive time.
Didn't lay the groundwork. Not using alternative activities. Not using support team.	Check that you've built a support team, brainstormed alternative activities, and alerted everyone your fast might affect.
Withdrawal symptoms.	Fasts and screen-scene changes may initially disrupt habits, trigger uncomfortable feelings, and create inconveniences that undermine your commitment. These symptoms are a natural result of your brain, communication practices, social life, and daily patterns adjusting to the changes.
	The symptoms can be uncomfortable and lead to abandoning the fast. But they *will* pass. Summon your resolve. Rely on your support team. Make it through the first hours/days/weeks, and you *will* feel better. Maybe better than ever.

Problem: Gave in to temptation. Not able to adhere to plan. Broke reset rules.

Possible Cause	Solution
Vague or incomplete action plan.	Make sure the steps, rules, behaviors, and/or attitudes that comprise your plan directly relate to and support achieving your goal. Make sure the tools you select also directly relate to and support carrying out your plan.
Failure to sufficiently identify triggers and temptations.	Intervene on triggers and temptations by investigating the nature and/or pattern of any "relapses." Identify the emotional or practical triggers that occur prior to "succumbing." Engage tools to resist those temptations (see page 316).
Unhelpful schedule.	Revisit the timeframes within your plan. You may find that switching the days or hours of an intermittent fast or rescheduling slots for certain activities will strengthen your ability to stick to your plan..

CONTINUED ›

Not using the best tools.	The right tools make all the difference in succeeding with your reset. Use your support team. Program your free time with socializing and alternative activities.
	Take another look at the tips in the relevant RESIST chapters (4–9) and the tools beginning on page 318. Find those that address your particular situation and temptations and pick one (or more) to try out.
	Bury an app in a folder. Disable notifications. Give your phone to a parent overnight. Exercise more. Make sure you create and keep handy your affirmation cards (see page 324) to remind you why you're doing a reset. Use your screen-time tracker to block access to an app. The tools are there to help. But *you* have to use them.
Too much unstructured time.	Don't leave yourself with large, unfilled chunks of time—those periods when you *used to* game, post, watch, etc. It's essential, especially during the early stages of a reset, to keep them filled. Plan enjoyable and stimulating activities for your newfound time. You may have heard the expression "Idle hands are the devil's tools."
	Can't say I have.
	Well, in this case, "idle hands are Big Tech's tools." So keep your hands (and all the rest of yourself) active, and you will be better able to resist temptations.
Unsupportive physical or social environment.	Certain situations (being alone at home or in your room, studying in a coffee shop, hanging out with a particular friend) may pose greater threats to your reset. Avoid temptation-laden locations and social settings, at least during the early stages of a reset. Do homework at the kitchen table, go to the library, alter your social patterns.

Problem: Successful reset but now backsliding into old behaviors.

Possible Cause	Solution
Human nature.	Maintaining healthy habits and vows, whether exercising, studying a language every day, or sticking to any New Year's resolution, can be difficult. Revisit your reasons for doing a reset in the first place. Look at the concerns you had, the warning signs you recognized. Are they reappearing? Recognize that it is easier to nip a backslide in the bud than if you wait until it's 50 feet tall.
	Identify the specific "old" behaviors that are returning. Conduct a new mini-App-endectomy (use the Reset Plan on page 342) to address their reappearance.

CONTINUED ›

Changed life circumstances.	Have there been any events in your life—moving to a new school, the death of someone you know, falling out with a best friend, parents getting a divorce, being sick, quitting a team, joining a new social circle—that might be causing stress, new feelings, or new activities and behaviors that could account for the backsliding?
	Look for connections between your life and your backsliding, identify triggers, and use the appropriate tools to counter them.
Success and feeling better, causing you to let your guard down.	Weirdly, a successful reset that improves your life can become a temptation in itself. It's as if your mind gets hacked by Big Tech whispering, "Hey, things are great! You're in charge now. You've changed. Look how great you feel. You can safely go back to your old habits and it will be different this time."
	But that's like being out in a rainstorm under the shelter of your umbrella and thinking, "Hey, I'm not getting wet! I guess I can fold up my umbrella." Your *reset* is like that umbrella. Give it up too soon and the screen-time deluge that led you to doing an App-endectomy may return.
	Now, it's certainly possible that with your new, post-reset self-awareness and self-control, you can modify your screen scene without backsliding to problematic use. Simply growing older and having different priorities, interests, friends, and life circumstances will naturally alter how you use your devices.
	But recognize that for some people, at some stages of a reset, and especially after its completion, the incredible improvement they feel can lead them to believe, falsely, that they can fully resume old behaviors without any ill effects.
	If you feel that backsliding is leading you to a bad place, conduct a new targeted App-endectomy. Set your goal, make your plan, and select your tools based on your most significant backsliding concerns and/or warning signs.
	Most of all, remember that you did a successful reset once. You can do it again.

Well, I'm exhausted from writing this chapter. But that's okay, since *you're* the one who needs energy to begin or restart your App-endectomy. As you do so, recognize that this type of change and self-work can be tough. But if you stick with your plan, it'll get easier. And the rewards—whether spending more time with friends, pursuing interests, getting better grades, improving relationships with your parents, or feeling free (wheee!)—will reinforce your efforts.

A time will come when you will be glad and proud that you reset your screen scene. And when that happens, reward yourself with a little bowl of ice cream. Just make sure I'm in a different state.

GREAT THINGS YOU CAN DO ONLINE (AND OFF!)

Making Your Screen Scene a Force for Good

Can you believe it? Here we are at the last chapter.

> YAY!

> Be nice. I know you'll miss me.

Just think of everything you've done, discovered, and digested over these pages.

> Like those burritos?

You've learned about the downsides, dangers, and disadvantages of disproportionately dwelling in the domain of digital dragons. (You can tell I perished in the Alluring Abyss of Alliteration back in chapter 2.) With all your newfound knowledge about screen time and Big Tech, your head must now weigh at least 30 pounds, making it even more important that you don't hunch over to look at your phone. (See Got Tech Neck? on page 60.)

Having come this far, I hope you have a better idea of the ways in which Big Tech seeks to manipulate and exploit you and how you can resist and defeat those efforts. If you took all the challenges, explored your screen scene, identified areas in need of a digital reset, and gave or plan to give yourself an App-endectomy, you're well on the way to achieving a healthy balance between your on- and offline lives.

As I've said umpteen-and-a-half times, I'm not against phones, social media, or the internet. Au contraire, I don't know what I'd do without them. But I *am* against the negative impact they have had on individuals, societies, and foundations of civilized life such as privacy, decency, democracy, kindness, truth, empathy, shared facts, and respect.

Hopefully you are now better equipped to confront and triumph over the unhealthy, invasive, and addictive aspects of the digisphere. But more than that, I hope you'll harness the incredible magic and power of the internet as a source of good in your offline life. To enjoy that goodness, you need to cultivate it. Here are a few ways you can do that.

Create More, Consume Less

You may recall my saying that not all screen time is the same.

> Yeah. All 233 times.

Well, here's a new twist. Think of screen time as "connecting" versus "creating" versus "consuming." Think of it as being "active" versus being "passive." Being sociable versus being solitary. And I suppose there's a kind of "mush in the middle" which I'll get to in a moment.

"Connecting" is easy to define. It's when communicating with others is the primary focus of your screen engagement.

"Consuming" is when you're the observer or recipient of somebody else's creations. Consuming in and of itself isn't bad. In fact, it can be useful and essential. We all need to escape and decompress from time to time. And there's absolutely nothing wrong with watching videos, checking your feeds, or scrolling your social. Entertainment, relaxation, and learning often embody "consuming," and can be important life-enhancing activities.

The problem comes when watching *one* video turns into spending half a day watching videos—YouTubing down a rabbit's hole rather than *you* tubing down a lazy river.

In today's world it's easy to waste huge chunks of time consuming and spend very little, or none, creating. That's because there's a seemingly infinite amount of content out there. Information overload. Social media saturation. As I write this it's estimated that there are 44 Zettabytes of data in the digital universe. For those of you who aren't math whizzes like me, one Zettabyte is equal to 1,000,000,000,000,000,000,000 bytes, or roughly a trillion Gigabytes, give or take a petabyte or two (I think a petabyte is what happens when your dog catches the mail carrier). Of course, by the time you're reading this we may have run out of Zettabytes. But that's okay. A larger number is waiting in the wings: Mosquitobytes.

We're drowning in so much data that content, new and archived, is always there for the taking. Human nature being what it is, it's often easier to just take it all in rather than create something new. And creating is just as important as consuming—*more* important, if you ask me.

> **I didn't ask.**

> **You would've.**

Creating is how you exercise your brain, itch your imagination, and discover who you are. So, you ask, what constitutes creating?

> **I didn't—oh, never mind.**

In the most basic sense, creating is when you bring something into existence. For example, you could create a painting, a go-kart, or a Lego banana split. A sonnet, a soufflé, or a symphony for armpit fart musicians. You could create a guinea pig maze, an edible birthday card, or a bird bath with a water slide and tiny beach umbrellas for migrating hummingbirds. My point is—

> **Yeah, could we get to the point?**

—everybody has a talent, something unique to say. And there's a lot of variety in what constitutes creating. I've known teens who tell me, "I don't have anything to say. There's nothing I'm good at." To that I would say, "Poo," except you-know-who would probably get on my case.

Right about that.

You have a *lot* to say. First and foremost, you are an expert on yourself and your world. You know a tremendous amount about what it's like to be you. You know what you're good at, what you like, what bums you out. You know what people your age stress about, care about, and get angry about. You know all about academic and social pressure, parents, making tough decisions, the best and worst parts of being a teen. You've created your own strategies for dealing with homework, family, friends, social media, washing dishes, working out, the ups and downs of life—whatever. You can express that knowledge—which nobody else has—and others will benefit from it. You can turn your experience into practical advice, moral support, humor, commiseration, inspiration—something others can relate to. That means you have *influence.* You can create "digital assets." These can be blog posts, comedy routines, artwork, stories, music, tutorials, a video journal—anything. They become part of your online trail, your *brand.*

Much of the joy and power of the internet is that you can share your creativity with others. You've surely come across teens who give make-up advice, review toys, sing their own compositions, perform amazing trick shots, create marble courses, offer gaming tips, or just talk about what's on their mind. The goal isn't money or fame or followers (although those are occasionally byproducts), but rather the pleasure of expressing yourself, connecting with people, and making a difference.

Here are some great ways to be creative using digital tools and/or the internet:

- Explore photography. Take creative photos of nature or people or architecture or whatever inspires you. Touch them up if you can get access to editing software. Post your best stuff online for feedback—or just keep it to yourself if that's more your style.

- Draw or paint. You can do it by hand and scan your creation and post it online, or you can use digital tools to make art right on a tablet or computer.

- Write a blog post, poem, story, screenplay, novel, or something else. How about a memoir about getting poison ivy when you went camping last weekend?

- Write jokes and post them on social media. (Just don't be mean.)

- Dream up a game or reality show and get your friends to be the contestants.

- Create an app.

- Build a website. Display and promote your creative ventures (artwork, writing, music, animation shorts, twig furniture).

- Be an entrepreneur. Use social media or build a website to promote your product or service to sell. Maybe you have a dog-walking or lawn-mowing business. Do you babysit? Tutor? Have a band looking for gigs? Make rainbow booties for French poodles to wear to Pride? Whatever your skill, between social media and a website you'll find people who want it.

- Make a video. It could just be you talking and being, you know, yourself. Give a tour of your bookcase, beauty products, or cacti collection. Show how your sock drawer is organized and explain how you decide which pair to wear in the morning. Make a stop-motion video with clay or Legos. How about a cooking video of you whipping up your favorite recipe? You could enlist a younger sibling to help, make a total mess in the kitchen, and then end the video with a fast-motion frenzy that shows you cleaning everything up. You could make a TikTok of your friend belly-flopping at the pool. (Just make sure you have her permission to post it.) Or a live-action mystery story that you and your friends write, star in, edit, and publish!

- Make music. Record yourself singing another musician's song and tweet it to them—maybe they'll respond! (Or their lawyer will tell you to cease and desist violating their copyright.) Or write your own song and record yourself performing that. You can form a band with friends and mix your tunes with Garage Band (which is free on Mac products) or similar programs.

You may want to share what you create with others. In fact, that may be the reason you made it. For example, there's no way I would ever write a book if it weren't going to be shared. Yes, there's huge personal satisfaction in writing about bytes and boogers (hmmm, I think that might be a great title for my next book), but the reason I write books is for other people—the more the merrier—to enjoy and learn from them. Other things I create just for myself or for a very few people.

So, while the internet offers an amazing platform for sharing work, don't feel that your creations have value only if others see them. Creating can be just for yourself. And it doesn't have to be earnest or serious. Of course it *can* be, and if you're tackling something serious, that's fantastic. But you can also be silly or whimsical. You can be silly and whimsical today and earnest and serious tomorrow. Or do it all in one great, creative morning. The point is that you are putting something of yourself into what you do. *That's* where the value is found.

And now, if you can take a break from creating, let's turn to other great things you can do online.

> **What about the mush in the middle?**

> Huh?

> **You said you'd get to the mush in the middle.**

> Oh yeah. I think there's mush in the middle of my mind at the moment.

What I meant by "mush" is that sometimes it's not totally clear whether an activity is connecting, consuming, or creating. Some activities may combine two or even all three of these elements. Or start as one and lead to another. Is watching a gardening video consuming? Uh, yeah. But what if you take what you learned online and plant it offline to grow some big, juicy tomatoes? What about listening to an audiobook? At first glance that seems like consuming, but you could argue that you're an active participant in that story because you're building the visuals in your mind. And maybe it inspires you to write your own story. Or (just Among Us) what if you play a video game where you are strategizing, interacting, and using all your gray cells to psych out your opponents or coordinate with teammates? How about a fast-paced, hilarious DM exchange with a friend where you're playing off of each other's comments like two comedians? "Consuming?" "Creating?" "Connecting?" Sometimes it's hard to tell. Sometimes it's all three.

The point, as far as I'm concerned, is this: As long as you are thinking about the balance between connecting, consuming, and creating and being *deliberate* about your choices (not getting sucked into a video vortex from which you emerge hours later), you're on the right digital path. The more you connect and create, and the less you consume, the more life-enhancing your screen scene (and your *offline* life) will be.

Lead More, Follow Less

Leadership doesn't only come from a position someone holds, like class president, team captain, or first person in line. That kind of leadership can be effective and important. But often, the most effective and important leaders are those who lead by acting on their values and showing others what they stand for. Here's how.

Stick Up for Others

Let's say you're in a group chat with several friends. One of your friends, let's call him Nathan, makes a joke about another friend's weight. We'll call the second friend Ralph.

> Ralph?

> Be glad it's not Barf.

Nobody calls Nathan out for his unkind dig, and maybe Ralph even laughs about it. But you know it hurts him. You have a choice here. You can go along with it like everyone else—that is, you can *follow*—or you can say something and *lead*.

"Hey, Nathan, that's not cool."

Sometimes, that's all it takes to make a change. Ralph knows you have his back. Nathan learns that cruel comments aren't acceptable in your group. The group culture changes a little bit. Little changes like that can add up, leading to big changes. They can lead to a more positive friendship group, a group that has empathy for others and shows it. All it took was a little leadership.

You can do this in any group—online or offline. Anyplace you witness instances of bullying, shaming, or bigotry. So, say something! And remember to keep your comments about the issue at hand, not about people.

Bad: "Hey @contrarydude99, you're a %#@!& piece-of-$#!+ for saying that."

Better: "Yo @contrarydude99, instead of trashing people you don't agree with, let's talk about what the protestors are actually saying. Put yourself in their shoes."

Sticking up for others can be hard. You are putting yourself in line for criticism from friends or strangers. I'm not saying it's a piece of cake. Or a lemon meringue pie cut into pieces with a Razor Laser Sword. The fact that it is hard is why most people don't do it. And it's why the people who *do* do it are leaders.

> Doo-doo?

> You're getting as bad as me.

Speak Up

Leadership is about using your voice to spread your positive values and inspire others. Standing up to rudeness or bullying is one way to do that, but you can also be more proactive. If there's a cause, problem, or issue that you feel strongly about, let people know. You can research just about anything online to learn more about it. Get the facts, solidify your argument, and speak up. You can write an opinion piece for your school paper, which is probably online, or post it on your social.

The point is, you have a voice. If you have something important to say, put it out there!

Be a Privacy Activist

You are now more aware than before of the widespread, invasive, and secretive surveillance conducted by Big Tech, social media, online platforms, and government agencies. This is a trend across the entire planet. With voice recognition, facial recognition, gait recognition, smell recognition (trust me, it's coming), location tracking, data collecting, and millions of CCTV cameras recording your every move, it is increasingly impossible to lead a modern life without intersecting with, and being monitored by, the digital world.

You read in chapter 7 about ways Big Tech infects your devices to learn everything it can about you. It may seem futile to expect that your actions of resistance will have any effect. But they can. Demand privacy and greater data protection from companies, services, and professionals with whom you interact by writing letters, posting on social media, not buying products, and closing accounts. When enough people ask, complain, boycott, comment, and "vote with their thumbs," that's when companies change their policies. Yes, you're "one person," but when enough "one persons" resist, it becomes a movement. People, politicians, and corporations often try to get away with unscrupulous or unethical actions. But when there's pushback and the public speaks or votes, that's when they back down and do the right thing.

Get Involved

Fight injustice. Join a cause. Protect the planet. The internet is a great way to connect with people and groups that share your vision and care about the things you care about. You can participate in existing efforts or launch your own. You can use social media to find, organize, and motivate people to band together *offline*— whether to join a march or protest, clean up trash along a beach, or flood your mayor's office with calls from local residents.

Activism can take many forms. It can be done at a local, state, national, or international level. Often, activism is political. And wow, do we need teens to get politically active if we are to ever get out of the mess adults have made of the world. Even if you're not yet able to vote, you can support a campaign, write letters, attend rallies and meetings, join phone banks, call your state and national representatives, get signatures on a petition.

You may have a passion for animals (like finding homes for abandoned dogs), the environment (like supporting green initiatives to combat climate change), or helping people who are struggling (like refugees or people who are homeless). Whether it's a playground near you that's in disrepair, a neglected piece of land that could become a community garden, or a senior center where you go once a week to play your violin for visitors—your contribution could make a huge positive impact in your community and people's lives.

Don't ever feel that one person, one teen, can't make a difference. Darnella Frazier was 17 years old when she took and posted the video of George Floyd's murder that broadened the Black Lives Matter protest movement and led to renewed focus on police brutality and systemic racism, not just in the United States but around the world. Greta Thunberg was a 15-year-old student in Sweden when she went on a school strike to demand stronger action on climate change from the Swedish government. Soon, with the amplification of social media, her activism inspired millions of students around the world to organize their own strikes. By the age of 17, Greta had given a speech at the United Nations, been named Person of the Year by *Time* magazine, and received two nominations for the Nobel Peace Prize. Think of the Parkland students who turned the tragedy of their school shooting into March for Our Lives and the nationwide #neveragain movement to reduce gun violence. I could go on and on about young people whose on- and offline actions, words, and efforts led to powerful movements and changes. But I won't.

> **I wish you would.**

> Me, too. But I gotta begin to wrap things up here.

In talking about these dramatic examples of activism, I wouldn't want you to think that "changing the world" is the measure of success. I'm sure these teens never anticipated the global impact of the stand they took. They did something courageous and principled, and their passion, amplified by the internet and social media, carried it to unimagined levels of visibility and influence.

It's just as important for thousands—no, millions—of teens to use their digital lives to add to the goodness in the world. No project is too small or too local to make a difference. Start a crowdfunding campaign for a desperately sick child who needs an operation but has no health insurance. Or a family that lost their home in a fire. Or an agency that provides housing and other resources for LGBTQ kids who run away or who are kicked out by their families.

Use the internet to research afterschool youth programs, children's hospitals, homeless shelters, food banks, or other places where you could clean, stock shelves, assemble food packages, tutor, mentor, or share a talent, whether it's model making, juggling, leading sing-a-longs, or fart—

> **I wouldn't go there if I were you.**

> Got it.

Cultivate Your Digital Footprint

All the things you post—all the comments, likes, rants, and photos—become part of your own unique online trail. But you know this. That mean comment you made about your algebra teacher? It's out there. That photo someone posted of you doing a beer bong in Larry's basement when his parents were out of town? It's out there. That sexy photo you sent to your BF? Out there.

But so are all the kind, generous, insightful, and creative things you put online. All the photos, videos, poems, comments, and posts you made that show what you care about, what you stand for, what you are willing to fight for, and what a great person you are.

Flowers and turds.

While you can't control everything your friends might post, you can control 100 percent of what you post. Think of your digital presence as a virtual museum you fill with the finest and most beautiful objects, relationships, thoughts, memories, wishes, and experiences of your life. Nothing gets in by accident. Everything in the Living Museum of You represents a choice you make to put it there. This doesn't mean you can't be silly and spontaneous. You shouldn't have to lead your life *constantly* thinking about whether a TikTok of you burping is going to ruin your future. But still . . .

So think of your digital footprint as something you shape mindfully, deliberately, and creatively so that when people check you out it says: "Hire me, I'm trustworthy!" "Admit me, I'm creative." "Date me, I'm interesting." "Invite me, I'm sociable!" "Count on me, I'm responsible." "Marry me, I'm cool, caring, funny, reliable, hardworking, empathetic, and like to change diapers."

Be OFFLine More, Online Less

By now, I'm sure hearing this from me doesn't come as a surprise.

> It does. I'm gobsmacked.

> Like that word, eh?

> I cannot obfuscate my pleasure.
> Neither can my doppelganger.

One of the best things you can do to help maintain a healthy, happy online life is to balance it out with a healthy, happy OFFline life. And by balance, I don't mean 50-50 like a level teeter-totter. I mean more of a teeter-totter with you on one end and an elephant on the other with, hmmm, let's see, I'm not sure which end is online and which is offline.

> **I think you mean we should spend more time offline than online.**

> Thank you.

> **Just trying to help wrap things up.**

Your online life should be in service to your offline life. The time you spend online should nurture your interests, strengthen relationships you care about, help you achieve goals, and fill your being with positive energy, feelings, and self-regard.

So how can you do that? Here are a few ideas.

Organize Screen-Free Expeditions, Activities, and Clubs

Have you heard of the law of inertia? It's almost as famous as the Pythagorean theorem of TikTok. It states that objects at rest tend to stay at rest unless a force puts them in motion. This applies to people, too. Teens glued to their screens may be considered objects at rest—even if their fingers are going at it Fast and Furious(ly). One thing you can do to balance your online life with a more robust offline life is to find a "force" that will change your inertia. That force is called a plan.

Just as kicking a ball sets it in motion, making a plan sets you in motion. Research backs this up. Voter turnout increases when people are coached to create a plan for voting. Where will you vote? On what day? At what time? How will you get there? The act of coming up with a strategy for action is what researchers call an *implementation intention.* I call it a *plan* (maybe because I don't get paid by the letter).

Same thing with exercise. People may be *motivated* to exercise—"I really want to get in shape"; "I hate looking in the mirror"; "I can't get into any of my clothes"—but motivation alone doesn't do the trick. Studies show that people who come up with a *plan* for when, where, and how they'll exercise are far more likely to follow through than people who simply have the desire to exercise but no plan for doing so.

That's why—and I'm about to let you in on another World of Psychology secret that you may have already guessed—the power of an App-endectomy is that it's a *plan*. The steps you go through in filling out the template lead you to create a specific, er, implementation intention: What's your goal? How will you achieve it? What are your tools? Who are your supporters? How will you overcome threats and temptations? What day and time will you start? What actions do you need to schedule? How will you measure your progress? Put it all together and it's a plan. And that plan maximizes your chances for success by turning "motivation" into a verb.

Keep this create-a-plan supertool in mind, not only as a way to reset your digital life anytime you feel it needs a tweak (or a kick in the pants), but as a way to achieve most any goal or solve any problem in your life.

Inertia hates plans. So, make plans to do things offline. If something's on the calendar, if friends are counting on you to show up, you're much more likely to get off your Bed, Butt, and Beyond.

Be an activities director.

Organize your friends and family. Be the one who says, "Hey, let's play kickball at the park at 3:00 p.m. every Saturday." Or, "Mom, wanna go with us to the Ice Cream Museum Thursday after school?"

Activities Director

Be an explorer.

Remember waaaaay back in chapter 6—

> **I can't remember that far back.**

—I talked about how adolescence is a time for developing independence, exploring, becoming self-sufficient, and building your street smarts? And that many teens, by spending so much of their time on screens, are leading much more sheltered lives and not developing these offline skills?

> **Oh yeah. I have a faint recollection.**

Well, one way to counter that trend is to get out there in the world. Be an adventurer. A swashbuckler. That's not somebody who buckles a swash, but, rather, somebody who leaps into life with bravado, pursuing daring, exciting, and romantic adventures with gusto (and sometimes a sword). I don't know about you, but I like that image. I wouldn't mind having "Swashbuckler" carved on my gravestone (right above "Recovered Ice Cream Addict").

Be a swashbuckler. Create a Band of Explorers. Plan adventures with your friends or family. Set a goal of riding every one of the 178 miles of bike trails in your region. Pick something you've never done, someplace you've never seen—a museum, park, parcourse, cemetery, observation tower, lake, cavern, Wally's Wacky World of Wallabies—and make it a target for a trek. Figure out how you'll get there, what preparation, supplies, or equipment is required to pull it off. You may need your phones to check schedules, hours of operation, public transportation, or directions, but it goes without saying—

> **Which is why you're about to say it.**

—that you should ditch your devices during the expedition unless they are integral to carrying out your mission.

Help Others

If you've struggled with managing your screen time, you surely know you are not the only one. You probably have plenty of friends who struggle with the same thing.

You know that person who is already on Steam every single time you go on, as if they just live there? Or that person who always throws a comment on your Insta within five seconds of you posting? Or that person who texts while driving? Or who can't hold a face-to-face conversation for ten seconds without checking their phone? Or who speaks in memes? Or who hasn't seen the light of day all summer, doesn't notice the buildup of Cheeto residue on their gaming controller, and has no discernable sleep schedule?

That person.

While you're working on improving your own life balance, consider if there's someone in your life who could also use some help.

Give a Friend "Help-Lite"

If you have a friend whose screen time is somewhat out-of-whack, but not too seriously, invite that person to do things off-screen with you. Include them in group events like shooting hoops, sleeping over, or playing a board game at someone's home. Look for one-on-one things you can do together such as taking a walk, going to a mall or a concert, or tossing a frisbee around. You don't have to account for every hour in your friend's life, but getting them involved in something non-virtual every now and then can add at least a little balance to their life and remind them of how much fun in-person activity can be.

Doing that together not only helps them, it's good preventative maintenance for you too.

If your friend's online-offline imbalance isn't too out-of-whack-i-tudinous, you can casually bring up the topic. You'll increase the chance of being heard by following three principles:

- Be empathetic.
- Don't judge.
- Use your own experience as an example.

Copping to your own problems or choices is a good icebreaker for approaching difficult topics without seeming nosy or accusative. "Gawd, I can't believe how much time I spend on my social." "I went way overboard with Minecraft myself and had to go cold turkey." "I was becoming addicted to Insta so I had to stop using it for a while to make a reset." "Do you ever feel like your phone is your whole life?"

Neutral statements and questions like these are most likely to encourage honest, non-defensive responses. You can see why if you compare them to blameful or accusatory language:

"All you ever do is play that stupid game."

"If your grades keep falling, you're going to ruin your college chances."

"Why do you waste so much time on TikTok?"

"Can't you pay attention to what I'm saying for one minute without checking your phone?"

The goal is to get your friend to engage with the idea that they might have a problem with excessive screen time. It may be enough just to mention it and suggest that you do more offline things together. If you've given yourself an App-endectomy, you could tell your friend about it and ask if they'd like to try one. Offer to show them how. Or, if *you* have some screen-related issues you want to address, you and your friend could tackle a reset together.

Intervene

For a friend in more serious screen-time trouble, you may need to be more direct. This carries some risk, since she might get defensive or angry. But if you feel her screen time is harming her (or others), step in and step up. That's what friends do. Here's how.

Prepare. Sharing your concerns with a friend about her screen scene requires a thoughtful approach. You can't just wing it. To prepare, read through the following pointers. Each will give you an idea of the type of preparation needed: how to begin, what to say, how to say it, and how to conclude. Write notes for yourself. Having a piece of paper that you refer to will impress upon your friend that you are serious and that you prepared for the talk.

Pick the right time. This is a serious issue, and the conversation could get heavy. So it's important to find a time and place where you can have privacy and quiet and not be disturbed.

Express your feelings. Start by letting your friend know how much you care. "We've been best friends since second grade. So I really care about you and how things are going in your life. There's something I wanted to talk with you about. I'm really concerned about the amount of time you spend on your phone."

Stick to the facts. Opinions can be challenged. Facts, less so. "I've noticed that you're spending more and more time on your phone. You and I used to do so many things together after school. I miss that. And when we are together, you're always checking your phone and sending messages, which makes me feel like you don't even care I'm there. I know you quit soccer and are flunking algebra. You used to keep your room so neat and organized and now it looks like a hurricane came through." (Of course, you'll overwhelm your friend if you recite a bunch of facts all at once. Do them one at a time or in like-minded clusters.)

Invite a response. "I see all these changes and it seems like they have to do with how much time you're spending on your phone. And you don't seem very happy these days. So I wanted to ask, are you okay? Do you think there's a connection? Are you worried about this? Have you tried to cut back?" (Here, too, you don't want your friend to feel interrogated or overwhelmed.)

At this point, your friend may be relieved that the "secret" is out, that somebody noticed and cares. She may open up and talk about her struggle to control her screen time. She may express fears, guilt, shame, anxiety, self-critical thoughts, or problems in her life that relate to her screen time.

It's also possible, if you've touched a nerve, that your friend will react with anger or denial. She may tell you everything's fine and to mind your own business. Or the response could be someplace in between—maybe she's open to hearing what you're saying, but doesn't really think she has a problem, but, hey, thanks for caring. No matter what the response, the next step is the same.

Offer to help. If your friend is appreciative and receptive to change, you want to be ready with suggestions for how she can tackle the problem. As part of your preparation for the intervention, do some research on programs, counselors, and support groups. These exist on- and offline. Hand her a list of resources that she can investigate.

Tell your friend about this book and how it helped you reset your digital life. Offer to share the book with her and guide her through giving herself an App-endectomy. If she's open to that, help her *make a plan.* (Remember, a plan is the gateway to action.) Depending on your friend's temperament and self-discipline, it might be enough to give her the book to read. Or, if you think your friend needs more structure, ask her to read a chapter or two, and you can then have a phone call or coffee to talk about it, kind of like a book club. While everything in the book would help her understand her screen scene, key steps would be taking the challenges in chapters 2 and 3, and then going through the App-endectomy chapter. Rather than presenting your friend with a plan, it's best if you can facilitate *her* making the plan. That gives her ownership. And then, offer to be part of her support team.

> ### What if she gets mad?

If your friend is defensive or angry, you can say, "I'm sorry that my mentioning this has upset you. But I care about you and wanted to say something. If you ever want to talk about this, I'm here for you." You could also loan her your copy of

Slaying Digital Dragons. Even if she responded with hostility to your concern, in the privacy of her bedroom she might sneak a peek at the book. And, obviously, once she starts reading, she won't be able to put it down.

If your intervention didn't get the result you hoped for, don't feel like you failed. Sometimes people aren't ready to change. But your friend heard what you said. She can't "unhear" it. And if she did have some worries of her own below the surface, you scratched them. Somebody else may come along and express concern about her screen time. Her parents may get after her about it. And over time, all those comments will add up. Your friend may reach a point where she can no longer ignore or hide from the negative consequences of her screen time, and then she will be ready to do something about it. And it all began with the seed you planted.

When the Person Spending Too Much Time on Screens Is a Parent

It's one thing to talk to a peer about something difficult like possible screen addiction. But when it's a parent, it's a whole different kettle of phish. Now, I don't know if your parent simply has an annoying habit or two, is occasionally lost in Phoneland, or is totally addicted to their screens. But no matter where they fall along the screen-scene continuum, it can be tricky business to approach a parent about *their* behavior.

Many parents invite the sort of openness that encourages kids to feel they can safely bring up any topic. If that's the sort of relationship you have, great! Your job will be that much easier. Other parents may be more authoritarian and "proud." They can't bear to admit a mistake or seem fallible to their kid. They may define criticism from children as disrespectful and automatically dismiss their children's concerns and ideas. They may get defensive. "I don't need you telling me about my phone use. You worry about you." And still other parents are total jerks. (Sorry, but I have tried to be "real" in this book.) But let's hope the parent in question would be open to hearing your thoughts.

Here are a few general tips for addressing parental screen time.

Think of it as an intervention. Even if it's a mini-mini-intervention—just one thing that you're concerned about, like, say, your parent checks his phone when you're trying to talk with him about something serious—it's a good idea to have the tips for intervening on a friend ringing in your head:

- *Prepare.* Think ahead of time about what you want to say and how your parent might respond.

- *Pick the right time.* Don't bring it up if your parent is stressed, rushing to meet a deadline, or just dropped a pot of spaghetti sauce on the floor.

- *Express your feelings.* Parents are more likely to respond positively to feelings than criticisms.

- *Stick to the facts.* Avoid judgments and blameful statements.

- *Invite a response.* Try to get their "buy-in" to whatever it is you're asking for or proposing.

Phrase your concern as a request. Let's say your mom is forever taking, tagging, and posting pics of you and putting every single thing you do on Facebook. It violates your privacy and you're not happy about it. You have every right to bring this up, but your chances for success depend on taking the right approach.

- *Right way:* "Mom, I have a favor to ask. It's important to me to have my privacy and be able to control what's online about me. I get embarrassed when I see some of the photos you post of me and the things you tell your friends. Could you please check with me before you post anything about me?"

- *Wrong way:* "I hate it when you put things up about me without my permission. You have no right to do that. If you don't stop, I'm going to start putting *your* private stuff online."

You can see how the "right way" involves owning your feelings (embarrassment), expressing your values (a desire for greater privacy and control of your online image), and inviting a response (asking your mom to agree to respect your feelings by getting your permission to post about you).

This approach is much more likely to succeed than asking her to stop her inconsiderate, invasive, obnoxious, hurtful behavior.

> **You think?**

Express a wish to improve your relationship. Decades ago, as the dangers of smoking and secondhand smoke became more widely known, kids were one of the most effective forces for getting parents to quit. Imagine the power of millions of parents hearing their kids say, "I don't want you to die." "Your secondhand smoke is going to give *me* lung cancer." "The house stinks." Many kids hid ashtrays, threw out cigarettes, and deftly guilt-tripped their parents. While I might have had some refinements to suggest to kids back then, their approach was primal and sound in the heartstrings it pulled: parental love for their children and the desire to maintain and improve parent-child relationships.

You can use those same tactics. Rather than criticize a parent for how much time they spend on their phone, ask them to spend more time with you. Let's say your dad drives you to school, but he's always on his phone. Tell him, "I really like having this time with you. But I get scared when you look at your phone while you're driving. Do you think we could make it phone-free and talk?" Now, of course, this means you would have to be off your phone as well. And up for talking to your dad.

Another example: Your parents set their phones on the dinner table and constantly check them over the course of the meal. They're so preoccupied you feel like you could tell them that 1,000 aliens invaded your school, the principal grew horns, the entire ninth grade went to the hospital with food poisoning, you're pregnant—and they would just nod and say, "Uh huh. That's nice."

Rather than focus on their behavior, focus on your desire for more family time. Propose dinners without devices. It's the difference between saying, "Can you guys turn off your phones when we eat?" and "I'd love it if we could make dinner phone-free and talk during that time instead. We never have enough time to do things as a family." (It's okay if a feeling shoots a little dart of guilt.)

Propose a family App-endectomy. Your parents may give you a lot of grief about your phone use. Yet they use their phones just as much as you do. More, you think. Why not suggest an App-endectomy for the entire family? With many parents addicted to their phones, they might be receptive.

The best way to do this is to have a family meeting. It can be casual (you bring the idea up during dinner) or more formal (you invite your family to a discussion you'd like to have).

Introduce the topic by saying that you've been giving a lot of thought to your screen time. Express your concerns about how much time you spend on screens, and talk about how you'd like to cut back. "And what would *really* help me is if the whole family could support this by doing a family reset." See how you've sneakily framed *their* cutting back as support for you?

You can ask questions designed to get them to think about their screen time and larger Big Tech issues: "Do you guys ever feel like your phone controls you?" "Have you ever thought about what you do online and how it affects you?" "What do you see as the best and worst things about your phone use?" Ask about their opinions on social media, the role of the internet in spreading conspiracy theories, likes and retweets, autoplay features, breaking up Big Tech monopolies, and other aspects of the online world.

Hopefully, you'll hear some answers that reinforce the idea of a family reset. If, however, people respond negatively, are in denial, or say that everything is hunky-dory, you can base your request on wanting more "quality" time together (rather than addressing their phone habits).

Once you get buy-in from some or all of your family, use the App-endectomy reset process to create and guide an action plan. You'll need to identify an initial family goal. It could be making dinner a phone-free time. Or taking a phone-free outing on Saturday afternoons. Or turning off phones when watching TV together. Once you select a family goal, you'll need to follow the relevant steps of the Reset Plan (pages 342–344). Each individual family member can also target a personal goal to shoot for during the all-family reset.

TIP: If you think you might already have allies for an all-family App-endectomy—maybe a sibling or one of your parents—it's a good idea to preview your idea with them ahead of the meeting. That way you know you'll have support if anyone responds negatively.

TIP: While it's best if your entire family jumps on board, it's not necessary. If, say, one sibling (or even a parent) refuses to participate—maybe he won't leave his phone at home during an outing—you can still engage the plan with other willing family members. It might be a bit awkward, but, hey, that's life. Your sib or parent might come around, and if not, the rest of you can still benefit.

TIP: Allowances will need to be made if someone's job requires constant phone availability. Obviously, if your mom's an on-call surgeon or your dad's a volunteer fireman, they may be required to keep their phones on. Nonetheless, you can construct "rules" that allow them to keep their phones handy to receive important messages while also adhering to the terms of a family reset.

TIP: If dangerous behaviors are an issue—for example, if your parents text while driving—you have my permission to escalate your efforts. Pull out all the guilt stops: "I don't want to die. And I don't want you to die. How will you feel if you make me an orphan?"

> They'll be dead. They won't feel anything.

> Are you sure?

The point is, illegal, dangerous behavior justifies stronger responses. Insist that your parent sets "no texting while driving" as a goal. Of course, you won't be able to know if they cheat. But you (and other members of your family) could refuse to get in the car with them if they're going to text or look at their phone while driving.

I realize this could get a little, er, awkward if they order you to "Get in that car this very minute!" But unless your parent might be physically abusive, you really have a lot of leverage. Now, they might say, "Okay, you can walk to school." Or,

"Fine by me, you can miss your soccer practice." So be prepared for the possibility of some initial sacrifice on your part. But your average loving parent will give in because of:

- guilt;
- the school calling to ask why you've been absent ("Well, you see, Mr. Grimm, Billy refuses to get in the car with me since I text while driving");
- knowing you're right; and/or
- realizing that their position that they should be able to text and drive is absurd.

TIP: If your parents are total phonaholics and reject all your requests and overtures for a family reset, remind them that by using their phones so much they are depriving you of essential parent-child bonding and nurturance, which is likely to lead to future psychiatric problems that will cause you to act out, be suspended from school, get in trouble with the law, be incapable of forming intimate relationships, and run up hefty shrink bills that they will have to pay.

Improve Your School's Screen Scene

Over the course of many pages—

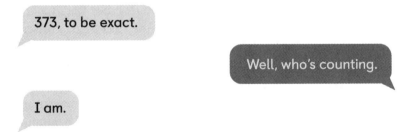

373, to be exact.

Well, who's counting.

I am.

—you've been examining your own screen scene and digital life. But what about your school's?

Schools are increasingly using technology and the internet to carry out their mission. Now, of course, COVID-19 triggered an extreme—and, I hope, rare—reliance on technology. But even before remote learning became the school experience for millions of kids during the pandemic, educational methods had embraced screens. In the same way that excessive screen time can harm an individual's physical, social, emotional, and cognitive health, excessive or ill-considered screen time in schools can harm not only student health, but the overall health of the school climate and community.

Some schools have hired Information Technology (IT) specialists and devoted considerable resources to developing thoughtful rules, guidelines, and plans for digital citizenship, privacy and security, personalized learning, student-teacher communications, managing homework, and using the internet and digital devices to enhance teaching and learning. Other schools have jumped willy-nilly onboard the tech train without much research or planning. Some educators view online learning as a way to enrich the human experience within the classroom. Others see it as a way to replace it.

In either case, issues of security, privacy, and the effectiveness of electronic learning have now taken a seat in every classroom (right next to the kid in the back row who picks his nose).

With your newfound deep, nuanced, and masterful understanding of the impact of screen time on your own life, you can be an advocate for making sure your school's use of technology is appropriate and beneficial, not only for you and your classmates, but for the entire school community.

Get InspirED

InspirED grew out of a collaboration between the Yale Center for Emotional Intelligence, Facebook, and Lady Gaga's Born This Way Foundation. (I know, who would've thunk those three would get together?) The project began by surveying tens of thousands of high school students to find out how they feel in school and how they *want* to feel. The majority of students said they feel tired, stressed, and bored. But they wanted to feel respected, valued, safe, passionate, purposeful, connected, supported, happy, excited, motivated, energized, empowered, and inspired.

This gap between how students felt and how they wanted to feel propelled the mission of inspirED: to "empower students to work together to create more positive school climates and foster greater well-being in their schools and communities." InspirED does this by providing free resources and support for students and schools that wish to launch an inspirED team to assess and improve school climate.

The inspirED process could be the perfect structure for improving your school's screen scene by tackling one of the following projects or one of your own invention. You can learn more by going to inspiredstudents.org. Read what they have to say, download their "Innovator's Guide" from the Resources page, and see if it might be a good fit for what you'd like to do.

Spearhead a Schoolwide Digital Health Project

Many schools have vague, inconsistent, or spotty policies regarding their use of technology. They haven't fully thought through the impact of these tools and platforms on student privacy, learning, or student-teacher relationships.

Members of the school community have a right to know the answers to the following questions:

- Does the school have a written policy regarding its use of technology? What is it? What are the priorities and objectives?

- What file-sharing and online learning services does the school use? Are they free in exchange for exposing students to ads, data mining, and/or possible identity theft? What are the privacy and security policies of any platforms the school uses? Could hackers gain access to a student's name, voice, email address, disciplinary record, and/or grades?

- Does the school use a portal for notices, homework assignments, and student-teacher communication? Does the portal facilitate learning with predictable, uniform procedures, or do students get caught in a maze of inconsistent practices across different teachers, courses, and classrooms?

- Do school disciplinary policies encompass online behavior? Smartphones and social media have blurred the lines between on- and off-campus life for students and staff alike. If a student is cyberbullied by a classmate outside of school hours, is that a school issue? If there's a secret "hot or not" website to rate classmates, is that a school issue? If a student posts racist or homophobic content on a personal website, is that a school issue? Can students and teachers text or email one another? Can they friend each other or like posts on personal social media sites?

- Does the school's emphasis on "innovation" and technology shortchange other budget categories such as health resources and counseling, arts, music, sports, libraries, repairs, safe school buildings, or teacher salaries?

- Do school tech policies account for economic differences in students' family backgrounds and whether students have at-home access to WiFi or devices?

- Have research findings on the emotional, social, academic, and even physical effects of on-screen learning influenced the school's technology policies?

A school's screen scene can have a positive or negative effect on students, the school community, and the quality of the educational experience. If you or your friends feel there's room for improvement in any of these areas, you can initiate a process as concerned "citizen-students" to learn more about the issues, with the ultimate goal of making recommendations for change. This could be done as an inspirED project or through your student council, a technology club, a parent-teacher association, or the school paper (where an enterprising student reporter might find this a ripe topic for investigation).

Cheer Up Your School Climate

School climate isn't about heat waves and hurricanes in the school cafeteria. It's about what it feels like to be at school. Given how much time you and your friends spend in school, you deserve a school climate that is welcoming, respectful, and purposeful. You should enjoy being there. This is important since positive school climate is associated with all sorts of good things, such as higher academic performance, improved student relationships, reduced truancy and disciplinary problems, and happier students and teachers. And we always like it when teachers are in good moods!

What determines school climate?

Many factors promote outstanding school climates:

- respect for diversity
- compassionate and uplifting solidarity among students
- shared values and a positive sense of community
- close, supportive student-teacher relationships
- a 12-foot-long ice cream buffet in the cafeteria with 97 different toppings

Pretty much all areas of school life influence school climate. In fact, run a search on "school climate" and you'll find numerous surveys and measurement instruments you can use to assess it. Let's look at a few more factors that determine what it feels like to be part of a school community. You can see how all of them can exist along a continuum from great to terrible, with each affecting school climate for better or worse.

- fair and equal enforcement of rules
- levels of drug use, bullying, student misbehavior, violence, and competition
- physical safety and appeal of the school building and grounds
- adequate resources for students' mental, emotional, and physical health needs
- high expectations for student behavior and achievement
- freedom to explore identity and express opinions without fear of bullying or reprisal
- teaching methods and classroom resources that allow all students to thrive
- school support for interests and areas of student development beyond academics
- broad range of extracurricular clubs, events, activities, and teams

As you looked through the list, I bet an inner voice reflexively answered how your school fares on each measure, saying, "*Yup, no, definitely, not my school, big problem, we're good on that, I wish, no way.*"

If you recognized areas where your school could do better, a project to improve school climate would be a great way to use the power of the internet to benefit the offline lives of members of the school community.

Be Empowered

I've been dreading this moment. It's the time when all good things, and by that I mean this book, must come to an end. Wrapping up a book is a lot harder than wrapping up half an egg salad sandwich. This is for two reasons.

One is that there's still so much I want to share with you. Like how in 1917 the artist Marcel Duchamp (using the name R. Mutt) submitted a urinal on a pedestal (*pissotière* in French) to an art exhibition. The work, which he titled "Fountain," was rejected. The next month, an article appeared deriding the exhibition for rejecting the piece: "*Whether Mr. Mutt* [who was Monsieur Duchamp] *with his own hands made the fountain or not has no importance. He CHOSE it. He took an ordinary article of life, placed it so that its useful significance disappeared under the new title and point of view—and created a new thought for that object."* Many people consider "Fountain" to be one of the most radical and influential works of 20th-century art.

The reason I like that story is because it shows how one person's original idea, action, insight, or innovation can transform how people see things, live, and behave. That one person could be you. Create versus consume. Oh, and that urinal that was rejected and ridiculed in 1917? A later edition sold for $1,762,500 in 1997.

The second reason it's so difficult to wrap up a book is because, as you know from learning about writing an essay, every essay is supposed to have a *beginning*, where you introduce the topic; a *main body,* where you make your case; and a *conclusion*, where you summarize the main points and draw your conclusion, leaving readers with a parting, insightful gem.

That's HARD! We've covered so much ground: Life balance. Boredom. Multitasking. Phone calls to eggs. Toasty testicles. Blue light. Sleep. Empathy. Cookies. Ice cream. Ice cream. Ice cream. Negative thought loops. Brand sanitizer. Sexting. Socrates.

> Don't forget boogers.

You battled Brain Snatchers, Time Suckers, and Demons of Denial to **REFLECT** on your own screen scene and online-offline balance. You learned how social media and Big Tech try to addict, manipulate, and stalk you. How too much or the wrong kind of screen time can harm your body, brain, relationships, social skills, psyche, privacy, reputation, and future opportunities. How online hate, lies, and conspiracy theories can destroy truth, societies, and the foundations of civilization.

You now have an arsenal of tips and tools to **RESIST** the assaults and negative forces of

The Dark Side.

And, most important, you possess a supertool—called an App-endectomy—that allows you to **RESET** your screen scene or any other area of your life you wish to target.

Despite my occasional rants against Big Tech throughout this book—

Occasional?!?

—I hope I've made it clear that I'm not against smartphones, digital devices, social media, or the internet. I wouldn't know what to do without them. I don't want to turn the world back to smoke signals and the Pony Express.

And I hope it's clear that I'm not pushing for you to change your digital life one way or the other. For all I know, maybe you should spend *more* time online.

But I am hoping that you, my dear reader, will do one thing as a result of reading this book:

Be empowered.

You can't control the digisphere or the forces behind it. It will continue to change—quickly and unpredictably—as virtual reality, artificial intelligence, and brain-computer interfacing evolve. There will be new platforms, technologies, and regulations. Time will tell if they make the internet a more humane, civil, and life-affirming place or push us in even darker directions.

No, you can't control the digisphere. But you *can* control your relationship to it.

You can be *empowered.* You can use your knowledge, confidence, self-awareness, and tools for personal growth to increase your control over your own life or situation. To make your own decisions. To think for yourself. To lead an examined life.

If you give more thought to your decisions, you are bound to make better ones. And overall, you are bound to live a healthier, happier life.

This doesn't mean you can never burn an entire day on YouTube or playing your favorite game—your fingers going numb, your stomach rumbling with hunger, your eyeballs cracked like the desert floor. While that's not the greatest thing for your brain or your body, if you do it every once in a while—say, three or four times over summer break—you're not going to wither away into a brain-drained pool of brain-pruned pudding.

Thinking of posting a revealing photo? Give it some thought. Thinking of Snapping a funny-but-mean insult? Posting an embarrassing pic of somebody? Take an extra few seconds to think about what will happen when you do—how the other person will think and feel. What your peers will think and feel about *you*. How *you'll* feel about you. How it will affect your reputation. Maybe you'll still decide to do it. But at least you gave it some deliberate thought.

Using your knowledge, goodness, empathy, and values to empower your choices is a virtue that applies to all of life, not just online life. Consciously decide how willing you are to let Big Tech invade your life, and what benefits or drawbacks that will bring. Make knowing decisions about how you want to spend your time. What kind of digital footprint you want to leave.

It's all about putting you in charge. So you can be an Ace of Apps. Soaring on golden wings of wisdom and willpower.

Being empowered.

Can you do that?

> **Count on it!**

Well then, I think my work here is done.

So with that, dear readers, I bid you goodbye, adieu, sayonara, au revoir, adios, arrivederci, ma'a as-salama, auf wiedersehen, aloha, ciao, namaste, shalom, do svidaniya—

> **WAIT!!!**

> What???

> **I have something for you.**

> Pour moi?

> **Pour what?**

> Never mind. It's French. You have something for ME? Like, a present?

> **Sort of.**

I don't know what to say.

Good. You've said enuf. Here it is!

My Resistance Manifesto

I will join the resistance against Big Tech by taking charge of my screen scene.

I will lead an empowered, examined life, always thinking for myself.

I will *REFLECT* (on my digital life), *RESIST* (any negative forces), and *RESET* (my life balance) if anything gets out-of-whack-a-doodle. *(Bet you liked that one.)*

I will use my screen time to do good things for myself and others.

I will maintain a healthy balance between my online and offline lives.

I will protect my body, brain, privacy, reputation, schoolwork, sleep, and psyche from Big Tech meanies.

I will resist the shallow, nasty, and judgmental aspects of social media.

I will resist negative thinking.

I will, without being a supercilious jerk about it, try to create more than I consume. *(Like that word? Supercilious?)*

I will stay away from platforms that make me feel bad.

I will post to share my life and not let posting become my life.

I will be an offline adventurer and look for opportunities to swash my buckle.

I will use my time on screens to benefit my relationships, personal growth, and future options.

I will be alert to the lies, misinformation, and biases found online.

I will listen to my gut and watch out for warning signs. *(And too many burritos.)*

I will use the Reset Plan as a tool to improve my screen scene or other areas of my life.

I will pause before acting to think about the consequences of anything I do online, like sending ice cream to Alex.

I will respect other people's privacy and feelings and not use my phone to hurt or embarrass them.

I will leave a digital trail of flowers, not turds. *(That's for you.)*

I will always remember that the most powerful app is my brain.

So what do you think?

I . . . I'm so touched. I . . . I . . . I'm speechless.

I thought the day would never come.

SELECTED BIBLIOGRAPHY

Books

Alter, Adam. 2017. *Irresistible: The Rise of Addictive Technology and the Business of Keeping Us Hooked.* New York: Penguin Press.

boyd, danah. 2014. *It's Complicated: The Social Lives of Networked Teens.* New Haven, CT: Yale University Press.

Dunkley, Victoria L. 2015. *Reset Your Child's Brain: A Four-Week Plan to End Meltdowns, Raise Grades, and Boost Social Skills by Reversing the Effects of Electronic Screen-Time.* Novato, CA: New World Library.

Freitas, Donna. 2017. *The Happiness Effect: How Social Media Is Driving a Generation to Appear Perfect at Any Cost.* New York: Oxford University Press.

Heitner, Devorah. 2016. *Screenwise: Helping Kids Thrive (and Survive) in Their Digital World.* New York: Bibliomotion.

Homayoun, Ana. 2018. *Social Media Wellness: Helping Tweens and Teens Thrive in an Unbalanced Digital World.* Thousand Oaks, CA: Corwin.

Kamenetz, Anya. 2018. *The Art of Screen Time: How Your Family Can Balance Digital Media and Real Life.* New York: PublicAffairs.

Kardaras, Nicholas. 2016. *Glow Kids: How Screen Addiction Is Hijacking Our Kids—and How to Break the Trance.* New York: St. Martin's Press.

Lanier, Jaron. 2018. *Ten Arguments for Deleting Your Social Media Accounts Right Now.* New York: Picador.

Miner, Julianna. 2019. *Raising a Screen-Smart Kid: Embrace the Good and Avoid the Bad in the Digital Age.* New York: TarcherPerigee.

Price, Catherine. 2018. *How to Break Up with Your Phone*. New York: Ten Speed Press.

Schneier, Bruce. 2015. *Data and Goliath: The Hidden Battles to Collect Your Data and Control Your World*. New York: W.W. Norton & Company.

Twenge, Jean M. 2017. *iGen: Why Today's Super-Connected Kids Are Growing Up Less Rebellious, More Tolerant, Less Happy—and Completely Unprepared for Adulthood—and What That Means for the Rest of Us*. New York: Atria.

Wu, Tim. 2016. *The Attention Merchants: The Epic Scramble to Get Inside Our Heads*. New York: Vintage Books.

Zuboff, Shoshana. 2019. *The Age of Surveillance Capitalism: The Fight for a Human Future at the New Frontier of Power*. New York: PublicAffairs.

Organizations

Campaign for a Commercial-Free Childhood (CCFC): commercialfreechildhood.org

Common Sense Media: commonsensemedia.org

ConnectSafely: connectsafely.org

Pew Research Center—Internet and Technology: pewresearch.org/internet

Savvy Cyber Kids: savvycyberkids.org

Newsletter

Ovide, Shira. "On Tech with Shira Ovide." *New York Times.* nytimes.com/newsletters/signup/OT.

Film

Orlowski, Jeff, director. 2020. *The Social Dilemma.* Exposure Labs. Argent Pictures. Netflix.

INDEX

To download the reproducible forms and other digital content for this book, visit freespirit.com/dragons. Use the password 2slay.

ABOUT THE AUTHOR

Alex J. Packer, Ph.D., is an educator, a psychologist, and the award-winning author of numerous books for parents, teenagers, teachers, and youth workers including *How Rude! The Teen Guide to Good Manners, Proper Behavior, and Not Grossing People Out.* His books have been translated into many languages including Spanish, German, Korean, Japanese, Thai, Mandarin, Greek, Romanian, and Serbian.

An expert on manners, adolescent development, child-rearing, substance abuse prevention, and ice cream addiction, Dr. Packer (but you can call him Alex) has led workshops and spoken widely at schools, events, and conferences across the United States and around the world. Talks have taken him to locations as far-flung as Venezuela, Thailand, Argentina, Spain, Germany, China, Colombia, Japan, and Mexico.

For 14 years, Alex was President and CEO of FCD Educational Services, the leading nonprofit provider of onsite K–12 substance abuse prevention services for schools throughout the United States and in over 65 other countries. Alex also served for eight years as head of an innovative alternative school in Washington, D.C., for children ages 11–15, and as Director of Education for the Capital Children's Museum. His feature-length screenplay, "Digby and Fly," won Grand Prize in the Massachusetts Film Office Screenwriting Competition.

Alex graduated from Phillips Exeter Academy and holds undergraduate and master's degrees from Harvard College and the Harvard Graduate School of Education and a Ph.D. in educational and developmental psychology from Boston College.

Alex has a love-hate relationship to the digital world. (He loves to hate it, and hates that he loves it.) Big Tech's creepy, invasive, unauthorized surveillance of Alex's online activities reveals that he has flown ultralight aircraft without crashing, spends five months a year in France, enjoys vintage sports cars, types with two fingers, turns his phone off at night, and is considering thumb-reduction surgery to improve his texting accuracy.

Other Great Resources from Free Spirit

How Rude!®
The Teen Guide to Good Manners, Proper Behavior, a nd Not Grossing People Out
(Revised & Updated Edition)
by Alex J. Packer, Ph.D.
For ages 13 & up.
504 pp.; PB; 1-color illust.; 7¼" x 9".
Free Leader's Guide
freespirit.com / leader

What's the Big Deal About Addictions?
Answers and Help for Teens
by James J. Crist, Ph.D., C.S.A.C.
For ages 13 & up.
168 pp.; PB; 6" x 9".

Dream Up Now™
The Teen Journal for Creative Self-Discovery
by Rayne Lacko, with community outreach advisor Lesley Holmes
For ages 13 & up.
176 pp.; PB with layflat binding; 1-color; 7¼" x 9¼".

LGBTQ
The Survival Guide for Lesbian, Gay, Bisexual, Transgender, and Questioning Teens
(Revised & Updated 3rd Edition)
by Kelly Huegel Madrone
For ages 13 & up.
272 pp.; PB; 2-color; 6" x 9".

Fighting Invisible Tigers
Stress Management for Teens
(Revised & Updated 4th Edition)
by Earl Hipp
For ages 11 & up.
144 pp.; PB; 2-color; illust.; 6" x 9".

What Are My Rights?
Q&A About Teens and the Law
(Revised & Updated 4th Edition)
by Thomas A. Jacobs, J.D.
For ages 12 & up.
240 pp.; PB; 6" x 9".

Interested in purchasing multiple quantities and receiving volume discounts?
Contact edsales@freespirit.com or call 1.800.735.7323 and ask for Education Sales.

Many Free Spirit authors are available for speaking engagements, workshops, and keynotes.
Contact speakers@freespirit.com or call 1.800.735.7323.

For pricing information, to place an order, or to request a free catalog, contact:

Free Spirit Publishing Inc. • 6325 Sandburg Road, Suite 100 • Minneapolis, MN 55427-3674
toll-free 800.735.7323 • local 612.338.2068 • fax 612.337.5050
help4kids@freespirit.com • freespirit.com